Administration and Management of Programs for Young Children

Cynthia Jones Shoemaker
The George Washington University

Merrill,
an imprint of Prentice Hall
Englewood Cliffs, New Jersey   Columbus, Ohio

Library of Congress Cataloging-in-Publication Data
Shoemaker, Cynthia
    Administration and management of programs for young children / by
Cynthia Shoemaker. — 1st ed.
        p. cm.
    Includes bibliographical references and index.
    ISBN 0-02-410041-2
    1. Early childhood education—United States—Administration.
2. Day care centers—United States—Administration.   I. Title.
LB2822.6S56   1995
372. 12—dc20
                                                                           94-3610
                                                                                  CIP

Editor: Ann Castel Davis
Production Editor: Christine M. Harrington
Production Buyer: Patricia A. Tonneman
Electronic Text Management: Marilyn Wilson Phelps, Matthew Williams, Jane Lopez,
   Karen L. Bretz
Illustrations: The Clarinda Company

This book was set in Century Schoolbook by Prentice Hall and was printed and bound
by R.R. Donnelley & Sons Company. The cover was printed by Phoenix Color Corp.

© 1995 by Prentice-Hall, Inc.
A Simon & Schuster Company
Englewood Cliffs, New Jersey 07632

Printed in the United States of America

10 9 8 7 6 5 4 3 2 1

ISBN: 0-02-410041-2

Prentice-Hall International (UK) Limited, *London*
Prentice-Hall of Australia Pty. Limited, *Sydney*
Prentice-Hall of Canada, Inc., *Toronto*
Prentice-Hall Hispanoamericana, S. A., *Mexico*
Prentice-Hall of India Private Limited, *New Delhi*
Prentice-Hall of Japan, Inc., *Tokyo*
Simon & Schuster Asia Pte. Ltd., *Singapore*
Editora Prentice-Hall do Brasil, Ltda., *Rio de Janeiro*

This book is dedicated to all early childhood administrators who support families by inviting parents as well as children into their programs. It is also dedicated to my husband Douglas Shoemaker, to our six children, and to their children.

PREFACE

Set in the context of early childhood organizations, *Administration and Management of Programs for Young Children* addresses the functions common to management and administration. This book offers discussion and application of administrative concepts and practices to those trained in early childhood education and child development. The principles presented here can be applied in many types and sizes of organizations (such as child care centers).

The importance of facilitating a "supportive workplace" (as opposed to a "defensive workplace") is discussed throughout this book. A supportive workplace allows for the openness, caring, and positive morale so needed by the adults who work with young children. Further, in a supportive workplace there is empathy, concern for the needs and development of others, and a positive regard for the self-esteem of all persons involved (children and adults).

The four functions common to administration—planning, implementation, operating, and evaluating—are presented in detail in this book. For example:

1. *Planning.* The chapters on leadership (Chapter 7), planning (Chapter 8), parent education and involvement (Chapter 2), and the proposal and grant writing section of Chapter 12 all relate to the planning function.

2. *Implementation.* The chapters on decision making (Chapter 9), motivation (Chapter 5), team building (Chapter 4), creative and analytical problem solving (Chapter 10), and staff development and training (Chapter 3) particularly relate to the implementation of programs. Many of these principles are useful in planning, too, of course. The sample time line in Appendix D is a reference for implementing new centers.

3. *Operation.* The chapters on challenges in early childhood education (Chapter 1) and operational issues (Chapter 11) offer some guidelines and concepts for the needed knowledge base for the operation of programs for young children. Also, the Program Enrichment Papers in the appendices offer one or two curriculum ideas to be used each month. The Home Learning Enablers and Parent Papers in the appendices also give some practical activities for par-

ent involvement, which is an important part of administering programs for young children.

4. *Evaluating.* Evaluation is an ongoing process in all parts of a program and is addressed in some way in almost every chapter. When seen as a continuous circle made by planning, implementation, operation, and evaluation, evaluation feeds back into planning to update goals and processes. On the administrative side, evaluation can include actual enrollments, and where the budget and accounts are in relation to where they should be. Since much has already been written on evaluation and staff performance, and on child outcomes, these topics are only touched on briefly here.

WHY THIS BOOK?

This book was written after the author spent many years teaching preschool and child-care administration and management at the college level. During this period the author's workshop sessions at the National Association for the Education of Young Children conferences on leadership, motivation, and decision making (taken from lectures in the courses) were so well received, with requests for written copies, that they eventually became three of the chapters for this book. Every course the author taught on early childhood management and administration led to requests for more courses until there were four: basic and advanced administration courses, a course on group settings for young children, and a course on special needs and problems of children. As the book developed, three of these four course concepts and materials were included. The special needs materials were eventually requested as well, and will be presented in the second edition of this book.

This book addresses only sound, developmentally appropriate care for children in groups of five or more. Similar suggestions exist for family child care and for groups of under five in the home, but that is not the focus of this book. Involvement of parents in their child's care and education is assumed to be an integral part in high quality early childhood programs, as is well documented in research. In fact, we believe that training and education for all adults involved with children in programs is the cutting edge issue for success or failure in meeting positive goals for child care.

Parent education coupled with parent involvement, or providing information plus modeling, always increases learning opportunities. These methods also work to ensure that a program is culturally and ethnically appropriate for children, helping child care contribute to, and enhance, the multifaceted diversity that makes a community (and, indeed, an entire country) unique. We believe that excellent, developmentally appropriate child care is a real service to the community in that it can (and does) have lasting positive effects on each child's life. Furthermore, the least expensive way to reach all the children is to reach all the parents, as parent education also benefits the children who are too young or too old for child care.

ACKNOWLEDGMENTS

I would like to acknowledge the valuable assistance received from Lori Biamonte, Pam Oliver, Peter and Diep Shoemaker, and from Barbara Scanlon, whose wonderful pictures grace Chapters 2 and 5. I would also like to thank Sandy Turner and Doug Shoemaker for their contributions to Chapter 6; and David Cavenaugh for his contribution to Chapter 12.

A special word of appreciation goes to the editorial and production staffs at Merrill and Prentice Hall. Thanks is also extended to the reviewers for this edition for their help and constructive suggestions: R. Eleanor Duff, University of South Carolina; Richard Fiene, Pennsylvania State University, Harrisburg; Craig Hart, Brigham Young University; John R. Hranitz, Bloomsburg University of Pennsylvania; Arminta Jacobson, University of North Texas; Kim A. Madsen, Chadron State College; Ramona E. Patterson, South Univeristy, Baton Rouge; and Pauline Davey Zeece, University of Nebraska, Lincoln.

CONTENTS

CHAPTER TWO
Parent Education and Parent Involvement   27

PART TWO
Human Resource Issues   57

CHAPTER THREE
Staff Selection, Development, and Evaluation   59

CHAPTER FOUR
Team Building and Small Group Interaction   71

CHAPTER FIVE
Motivating Staff, Parents, and Children   83

CHAPTER SIX
Professionalism: More Than Meets the Eye   105

PART THREE
The Role of the Director   119

CHAPTER SEVEN
Understanding Leadership and the Use of Power   123

CHAPTER EIGHT
Planning   141

CHAPTER NINE
Decision-Making for Administrators   155

CHAPTER TEN
Creative and Analytical Problem-Solving   173

PART FOUR
Operational Issues   191

CHAPTER ELEVEN
Facilities, Equipment, Room Arrangement, and
Scheduling   193

CHAPTER TWELVE
Finances, Record-Keeping, and Proposal Writing   213

PART ONE

Challenges and Trends in Early Childhood Education

There are many new challenges in education in the 1990s, and early childhood education, which includes the youngest children in the educational process, is on the leading edge. The following are just a few of these challenges:

1. Children are attending group care programs at an earlier age.
2. The number of working parents has dramatically increased; the workplace pressures placed on them have increased as well, with longer days and longer commutes, and these working parents need to find the best alternatives for their children.
3. There are diverse opinions about what is good for children.
4. There are differing attitudes toward the value of play, resulting in programs that allow too little freedom for play and programs that allow too much freedom for play.
5. It often is difficult to work well with parents and to provide them with parent education information, whether it be in the form of courses, books, or send-home information. Chapter 2, "Parent Education and Parent Involvement," deals with this subject more intensively since parent involvement is one of the major trends in early childhood education today.

The certification of teachers and the accreditation and licensing of programs for young children also reflect the challenges and trends in today's world of early childhood education. Many other countries that have early childhood programs and that have enacted supportive legislation might serve as examples for the United States. Early childhood educators from England, New Zealand, and Australia consistently find U.S. regulations weaker than their own. In terms of accreditation of preschools and child-care programs, in addition to the National Association for the Education of Young Children (NAEYC) accreditation, most states require that child-care centers be licensed through the state's health or social services departments; a few states, however, provide state accreditation of early childhood educational programs through the Department of Education. In one state, accreditation of nursery schools by the Department of Education was added in the 1940s. When dog and horse training facilities and programs for veterans were being accredited, early childhood personnel at that time had to *ask* to have their schools included in the accreditation process. One value of accreditation lies in its ability to regulate the ever-expanding numbers of children in classrooms.

There are two major changes occurring in society today that affect the early childhood field and its relationship to formal education, and these same circumstances also can be seen in the workplace. The first change is the ongoing transition into the information age, which has resulted in the use of computers in early childhood program administration and in classroom curriculum. The second change is the increasingly multicultural population of the nation (U.S. Dept. of Labor, 1989). Cultural diversity in the classroom is not new in early childhood education, but it is a challenge and a trend. Active parent involvement of many kinds helps to ensure that children's needs will be met in a way that is meaningful and understandable related to cultural background.

Finally, the results of research focusing on the long-term effects of child care for young children are a challenge to all in the early childhood field. These discovered effects are far-reaching, affecting even teachers and principals in the elementary schools into which these children matriculate. The lack of high-quality, developmentally appropriate child care for children now causes school problems and expense later. For example, a child who receives poor-quality child care might find it necessary to repeat grades in school or participate in special education programs. Poor-quality child care also results in low self-esteem, and fosters negative attitudes throughout life. Mental health problems leading to institutionalization, and crime leading to prison crowding problems, cost public budgets far more than would developmentally appropriate child care with encouraged parent involvement.

It is important that parents retain their perception and their role as their children's most important teachers. Going along with this belief, parent involvement and parent education are key factors in any child-care system. Studies done in Israel by Jerome Kagan (1970) in the Kibbutz system, where parents see their children for one half hour per day, show that almost no matter what the circumstances, the child always turns to the parent first.

Setting up learning opportunities to educate all adults who are involved with children in early childhood programs is an important indicator of success or failure in meeting the challenges and problems just discussed. This training must include parents as well as teachers, aides, and administrators.

Citizens who support early education legislation and funding at the federal and state levels for the care of young children cite the damage being done to young children who are left alone at home while single mothers work; children who are taken to the workplace with their mothers where there are no adequate care arrangements; and children who are cared for in unlicensed centers in states with low standards, sometimes even with child abuse resulting. These concerned citizens see child care as a societal problem, not as an individual problem, and one that will be destructive to society if not regulated and supported. Indeed, the society will suffer if large numbers of young children are damaged.

CHAPTER ONE

Challenges in Developing Programs for Young Children

The need is greater than ever to develop a warm, trusting, sincere environment for children and to have this goal be top priority for staff, parents, and children. Children have a desire to learn, to be curious, and to take risks. They need to have their parents involved in their learning at least some of the time.

Goals for children that will wear well through challenges and trends include developing a positive self-image; growing physically, intellectually, and socially; building imagination and thinking skills; and being encouraged to participate, to feel important, to feel relaxed, and to be a part of the program or center.

Treating each child as an individual, providing a well-rounded program with many experiences, and maintaining a provision for health concerns are all components of integrating children's needs into a child-care program, regardless of the curriculum model or models used. Children with special needs or who speak English as a second language will need special attention. A child with limited English proficiency who also has special education needs or disabilities will particularly need assistance.

PHILOSOPHY

The philosophy of the preschool or child-care center is the foundation on which the total program is built. If this statement of purpose is carefully developed and easily understood by all, many of the problems that occur in child-care administration could be prevented: interstaff problems; staff-to-parent problems; and parent-to-parent problems. A typical statement of educational philosophy might discuss what is meant by individual acceptance. It might use terms such as "freedom within limits" and espouse a "child-sized world." It might advocate a relaxed and friendly atmosphere where a child can explore, share, play, and communicate with other children his or her own age. Parent participation and teacher-parent-child, or three-way, sharing should be included.

A group decision to plan for children who are happy, confident, productive, whole individuals, and who are able to face and cope with the problems that come before them, is a good first step toward a high-quality program philosophy. Parents and staff need to agree on goals such as the following: children can learn to respect themselves; they can establish a sense of confidence and self-esteem, while learning to respect others and their ideas and rights; they can learn to make choices, to solve problems, and to explore new ways of doing things without being afraid to try; they can become confident, whole individuals who are able to cope with what lies before them. Once such goals are established, mutual understanding about the curriculum and activities can follow in an atmosphere of discussion and learning.

ESTABLISHING THE CENTER

The first step in organizing a preschool or child-care center is taken when a number of interested persons call a meeting to discuss plans for organization. Assuming they agree on the need for an early childhood program in their geographical area and on the general kind of education they desire, they then will want to sound out the community and evaluate the facilities already available. To do so, the group may wish to form a committee to do some research.

The first task for a research committee should be to check the U.S. census tracts (in the public library) for demographics, numbers of small children, births, socioeconomic level, and other available information as desired. One research committee such as this developed a census tract map and colored in the areas with the most young children. Then they looked for a location in the center of a shaded-in area.

For the committee's second task, committee members might use the survey shown in Figure 1.1 to compare three or four programs for young children. Many ideas for using indoor and outdoor space emerge from this exercise, in addition to discovering needs and a market niche.

Once a general location and perhaps one or two alternatives are selected, a committee member can approach employers in the area to generate support. Options to present to employers might include housing the center, publicizing and supporting the center by giving flyers about it to their employees and prospective employees, and/or supporting the center by purchasing 5, 10, or 15 "contract" slots to be paid for in advance and then held for their employees, perhaps as part of their benefit package. At this stage, developing a decision tree, as described in Chapter 9, can be very useful for sorting out the benefits of purchasing an existing site, remodeling a site, or building a center, if all these options exist in the desired location. As the group identifies and critiques the options, more information will emerge.

FIGURE 1.1
Competition Survey

Center name	Price	Number of children	Use of indoor space	Use of outdoor space	Special features or theme	Characteristics missing or poorly handled (lighting, space, teachers, education, etc.)
Center A						
Center B						
Center C						
Center D						
Our Center						

If these preliminary investigations yield positive results, the group goes to work. Committees are selected to do the following:

1. Find out about county and state requirements and, at the appropriate time, make application for licensing.
2. Find suitable housing as previously discussed.
3. Plan the budget.
4. Develop the philosophy and its statement.
5. Hire the staff.
6. Publicize the service available for children or visit a social service agency or corporation to determine the number of funded children that might be available in the area.

If the organizing group feels unprepared to decide on an educational program, and hence to select a teacher, they might find it useful to arrange several meetings with an experienced early childhood teacher in order to discuss child development and preschool education. This would help the group set the goals for their projected center. The all-important philosophy really is the first step.

ORGANIZING STRUCTURES

The Executive Board

In most organizing groups, an Executive Board is elected by the interested parties to manage the business operations of the center or school. The Board, which carries out the administrative duties in accordance with the purposes and bylaws of the group, leaves the teachers free to concentrate on the educational philosophy and the program. Board members should be members of the community who have a high level of interest in the proposed center; prospective parents are a good resource. Assigning Board members specific roles—that is, involving them in tasks with which they feel comfortable—provides an excellent opportunity for them to learn about good early childhood education. This learning takes place through the "hands-on" process of researching a particular area, which might be the equipment needed, or the budget, or the regulations that must be met. Such involvement also provides group cohesiveness and good public relations in the community. This source of energy and interest, leading to "buying into" the goals of the center, should not be underestimated, even by profit-making centers.

During the organizing period, an interim Executive Board may be established. Later, as the center becomes operational, the interim Board is replaced by a permanent Executive Board, the members of which are elected for one, two, or three years. The usual officers of President, Vice President, Recording Secretary, and Treasurer may be augmented by advisors from the community and by permanent committee chairs for the following areas:

- Housing and Licensing
- Bylaws and Incorporation
- Membership/Enrollment and Public Relations
- Equipment and Supplies (The teacher/Director, if hired by this point, is an ex-officio member of this committee.)
- Teacher Hiring and Personnel Committee
- Treasurer and Finance Committee

Additional committees may include:

- Educational Standards Committee
- Handbook Committee
- Communications Committee (responsible for a newsletter, calendar, and bulletin board)
- Hospitality/Social Committee
- Parent Education/Program Committee

There is a lot of work to be done in organizing a center or school. Each committee has its own job and set of objectives. Those committees found in the first list are the ones that must be organized as soon as possible. In the beginning, there may not be enough people to cover all of the needed committees, so organizers should prioritize which needs are the most urgent until there are enough interested persons to cover all aspects.

The Child-Care Center or Preschool Board

After the center is organized, a working Board of Advisors or Board of Directors is a must in a child-care center unless the Director wants to work 50 or 60 hours a week (see Part 3, "The Role of the Director"). A child-care center with a prestigious Board of Advisors or Board of Directors whose members are drawn from professionals from a possible church or business sponsor and from the community may want to consider setting up a second Executive Board (or choose another appropriate title that will give some honor to the participants). The purpose of this second group should be to work and not just to oversee and advise, and at least 51 percent of its membership should be parents whose children are presently enrolled in the center. In fact, all members of the Executive Board may be drawn from parents currently involved with the center; however, some of the members of this Executive Board also may be drawn from alumni parents of other programs (perhaps necessary at start-up); alumni parents from your center as you develop them; and interested community or church persons (if the center is housed in a church).

The Director and teachers may be voting members of this Executive Board, depending on whether the parent members feel this is beneficial. Whether or not they are voting members of the Executive Board, the job of the professional staff in the center is to design an educational policy and curriculum that recognizes the philosophy of the parents, staff, and Executive Board. The professional staff is to choose and implement the specific education curricula and to give advice and guidance on areas of administration in which the Executive Board is involved. In other words, the Director's job is to educate the parent Executive Board in practices that are supportive of children and to interpret the preschool program. Many more persons in today's world are experts in administration than are experts in early childhood education, as evidenced by the popularity of master's degrees in business administration versus master's degrees in early childhood education. The help of the latter group certainly can be used.

Bylaws and Operating Rules

Each preschool program should develop a set of bylaws to organize their group, give it structure, and to send in for the center's nonprofit incorporation, should they choose to pursue this. Bylaws are similar to each other in form and should be kept simple. If the parent group as well as the Executive Board is required to vote on major changes in the bylaws, much more participation and "buying into" the goals of the program are possible. Using a democratic structure such as this for the group develops teamwork right from the start.

Operating rules or policy regulations can be added to the bylaws in a separate section or can be made into a separate document, which makes them easier to change. These rules and regulations are not addressed here since they will be unique to each group; for example, such a document may even include job descriptions for paid and volunteer jobs. Usually the Executive Board sets these policy regulations without a vote of the parent group, unlike the bylaws.

A table of contents for a typical set of bylaws follows. As can be seen, the decisions that need to be made in order to write these bylaws are a useful part of the development of a center or a school.

Sample Table of Contents for Bylaws

A. Statement of Purpose or Philosophy

B. Name of Program

C. Enrollment

    1. Methods of applying for children

    2. General responsibilities of parents

       3. Health requirements

       4. Meeting attendance requirements and committee participation requirements for parents

    D. Organization

       1. Board of Advisors

          a. Election and duration of term

          b. Duties

          c. Meetings

       2. Executive Board

          a. Election

          b. Duties and Powers

          c. Meetings

       3. Staff

          a. Duties

          b. Contract Procedure

       4. Standing Committees

          a. Appointment

          b. Duties (job descriptions can go in the operating rules/policy regulations section)

    E. Treasury

       1. Amount of tuition and fees

       2. Method of payment

       3. Fee arrangements in the event of withdrawal

       4. Insurance and fees

       5. Hours and holidays

       6. Late tuition payment policy

    F. Amendment Procedure

    G. General Rules

    H. Dissolution

Incorporation

Incorporation, whether as a nonprofit educational organization or as a profit-making corporation, is highly recommended for child-care programs that are separate entities. Unless a center is incorporated, Executive Board members can be individually responsible for damages awarded to any person claiming negligence, on the part of the center, resulting in personal injury. Incorporation also protects Executive Board members from responsibility for financial difficulties, and allows the program to enter into legal contracts such as a contract with a teacher or a rental lease. Incorporation may require legal advice.

In many states, a *nonprofit corporation* is specified as an organization that does not sell stock, and, upon dissolution, its assets go to another nonprofit corporation (such as a church or another nonprofit child-care center). To incorporate, a copy of the organization's bylaws must be attached to the Articles of Incorporation, and then must be submitted to the State Department of Assessments and Taxation of the state in which the center is located. Often this department will have a brochure available that contains helpful advice on incorporating. Tax-exempt status for state sales tax, which is different from the nonprofit exemption from federal income tax, may be requested separately once nonprofit status is granted, and can result in quite a savings in the purchases of equipment and supplies. A surplus line in the budget, that carries over into the next year's operating expenses or is kept as a contingency fund, is permissible in a nonprofit corporation, since *nonprofit* does not mean *nonsurplus*.

Individual incorporation of a center protects the housing facility, such as a church or other institution in which the center is located, from damages in case of a negligence suit. The process of becoming incorporated is slow, so the necessary papers can be sent in while other start-up tasks are being addressed.

Site Selection

Site selection can be a difficult problem, unless a suitable site is obvious. For many years, obtaining housing has been the most difficult problem for those starting a child-care program. A rough outline of the information presented in the bylaws could be combined with the following information to serve as a useful packet for prospective landlords: the hours during which children's classes and parent meetings will occur; the facilities required (indoor and outdoor, including parking); the qualifications of the educational staff; and the name, address, and telephone number of contact persons. The proposed rent should be high enough to cover the expenses of the housing institution, including janitorial services, but also should be low enough to allow lower income families access to the program. Housing a center in a rent-free facility often leads to troubles with the landlord, who may lose patience with a non-paying group in a shorter period of time than with a rent-paying operation.

Licensing in most areas is handled by local and state agencies who inspect nursery schools and child-care centers. Although licensing takes time, an interim permit often is issued to allow the program to get under way while awaiting health, fire, and safety inspections. It may be necessary to alter a building to meet necessary regulations and obtain a license (one example of an alteration might be installing fire doors). The cost of such alterations may be covered or shared with the landlord in many instances.

In choosing a site, it may be necessary to deal with regulations or standards in any or all of the following areas:

Zoning

Business licensing

Fire safety regulations including fire extinguishers, smoke alarms, fire alarms, exits, and escape plans

Educational standards including teacher/pupil ratio, indoor space/child ratio, outdoor space/child ratio, staff qualifications, and health requirements

Equipment

Parking regulations

Building codes, including those for electricity, plumbing, heating capacity, and access

Health regulations including food preparation, food storage, number of bathrooms, lighting, and ventilation

Transportation regulations or licensing

Most high-quality early childhood programs have educational standards that far exceed any regulations that may be required by legislation. Thus, when government standards are raised, these programs do not find themselves having to lobby for the standards to be lowered, thereby finding themselves in a position of fighting against the best interests of the children.

Membership Committee

The task of the membership committee is to recruit families for the program. Committee members must have a good understanding of the philosophy, goals, and curriculum of the program. This committee is the outreach and public relations arm of the program, and, together with a committee for publicity, plans ways to present the child-care program through all types of news media: newspapers, radio, television, bulletin boards (electronic ones as well as physical ones), and flyers to corporations and company personnel offices. This committee may plan an open house, take pictures of classes in session after the center opens, distribute recruitment posters, and develop brochures. The duties of the membership committee may be extensive, so occasionally the membership chairman is given a partial scholarship or tuition remission in return for these services.

An enrollment committee may be separated out from the membership committee as the center grows. They maintain enrollment forms, a waiting list, and arrange admission interviews for children. They also help to plan orientation meetings in the fall and perhaps offer orientation every quarter for a year-round child-care program.

Teacher Hiring or Personnel Committee

It is very useful to have a committee to help advertise, help schedule interviews, and help conduct interviews of the prospective teaching staff, and even, on occasion, of the Director. The quality of the early childhood program will depend largely on the knowledge and skills of the Director and the teachers. If an Executive Board of a community group or of an already existing center is establishing the new child-care center, key personnel to be hired may already be identified. However, an interviewing procedure that spreads the decision-making responsibility over several persons is always wise for future hiring and for the additional hiring that needs to be done at the time the center is established. More information on this important topic can be found in Chapter 3.

Advertisements for teaching staff may be placed at local colleges and universities, and in newspapers. These listings should include educational requirements for the job, hours, and a range for salaries. List at least two contact phone numbers, or if it is preferred, have applicants mail in resumés to an address given in the advertisement.

As inquiries begin to come in, send out an application form in response to each. The application should include a deadline for return. In partnership with the whole personnel committee (three to five persons), screen the completed applications for the person's experience, education, and qualifications. Rank the applicants in priority and set up an interview schedule.

Preplanning the interview questions, so that each candidate is asked the same questions, is important for fairness. (Suggestions for questions are given in Chapter 3.) The committee may wish to reinterview the top two or three candidates after the first round of interviews. A note of thanks should be sent to all interviewees for their time and to let them know when the position has been filled.

A formal contract should be signed by the teacher/Director selected. At this point, the teacher is introduced to the interim Executive Board and is invited to participate immediately in selecting equipment, planning classroom space, developing the educational program, and planning parent orientation meetings.

A final organizational note: The secretary should maintain a personnel file for each employee, which includes their application form, contract, reference letters, health form, and yearly evaluation.

Treasurer and Finance Committee

A sound financial structure is essential to a successful child-care program. Initial tasks of the finance committee include formulating a budget, establishing tuition fees based on budgeted expenses, and setting up the books. If financial policies and structures are well thought out, these tasks will be easier in succeeding years.

The budget should be figured with the income at 90 percent of enrollment rather than 100 percent, since this provides a leeway that allows for variability and turnover. A reserve fund of one or two months income, minimum, should also be maintained. The first and last month's tuition may be collected upon enrollment to help start this fund.

Most programs also collect a nonrefundable registration fee at the time a child's application is received; this money enables the program to open its bank account. If the child withdraws before opening day, however, this fee should be refunded. Some schools earmark these registration fees to go toward large equipment purchases.

A well-designed budget is a guide to growth and improvement, and, along with other expenditures, should allow for planned purchases of equipment and annual personnel salary increases.

Written financial policies are important for consistency and fairness. A date by which tuition must be paid and a late fee should be established. Sometimes a provision is made for lower tuition fees if more than one child from the same family is enrolled in the program. The finance committee also should look into possible insurance requirements of the program, which may include: tenant's liability, owner's liability, program liability, employer's liability, bonding (for the Treasurer), fire and theft insurance, unemployment insurance, and medical and accident insurance for children and employees.

Equipment and Supplies Committee

A rich variety of equipment is needed for a preschool program since children learn through interaction and the stimulation of play. A short-term, two- to five-year loan for start-up expenses prevents the burden of initial equipment costs from falling on first-year enrollees. The equipment list should be developed while working with a trained early childhood teacher. Members of the equipment and supplies committee might also visit other children's programs and preschools for ideas as well as subscribing to educational supply catalogs. Conferences and early childhood magazines also are good resources for equipment information. More detail on categories of equipment and supplies is given in Chapter 11.

As committee members gather ideas, they begin to compile lists. Once purchases have been made, as the year goes on, committee members are responsible for checking to see if the equipment is wearing well, or needs repair. Small toys and puzzles may have pieces missing, and repairing or replacing these is part of the committee's task.

The "job descriptions" for other possible and helpful committees are given in Chapter 12, but the ones that were described here are especially helpful for the initiation of a program for young children.

LEGISLATION, CERTIFICATION, AND ACCREDITATION

The staff of child-care centers as well as parents need to keep current with local, state, and national legislation and with the variety of teacher certification and center licensing regulations that are held by each state. At the time of this writing, many regulations are under review (at all levels), and should be obtained from the appropriate agency in the particular state in which a center is located.

Within each state, licensing is usually granted by one or more agencies which include Health, Welfare or Social Services, and (in very few states) Education. Accreditation by state departments of education and by the National Association for the Education of Young Children (NAEYC) is also desirable. Possible and desired trends in legislation include the greater involvement of parents and families in their children's education. The Council of Chief State School Officers (CCSSO, 1991) says, "If the potential resources available to the school and the family resulting from the synergy of their partnership is realized, schools and families will have powerful new tools for ensuring education success for children." (p.1).

The *Families in School* booklet put out by the Council of Chief State School Officers (1991) encourages educational agencies at several levels to implement programs that enhance teachers' capacity to work with families as partners in the improvement of their children's education. The booklet also guides families in making decisions that affect the quality and content of the education programs and schools for their children.

At the preschool level, this involvement is especially important since the foundations are being laid for the education system of school-age children. As family involvement becomes an integral component of setting standards for good schools and quality education in the K through 12 age group, it will be following the lead that good early childhood programs have established for several generations of children and parents (Parent Cooperative Preschools International, 1985).

Family involvement can and should become a key component of school and center improvement, while also lending energy, talent, and other scarce resources to these educational programs. As a result, it is hoped that local districts and state education agencies would continue developing and implementing family involvement in new education programs and initiatives (CCSSO, 1991).

Legislation involving early childhood education in other countries makes "setting up" grants available. For example, the funding in New Zealand to cover the cost of start-up is granted after the center has passed accreditation standards. International legislation for early childhood programs is indeed a fertile source of new ideas for some of the problems faced in the United States today (New Zealand, Education Department Standards, 1968, p. 42).

CURRICULUM MODELS IN EARLY CHILDHOOD EDUCATION

The administrator and teaching staff should discuss whether their philosophy, as spelled out in the curriculum, will be activity oriented, cognitively/academically oriented, or process oriented. It is possible to blend these or other curriculum models, and different philosophies can be utilized by different teachers, but it is best within one center not to have too many divergent classroom curriculum approaches.

There are many excellent curriculum models in early childhood education; in fact, an entire university course could be devoted to curriculum alone. Presented here are three broad curriculum approaches that should give an overview of the possibilities. The multiplicity of curriculum choices is yet another challenge and change in early childhood education. It is best to keep in mind that choosing developmentally appropriate curriculum, whatever its approach or slant, is the overall goal in developing a successful program (Bredekamp, 1990).

Activity Approach

The activity approach is the traditional, whole-child development curriculum. Goals and objectives are often listed in relationship to holidays, seasons, themes, or units. This approach provides a wide range of experiences that build self-confidence and competence. The materials for this approach allow children to see, hear, feel, smell, and experience. The child is encouraged to learn through his or her senses and the materials provide for this.

Subject Matter Approach

This approach can be identified by goals that are academic in nature and by content that is the same as subjects the child will encounter later in schooling. Much of what is done in the early years builds foundations for later learning in all approaches. By highlighting subject matter skills, this approach sometimes provides fewer concrete experiences and more teacher-directed learning than does other approaches. A good teacher can be aware of this pitfall and guard against it. Goals in the subject matter curriculum are listed by subject, such as language, math, science, or social studies.

Process Skills Approach

The process skills approach has as its goal the enabling of the child to adapt to an ever-changing society. Units or goals in this curriculum approach are labeled creative skills, interactive skills, or cognitive skills. These skills or processes include decision-making, cooperating, caring, communicating, creating, perceiving, observing, loving, knowing, and problem-solving. The child is active in experimentation, exploration, construction, and selection. An example activity or learning opportunity of the process skills approach might be: Children will use decision-making skills as they choose alternatives and predict implications during free-choice time.

HISTORICAL FOUNDATIONS AND CURRENT TRENDS

In early-era America, child care on a large scale was unnecessary, since children were physically close to their parents who were working on the family farm, tending the family store, or working outside but nearby the family home. Even as recently as 50 years ago, the majority of American families were "traditional" in the sense that fathers worked fulltime while mothers stayed at home to care for the children; however, child care connected to the workplace does have a place in American history.

The beginning of large-scale child care associated with the workplace is linked to funding by the federal government, which at the time had the needs of the nation in mind rather than the needs of individual children or their families.

In August of 1942, the office of Defense, Health, and Welfare was directed by the War Manpower Commission to set up a program of federally supported child-care centers for children of working mothers in war-related industries. The Lanham Act was passed at this time, which made an additional $150 million available for facilities, including child-care centers, operating in expanded war-industry areas.

One company that took advantage of the Lanham Act was the Kaiser Shipbuilding Corporation in Portland, Oregon, which opened two child-care centers that served 4,014 children from eighteen months to six years of age. The buildings and equipment for these programs were provided by the United States Maritime Commission. In addition to the preschool program, the centers were open to school-age children during holidays, weekends, or whenever necessary. Other nonenrolled children of working parents could attend if their regular child-care arrangements broke down. Some comprehensive services such as health care, home service food, parent information, and other benefits were also made available. The purpose of these centers was to provide services to parents who were required to work long hours.

The federal funding stopped with the end of the war, so most child-care centers closed. Many mothers returned to their homes and families. However, if a family still needed child care, it was most often filled by family home-care providers.

It was not until 1969 that corporations became active in child care. Service areas in which women were expected to work, such as textiles, light manufacturing, assembly-line work, and hospitals, were the first to respond. These programs offered very little parent involvement and often were seen as instruments to make working women more vulnerable. Industry-owned and industry-managed child-care facilities controlled the possibility of employees striking for better conditions and turnover by threatening to withdraw child-care programs.

The diversity of child-care programs utilized by working parents and the complexity of emotions concerning who should be responsible for the care of children did not encourage widespread employer involvement in quality-child-care issues. Although the economic recessions of the 1970s and the women's movement brought more women into the workforce and created a greater need for child care, the federal and state governments, also affected by the recessions, provided little legislation to support child care. A 1978 survey by Perry, cited by Waxman (1991), found there were only nine industry-sponsored child-care centers in the United States. Also in 1978, just 110 U.S. employers offered their employees some type of child-care assistance (Smith, 1991).

Although the 1980s saw increasing demands for quality child care for the growing number of working women, there were conflicting reports on the effects of child care on the healthy development of children. Early studies of child care in the 1960s had shown positive results; however, by the late 1980s, contradictory evidence had been reported. While children were reported to demonstrate positive gains in social, language, and cognitive development, disturbing evidence of negative emotional, aggressive, and uncooperative behaviors was found. The evidence was most disturbing in regard to infants who were in child care during their first year (National Research Council, 1990). Much of the detrimental evidence was correlated to the quality of child care and the large size of the groups to which the children were exposed. While the quality of child care was accepted as a major concern, the delivery and regulation of quality child-care service was a major debate.

In the 1990s, many child-care options have been developed in response to the needs' assessments of employees. In 1990, 5,400 employers offered child-care *assistance* to their employees (Smith, 1991). Waxman (1991) noted that as of 1991, the number of industry-sponsored child-care *centers* had grown to between 500 and 1000 centers in just 13 years. A research group based in New York, called the Families and Work Institute, has created a "family friendly index" to help companies develop a plan of action in addressing work and family issues (Bernstein, Weber, Driscoll, & Cunes, 1991).

Quality on-site or near-site employer-sponsored child care can lead the way for meeting the comprehensive needs of families and children. It can also address the national need for quality early childhood education. The rapid growth of the relationship between employers and quality child care, in addition to provisions for the uniqueness of the development and management of these centers, must be closely monitored.

As can be seen from the previous discussion, child-care arrangements increasingly are moving outside the home, with children's development often placed in the hands of strangers or near-strangers. As late as 1985 only 14 percent of preschool children were cared for in an organized child-care setting. By 1990, this figure doubled and half the children of working parents were either being cared for in a center or in another home. In 1985, 25 percent of working mothers with children under five used a child-care facility as their primary form of care, compared with only 13 percent in 1977 (Hamburg, 1991, p.7). However, while today there are three times as many children enrolled in child care, there are only two times as many centers, leading to overcrowding and staff turnover. The number of children in child care is due to double again by 1995, and even if the number of centers doubles as well, the gap will grow even larger since the number of centers is behind enrollment numbers already.

On the whole, this transformation in child-care arrangements was unforeseen, unplanned, and is still poorly understood. Many American parents are reporting to public opinion surveys that they are deeply troubled about raising their children in today's society (Hamburg, 1991).

A shift toward placing younger children in centers has also occurred, reflecting the increased proportion of mothers of very young children who are in the labor force. Between 1976 and 1990, the proportion of infants under 12 months of age in center care increased from 1 percent to 4 percent, and the number of toddlers ages 1 to 2 nearly doubled from 3 percent to 5 percent (Willer et al., *The Demand and Supply of Child Care in 1990*, 1990, p.45). The proportion of infants in family child care remained stable at 25 percent from 1976 to 1990. The proportion of employed mothers of children under 5 who use center care has increased four times since 1965, from 6 percent to 28 percent, with an accompanying decrease in the use of in-home providers (Willer et al., 1990). Some put this number of children at 5 million.

A major challenge of the 90s will be to increase the number of high-quality child-care centers. The number of children needing care may continue to increase and more options for increasing the number of developmentally appropriate centers will be needed. One such option, discussed in Chapter 12, is the possibility of existing accredited centers marketing their services to, and perhaps adding satellite centers for, nearby corporations at a corporate group rate. This option would provide a certain number of reserved enrollment slots for company employees and would help the center to maintain and expand their operations (Duncan & Thornton, 1993). A 1991 National League of Cities Survey of 278 of America's larger cities reported that 96 percent of these cities said that child care was the most pressing need for city children. This becomes completely understandable when the current number of good care options are reviewed (Child Care Information Exchange, 1991).

Brainstorming for Solutions

In the first and last class of the semester, conduct a class activity in which students brainstorm ideas in answer to the question, "What would lead to better child care in the United States?" (Brainstorming is a technique in which students generate ideas without sorting them. Chapter 10 provides more details on this activity.) To assist the class in finding solutions, have them build a discussion around each of the following questions:

1. What is the problem? (It often needs redefining.)
2. What more do we need to know?
3. Who needs to be involved?
4. What would a solution look like?
5. What is the first step?

When a number of ideas have been generated, the class can vote to select 10 or fewer solutions, along with their respective first steps, as the ideas that should have priority. These ideas can be developed as small-group projects, term papers, or even as a graduate thesis.

This problem-solving framework can be used for both large and small problems. Initially, one problem should be done with the whole group for practice, then other problems can be worked on by small groups that report back to the whole group. One method of generating problems to discuss might be to have class participants, at the beginning of the class period, hand in problems they would like "think tank" help on.

The following list was generated by one class at the end of a semester in answer to the question, "What would lead to better child care in the U.S.?"

1. Learn from/copy England and New Zealand for ways to develop more slots/spaces to serve children. (In England, they receive extra grants for creating more spaces, for creating spaces for children with disabilities, for involving the elderly, and for meeting other special requirements. In New Zealand, they have "setting up grants," which are disbursed once the standards for a new center are met.)
2. Require NAEYC accreditation for centers to receive public funding.
3. Require parent education and parent involvement for centers to receive public funding.

4. Have many paths to better child care be accepted: public school prekindergarten; federal and other public programs; accredited nonprofit and profit-making programs.

5. Build centers on public school grounds.

6. Encourage corporate-sponsored child care and publicize the benefits (to children, parents, and the corporation).

7. Encourage corporate personnel benefits offices to give corporate vouchers to approved/accredited child-care programs; these vouchers can be redeemed for tuition assistance that is billed to the corporation. "Cafeteria-style" benefits allow for this.

8. Require Parent Board Chairpersons to sign grant and budget documents (as is required in some Federal programs).

9. Attach accredited child-care centers to hospitals.

10. Attach accredited child-care centers to government agencies at all levels of government (county, state, federal).

SUMMARY

The very words *child care* bring a different image to everyone's mind. Some see a brightly decorated, modern facility filled with the sounds of children's laughter and tumbling block towers. For too many others, the vision is one of an overcrowded room filled with unruly children and frustrated teachers. In a country as wealthy as the U.S., a country which houses some of the finest universities in the world, a country which considers itself to be the leading world power, it is sad that an issue as crucial as the future of its own children is not receiving the attention it deserves. Why is the U.S. entrusting its future to child-care facilities that have little or no minimum standards for their teachers? Why is one teacher permitted to be responsible for as many as 12 infants at one time, as is the case in Idaho (Wingert & Kantrowitz, 1990)? Some continuing challenges in child care include:

> *Lack of federal regulations with regard to the care of young children.*
> As Wingert and Kantrowitz so aptly wrote, "The government offers consumers more guidance choosing breakfast cereal than child care" (1990, p. 227).
>
> *Parental fear about the long-term effects on children of child care.* More and more studies, such as those done by Jay Belsky (1984) at Pennsylvania State University, suggest that children who attend daycare/child-care programs are at a greater risk of exhibiting social and emotional problems later in life, as well as at risk of demonstrating higher levels of aggression and disobedience.
>
> *High turnover among child-care workers.* Those who work in child care often fall victim to the stresses of overcrowded classrooms, understaffing, and lack of financial incentives, and they leave the profession. A high turnover in caretakers leaves children with a sense of insecurity. (Some studies show that 50 percent of child-care centers have a 50 percent turnover rate.)
>
> *Lack of alternatives for caring for children when they are sick.* Parents are not always able to stay home with a child who has a cold. Sending him or her to school puts all of the other children and teachers at risk of infection.
>
> *High cost of child care.* Lower cost alternatives in child care, such as hiring immigrants as nannies who do not have proper papers or placing children in vastly overcrowded classrooms, are sometimes illegal. Low-income parents need sliding scales for fees, and parents of all incomes need proof that the facility in which they are placing their children is certified, licensed, and has valid references; this provides peace of mind that their children will not be harmed and will be helped to grow developmentally.

In conclusion, it is known that what happens to a child in the first several years of life lays the foundation for a long, healthy lifespan (Hamburg, 1987). It is important to be resourceful in finding ways of putting this knowledge into practice for healthy child development. Meeting the challenges of developing a program for young children is one step.

Integrating some of the challenges and trends in early childhood education into programs to meet the needs of young children is another step. Caring for children is important work for any human being, and is fundamental to the future of society. Parents can and must help with this work, as we shall see in the next chapter.

BIBLIOGRAPHY

Association of Teacher Educators, & National Association for the Education of Young Children. (1991). Early childhood teacher certification. *Young Children, 47*(1), 16–21.

Belsky, J. (1984). Two waves of daycare research. In R. C. Ainslie (Ed.), *Quality variations in daycare*. New York: Praeger.

Bernstein, A., Weber, J., Driscoll, L., & Cunes, A. (1991). Corporate America is still no place for kids. *Business Week* (3241), 234–238.

Bredekamp, S. (Ed.). (1990). *Developmentally appropriate practice in young childhood programs serving children from birth through age 8*. Washington, DC: National Association for the Education of Young Children.

Breitbart, V. (1974). *The day care book: The why, what, and how of community day care*. New York: Alfred A. Knopf.

Child Care Information Exchange. (1991, March/April). Did you know? *Child Care Information Exchange, 78*, 15.

Click, P. M., & Click, D. W. (1990). *Administration of schools for young children*. Albany, NY: Delmar.

Council of Chief State School Officers. (1991). *Families in schools*. Washington, DC: Author.

Duncan, S., & Thornton, D. (1993, January/February). Marketing your center's service to employers. *Child Care Information Exchange, 89*, 53–56.

Eiselen, S. S. (1992). *The human side of child care administration: A how to manual*. Washington, DC: National Association for the Education of Young Children.

Essay. (1993, February). *U.S. News and World Report*, p. 51.

Finn, M. (1991). *Fund raising for early childhood programs*. Washington, DC: National Association for the Education of Young Children.

Galinsky, E. (1990). The cost of not providing quality early childhood programs: Reaching the full cost of quality in early childhood programs. *Young Children, 45*, 229–236.

Godwin, A., & Schrag, L. (1988). *Setting up for infant care: Guidelines for centers and family day care homes*. Washington, DC: National Association for the Education of Young Children.

Gonzalez-Mena, J. (1990). *A guide to routines*. Sacramento: California Department of Education.

The Governors' 1991 Report on Education. (1990). *Results in education*. Washington, DC: National Governors' Association.

Halpern, R. (1989). Community-based early intervention: The state of the art. In J. Shonkoff & S. Meisels (Eds.), *Handbook of early intervention*. New York: Cambridge University Press.

Hamburg, D. A. (1987). *Fundamental building blocks of early life*. New York: Carnegie Corp.

Hamburg, D. A. (1990). *A decent start: Promoting healthy child development in the first three years of life.* New York: Carnegie Corp.

Hamburg, D. A. (1991). *The family crucible and healthy child development.* New York: Carnegie Corp.

Hayes, C. D., Palmer, J. L., & Zaslow, M. J. (Eds.). (1990). *Who cares for America's children: Child care policy for the 1990's.* Panel on Child Care Policy, Committee on Child Development Research and Public Policy, Commission on Behavioral and Social Sciences and Education. Washington, DC: National Academy Press.

Hechinger, F. M. (Ed.). (1986). *A better start: New choices for early learning.* New York: Walker.

Hetherington, E. M., & Parke, R. D. (1986). *Child psychology: A contemporary viewpoint* (3rd ed.). New York: McGraw-Hill.

Hewlett, S. A. (1991). *When the bough breaks: The cost of neglecting our children.* New York: Basic Books.

Isenberg, J., & Quisenberry, N. L. (1988). Play: A necessity for all children. *Childhood Education,* 138–145.

Kagan, J. (1970). White House conference on children. Washington, DC: U.S. Government Printing Office.

Kagan, S. L. (1990). *Excellence in early childhood education: Defining characteristics and next-decade strategies.* Office of Education Research and Improvement, U.S. Department of Education. Washington, DC: U.S. Government Printing Office.

Kostelnik, M. J. (1992). Myths associated with developmentally appropriate programs. *Young Children, 47*(4), 17–23.

Lazar, I., & Darlington, R. (1982). Lasting effects of early education: A report for the consortium for longitudinal studies. *Monographs for Research in Child Development, 47*(2-3, Serial No. 195).

Maughan, B., & Rutter, M. (1985). Education: Improving practice through increasing understanding. In R. N. Rapaport (Ed.), *Children, youth, and families* (pp. 26–49). New York: Cambridge University Press.

Minnesota Department of Education. (1990). *Challenge 2000: Success for all learners.* St. Paul: Minnesota Department of Education.

Modigliani, K., Reiff, M., & Jones, S. (1991). *Opening your door to children: How to start a family day care program.* Washington, DC: National Association for the Education of Young Children.

National Association for the Education of Young Children. (1991). *Accreditation criteria and procedures of the National Academy of Early Childhood Programs.* Washington, DC: Author.

National Governors' Association Committee on Human Resources and Center Policy Research. (1987). *Focus on the first sixty months: A handbook of promising prevention programs for children zero to five years of age.* Washington, DC: Author.

National Institute for Early Childhood Professional Development. (1991). A Vision for Early Childhood Professional Development. *Young Children, 47*(1), 35–37.

National Research Council. (1990). *Who cares for America's children?* Washington, DC: National Academy Press.

New Zealand, Education Department Standards. (1968). *Standard for the administration and organization of play centres recognized by the director-general of education.* Appendix XI, circular memorandum B16613, pp. 42–43.

Overman, S. (1989). States offer incentives for corporate child care programs. *Personal Administrator, 5,* 31–41.

Parent Cooperative Preschools International. (1985). *How to start a co-op.* Indianapolis, IN: Author.

Recio, I. (1991). Beyond day care: The company school. *Business Week* (3239), 142.

Rutter, M. (1985). Family and school influences on cognitive development. In R. A. Hinde, A. N. Perret-Clermont, & J. Stevenson-Hinde (Eds.), *Social relationships and cognitive development* (pp. 83–108). Oxford, UK: Clarendon Press.

Seitz, V., & Provence, S. (1990). Caregiver-focused models of early intervention. In S. J. Meisels &

J. P. Shonkoff (Eds.), *Handbook of early childhood intervention*. New York: Cambridge University Press.

Sher, M., & Brown, G. (1989). What to do with Jenny: A corporate child care decision that greatly affects the bottom line. *Personnel Administrator, 5,* 31–41.

Smith, D. M. (1991). *Kincare and the American corporation solving the work/family dilemma*. Homewood, AL: Business One Irwin.

U.S. Department of Labor, Bureau of Labor Statistics. (1989, November). New Labor Force Projections Spanning 1988–2000, *Monthly Labor Review, 112*(11), 3–11.

Waxman, P. L. (1991). Children in the world of adults—On site child care. *Young Children,* 16–21.

Willer, B. (1992). An overview of the demand and supply of child care in 1990. *Young Children,* 19–21.

Willer, B., Hofferth, S. L., Kisker, E. E., Divine-Hawkins, P., Rarquhar, E., & Glantz, F. B. (1990). *The demand and supply of childcare in 1990*. Washington, DC: National Association for the Education of Young Children.

Wingert, P., & Kantrowitz, B. (1990, Winter/Spring). The daycare generation. *Newsweek,* pp. 226–228.

Zaslow, M. J. (1991). Variation in child care quality and its implications for children. *Journal of Social Issues, 47*(2), 125–138.

Zigler. M. J., & Lang, M. E. (1991). *Child care choices: Balancing the needs of children, families, and society*. New York: The Free Press.

Zigler, E. F., & Weiss, H. (1985). Family support systems: An ecological approach to child development. In R. N. Rapaport (Ed.), *Children, youth, and families* (pp. 166–205). New York: Cambridge University Press.

CHAPTER TWO

Parent Education and Parent Involvement

B eing supportive of children means involving their parents. Parent education precedes and then goes hand-in-hand with parent involvement as a vital part of any child-care center's efforts on behalf of children. As parents try ideas and materials with their children, they become involved and want to learn more, whether through parent education meetings, study groups, or send-home papers. (See Appendix A for Home Learning Enablers and Appendix B for Parent Papers.) As parents learn more about their children, such as how they develop and think, parents often become more interested in being active and involved with their children (Figure 2.1).

FIGURE 2.1
Parent Education and Parent
Involvement Develop Together

Parent education

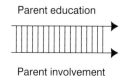

Parent involvement

Research shows the tremendous positive impact that even the smallest efforts on the part of parents can have on children. When parents are given help in supporting their children's learning, it has been found that children hold their gains longer (Henderson, 1987; Moles, 1982; Linney & Vernberg, 1983; Clark, 1983). In a review of 37 studies, the most clearly positive results were found when parent participation of almost any kind was a critical ingredient in the program. In follow-up studies 10 years later, these children were still performing at higher levels both academically and socially (Henderson, 1987), as shown in Figure 2.2.

These studies also showed that the more intensely and longer the parents supported their children, the better the children did (Linney & Vernberg, 1983; Henderson, 1987). When parents were involved in activities with their own young children, although a small additional cost to the center was involved (for example, the cost of one ream of paper for send-home activities, which actually could be charged to the parents), the impact of state, federally funded, and any well-organized early childhood programs in some cases almost doubled (Jones, 1981). Susan Gray (1971) found that, along with the gains of the children involved in the child-care program, the I.Q.s of younger and older siblings also went up when home visits and parent activities were part of the program. It has been stated that the least expensive way to reach every child is to reach every parent.

FIGURE 2.2
Short-Term Gains versus Lasting
Gains with Parent Involvement

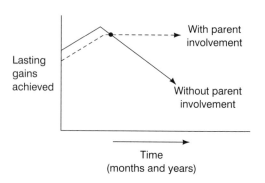

PARENT-CHILD INTERACTION

Rich empirical and philosophical literature has existed for many years describing the deep and lasting benefits of parent-child interaction. This literature includes concepts about the nature and development of infant learning, insight into the ways children develop thought processes, and new interpretations of the structure of knowledge and early learning.

Environmental influences on learning, the effects of the family upon achievement, and the effect of early stimulation upon later life have also been studied. It has been noted that the most familiar sound to a baby or young child is the sound of his or her mother's voice. Babies can distinguish the timbre and pitch of their own mother's voice from the day of birth, partly because they heard her voice before they were born (Friedman, 1978). The impact of the mother-child bond on learning, and of the father-child bond (since his voice is usually the second-most familiar) on learning, has only been peripherally explored. However, it seems that family members who were present during the pregnancy have the most direct impact on learning, and all family members have a very strong impact (Bornstein and Tamis-Lemonda, 1989).

Professional educators who work directly with children, especially children over six years of age, have much less influence on children's learning than was previously thought, according to Burton White (1974). With this perspective in mind, the family must receive increasing priority as the first educational delivery system.

Hamburg (1990), as well as White and many others, list three main obstacles confronting families as they attempt to educate their young children: ignorance (not knowing what is helpful), stress (economic stress and physical stress, such as tiredness from coping), and a lack of assistance from local, county, state, or federal resources. Many programs for parents have been designed to help parents overcome at least the first and last of these obstacles—ignorance and lack of assistance. Parent education and assistance programs might benefit from addressing four areas that make up the foundation of educational capacity: language development, curiosity, social development, and cognitive intelligence (White, 1974).

Clark (1983) isolated some characteristics of families whose children do well in school; these qualities appeared in both single and two-parent homes, and in both poor and middle-class families:

- Clearly expressed valuation and support of education and achievement;
- Parents' sense of self-mastery and control over their own lives;
- Frequent discussions, positive expectations, and support and reinforcement of interests and schoolwork; and
- A family climate that includes regular routines and mealtimes and encourages purposeful use of time and space.

Providing support to families, with two-way communication being a key ingredient, can help more of these characteristics to occur.

Bloom's studies (1964, 1981) also support the critical importance of the home and of parents as teachers of their children. The findings confirm the statements of Goodson, Swartz, and Millsap (1991) that parent involvement produces the most lasting retention of gains made. Bloom (1981) indicated that differences in children's academic and cognitive development can be traced to the value placed on education by the family and specifically to parents' reinforcement of the child's activities in school. Bloom (1964) also found that one-half of all intellectual differences that exist at age 17 can be found in the range of differences seen in that child at age 4.

Parent–Child Interaction and Intelligence

A significant group of early education projects sprang up following the publication of Benjamin Bloom's book *Stability and Change in Human Characteristics* (1964), which brought out the importance of early education. Earl Schaefer, who was part of the Infant Education Project at Catholic University in Washington, D.C., was a leader in one of the first of these projects. Schaefer was knowledgeable about the differences in mental test scores that emerge in the second and third years of life. In a presentation entitled *Parenting and Child Behavior Predictors of Retention in Grades K, 1, 2* (1986) he revisited these important concepts.

Schaefer believed in the importance of early education, and designed an experiment in which tutors visited the homes of disadvantaged boys between the ages of fifteen months and three years. This was a child-centered tutoring program in which the tutor worked with the children one hour a day, five days a week. The children did very well, confirming the experimenter's hypothesis on the benefits of early education.

After tutoring stopped at three years of age, follow-up testing showed that the I.Q.s of the experimental children began to decline, while the I.Q.s of the control group began to come up. The parents of the children in the control group had seen only the testing activities, but had not seen the tutoring used with the experimental group. Schaefer (1974) states about these parents:

> To some extent they grew interested in their child's intellectual development. I think it is conceivable that our control groups' parents grew more interested in helping their child develop than our experimental groups' parents were when we tutored their children—we are the experts; we have the competence; we have the skills; we will take responsibility for educating your child. And that's always wrong. Professionals can't do it. They are there for only a limited time each day. And a limited time isn't enough. So this dialectic process started out—the need for early education, which was confirmed. Then the drop in test scores after we stopped lead to an antithesis—the need for continuing education. The only synthesis and antithesis is to develop the family as an educational institution right from birth to maturity. (p. 18)

Schaefer (1974) then went on to examine studies that did involve the family. He says:

> Look at Phyllis Levenstein's early study, don't look at my study. The I.Q.s of the children in the Mother's Home Training Program went up 17 points in 7 months, whereas the I.Q.s of the children in my study went up 17 points in 21 months and then dropped. (p. 18)

In addition to the Mother's Home Training Program (Levenstein, 1975), Schaefer also recommended Susan Gray's study (1971), which shows the impact of parents' interaction with their children on lasting improvement in I.Q. scores, as do many other studies (Asp & Levine, 1985; Clark, 1983; Epstein, 1984a, 1986, 1987b, 1987c, 1988b; Hess & McDevitt, 1984; Lazar, 1977).

In Levenstein's Mother's Home Training Program, the decline in I.Q. scores did not appear, suggesting that this project's model of verbal interaction between parent and child (in contrast to the tutor-child model in the Schaefer project) shows that parent participation is a crucial factor in the maintenance of long-term effects.

The Family Development Research Program at Syracuse University (Honig, 1978) in reporting their longitudinal findings obtained from observing families with normal and special needs children interacting at home, found many benefits in helping families to improve parenting skills, as did many of the other studies already mentioned. A summary of Honig's findings indicated that mothers who planned and organized their infants' experiences and routines produced the most competent babies. Her studies also indicated that those children exposed to typical nursery-school toys, such as crayons, paper, and puzzles, appeared more competent than those lacking this exposure (Honig, 1989).

Another positive factor connected with competent children was that they were allowed to help a lot with household chores, such as dusting, hammering, raking leaves, and helping to sort the laundry. Other factors contributing to the children's level of competence (according to Honig, 1978) included limiting television viewing time, reading to the children, and allowing the children to delve into "messy" and perhaps even slightly dangerous processes. In other words, the most competent children had parents who (1) severely limited and supervised television viewing; (2) read to the children regularly on a daily basis; and (3) allowed the children to experiment with blunt scissors, for example, or wash dishes.

The mothers of the competent children modeled appropriate activities; were good observers; praised, encouraged, suggested options, and served as facilitators; and behaved as teachers. The fathers in these families inject a positive aspect also. The study indicated that the fathers of the competent babies also spent more positive interaction time with their children. The competent children's parents had firm, consistent household rules, for which they provided explanations. They engaged in role-playing games as well as other games and entertainment with their children that provided intellectual content. As a result of these findings, Honig suggested that some children have a higher level of competence which results from their relationship with their parents (Honig, 1978).

Lally and Honig (1977) reported the results of a comprehensive "omnibus" program of family services that included home visits plus center child care for 2½ years to 108 families low in income and education. Data indicated that families in this program saw their participating children, in comparison with siblings and peers, as more likely to ask questions, make their own choices, teach other children, try new and difficult tasks, and fight less often.

In 1981, Jones conducted a study that tracked I.Q. changes that occurred after using parent-involvement send-home papers (see Home Learning Enablers, Appendix A) weekly for 14 weeks with 127 three-year-olds in 15 federally funded child-care centers. Overall, the treatment children (those whose parents were given the Home Learning Enablers) gained an average of almost 4 points more than did the control children, and the children in both groups gained an average of 5 points just from being in a well-organized child-care program (with some variation across the centers, of course). Thus, nearly 9 points were gained in the 14 weeks for the treatment children.

One negative development also appeared in the study: The higher I.Q. children *lost* I.Q. points over the 14-week period. The more-able treatment children lost an average of 5 points *less* than did the more-able control children, but both groups lost points since there were no provisions for gifted children in the centers. I.Q. fluctuations also occurred for children who had traumatic experiences during the 14-week period (e.g., one child stated, "The police come and take my Mommy away."). These children dropped in scores, but started to regain ground before the end of the study. Some children showed extremely high gains.

Overall, however, the study results backed the current research findings, showing that by implementing 14 weekly home-learning, send-home papers per child, the gains sought by the center's program could be nearly doubled (Jones, 1981).

Parent–Child Interaction and Language

A number of studies and programs have focused specifically on the impact of the parent-child relationship on language development. Studies have ranged from naturalistic home observations of behaviors that encouraged children verbally, to quite structured approaches aimed at changing a mother's syntax and grammar and thus improving her child's.

Many writers have focused on ways to help parents during the crucial years of their children's language development. Larrick (1976), for example, concentrates on ways parents can help their children develop oral language facility and build positive attitudes toward the printed language so they will learn to read easily and happily. Reading aloud to children from an early age (6 to 24 months and up) continues to be supported by study after study (Fredericks & Rasinski, 1990; Hess, Holloway, Dickson, & Price, 1984; Mavrogenes, 1990; Norman-Jackson, 1982). The parents' reading level seems to be less important than the activity itself.

Thus, in summing up current research results, the importance of the home environment in language development can only be underlined (Anderson, Fielding, & Wilson, 1988; Clay, 1987; Jenson, 1985; Silvern, 1985).

Parent–Child Interaction and School Achievement

To understand the roles of parents in schools today, it might be useful to look at how parents' interaction with schools came into being. According to Hobbs (1976), at one time many schools regarded parents as a nuisance and many parents regarded schools as forbidden places in which they should have no legitimate interest. The view of "let the experts do it" was prevalent among parents and was encouraged by schools (Schaefer, 1974). However, in the past two decades, families and programs for young children have been coming together in many interesting ways as they begin to realize the importance of the relationship of parent-child interaction to later school achievement (Council of Chief State School Officers, 1989).

Schools at one point followed the industrial model. They removed the children from the family, set up a system of authority based on state-level sanctions and expertise, and instituted a "work" discipline similar to that of adult organizations. As time has progressed, the relationship between educational settings and parents, and between teachers and parents, has improved, but not to its fullest extent.

As we have seen, there is a need to build stronger parent-child interaction in the early years of a child's life, not only to help later school achievement, but also for other reasons. As many researchers are beginning to document, perhaps strengthening the parent-child relationship may become the answer to the cries of teachers who are frustrated because they are not able to bring about the results they want from the children in their classrooms. Perhaps this will be the answer for those frustrated and disappointed parents who see their children not achieving satisfactorily at school and feel that it must be the school's fault. These attitudes can be seen spilling over into the classrooms of child-care programs.

It has been said that achievement starts and builds at home (Rich & Jones, 1978; Schaefer, 1974). From parents, children learn basic attitudes toward learning and develop the values that will later be infused into academic tasks. Parent-child interaction is important in the educational process because children's first and most potent teachers are their parents (Taylor, 1967). It is not the sole responsibility of schools and child-care centers to educate children, nor should they try to do it alone. In order to maximize the learning process, it is necessary for schools and centers to seek the aid of parents.

Coleman (1966, 1973) demonstrated that reading achievement is more fully an outgrowth of home influences than it is a function of what takes place in school. Moore and others (1976) discuss research into the role of in-home and out-of-home early childhood education and the effects of both on later academic achievement. In this discussion, the importance of the role of the family and home environment in early education is emphasized, and it is suggested that providing education in parenting skills and in improving the home environment should be primary goals of early childhood education (Gordon, 1977; Henderson, 1987; Swap, 1987).

Research suggests clearly that the home has as much or more influence on student learning as do teachers and the educational setting. The most effective children's program, therefore, will be one in which the home and the school or center work together on behalf of the child. Even with this knowledge, parent involvement still has not entered into the mainstream of teacher education but remains on the edges. This may continue to be the case unless teacher educators, teachers, administrators, parents, and politicians see the need to change the situation. If they choose the path of greater parent involvement, the child is likely to emerge the winner (Greenwood & Hickman, 1991).

INSTRUCTIONAL MATERIALS

An emphasis on children's interaction with specific learning materials has a long tradition in early childhood education, beginning with Frederich Froebel (1782–1852). Froebel (1902) created a variety of toys, or "gifts" as he called them, designed to help children learn about the world and about themselves. Froebel's ideas greatly influenced programs for young children in the late 1800s, especially his emphasis on the importance of children's play.

Maria Montessori (1870–1952) also designed an elaborate set of materials (1968). Her goal was to increase children's abilities to discriminate among stimuli and to order stimuli among various dimensions, such as height, weight, and color. In the Montessori system, the critical relationship is that between the child and his or her learning materials.

According to Dewey (1938), thinking is best promoted by allowing children the opportunity to engage in experiences that suggest problems to be solved. Most interpretations of this position suggest that such experiences need to be concrete in nature. For example, field trips and excursions into the immediate community provide experiences and thinking activities.

Piaget (1973), in studying the way children come to understand their world, concluded that early sensorimotor experience with concrete objects plays a crucial role in the development of thought. This belief suggests that children younger than age 5 need to have a variety of experiences with concrete manipulatives, both at home and in group settings.

Most child-care centers provide opportunities for a wide range of experiences. The typical materials found in early learning settings show a high level of consistency. This array of materials provides a range of opportunities to develop or build upon skills and concepts. Children in these programs are encouraged to explore and experiment with these materials in a variety of ways.

Science, math, language, and other academic subjects can be the basis of a host of learning activities involving manipulation, observation, and record-keeping. Cooking and nutrition-oriented activities also make use of sensorimotor experiences as a means for learning.

Each type of manipulatable material requires a slightly different combination of skills and competencies. When using these manipulatives, children are also required to answer different questions that help them build on the skills and competencies they are learning. Helping adults understand the purpose of these questions can help adults, whether parents or teachers, to make full use of the materials as mediums or catalysts in children's thinking and learning. The Home Learning Enablers in Appendix A provide this type of help in a send-home format for parents.

Instructional Materials and Programs for Parents

Many kinds of instructional programs and materials are available to parents. Some—such as study groups, books and manuals for improving parenting skills, home visits and parent participation opportunities in early childhood programs—do not focus, except peripherally, on the parents' use of instructional materials with their own children. Some parent involvement or outreach efforts, however, do provide activities and materials to give parents. Often these are provided all together in a book or packet.

A literature search reveals very little information about the types of materials prepared by instructional programs that are meant to be used by parents. There is little description of these materials in terms of time needed, complexity, attractiveness, or adaptability to individual home situations. There are a few exceptions, however. For example, the *Family Math* book (Stenmark, Thompson, & Cossey, 1986) contains specific activities for kindergarten and older children. Another simple yet effective program for sending home materials, developed by Carol Rountree for a class project in 1992, is the PAL (Parent Assisted Learning) bag. This canvas tote bag, containing a book the child selects along with specific activities related to the book, is sent home for one to two weeks by the center or program. (A software program disk or CD ROM disk could also be sent home this way.) If funds are available, a blank tape can be included in the bag with a request for parents to record the reading of the story and the child's innovations. Parents are also asked to keep a journal of activities.

It is a developmentally appropriate practice, according to Bredekamp (1990), "to view parents as integral partners in the educational practice." However, many parents neither appreciate nor understand the critical role they play in literacy development (Jewell & Lintz, 1990). Egawa (1990) encourages adult participation in activities that connect a child with a book; it is often through an adult's reaction to a given book that a child's perceptions and emotional responses are born, thus building purposefulness into the literacy activity. Jacqueline Norman-Jackson (1982) found that successful readers in second grade differed from unsuccessful ones in the amount of verbal interaction that took place with family members during the pre-elementary school years. Thus, active participation by parents and families in a child's education is as essential for academic success as are multisensory activities that address a child's individual learning style (Kennedy, 1991; Hess & McDevitt, 1984; Carbo, Dunn, & Dunn, 1986).

Epstein (1989) reported that when teachers encouraged parents, parents' involvement in their children's education increased. Many programs utilize a number of strategies to encourage parents, including newsletters that suggest home activities for parents to do with their children. The goals for such programs are to promote a home environment that reinforces the school or center environment, and to help the program director assist parents with their expectations of their children.

A newsletter, in addition to home learning activities, is a must for a well-run center or program. Child development information and current curriculum topics make good columns to include, as do activity ideas for parents to do with their children. (These ideas can even include cooking recipes.) Many Directors and teachers find it helpful to share samples of their program's Parent Newsletters at professional meetings or at local Director/Teacher Council meetings. Directors or teachers who do not have time or do not have a committee to produce a monthly newsletter can buy or subscribe to inserts for newsletters; for example, the Parent Papers in Appendix B make good newsletter inserts. The sample newsletter in Figure 2.3 can be used as a model, with different news items printed or typed in the boxes. A prepared insert could then be stapled to this "cover sheet," and communication is under way. The Parent's Helping List shown in Figure 2.4 is another sample newsletter insert appropriate for kindergarten programs.

Training manuals are available to instructors of parent study groups whose members are interested in learning new parenting skills. It is hoped that with this assistance, these study groups will foster home-based early childhood education. Although no materials are provided specifically for parent members, many study groups suggest ideas for nonconcrete activities, such as games and songs for parents and children to enjoy together. Group discussions in these study groups might include topics such as using behavior modification techniques and helping children develop self-control. Parent Papers (Sets 1 and 2) in Appendix B also provide a springboard for discussions on a variety of topics with a child-development focus including discipline.

FIGURE 2.3
Sample Newsletter Cover Sheet

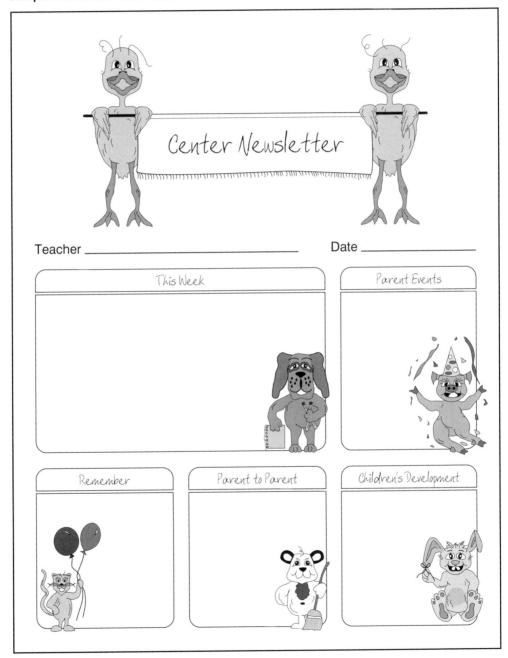

FIGURE 2.4
A Parent's Helping List

Parent's Helping List

1. *Kitchen/Cooking Parent (need at least 2)*
   To bring to class the prepared food items needed for class projects (i.e., celery washed and cut).

2. *Art Room Parent (need at least 2)*
   Assist weekly in the Art Room from 9:30 to 10:30 a.m. Take home art smocks and wash weekly so they are clean and fresh for next class project.

3. *Field Trip Parents (need at least 5)*
   Accompany class of approximately 22 students on field trips throughout the year to make it enjoyable and safe for the children.

4. *At Home Projects Volunteers*
   Prepare classroom items as needed (i.e., cut out pictures, gather colored leaves, etc.).

5. *Class Party Parents (need 4)*
   To set up, make materials for, and clean up after the classroom parties.

6. *Woodworking Parent*
   Collect and donate wood.

7. *Typing (2nd semester) (need 2)*
   To prepare students' stories into finished products. Another parent should be available to work directly with children in our room. (Flexible hours)

8. *Garage Sale Parents*
   All parents can participate in this area. The class needs at least 4 diligent parents to actively search for safe, inexpensive roller skates, small bikes, and Big Wheels to help upgrade the dwindling classroom supply.

9. *Computer Volunteers*
   Volunteer to help directly with kids in our room with our computer as needed. Prior computer skills needed. We supply software and computer.

Name:

Phone #:

Child's name:

Home Visits as Instructional Programs/Opportunities for Parents

Regardless of the socioeconomic status of the home, all parents want their children to achieve in education, but often they do not know how to help their children attain that goal (Kennedy, 1991); many of these parents desire teacher or center direction in this endeavor (Mavrogenes, 1990). Home visits are one way of helping parents achieve educational goals for their children. One example of a research program that included home visits is the Family Development Research Program (Honig, 1979). This program offered a quality infant day-care service that incorporated a home visitation component. The goals of the home visit program were to maximize family functioning, contribute to parental knowledge of child development, and foster parent involvement in their children's cognitive and psychosocial development. Materials were not given directly to the parents, only to the home visitors.

Another project that utilized home visits is the Houston Parent-Child Development Center, which developed a program to meet the needs of low-income Mexican-American families with preschool children. The program included home visits and family workshops in its agenda, as do many similar programs.

During instructional home visits, parents often are given or shown educational activities to participate in with their children. To make sure that these brief home activities are used in developmentally appropriate ways, it is important for the program representative to model the activities during the home visits, as well as in the program setting. This is best accomplished after establishing trust with the parents and perhaps other family members. Many other examples of successful home visit models are listed in this chapter. Head Start and other federally funded programs use home visits as a vital part of building the home-school link that, according to Bronfenbrenner (1979), helps a child feel secure and successful. Developing and using self-evaluation checklists for home visitors may be useful in helping participating programs meet their goals for home visits.

Parental Participation in the Classroom as Instructional Opportunities for Parents

The Compensatory Education Program for Preschoolers in Fresno, California, offered a school setting for two-, three-, four-, and five-year-olds with the requirement that parents in the program participate one day a week. Advice was given to parents about how to interact with the children during the one-day period per week the parents would spend participating in the program. Parents learned about the specific needs and abilities of preschool children, and materials helpful to parents also were listed in the newsletter. Cooperative nursery schools offer many of these same benefits.

A few programs combine some of the characteristics previously discussed, such as group discussions, home visits, classroom participation, and activities for parents to use with their children as a follow-up to training sessions. Head Start, Home Start, and Even Start are some programs that combine approaches and that provide suggested home activities.

Home Instructional Materials Used by Parents

Activities that parents actually engage in with their children, whether for the purpose of building social or cognitive skills, fall into several categories depending on the type of instructional materials needed. The first category includes activities that make use of common household items; the second category includes activities organized around specific instructional materials either provided to the parent or carefully described; and the third category includes activities such as reading stories, playing games, or taking part in general arts and crafts projects that either build language or positive self-concepts.

Activities with Common Household Items

Gray and Ruttle (1976) designed a longitudinal study in which 51 low-income families, each with two children under the age of five, participated in a 5-year home-based intervention study designed to help mothers become more effective educational agents. One group of families received a 9-month treatment based on the needs and characteristics of the specific families; another group received a treatment that focused on materials the mothers were to use in the homes with their children; a third group was made the control group. When mothers and children were pretested and posttested on a range of instruments relating to maternal and child competency, the results of the first two groups were positive and above those of the control group (Gray & Ruttle 1976; Gray, 1984).

The Demonstration and Research Center for Early Education (DARCEE), in a report compiled by the Far West Laboratories (1971), described a training program designed for three groups of parents. One group would participate in the training program within the environment of a demonstration center; the second group would be given the training by a home visitor; the third group of parents and children were in a school setting that did not incorporate parent involvement or parent training (this was the control group). The training consisted of teaching parents to use common household items as teaching tools and to take advantage of everyday home situations as opportunities for teaching specific skills, such as using laundry to teach the child about colors and sorting. Parents participating in the training also received instructional materials used by the teachers and samples of the work done by the children for their own use with their children.

Gray and Klaus (1970) and Gray, Ramsey, and Klaus (1981), who worked closely with this project, reported that the results for the group attached to the center were superior to those for the home visitor group and for the control group. The target children and their younger siblings in the home visitor group did show significant gains in I.Q., but their gains were not as high as those of target children whose parents were trained in the center. After two years of public school, all three groups were again tested, and it was found that in the two target groups, the children's I.Q.s had remained stable. In the group in which the mothers were not involved, however, there was a decline in I.Q.s. As a result of these findings, Gray suggests that perhaps working with parents is not only highly economical from the standpoint of immediate cost efficiency, but also has long-lasting benefits for the child.

Hess and McDevitt (1984), in their longitudinal study of maternal intervention techniques and their effects on cognition, also found lasting benefits to working with parents, but found that the method in which a mother interacted with her child in learning situations had a direct influence on the child's performance. The more controlling the mother's directions were, the poorer the child's outcome. The authors found that children who were guided and encouraged to discover solutions for themselves were more likely to see themselves as capable problem-solvers and to transfer that sense of competency to other settings (Hess & McDevitt, 1984). Suggestions by professionals for appropriate parental and family responses to children's efforts, and guidance for implementing these responses, are therefore also needed when setting up training programs for parents.

In an English-Chinese program in California, called "Parents Helping Children to Learn" (Fuduka, 1976), activities were suggested that parents could do with their children to supplement the school program. Twelve monthly "letters" were sent home that contained four to six ideas for each month. These ideas included practical exercises such as setting the table, sorting the laundry, and cooking, as well as such activities as outings to the library and to the park, playing games, making handicrafts, coloring and painting, and reading picture stories with simple words.

Shoemaker, in *Home Learning Enablers and Other Helps* (1994), suggests activities categorized by age and subject matter for parents to do with their children. These activities make use of common household materials or daily routines. Cooking, making trips to the supermarket or the gas station, and using materials such as newspapers, toilet paper, kitchen cans, and jars are just a few suggestions specific to ages three, four, five, six, and seven; third, fourth, fifth, and sixth grades; and middle school/junior high. A section in each activity is devoted to adapting the activity for older or younger children, the parents' evaluation of the success of the activity, and space for "new ideas" from the parent or the child. While these Home Learning Enablers suggest specific materials to use in each activity, the materials are common to most homes. These Home Learning Enablers are to be sent home weekly, biweekly, or monthly. (See Appendix A for Home Learning Enabler samples for ages three, four, and five.)

Activities with Specific Instructional Materials

One well-documented project that made use of specific instructional materials was Phyllis Levenstein's Mother's Home Training Program. This study utilized specific curriculum materials composed of 12 books and 11 toys, which were all carefully selected based on well-defined criteria. All components of the curriculum were designed to promote verbal interaction between mother and child, and family and child. Between 1967 and 1974, more than 300 children and their mothers participated in the program, accomplishing both its cognitive and affective objectives. Over a period of 32 home visits in 7 months, Levenstein reported a 17-point I.Q. gain in her population (Levenstein, 1975).

One of the most valuable aspects of the program, reports Hess and Goodson (1975), is that its design allowed for specification of some of the variables. For example, situations that did not involve the mother/child dyad or the specified toy or book were not nearly as effective as were situations involving three variables: a toy demonstrator, the mother and child, and the toy or book. Follow-up results support the active role of the parent as teacher in a child's development.

Fourteen years after the beginning of Levenstein's project, Levenstein was able to say that the effects of the Mother's Home Training Program last into the third grade (Russell, 1979). Learning takes place, according to Levenstein, because the child is *in* the mother-child relationship. Those aware of the mother-child bond often are tempted to try to intensify it—to give mothers child-rearing advice when listening to their troubles. Levenstein views this as an invasion of privacy and favors a "light touch," or a nonintrusive approach. This strategy, she feels, ensures respect for families, and promotes the learning that occurs in the constant reciprocal process between mother and child, which is the heart of this program. Father-child and family-child programs have also shown gains. Levenstein is dismayed by programs that show disdain for the people with whom they are working. She also deplores programs that do not give top-quality curriculum materials to the families as a long-lasting focus of verbal stimulation and a bridge to later school experience.

Instructional materials need not be commercial, of course, to be beneficial. For instance, parent education manuals for parents of preschool children with disabilities describe specific instructional materials or toys that can be made. Some of these toys include spools for stringing, spools of graduated sizes, graduated cans, a lacing shoe, a sandpaper alphabet, a lotto game, sequence cards, lacing cards, and rough and smooth cards. Children without disabilities would also enjoy these activities.

Early childhood is a time ripe with opportunities for instruction. Burton White (1975b), in describing the last half of a child's second year and the child's third year, states that this is a time for nurturing the roots of intelligence—the learning to learn skills—as well as a time for development of language, social skills, and curiosity. He gives general suggestions for encouraging competence and suggests specific materials that he especially recommends for the 2- to 3-year-old. White's list includes commercial toys and household materials such as cans, pots and pans, and plastic refrigerator containers with lids of all sizes. He does not, however, suggest activities or skills that might be developed with these materials.

Gordon, Guinagh, and Jester (1972) state that "the years between two and four are special because so much happens in the child's use of speech and language" (p.1). They go on to say that the way in which parents and adults play and work with children at these ages is of special importance.

Activities to Build Language and Self-Concept at Home

Newsletters or handouts for parents of preschool children can be used to provide ideas for play experiences that are informal learning activities. Language games, mathematical concept games, and creative activities can be suggested and explained in detail. Such activities have the potential to enhance the social, emotional, cognitive, motor, and language development of preschool children. No materials need be provided, although any materials needed for creative activities can be listed in that section. Hints for parents on interacting with their children also could be included. A section on traditional arts and crafts for children, as well as science, cooking, gardening, drama, and woodworking, can be worked into the newsletter schedule also. Family outings, pet care, and chores are also good topics.

Preparation of Instructional Materials for Parent Use

While so much has been written on preparing instructional materials for use by educators, very little has been written on preparing instructional materials that might be used especially by parents. Indeed, a great many of the parent education programs and handbooks provide parents with instructional activities involving only spoken words to use as instructional tools, despite the evidence that preschool children learn best through concrete experience.

The Home Learning Enablers (Shoemaker, 1992, 1994; see Appendix A) and *Family Math* (Stenmark, Thompson, & Cossey, 1986) are two resources written with parents in mind. They both use formats for each activity that are easy for adults to scan; each activity lists the components of the exercise, and leaves plenty of white space to visually separate the logical sequence of needed steps.

The following steps are included in the Home Learning Enablers: name of activity, materials needed, how to do it, time needed, age of child, evaluation, and adaptation. Many of the Learning Enablers also list subject-matter categories for areas in which an activity builds skills.

The "time needed" step is a unique feature of the Home Learning Enablers in that many programs do not incorporate the variable of time into their procedures. White's (1975) extensive research in the Harvard Preschool Project points to the importance of time as a learning variable, noting that 30- to 60-second "brief enrichments" are most beneficial to young children since their attention span is short. The time length of the Home Learning Enabler activities starts with two or three minutes for toddlers, and works up to 15 minutes for junior-high-age children.

The *Family Math* activities are all math-related, of course, but do list objectives and explain how to do each activity, which is very helpful. These activities are for kindergarten age and older. Some of these might be very useful as send-home resources from child-care programs for school-age children.

The Home Learning Enablers and *Family Math* both feature brief one-page activities for easy assimilation by parents. Many activity books cram several activities onto each page. Another drawback to such activity books is that while many of the materials are suggested for use by parents or are given to the parents, the simple language meant to make these materials accessible is often lost in the paragraph-style writing and in the small print.

When preparing instructional materials for parents, videos for parent groups also might be included. The usefulness of these materials is somewhat limited, however, since they rely on the spoken word and visual impact rather than on concrete materials the parents use with their children.

In conclusion, it seems that very little is available to assist in the preparation of materials for parents to use with their children. The materials available for parents of children with disabilities or of bilingual children are quite specific to families in those particular situations, and are also specific in terms of the suggested concrete materials to be used. There are a few programs for parents, however, that benefit a wider range of families, and that are unique in utilizing common household items in a specific, logical way that is easy for most parents to follow.

INVOLVEMENT OF PARENTS WITH LIMITED ENGLISH PROFICIENCY

In order to promote the healthy self-esteem and success of each and every young child, early childhood programs must be thoughtfully designed to serve both parents and children. This is a particularly challenging task when the families to be served speak a language other than English at home. Programs for young limited English proficiency (LEP) children need to be designed to reinforce the strengths of the individual child and his or her family. Because families are the groups of greatest importance to young children, programs must serve the whole child within the context of the family (Derman-Sparks & A.B.C. Task Force, 1989).

According to Dixon and Fraser (1986), having parents of LEP students participate is a reliable way to gain information about children's family traditions and attitudes, particularly when these children are from cultural backgrounds unfamiliar to the teacher.

Early intervention is key to the academic success of educationally and economically disadvantaged students, many of whom are LEP students. Research has found that a combination of early intervention and parent involvement increases children's educational achievement (Vargas, 1988).

Research in the field of early childhood education indicates that parental involvement is a necessary condition to ensure the success of all children in early childhood programs (Nissani, 1990). Parents provide the needed link between home and school or center. Much of the research involving bilingual/multicultural education in early childhood emphasizes the role of parents, either directly in the classroom or in auxiliary programs. Data gathered from several programs shows that in programs where children make the greatest gains, parents have been actively involved (Arnberg, 1983). In a review of 20 bilingual preschool education programs around the world, almost 70 percent of them reported parental involvement as a major component of their program (Arnberg, 1983).

Overall, research has demonstrated that even a modest degree of parental involvement has a positive effect on a child's later academic achievement and promotes a generally improved attitude towards learning. The effects are even more powerful among lower socioeconomic and minority students. Studies undertaken in New Haven, Connecticut, between 1969 and 1984 indicated that parent participation activities improved parent-teacher relations, energized both the parents and the teachers, and had a favorable impact on the students (Ornstein & Levine, 1989).

The focus or goals of a program can be more easily understood and learned by a parent who is visiting the classroom, with an interpreter when necessary. In addition to observing, often parents can be directly involved in working in the classroom. In some programs, parent involvement may be gained through home visits, which encourage and support parents as they work with their children at home.

Social events, such as a potluck supper or a Saturday flea market/yard sale, are often a first step in making parents feel comfortable and involved, since eating and socializing together in this context just naturally brings about conversations about children and school. A special parent education committee could be organized to compile a list of possible activities, from which the most popular ideas could be selected and voted on. Two or more parents might be put in charge of each event, which could occur monthly or at times and intervals parents prefer. One center felt its surrounding neighborhood was unsafe, and held parent gatherings at breakfast or supper times to coordinate with drop-off and pick-up times.

Parent involvement opportunities should be made available to all parents. Often language-minority parent involvement in their children's education is inhibited by language barriers, lack of knowledge about the program, high mobility rates, insufficient incentives to become involved, and shortage of staff time to encourage and nurture parental involvement while trying to fulfill the basic curriculum objectives. Early childhood programs that serve language-minority students should employ staff familiar with the needs of the families they serve. This includes bilingual and culturally sensitive personnel who are trained in parent involvement concepts and methods and so are able to attract parent participation. A responsive staff will make a parent feel welcome and important, and this will affect the parent's decision to respond to and participate in the program's activities. It is critical that early childhood education programs communicate with parents in a language and form the parents understand (Vargas, 1988).

Issues of sociocultural differences and the importance of teacher attitudes in establishing home/child-care program interdependence are certainly very relevant to the education of language-minority children. To date, neither parents nor centers and schools have taken full advantage of the benefits of parent involvement.

Parental involvement in the classroom ultimately benefits children, because by observing teachers and the way in which children learn and interact in school, parents can become aware of ways in which they can help their children learn (Arnberg, 1983). Programs that incorporate home visits, particularly if the professional involved in the visit is bilingual and/or is a member of the parents' minority group and so is not seen as a threat by the parents, can demonstrate ways in which parents can stimulate their children's growth in the home. Parents are not uninterested in their children's development and education, but often lack skills and knowledge concerning how they can positively influence their children's growth. Home visits have been demonstrated to increase parent involvement, enhance children's self-esteem, support the curriculum, and help alleviate communication problems for some bilingual families (Fox-Barnett & Meyer, 1992). The visits give parents an opportunity to communicate with the teacher without the boundaries of an institution. When such visits are not judgmental or critical, the parents may in turn feel that the center or school is a more approachable place (Fox-Barnett & Meyer, 1992).

Another commonly used method for involving parents in the classroom is to provide workshops or classes on ways to develop children's skills at home and to reinforce what is learned at the center or nursery school. With this goal in mind, the focus of early childhood education for parents should be topics such as emergent literacy and whole-language skills, ways to reinforce basic math concepts, oral language development, the role of self-concept, and the use of games for skills development. Since the most common reason given for seeking parent involvement is that it improves academic achievement, it may be argued that a crucial focus of parent involvement should be in activities that relate directly to academic tasks (Cervantes, Baca, & Torres, 1979). While the role of minority parents in the classroom is often limited to such activities as cooking or making music, some more academic programs have been established with language minority families in mind. For example, programs have been developed to enhance language minority parents' and children's reading attitudes as they participate in a series of instructional sessions. Activities for building communication skills as well as methods of reading aloud to children are modeled for parents, and the parents have an opportunity to practice the activities in the classroom as well as at home. Researchers have concluded that modeling is an effective method for training parents in skills for working with their children at home (Ovando & Collier, 1985).

Parents want the best for their children, and they rely on educational programs to enable their children to succeed. Although parents may not always have the time, self-confidence, or clear understanding of the program's goals to demonstrate that concern in a fashion that is recognizable to the school or center, language-minority parents, as well as other parents, must make it a priority to be an active and integral part of the center's program. The success and strength of parent-center relationships in multilingual communities will depend on parents reinforcing their children's cognitive development at home. Ethnic parents, like all parents, will appreciate and help work toward community and center efforts that value their contributions, yield positive academic results, and encourage positive interpersonal and intercultural relationships.

One way to foster positive community participation is to allow parents to plan a day or days in which emphasis is placed on their particular culture. This event could involve activities such as reading brief stories to the children in parents' native languages (other than English), bringing artifacts or pictures from home to share, preparing a typical dish with the children, bringing music and/or clothing from their country, or teaching the children a typical game, song, or craft. This not only increases parents' self-esteem, but also reflects positively on their children, since this is an opportunity for the children of this particular culture to play an important role by having their parents share something that is such an important part of their lives. In addition to exposing children to artwork and materials from different cultures, by integrating the cultures that are represented in the classroom *into* the classroom throughout the year, a mere "tourist curriculum" approach is prevented.

When incorporating home visits into a program, it is beneficial to locate community bilingual volunteers to accompany the program representative on the visits, so that the parents and educators are certain to communicate. An even better situation would be to use other family members as interpreters (aunts, uncles, etc.) who are bilingual, thereby decreasing the parents' anxiety at having so many strangers in their home.

INVOLVEMENT OF PARENTS WITH SPECIAL NEEDS CHILDREN

When dealing with children with special needs and their parents, provide parents with general developmental guidelines and activities that are not age-graded. The Home Learning Enablers in Appendix A, with the age section blocked out, are useful for send-home activities, since they move sequentially from easier to more difficult and can be used with older children who are delayed for a variety of reasons. For instance, an activity specified for a three-year-old could be sent home with a five-year-old, and little or no adjustment may need be made to the activity. However, remind parents that they are responsible for making the final judgment on the care of their children. Parents of special needs children should consult with their pediatrician and developmental specialist regarding the most appropriate activities for their children. In other words, suggestions from a center should not be used as a replacement for recommended therapy (Baker & Long, 1989).

SUMMARY

Mother-child and family-child communication has been found to be a central factor in a child's scholastic ability, and the lack of it a central factor in the effects of cultural deprivation. Obviously, there seems to be great benefit in encouraging more family-child and mother-child interaction and verbal communication (Lazar, 1977).

An emphasis on children's activities and interactions with specific materials has a long tradition in early childhood education. Piaget (1952), in studying the way children come to understand their world, concluded that early sensorimotor experiences with concrete objects play a crucial role in the development of thought. This suggests that children younger than age seven need to have experiences with concrete manipulatives both at home and in a group setting. However, parents often are not provided with materials or suggestions about materials for their children. If educators need instructional materials, it is reasonable to assume that parents need materials too. Bilingual and special needs children especially need their parents involved in early learning programs and in parent-child activities that make use of concrete instructional materials.

BIBLIOGRAPHY

Ainsworth, M. D. S. Object relations, dependency, and attachment: A theoretical review of the infant-mother relationship. *Child Development, 40,* 969–1025.

American Speech and Hearing Association. (1981). *Partners in language: A guide for parents.* Rockville, MD: Author. (Available from ASHA, 10801 Rockville Pike, Rockville, MD 20850; Telephone 301-897-5700)

Anderson, R., Fielding, L., & Wilson, P. (1988). The growth in reading and how children spend time outside of school. *Reading Research Quarterly, 23,* 285–303.

Andrews, S. R., Blumenthal, J. B., Johnson, D. L., Kahn, A. J., Ferguson, C. J., Lasater, T. M., Malone, P. E., & Wallace, D. B. (1982). The skills of mother: A study of parent-child development centers. *Monographs of the Society for Research in Child Development, 6* (Serial No. 198), 47.

Anselmo, S. (1978, November). Improving home and preschool influences on early language development. *Reading Teacher, 32,* 139–143.

Arnberg, L. (1983). *Bilingual education for preschool children.* Sweden: Department of Education, Linkoping University. (ERIC Document Reproduction Service No. ED 245 535)

Asp, E., & Levine, V. (1985, April). *The social context of home environment and achievement at school.* Paper presented at the annual meeting of the American Educational Research Association, Chicago.

Baker, C., & Long, T. (1989). *Tips from tots: A resource guide for your infant and toddler.* Los Angeles: Vort Corporation.

Baratta-Lorton, M. (1972). *Workjobs.* Menlo Park, CA: Addison-Wesley.

Baratta-Lorton, M. (1975). *Workjobs . . . for parents. Activity centered learning in the home.* Menlo Park, CA: Addison-Wesley.

Bauch, P. (1985, April). *Parent involvement: Exploring roles for parents in curriculum and school improvement.* Paper presented at the annual meeting of the National Catholic Education Association, Washington, DC.

Bell, K. (1991). *Home visits revisited*. New York: National Center for Children in Poverty, School of Public Health, Columbia University.

Bettelheim, B. (1987). *A good enough parent*. New York: Knopf Books.

Bernstein-Tarrow, N., & Lundsteen S. W. (1981). *Activities and resources for guiding young children's learning*. New York: McGraw-Hill.

Blank, S. (1987). *Contemporary parenting education and family support programs: Themes and issues in an emerging movement*. New York: Foundation for Child Development.

Bloom, B. (1964). *Stability and change in human characteristics*. New York: Wiley.

Bloom, B. S. (1981). *All our children learning: A primer for parents, teachers and other educators*. New York: McGraw Hill.

Bornstein, M., & Tamis-Lemonda, C. (1989). Maternal responsiveness and cognitive development in children. In M. Bornstein (Ed.), *Maternal responsiveness characteristics and consequences*. San Francisco: Jossey Bass.

Bowlby, J. (1988). *A secure base: Parent child attachment and healthy human development*. New York: Basic Books.

Bowman, B. T. (1989). Educating language minority children: Challenges and opportunities. *Phi Delta Kappan, 71*(2), 118–121.

Bradley, B. (1988, March). School: The parent factor. *Parents*, pp. 111–114.

Bredekamp, S. (Ed.). (1987). *NAEYC position statement on developmentally appropriate practice in programs for 4- and 5-year-olds*. Washington, DC: National Association for the Education of Young Children.

Bredekamp, S. (Ed.). (1990). *Developmentally appropriate practice in early childhood programs serving children from birth to age 8*. Washington, DC: National Association for the Education of Young Children.

Bronfenbrenner, U. (1979). *The ecology of human development*. Cambridge, MA: Harvard University Press.

Brown, D., & McDonald, P. (1969). *Learning begins at home: A stimulus for a child's I. Q.* Los Angeles: Lawrence Publishing.

Bruner, J. (1960). *The process of education*. New York: Vintage Books.

Bruner, J. (1964). The course of cognitive growth. *American Psychologist, 19*, 1–15.

Bruner, J. (1966). *Studies in cognitive growth*. New York: Wiley.

Burket, L. L. (1981, April). *Positive parental involvement in the area of reading during pre school years and primary grades*. (Report No. CS006658) Bloomington, IN: Resources in Education. (ERIC Document Reproduction Service No. ED 216 324)

Caldwell, B. M., & Smith, L. E. (1970). Day care for the very young—prime opportunity for primary prevention. *American Journal of Public Health, 60*, 690–697.

California Department of Education. (1991). *Parent involvement programs in California public schools: Families, schools and communities working together*. Sacramento: Parent and Community Education Office, California Department of Education.

Canter, L. (1991). *Parents on your side materials workbook*. Santa Monica: Lee Canter & Associates.

Canter, L., & Canter, M. (1991). *Parents on your side*. Santa Monica: Lee Canter & Associates.

Carbo, M., Dunn, K., & Dunn, R. (1986). *Teaching children to read through their individual learning styles*. Englewood Cliffs, NJ: Prentice-Hall.

Cervantes, H. T., Baca, L. M., & Torres, D. S. (1979). Community involvement in bilingual education: The bilingual educators parent trainer. *NABE Journal, 3*(2), 73–82.

Cherlin, A. J. (Ed.). (1988). *The changing American family and public policy*. Washington, DC: The Urban Institute Press.

Children's Defense Fund. (1989). *A vision for America's future*. Washington, DC: Author.

Chomsky, C. (1972). Stages in language development and reading exposure. *Harvard Educational Review, 42*(1), 1–33.

Chrispeels, J., Boruta, M., & Daugherty, M. (1988). *Communicating with parents*. San Diego: San Diego Office of Education.

Chud, G., & Fahlman, R. (1985). *Early childhood education for a multi-cultural society*. British Columbia, Canada: Pacific Educational Press.

Cicchetti, D., & Carlson, V. (Eds.). (1989). *Child maltreatment: Theory and research on the causes and consequences of child abuse and neglect*. New York: Cambridge University Press.

Clark, R. (1983). *Family life and school achievement: Why poor black children succeed or fail*. Chicago: University of Chicago Press.

Clay, M. (1987). *Writing begins at home*. Portsmouth, NH: Heinemann.

Cole, M., & Cole, S. R. (1989). *The development of children*. New York: W. H. Freeman.

Coleman, J. S. (1973, November). *Effects of school on learning: The IEA findings*. Paper presented at the Conference on Education Achievement, Harvard University, Cambridge, MA.

Coleman, J. S., Campbell, E., Mood, A., Weinfeld, E., Hobson, C., York, R., & McPartland, J. (1966). *Equality of educational opportunity*. Washington, DC: U. S. Government Printing Office.

Comer, J. P. (1988, November). Educating poor minority children. *Scientific American, 259*(5), 42–48.

Comer, J. P. (1990). Home, school, and academic learning. In J. I. Goodlad & P. Keating (Eds.), *Access to knowledge: An agenda for our nation's schools*. New York: New York College Entrance Examination Board.

Council of Chief State School Officers. (1989). *Family support, education, and involvement: A guide for state action*. Washington, DC: Author.

Council of Chief State School Officers. (1991). *Families in schools*. Washington, DC: Author.

Davies, D. (1991). Schools reaching out. *Phi Delta Kappan, 72*(5), 376–382.

Derman-Sparks, L., & A. B. C. Task Force. (1989). *Anti-bias curriculum: Tools for empowering young children*. Washington, DC: National Association for the Education of Young Children.

Dewey, J. (1938). *Experience and education*. New York: Collier.

Dix, T., & Gruesec, J. E. (1983). Parent socialization techniques: An attributional analysis. *Child Development, 54*, 645–652.

Dixon, G. T., & Fraser, S. (1986, March/April). Teaching preschoolers in a multilingual classroom. *Childhood Education*, pp. 272–275.

Douglas, J. W. (1964). *The home and school: A study of ability and attainment in the primary school*. London: MacGibbon and Kee.

Education Research Service. (1990). Effects of open enrollment in Minnesota. *ERS Research Digest*. Arlington, VA: Author.

Egawa, K. (1990). Harnessing the power of language: First grader's literature engagement with "Owl Moon," *Language Arts, 67*, 582–588.

Epstein, J. L. (1984a). A longitudinal study of school and family effects on student development. In S. A. Mednick & M. Harway (Eds.), *Handbook of longitudinal research*. New York: Praeger.

Epstein, J. L. (1984b). *Single parents and the schools: The effects of marital status on parent and teacher evaluations* (Report 353). Baltimore, MD: The Johns Hopkins University Center for Social Organization of Schools.

Epstein, J. L. (1986). Parents' reactions to teacher practices of parent involvement. *The Elementary School Journal, 86*, 277–294.

Epstein, J. L. (1987a). Parent involvement: State education agencies should lead the way. *Community Education Journal, 14*, 4–9.

Epstein, J. L. (1987b, February). Parent involvement: What research says to administrators. *Education and Urban Society*, 119–136.

Epstein, J. L. (1987c). Toward a theory of family-school connections: Teacher practices and parent involvement across the school years. In K. Hurremann, F. Kaufmann, & F. Losel (Eds.), *Social intervention: Potential and constraints*. New York: de Gruvter.

Epstein, J. L. (1988a). Effective schools or effective students: Dealing with diversity. In R. Haskins & D. MacRae (Eds.), *Policies for*

America's public schools: Teachers, equity, indicators. Norwood, NJ: Ablex.

Epstein, J. L. (1988b). How do we improve programs for parent involvement? *Education Horizons, 66*(2), 58–59.

Epstein, J. L. (1991, January). Paths to partnership: What we can learn from federal, state, district, and school initiatives. *Phi Delta Kappan,* 344–349.

Epstein, J. L. (in press). Effects of teacher practices of parent involvement on student achievement in reading and math. In S. Silvern (Ed.), *Literacy through family, community, and school interaction.* Greenwich, CT: JAI Press.

Evans, E. D. (1971). *Contemporary influences in early childhood education.* New York: Holt, Rinehart and Winston.

Far West Laboratory for Educational Research and Development. (1971). *Demonstration and Research Center for Early Education program report.* Nashville: George Peabody College for Teachers.

Ferber, R. (1986). *Solve your child's sleep problems.* New York: Simon and Shuster.

Finnie, N. R. (1975). *Handling the cerebral palsied child at home.* New York: E. P. Dutton.

Flaxman, E., & Inger, M. (1991). Parents and schooling in the 1990s. *The Education Digest, 57*(4), 3–7.

Fox-Barnett, M., & Meyer, T. (1992). The teacher's playing at my house this week! *Young Children, 47*(5), 45–50.

Fraiberg, S. (1981). *The magic years.* New York: Macmillan.

Fredericks, A. D., & Rasinski, T. V. (1990). Working with parents: Factors that make a difference. *The Reading Teacher, 44*(1), 76–77.

Friedman, R. (1978, Fall). First cry of the newborn: Basis for child's future musical development. *Journal of Research in Music Education, 21,* 264–269.

Froebel, F. (1902). *Pedagogies of the kindergarten.* (J. Jarvis, Trans.). New York: D. Appleton and Company.

Fuduka, A. (1976). *Parents helping children to learn.* San Francisco: Chinese Bilingual Pilot Program.

Galinsky, E., & David, J. (1983). *The preschool years.* New York: Random House/Time Books.

Garlana-Burtt, K., & Kalkenstern, K. *Smart toys.* St. Paul, MN: RedLeaf Press.

Gelfer, J. (1991). Teacher-parent partnerships: Enhancing communication. *Childhood Education,* pp. 164–167.

Gesell, A. (1945). *The embryology of behavior: The beginnings of the human mind.* New York: Harper.

Goldsmith, S. (1984). *ABC123—a teacher/parent resource for teaching beginning concepts.* Nashville, TN: Incentive Publications.

Goldstein, R. (1990). *Everyday parenting: The first five years.* New York: Viking/Penguin.

Goodson, B. D., Swartz, J. P., & Millsap, M. A. (1991). *Working with families: Promising programs to help parents support young children's learning.* Cambridge, MA: Abt Associates.

Gordon, I. J. (1969). Developing parent power. In E. Grotberg (Ed.), *Critical issues in research related to disadvantaged children.* Princeton, NJ: Educational Testing Service.

Gordon, I. J. (1977). Parent education and parent involvement: Retrospect and prospect. *Childhood Education, 34,* 71–77.

Gordon, I. J., & Breivogel, W. F. (Eds.). (1976). *Building effective home-school relationships.* Boston: Allyn & Bacon.

Gordon, I. J., Guinagh B., & Jester, R. E. (1972). *Child learning through child play.* New York: St. Martin's Press.

Gotts, E. E., & Purnell, R. F. (1986). Communications: Key to school-home relations. In R. P. Boger & R. T. Griffore (Eds.), *Child rearing in the home and school.* New York: Plenum.

Gray, S. T. (1984). How to create a successful school/community partnership. *Phi Delta Kappan, 65*(6), 405–410.

Gray, S. W. (1971, January). Home visiting programs for parents of young children. *Peabody Journal of Education, 48,* 106–111.

Gray, S. W., & Klaus, R. A. (1970, December). The early training project: A seventh year report. *Child Development, 41,* 909.

Gray, S. W., Ramsey, B., and Klaus, R. (1981). *From three to twenty: The early training project.* Baltimore, MD: University Park Press.

Gray, S. W., & Ruttle, K. (1976). *The family-oriented home visiting program: A longitudinal study.* Bethesda, MD: National Institute of Child Health and Human Development.

Greenwood, G. E., & Hickman, C. W. (1991). Research and practice in parent involvement: Implications for teacher education. *The Elementary School Journal, 91*(3), 279–288.

Halpern, R. (1989). Community-based early intervention: The state of the art. In J. Shonkoff & S. Meisels (Eds.), *Handbook of early intervention.* New York: Cambridge University Press.

Halpern, R., & Weiss, H. B. (1990). Family support and education programs: Evidence from evaluated program experience. In *Helping families grow strong: New directions in public policy* (Papers from the Colloquium on Public Policy and Family Support). Washington, DC: Center for the Study of Social Policy.

Hamburg, D. A. (1990). *A decent start: Promoting healthy child development in the first three years of life.* New York: Carnegie Corp. (Annual Report).

Hayes, C. D., Palmer, J. L., & Zaslow, M. J. (Eds.). (1990). *Who cares for America's children: Child care policy for the 1990's.* Panel on Child Care Policy, Committee on Child Development Research and Public Policy, Commission on Behavioral and Social Sciences and Education. Washington, DC: National Academy Press.

Hechinger, F. M. (Ed.). (1986). *A better start: New choices for early learning.* New York: Walker and Co.

Henderson, A. T. (1987). *The evidence continues to grow: Parent involvement improves student achievement.* Columbia, MD: National Committee for Citizens in Education.

Henderson, A., Marburger, C., & Ooms, T. (1986). *Beyond the bakesale: An educator's guide to working with parents.* Columbia, MD:

National Committee for Citizens in Education.

Hedrick, V. (1977, July). The winning play at home base. *American Education, 13,* 27–30.

Hess, R. D. (1969). Parental behavior and children's social achievements. In E. Grotberg (Ed.), *Critical issues in research related to disadvantaged children.* Princeton, NJ: Educational Testing Service.

Hess, R. D., Beckum, L., Knowles, R., & Miller, R. (1971). Parent training programs and community involvement in day care. *Day care: Resources for decisions.* Washington, DC: U.S. Government Printing Office.

Hess, R. D., Block, M., Costello, J., Knowles, J. R., & Miller, R. (1971). Parent involvement in early education. *Day care: Resources for decisions.* Washington, DC: U.S. Government Printing Office.

Hess, R. D., & Goodson, B. (1975, May). *Parents as teachers of young children: An evaluative review of some contemporary concepts and programs.* Palo Alto, CA: Stanford University.

Hess, R. D., & Holloway, S. D. (1984). Family and school as educational institutions. In R. D. Park (Ed.), *Review of child development research* (Vol. 7). Chicago: University of Chicago Press.

Hess, R. D., Holloway, S. D., Dickson, W. P., & Price, G. G. (1984). Maternal variables as predictors of children's school readiness and later achievement in vocabulary and mathematics in the sixth grade. *Child Development, 55,* 1902–1913.

Hess, R. D., & McDevitt, T. M. (1984). Some cognitive consequences of maternal intervention techniques: A longitudinal study. *Child Development, 55,* 2017–2030.

Hetherington, E. M. (1989). Parents, children and siblings six years after divorce. In R. Hinde & J. S. Hinde (Eds.), *Relationships within families.* Cambridge, England: Cambridge University Press.

Hobbs, N. (1975). *The future of children.* San Francisco: Jossey Bass.

Hochschild, A., & Machung, A. (1989). *The second shift: Working parents and the revolution at home.* New York: Viking Publishing.

Honig, A. S. (1972). *The family development research program: With emphasis on the children's center curriculum.* Syracuse, NY: The New York College for Human Development.

Honig, A. S. (1978). *Parent involvement and the development of children with special needs.* Syracuse, NY: Syracuse University.

Honig, A. S. (1979). *Parent involvement in early childhood education.* Washington, DC: National Association for the Education of Young Children.

Honig, A. S. (1989). Quality infant/toddler caregiving: Are there any magic recipes? *Young Children, 44*(4), 4–10.

Hoover-Dempsey, K. V., Bassler, O. C., & Brissie, J. S. (1992). Explorations in parent-school relations. *Journal of Educational Research, 85*(5), 287–293.

Horowitz, J., & Faggella, K. (1986). *Partners for learning.* Weston, MA: First Teacher Press. (Parent-teacher involvement suggestions and reproducible letters are featured in this early childhood book.)

Hunt, J. M. (1961). *Intelligence and experience.* New York: The Ronald Press.

Hunt, J. M. (1972). *Human intelligence.* New Brunswick, NJ: Transaction.

Jenson, M. A. (1985). Story awareness: A critical skill for early reading. *Young Children, 41*(1), 20–24.

Jewell, M. G., & Miles, V. Z. (1986). *Learning to read and write naturally.* Dubuque, IA: Kendall/Hunt.

Jewell, M. V., & Zintz, M. G. (1990). *Learning to read and write naturally.* Dubuque, IA: Kendall/Hunt Publishing.

Johnson, D. L., and others. (1976). *Houston parent-child development center.* Houston, TX: Houston University.

Jones, C. C. (1981). *The relationship of selected instructional materials used by parents and intelligence of three-year-old day care children from lower socio-economic families.* Ann Arbor, MI: UMI.

Kagan, J. (1977). The effect of day care on early development. In B. Persky & L. Golubchick (Eds.), *Early Childhood.* Wayne, NJ: Avery Publishing.

Kagan, S. L. (1990). *Excellence in early childhood education: Defining characteristics and next-decade strategies.* Office of Education Research and Improvement, U.S. Department of Education. Washington, DC: U.S. Government Printing Office.

Kahn, A. J., & Kamerman, S. B. (1987). *Child care: Facing the hard choices.* Dover, MA: Auburn House Publishing.

Kalt, B. R., & Bass, R. *The mother's guide to child safety.* New York: Grosset and Dunlap.

Kamii, C., & Radin, N. (1967). *The Ypsilanti early education program.* Ypsilanti, MI: Ypsilanti Public Schools.

Karnes, M. B. (1969). *A new role for teachers: Involving the entire family in the education of preschool disadvantaged children.* Urbana, IL: University of Illinois.

Kennedy, C. (1991, March). Parent involvement: It takes PEP. *Principal,* 25–28.

Lally, J. R., & Honig, A. S. (1977). *The family development research program: A program for prenatal, infant and early childhood enrichment.* Syracuse, NY: The New York College for Human Development.

Lancy, D. F., & Nattiv, A. (1992, Summer). Parents as volunteers. *Childhood Education,* pp. 208–212.

Larrick, N. (1976). From "Hands off" to "Parents, we need you!" *Childhood Education, 52,* 134–137.

Lazar, I. (1977). *The persistence of preschool effects: A longterm follow up of fourteen infant and preschool experiments.* Washington, DC: Administration for Children, Youth and Families.

Levenstein, P. (1975). *The mother-child home program.* New York: Carnegie Corp.

Linney, J., & Vernberg, E. (1983). Changing patterns of parental employment and family-school relationships. In Hayes and Kamerman (Eds.), *Children of working parents: Experiences and outcomes.* Washington, DC: National Academy Press.

Maring G. H., & Magelky, J. (1990). Effective

communication: Key to parent/community involvement. *Reading Teacher, 43*(8), 606.

Marzollo, J. (1987). *The new kindergarten full day, child centered academic.* New York: Harper & Row.

Mavrogenes, N. A. (1990). Helping parents help their children become literate. *Young Children, 45*(5), 35–40.

McInerney, B. L., and others. (1968). *Preschool and primary education project.* Harrisburg, PA: Pennsylvania State Department of Public Instruction.

McKay, D. (1981). *Introducing pre-school children to reading through parent involvement* (Report No. PS0123708). Paper presented at the Annual Meeting of Parents and Reading Conference, New York. (ERIC Document Reproduction Service No. ED 206 406)

Meade, M., & Hyman, K. (1965). *Family.* New York: Macmillan.

Minnesota Department of Education. (n. d.). *Minnesota early childhood family education: Answers to commonly asked questions.* St. Paul, MN: Author.

Moles, O. C. (1982, November). Synthesis of recent research on parent participation in children's education. *Educational leadership.*

Montessori, M. (1968). *Dr. Montessori's own handbook.* New York: Schocken Books.

Moore, R. S., and others. (1976). *The balanced development of young children.* Berrien Springs, MI: Hewitt Research Center.

Morgan, E. L. (1989, October). Parent-teacher communication techniques. *Education Digest,* p. 32.

Mosteller, F., & Moynihan, O. P. (Eds.). (1972). *On equality of educational opportunity.* New York: Random House.

Nardine, F. E., Chapman, W. K., & Moles, O. C. (1989). *How involved are state education agencies in parent involvement?* (Report No. 17). Boston: Institute for Responsive Education.

Nardine, F. E., & Morris, R. D. (1991). Parent involvement in the states: How firm is the commitment? *Phi Delta Kappan, 72*(5), 363–366.

National Association for the Education of Young Children. (1972). Parents as educators: Evidence from cross-sectional, longitudinal, and intervention research. In W. Hartrup (Ed.), *The young child: Reviews of research.* Washington, DC: Author.

National Association for the Education of Young Children. (1986, May). Accreditation: A new tool for early childhood programs. *Young Children,* pp. 31–32.

National Association for the Education of Young Children. (1991). *Accreditation criteria and procedures of the National Academy of Early Childhood Programs.* Washington, DC: Author.

National Commission on Children. (1991). *Beyond rhetoric: A new American agenda for children and families.* Washington, DC: Author.

Nevius, J. R., & Filgo, D. J. (1977). *Home start education: A guideline for content areas* (Report No. PS009645). Washington, DC: U.S. Educational Resources Information Center. (ERIC Document Reproduction Service No. ED 147 013)

Norman-Jackson, J. (1982). Family interactions, language development, and primary reading achievement of black children in families of low income. *Child Development, 53,* 349–358.

Ornstein, A. C., & Levine, D. U. (1989). *Foundations of education.* Boston: Houghton Mifflin.

Ovando, C. J., & Collier, V. P. (1985). *Bilingual and ESL classrooms.* New York: McGraw-Hill.

Parents and schools make a difference! (1989). Sacramento: California State Board of Education Policy on Parent Involvement.

Piaget, J. (1952). *The origins of intelligence in children* (M. Cook, Trans.). New York: International University Press.

Piaget, J. (1973). *To understand is to invent.* New York: Viking Press.

Radke-Yarrow, M., & Zahn-Waxler, C. (1986). The role of familial factors in the development of prosocial behavior: Research findings and questions. In D. Olweus, J. Block, & M. Radke-Yarrow (Eds.), *Development of antisocial and prosocial behavior.* Orlando, FL: Academic Press.

Raines, S. C. (1990). *The whole language kindergarten.* New York: Teacher's College.

Ramsaur, M. C. (1992). From teacher to parent to child. *Teaching K–8,* pp. 78–84.

Rich, D., & Jones, C. (1977). *A family affair: Education.* Washington, DC: The Home and School Institute.

Rich, D., & Jones, C. (1978). *The three R's plus: Teaming families and schools for student achievement.* Washington, DC: The Home and School Institute.

Rogers, D. E., & Ginzberg, E. (Eds.). (1990). *Improving the life chances of children at risk.* Boulder, CO: Westview Press.

Roopnarine, J. L., & Lamb, M. E. (1978). The effects of day care on attachment and exploratory behavior in a strange situation. *Merrill-Palmer Quarterly, 24,* 85–97.

Russell, A. (1979, Fall). Hidden curriculum in the mother-child home program: Update from Phyllis Levenstein. *Human Ecology Forum, 10,* 8–12.

Rutter, M. (1985). Family and school influences on cognitive development. In R. A. Hinde, A. N. Perret-Clermont, & J. Stevenson-Hinde (Eds.), *Social relationships and cognitive development.* Oxford, England: Clarendon Press.

Schaefer, E. S. (1974). New perspective in learning—the parent centered approach. In *Proceedings.* Rockville, MD: Conference of the Montgomery County, Maryland, Parent Cooperative Preschools.

Schaefer, E. S., Hunter, W. M., & Watkins, D. B. (1986). *Parenting and child behavior predictors of retention in grades K, 1, 2.* Paper presented at the annual meeting of the American Education Research Association, San Francisco.

Schweinhart, L., & Wekart, D. (1983). The effects of the Perry preschool program on youths through age 15—a summary. *Consortium for longitudinal studies: As the twig is bent . . . lasting effects of preschool programs.* Hillsdale, NJ: Erlbaum.

Scott-Jones, D. (1984). Family influences on cognitive development and school achievement. In E. Gordon (Ed.), *Review of research in education* (Vol. 11). Washington, DC: American Educational Research Association.

Seefeldt, C., & Barbour, N. (1990). *Early childhood education: An introduction.* New York: Merrill/Macmillan.

Seitz, V., Rosenbaum, L. K., & Apfel, N. H. (1987, April). *Long term effects of the Yale-New Haven family support intervention project.* Paper presented at the biennial meeting of the Society for Research in Child Development, Baltimore, MD.

Seitz, V. (1977, February). *Long term effects of intervention: A longitudinal investigation.* Paper presented to AAAS Conference, New Haven, CT.

Seitz, V., Apel, N., Rosenbaum, L., Zigler, E., & Abelson, W. (1983). *Long term effects of projects Head Start and Follow Through: The New Haven project.* Hillsdale, NJ: Erlbaum.

Shaw, J. W., & Schoggin, M. (1969). *Children learning: Samples of everyday lives of children at home.* Nashville, TN.: Demonstration and Research Center for Early Education.

Schoumacher, S., & Cadden, V. (1989, September). Preparing your child for the 21st century. *McCall's,* p. 41.

Shoemaker, C. J. (1992). *Home learning enablers and other helps.* Rockville, MD: ECEA Institute.

Shoemaker, C. J. (1994). *Home learning enablers and other helps* (2nd ed.). Rockville, MD: ECEA Institute.

Shonkoff, J. P., & Meisels, S. J. (Eds.). (1990). *Handbook of early childhood intervention.* New York: Cambridge University Press.

Sigel, I. E., & McGillicuddy-Delisi, A. V. (1984). Parents as teachers of their children: A distancing behavior model. In A. D. Pelligrew & T. D. Yawker (Eds.), *The development of oral and written language in social contexts* (pp. 71–92). Norward, NJ: Ablex.

Silvern, S. (1985, September/October). Parent involvement and reading achievement: A review of research and implications for practice. *Childhood Education, 62*(1), 44–50.

Skeels, H. M., & Dye, H. B. (1939). A study of the effects of differential stimulation on mentally retarded children. *Proceedings of American Association of the Mentally Deficient, 44,* 114–136.

Solomon, Z. P. (1991, January). California's policy on parent involvement. *Phi Delta Kappan, 72*(5), 359–362.

Spewock, T. (1991). Teaching parents of young children through learning packets. *Young Children,* pp. 28–30.

Sroufe, L. A. (1988). The role of infant-caregiver attachment in development. In J. Belsky & T. Nezworski (Eds.), *Clinical implication of attachment.* Hillsdale, NJ: Erlbaum.

Stenmark, J., Thompson, V., & Cossey, R. (1986). *Family math.* New York: Carnegie Corporation.

Stevens, J. H., Jr., & Matthews, M. (1978). *Mother/child, father/child relationships.* Washington, DC: National Association for the Education of Young Children.

Swap, S. (1980). *Parent involvement and success for all children.* Boston, MA: Institute for Responsive Education.

Swap, S. (1987). *Enhancing parent involvement: A manual for parents and teachers.* New York: Teachers' College Press.

Taylor, K. W. (1967). *Parents and children learn together.* New York: Teachers' College Press.

Tizard, J., Schofield, W. N., & Hewison, J. (1982). Collaboration between teachers and parents in assisting children's reading. *British Journal of Educational Psychology, 52,* 1–15.

Trelease, J. (1998). *The new read-aloud handbook.* New York: Penguin Books.

U.S. General Accounting Office. (1990, July). *Home visiting: A promising early intervention strategy for at risk families* (Report GAO/HRD 90-83). Washington, DC: Author.

Vandegrift, J. A., & Greene, A. L. (1992). Rethinking parent involvement. *Educational Leadership, 50*(1), 57–59.

Vargas, A. (1988, June). *Smart start: The community collaborative for Early Childhood Development Act of 1988.* Paper presented before the Senate Committee on Labor and Human Resources, Washington, DC.

Warner, I. (1991, January). Parents in touch: District leadership for parent involvement. *Phi Delta Kappan,* 372–375.

Weikart, D., & Lambie, D. (1967). Preschool intervention through a home teaching program. In J. Hellmuth (Ed.), *The disadvantaged child* (Vol. ii). Seattle: Special Child Publications.

Weiss, H., et al. (1991). *Raising our future: Families, schools, communities joining together.* Cambridge, MA: Harvard Families Research Project.

Wherry, I. (1992, April). Getting parents involved. *Educational Digest,* pp. 49–50.

White, B. L. (1974). *Reassessing our educational priorities.* Paper presented to the Education Commission of the States, Boston.

White, B. L. (1975a). *Experience and environment.* Englewood Cliffs, NJ: Prentice-Hall.

White, B. L. (1975b). *The first three years of life.* Englewood Cliffs, NJ: Prentice-Hall.

Wikelund, K. R. (1990). *Schools and communities together: A guide to parent involvement.* Portland: Northwest Regional Educational Laboratory.

Williams, D., & Stallworth, J. (1983/84). *Parent involvement in education project.* Austin, TX: Southwest Educational Development Laboratory.

Wittes, G., & Radin, N. (1969). *Two approaches to group work with parents in a compensatory preschool program.* Ypsilanti, MI: Ypsilanti Public Schools.

Zigler, E. F., & Lang, M. E. (1991). *Child care choices: Balancing the needs of children, families and society.* New York: The Free Press.

Zigler, E. F., & Weiss, H. (1985). Family support systems: An ecological approach to child development. In R. N. Rappaport (Ed.), *Children, youth, and families.* New York: Cambridge University Press.

PART TWO

Human Resource Issues

As was discussed in Part 1, the first task in establishing an early childhood center is to determine the center's philosophy. Once that philosophy has been decided, the task of assembling a team to carry out this philosophy can begin. Staffing, training, motivating, team building, and displaying professionalism are all part of the reality of today's well-run programs for young children. These concerns go hand-in-hand with leadership, planning, decision-making, and problem-solving. Directors who are already experienced in running a child-care facility, but who are setting up a new center, might want to read Part 3 of this text first. These chapters discuss the topics just listed, and might be a helpful review of the leadership foundations that successful human resources management rest upon. Although this book addresses center child care only, some suggestions could be adapted to family child-care settings as well.

Since human resources are the most valuable resources an organization has (Peters & Waterman, 1982), issues relating to this area are addressed before those relating to leadership and operations (Parts 3 and 4), and following the parent involvement/program development section (Part 1). While reading through these chapters on human resource management, readers who are would-be practitioners can think about how they would handle various situations if they *were* the administrators. Current administrators can adapt and apply suggestions. Every organization should be a learning organization, and this section is based on that premise. As Peter Senge (1990) laments, some organizations are not learning organizations but have "learning disabilities."

When the professional team within an organization becomes aligned in a common direction, these individuals' energies harmonize. Less energy is wasted, and a shared vision and understanding of how to complement one another's efforts emerges. The shared vision becomes an extension of individuals' goals, such as "working for the best center in town," or "helping children reach their potential." When individual goals and directions are aligned, as many of the exercises in the following chapters try to promote, then empowering the individual leads to empowering the whole team (Senge, 1990).

To maintain common goals and vision, however, there needs to be an ongoing "visioning process" in which local and personal ideas and visions continually interact with organizational ideas and visions. Part 3 of this text develops more strategies on how those in leadership can accomplish this task. An organization's combination of shared purpose, vision, and values creates a common identity that can demonstrate great strength. Senge (1990) sees the chief task of Directors, along with other leaders, as working to develop this common identity.

The idea of planning as a learning tool appears over and over in the next eight chapters. Since children are always learning from others and from their environment, it is appropriate that adults be in a continuous learning environment also. Today's learning organizations demand a new view of leadership, and the activities in the following chapters will help in building a learning organization that espouses such leadership. Once an organization clearly develops its vision and posts it in many ways for all to see, the educational team can work together with energy and enthusiasm to make that vision a reality.

CHAPTER THREE

Staff Selection, Development, and Evaluation

The careful choice of teaching and support staff is essential to the administration and management of a child-care center. The staff, and the staff training made available, are two key elements in a successful program. This chapter discusses the hiring committee, staff training and meetings, evaluation, and Advisory or Executive Board training. Sample staff evaluation forms are provided for use in programs, policies, and meetings.

SELECTION

Careful staff selection, with a high priority given to "the most crucial staff characteristic" of combined training in early childhood education and child development, has an effect on whether child care "helps or harms children" (Kuykendall, 1990, p. 48). The National Day Care Study (Abt Associates, 1987) found that "only one teacher characteristic predicts program quality and effectiveness: the amount of job-related training in early childhood education that a teacher has received" (Schweinhart, Koshel, & Bridgeman, 1987, p. 527). In this study, caregivers with such training delivered better care resulting in somewhat better developmental effects for children (Snow, 1983; Abt Associates, 1987). By establishing specific requirements that caregivers must meet in order to be hired, such as having a background in early childhood education and child development education, a Director can ask the Executive Board for help with the hiring process. This spreads the decision-making over a larger group (i.e., larger than just the Director herself or himself) and provides a learning opportunity for the parents and/or community Board members involved.

The Hiring Committee

An Executive Board with a 3- to 5-member hiring committee can be extremely helpful to a Director, both by giving assistance in telephoning and screening tasks as well as by spreading the decision-making over a larger group, as previously mentioned. The Director should make clear to the chairperson of the hiring committee the amount of education and experience that are minimum requirements for the job. Application forms should be sent to those applicants who are above this minimum; interviews can then be scheduled, with these being handled by the hiring committee, the Director, and perhaps a teacher. The interview sessions should be conducted as a group interaction, with one person, perhaps the committee chairperson, acting as the lead speaker. The Director may want just one teacher present rather than the entire hiring committee when going through the process of hiring aides, or he or she may prefer to have the committee's help.

The Interview

Since the interview is very important, the following sample format is provided to help readers construct a pattern that benefits their own specific situations. At the beginning of the interview, after introductions, the chairperson might open by asking the applicant to describe his or her education and training. Following this, questions relating to experience in the field and how the applicant would handle various situations that can arise with individual children yield much useful information. Some sample questions might be:

- How would you handle two children that are fighting?
- How would you handle a child who stands outside the group, continuously sucking his thumb?
- How would you handle a child who disrupts quiet activities by running about and hitting?
- How might you further enhance learning during art experiences or during story time?

Always remember to ask "How is your health?" and to check references carefully. In some areas, fingerprinting and a negative TB test are also required. Be aware that the person may have strengths in interacting with adults but not with children, or with children and not with adults. The reference check will help uncover these possibilities. Qualities of loving and caring for and about children are, of course, paramount.

Applicants should be made aware of expectations that go along with becoming a part of the center's team. For example, regular training and staff meetings that feature new ideas for the curriculum should be offered at least once a month; such programs are important components in having employees become assets to the center, and in offering a quality program that is developmentally appropriate for children.

DEVELOPMENT

The importance of providing training and development updates to all the adults involved with a child-care center (staff, Executive Board members, and parents) cannot be emphasized too highly. The more these involved adults understand the goals of developmental children's programs and know what excellent programs look like and aspire to, the more a center will be helpful to children and families. As a center "thinks children," excellence and quality will emerge in the program. This quality is characterized by establishing goals that go beyond state regulation or certification minimums in terms of meeting the needs of children and families, and in terms of building a professionally accepted knowledge base. To make such goals a reality, funding in the budget as a line item is needed for the development of staff, Executive Board members, and parents.

Staff Training

Position statements from professional organizations consistently mandate knowledge of child development and early childhood education as a requisite for teaching (Bredekamp, 1987; Association for Childhood Education International, in Gotts, 1988; National Association of State Boards of Education, 1988). As part of the staff, Directors also need this knowledge base; a Director's lack of education in child development and/or curriculum can "frustrate and impede the work of skilled teachers" (Kuykendall, 1990, p. 49). Directors who lack child development knowledge, and who consequently hire staff without making child development expertise a priority, can perpetuate this frustration on the part of the staff. A Director without this background can take courses to gain it.

Meeting Format and Structure

Regular weekly meetings for all staff, during which announcements are made and one learning area is explored each week, builds a firm foundation of excellence for a child-care center. If all the aides and teachers cannot be free at the same time (such as the children's nap time), a rotating schedule could be established, or half the group could meet on each of two days; such an arrangement allows all the staff to participate without dividing it along lines of educational background (which can create conflict and a "we-them" atmosphere).

Meeting Content

In deciding what topics to cover in staff training meetings, one successful format is to have two weekly meetings per month on curriculum content areas, a third meeting on administrative matters and problem-solving, and a fourth meeting on special topics such as working with parents; special problems children encounter including divorce, death, adoption, and foster care; caring for children with disabilities; and other topics drawn from the multitude of child-care issues.

As training sessions are set up, keep in mind that the best learning, for adults as well as for children, occurs as a result of doing. A center might select 10 to 12 curriculum topics that they want to cover over a 6- to 12-month period, such as block building, art, science, nature, or physical fitness, plus supervisory topics. Then, as the Director sees good examples of these topics in classroom activities, he or she can ask different teachers to make half-hour presentations of their activities and then allow a second half hour for the staff members to actually *do* the activity. These training sessions might be preceded by distributing handouts or articles from journals on the "Topic of the Week." The opening or closing half hour of a 90-minute meeting could be used for the usual announcements and routine business.

Teacher aide curriculum meetings might include developing classroom activities similar to the Program Enrichment Papers in Appendix C. Small groups could be made responsible for designing an activity focused on the theme under discussion in that particular week's meeting. A craft library or resource center that is stocked with books and materials relating to discussion topics and activities can be a valuable resource for a center.

The once-a-month special topics training session can be facilitated and enhanced by distributing and then discussing articles on given topics; by scheduling guest speakers; by watching films or other resources; by reading and discussing a particular book; or by listening to a report from a staff member related to a college or university course he or she is taking. Some centers use these types of training sessions to discuss particular children who might exhibit a problem that is the topic of discussion, but others consider this an invasion of privacy. Often, scheduling a "toy patching" session quarterly or twice a year provides a valuable learning time by allowing a chance for staff members to openly share feelings while their hands are busy. The Program Enrichment Papers in Appendix C also give more ideas for teachers' and aides' curriculum planning.

The monthly meeting on administrative topics provides a scheduled time for discussing organizational matters. Directors of large centers might want to divide up extra responsibilities among the staff, one for each, according to their preferences, such as

1. planning and scheduling field trips
2. checking supplies inventory
3. checking playroom maintenance
4. organizing parent education programs
5. serving as liaison for continuing education
6. serving as representative to mental health groups

These assignments can change each year, and, in addition to spreading the responsibilities over a wider group, this system enables other professionals in the center to have input and learn about the over-all needs of the program. Chapter 1 lists more "job descriptions" that can be shared with parents, volunteers, or paid staff.

Board Member Training

If the center has an Advisory Board and/or a Parent Executive Board, the Director will need to plan to train these Board members, or to assist with training if this is the responsibility of others. As the principal proponent of and educational resource for excellent early childhood education in the program, the Director's input into Board training is invaluable and should not be omitted, even though Board members serve on a volunteer basis. Understanding the goals and needs of a good child-care program and its facility is essential if Board members are to do a good job on the ongoing Board committees. A Board manual with job descriptions is very helpful and enables the Director to do his or her job more easily. A Board manual should be written early in the operation of the center.

When training Board members, the Director should have in mind the kinds of committees the Board will comprise. Some useful Board committees include an equipment and supplies committee, a purchasing committee, a marketing and public relations committee, a hiring committee, a newsletter committee, and a parent education committee. One center, for one of its fall orientation meetings which included both the Board and the staff, had the group watch a film showing good developmental child care. Before the film, assignments were made in which one-third of the group was to observe the teacher's interactions with the children; one-third was to observe the equipment and supplies in use; and one-third was to watch for ideas that could be used in public relations and advertising. A discussion of quality child care followed the film, and then each group reported back with their observations. Other films could be analyzed in a similar way. Other ways to involve Board members and to utilize their expertise are listed in Chapter 1.

Attending Professional Meetings

Attending professional association meetings and conferences is another valuable form of staff and Board member training. The overall effectiveness of the center can be greatly enhanced if the attenders are asked to report back on interesting new ideas they have learned from a meeting or conference. Communication research reports that if an individual member of a group sorts through material and reports back to the group, the group makes an assumption that useless aspects of the material have been discarded; as a result, group members attend to the presentation with more interest (Rogers & Shoemaker, 1971).

EVALUATION

Yearly evaluations along with self-evaluation exercises keep an employee improving his or her own performance and goals. For example, the teacher checklist in Figure 3.1 shows a sample self-evaluation form that helps the teacher determine whether decision-making in his or her classroom is based on structure or child preferences.

The group evaluation sheets shown in Figures 3.2, 3.3, and 3.4 will help facilitate yearly evaluations. All of these evaluations (Figures 3.1 to 3.4) can be distributed and collected once or twice a year, kept in a folder, and then reviewed in a one-to-one meeting with a staff member to see how (or if) things have changed for the center in general, or the individual in particular.

FIGURE 3.1
Teacher Checklist

Yes	No	Child-Care Center Characteristics
___	___	1. Children move freely about the playroom and playground.
___	___	2. Children select and use materials without adult interference.
___	___	3. All children usually engage in the same activity at the same time.
___	___	4. Children are expected to join in and remain with a group activity that is directed.
___	___	5. Children's activities are interrupted when the clock says it is time for the next scheduled activity.
___	___	6. Children may spend as much time as they choose to complete their work or their play.
___	___	7. Group activities are encouraged more than are individual activities.
___	___	8. Loud and boisterous play is prohibited at all times.
___	___	9. The teacher requires materials and equipment to be shared, regardless of the child, situation, or activity.
___	___	10. Materials and equipment are always put away by the children following their use of them.
___	___	11. The teacher often sits near an activity without entering into it, indirectly encouraging and facilitating play.
___	___	12. Adults talk and listen to a child on a face-to-face level.
___	___	13. When children speak, offer ideas, contribute suggestions, share an experience, etc., adults listen to them.
___	___	14. The teacher and other adults tell children what to do.
___	___	15. The physical environment, with its clearly defined centers of interest, tells children what they may do.
___	___	16. Children are required to walk in line when moving from place to place.
___	___	17. Children speak only when given permission.
___	___	18. The teacher positively acknowledges children's contributions whether they are ideas, suggestions, experiences, or actions.
___	___	19. Children wait for teacher instructions and patterns before constructing their own products.
___	___	20. The teacher and other adults speak to children in positive language.
___	___	21. Children's requests, desires, or wishes often are ignored.
___	___	22. The teacher and other adults freely give praise to children for each child's efforts.
___	___	23. Children initiate ideas and plans for work and play, and adults are available to help the children carry them out.
___	___	24. The schedule of the day's events or plans is rigidly adhered to.
___	___	25. Materials and equipment for the children's use are placed where children can help themselves to them.

FIGURE 3.2
Program Evaluation

Program Evaluation for 19____ to 19____ (year)

Please fill in the blanks as honestly as you possibly can, so we can strive for better programming in the coming year. You do not have to sign this.

1. The working conditions are _____
   _____

2. The staff I work with is _____
   _____
   _____

3. The equipment is _____
   _____
   _____

4. The food is _____
   _____
   _____

5. The supplies are _____
   _____
   _____

6. The coordinators are _____
   _____
   _____

7. My working surroundings are _____
   _____
   _____

8. My training was/is _____
   _____
   _____

9. Communication is _____
   _____
   _____

10. The growth of the children has been _____
    _____
    _____

11. My supervision/supervisor has been _____
    _____
    _____

---

12. Cleanliness of site/office/classroom, etc., has been _____

_____

_____

13. Administration is _____

_____

_____

14. The Director has _____

_____

_____

_____

15. The agency (if appropriate) has _____

_____

_____

16. The parents have _____

_____

_____

_____

17. The volunteers have _____

_____

_____

_____

18. Other: _____

_____

_____

_____

Additional Comments:

FIGURE 3.3
Policies and Procedures Worksheet

> **Policies and Procedures**
> **Worksheet for 19____ to 19____**
>
> Please list items that you would like to see specific policy on to avoid confusion and disagreement. This will aid in better communication come September of the coming year.
>
> Policy: _____
> _____
>
> Procedure: _____
> _____
> _____
>
> Policy: _____
> _____
>
> Procedure: _____
> _____
> _____
>
> Policy: _____
> _____
>
> Procedure: _____
> _____
> _____

As stated previously, updating both new and experienced employees on new developments in early childhood education and building a climate of respect help employees reach their peak performance. Encouraging new employees to ask questions also contributes to their smooth transition onto the center staff.

SUMMARY

Hiring the best staff possible and providing regular, well-organized staff training is very important to a well-run center. By providing opportunities for inter-action in a number of ways while keeping all eyes on the goal of a developmentally appropriate curriculum and center, a happy and productive adult team can be established. The following chapters on team building, motivation, and professionalism give more insights into the dynamics of human resource issues. However, leadership issues are also of central importance in human resource management. Part 3 addresses the leadership role of the Director and includes discussions on power, planning, decision-making, and creative and analytical problem-solving.

FIGURE 3.4
Staff Meeting Evaluation

1. The staff meeting was:
   Boring ____   Too Long ____   All Right ____
   Exciting ____   Well-organized ____   Unplanned ____

2. I am glad ____   sorry ____   I came.

3. I think staff meetings should be _____
   _____
   _____

4. The luncheon was tasty ____,   enough ____,   not enough ____,
   unnecessary _____,   nice _____.

5. I suggest _____ at _____ for staff
                    day   time
   meetings in September.

BIBLIOGRAPHY

Abt Associates. (1987). *Preliminary findings and their implications: National day care study.* Cambridge, MA: Author.

Bredekamp, S. (Ed.). (1987). *Developmentally appropriate practice in early childhood programs serving children from birth through age 8.* Washington, DC: National Association for the Education of Young Children.

Bredekamp, S., & Willer, B. (1992, March). Of ladders and lattices, cores and cones: Conceptualizing an early childhood professional development system. *Young Children, 47*(3), 47–50.

Child Care Employee Project. (1992, July). On the horizon: New policy initiatives to enhance child care staff compensation. *Young Children, 47*(5), 39–42.

Daniel, J. (1990, May). Child care: An endangered industry. *Young Children, 44*(5), 23–26.

Galinsky, E. (1989). The staffing crisis. *Young Children, 44*(2), 1–4.

Galinsky, E., & Friedman, D. (1986). *Investing in quality child care: A report to AT&T.* Basking Ridge, NJ: AT&T.

Gotts, E. E. (1988). The right to quality child-care. *Childhood Education, 64*, 268–275.

Jorde-Bloom, P. (1988). Closing the gap: An analysis of teacher and administrator perceptions of organizational climate in the early childhood setting. *Teaching & Teacher Education: An International Journal of Research and Studies, 4*(2), 111–120.

Jorde-Bloom, P. (1989, Winter). Professional orientation: Individual and organizational perspectives. *Child and Youth Care Quarterly, 18*(4), 227–240.

Jorde-Bloom, P. (1993). But I'm worth more than that: Addressing employee concerns about compensation. *Young Children, 48*(3), 65–68.

Kisker, E., Hofferth, S. L., Phillips, D., & Farquhar, E. (1991). *A profile of child care settings: Early education and care in 1990.* Washington, DC: U.S. Department of Education, Office of the Under Secretary.

Kuykendall, J. M. (1990, July). Child development: Directors shouldn't leave home without it!! *Young Children, 45*(5), 47–50.

Leavitt, R. L., & Krause-Eheart, B. (1985). Maintaining quality and cost effectiveness through staffing patterns. *Child Care Information Exchange, 45,* 31–35.

Morgan, G. (1987). *The national state of child care regulations, 1986.* Watertown, MA: Work Family Directions, Inc.

National Association for the Education of Young Children. (1990). NAEYC position statement on guidelines for compensation of early childhood professionals. *Young Children, 46*(1), 30–32.

National Association for the Education of Young Children. (1992, November). *NAEYC model of early childhood professional development.* Washington, DC: Author.

National Association of State Boards of Education. (1988). *Right from the start: The report of the NASBE task force on early childhood education.* Alexandria, VA: Author.

Peters, T. J., & Waterman, R. H. (1982). *In search of excellence.* New York: Harper & Row.

Rogers, E. M., & Shoemaker, F. F. (1971). *Communication of innovations: A cross-cultural approach.* New York: MacMillan.

Schweinhart, L. J., Koshel, J. J., & Bridgeman, A. (1987). Policy options for preschool programs. *Phi Delta Kappan, 68,* 524–530.

Senge, P. (1990). *The fifth discipline: The art and practice of a learning organization.* New York: Doubleday.

Snow, C. (1983, November). *As the twig is bent: A review of research of the consequences of day care with implications for caregiving.* Paper presented at the Annual Conference of the National Association for the Education of Young Children, Atlanta, Georgia.

The staff shortage: 41 ideas on how to respond. (1986). *Child Care Information Exchange, 47,* 33–41.

Stephen, K. (1990, June). Is child care a good business? *Child Care Information Exchange, 13.*

Whitebook, M. (1986). The teacher shortage. *Young Children, 41*(3), 10–11.

Whitebook, M., & Ginsburg, G. (1985). *Comparable worth: Questions and answers for childhood staff.* Oakland, CA: Child Care Employee Project.

Whitebook, M., Howes, C., & Phillips, D. (1989). *Who cares? Child care and the quality of care in America. Final report of the National Child Care Staffing Study.* Oakland, CA: Child Care Employee Project.

Whitebook, M., Pemberton, C., Lombardi, J., & Galinsky, E. (1990). *From the floor: Raising child care salaries.* Oakland, CA: Child Care Employee Project.

Willer, B., & Johnson, L. C. (1989). *The crisis is real: Demographics on the problems of recruiting and retaining early childhood staff.* Washington, DC: NAEYC.

CHAPTER FOUR

Team Building and Small Group Interaction

S mall groups, whether they exist in the workplace or in voluntary organizations, provide an important source of satisfaction to the group members. What is accomplished in these small groups is vital to any leader. A small group is usually considered to be less than 20, and is often less than 12. To gain the most benefit from a group this size, it is necessary to understand some of the processes that go on within small groups (or teams); such an understanding helps develop group stability, group health, and group effectiveness. The internal dynamics and factors within a group can make it more or less productive. Since the staff of many small centers may comprise just one "small group," it is important that it be productive.

THE IMPORTANCE OF SMALL GROUPS

The basic reason why group membership proves so beneficial is that groups provide their members with social support and a feeling of personal worth. The foundations for mature social exchange are established early in life through child-to-child and child-to-adult interactions; favorable interactions are quickly perceived by children as indications of acceptance and approval. Thus, acceptance and approval continue to be important motivators in adult life.

It has long been established that small groups or teams in the workplace will be more effective if they contain "friendship groups," that is, if they take into account the small groups that already exist in the "informal organization." Individuals like to interact with people who like them. Sometimes the thoughts of others are the only basis on which a person can evaluate his or her own perceptions. People like to have a feeling of certainty about their beliefs, opinions, and attitudes, and often gain affirmation through the shared values in a small group.

A negative aspect that affects the dynamics of small groups is that members with a low self-esteem tend to find frustrating conditions *more* frustrating than do members with a higher self-esteem. Consequently, in difficult circumstances, those with a very low self-esteem may give up while those with a high self-esteem might stay.

STAGES OF SMALL GROUPS

According to Jacobs (1970), there are three observable stages that occur when establishing a new small group: forming, storming, and norming. These stages can be observed in any small-group situation, whether it be during an evening parent meeting or during a three-month-long staff assignment.

The *forming stage* occurs as the group gets going and a status hierarchy develops within the group. Status can be based on a person's performance skills, interpersonal skills, or the job he or she holds. Different roles begin to emerge in the group during this stage: the "tough leader," the "friendly helper," and the "clear thinker," for example. Providing the group with clear expectations helps speed this forming process along; for example, by appointing a discussion leader, a group will get into a discussion more quickly. Sometimes a group leader might be chosen merely on the basis of resources, such as designating the person who has the pencil and paper as the leader.

The *storming stage* can cause tension, and occurs when one or more group members think the leader of the group is going in a direction with which they disagree. An example of this occurred during a teacher training activity for which the assigned task was to write out a philosophy of discipline for the center. Several small groups were working on the same task as a first step towards developing a unified written statement. One person started her group off with a strong statement about her views, which favored a fairly harsh philosophy of discipline. Another teacher, in obvious disagreement, said, "Now, *wait* a minute." The possible impasse was avoided when a "clear thinker" type in the group suggested checking other written philosophies, thus channeling energies along another line. This person who broke the deadlock, incidentally, became the leader. It should be noted that this rough start was partially created by assigning an "unclear task," the characteristics of which are discussed later in the chapter.

The *norming stage* follows quickly in a short-term small-group situation, or can last several weeks or years for a work group assigned to a large task. *Norming* is defined as creating a social standard for the group. In the workplace, this norm can be a performance standard imposed from the outside, or a standard of behavior (perhaps unspoken) expected of informal group members who share the same or some of the same values. In at least some areas of reference (social, work, church, political), norming is based on shared beliefs and opinions. Group members need to feel that their objectives are worthy of attainment. They develop expectations about how people should feel about certain issues. There is usually some agreement about what is relevant and what is not. Interestingly enough, if group members perceive a difference in one of these areas, they will talk more about it rather than less, perhaps trying to persuade the others to their point of view.

Group norming leads to group members exerting pressure on others to conform. In the workplace, for example, an informal group might together define what constitutes "a fair day's work." Then the group members, as well as other workers, might work towards achieving this specific goal. Such group norming can increase overall effectiveness when the goals of the group are lined up with the goals of the organization. On the other hand, a negative group norm can be detrimental to the organization. If the informal group, for example, defines a fair day's work as very limited, other workers might feel pressured to not go beyond that "norm."

Rules or norms also benefit the group or team by making the group more effective and fairer for all. Norms or standards reduce the need for making decisions on routine matters and also reduce the need for using personal power.

In the context of discovering how groups begin to develop norming behaviors, Figure 4.1 provides an interesting exercise for a class, for a staff meeting, or for a group just wanting a review of the ways in which people interact. To use the chart, the observer checks off behaviors that occur in the twosome or group under observation. This exercise is good practice in that it helps sharpen one's observation skills in the context of a small group. The behaviors described on the chart are arranged from least beneficial (number 1) to most beneficial (number 10). For example, the comment "What date shall we set for our next meeting?" is beneficial; it demonstrates a means of facilitating the attainment of group goals (number 10). The behavior given in number 6, "to become aware of the high cost of coercion," is beneficial because becoming aware that coercion sets back the whole group's ability to interact helps group members avoid this approach.

Figure 4.1 can be used either as a formal exercise or as an informal one. The observer might want to tally one person's behaviors in the left-hand column and a second person's behaviors in the right-hand column. This chart is particularly useful during staff meetings; for example, the group can do this exercise while two staff members role play a teacher-parent conference. The person role playing the part of the parent might be asked to exhibit a specific personality style that the staff selects. For instance, when the personality style chosen is that of an abusive or neglectful parent, a number of behaviors often surface. Such parents, if they talk much, usually will exhibit an overwhelming array of problems. Often, however, they do not say much at all. The leader of this exercise can interrupt the role play and ask each of the participants how they feel. The person in the teacher role usually feels frustrated and unsuccessful. The person in the parent role, however, sometimes feels more trusting and supported, and may plan to work more with the next younger child. This activity can therefore be very encouraging to teachers who are dealing with difficult situations. They become motivated to see the situation from a more long-term viewpoint and to realize that even when they see no obvious success, it does not mean that success is not happening.

SPECIALIZED ROLES

As a small group develops, two or three types of leaders can emerge. One person, for example, might focus on the task and then compete for, or take over, the position of power and influence in the group. Some researchers call these types of behaviors *goal behaviors*. Another person might work to reduce tensions in the group by telling jokes and might have an ability to develop a high interaction rate with individual group members. These people-oriented behaviors can also be called *maintenance behaviors*. The first type of leader could be said to fill the role of "tough leader," and the second, to take on the role of "friendly helper." Another label for "tough leaders" is task specialists, and for "friendly helpers," social specialists. A third role that often can be seen in small groups is the "clear thinker," which occasionally is combined with the personality characteristics of the "tough leader."

These roles are so important for group or team success that certain individuals might find themselves filling different roles in different groups, because they understand that the group will not be effective without someone stepping into a particular role. Some people might also fill different roles and provide different services at different stages in their lives. For example, a person just beginning a career might act as the "friendly helper." A person new in the community might offer to serve on the telephone committee. These different role structures in a group permit the organization to rapidly fulfill assigned tasks.

FIGURE 4.1
Behaviors Demonstrating Social Change

Tally
Behaviors
Used

	1. To obtain approval of others: Agreement, compliments, conformity—generally spontaneous	
	2. To reward others: Asking advice, compliments, positive responses—generally calculated	
	3. To reciprocate: Interacting or responding on the same level	
	4. To obtain marginal return: Supplying rewards that benefit, yet obligate the other person	
	5. To maximize benefit/cost ratio: Consulting indirectly, i.e., talking about a problem to get advice rather than asking for it directly; seeking advice from a group member percieved to be more like self	
	6. To become aware of the high cost of coercive attempts: Showing shrewd manipulation of the group toward the leader's point of view, perhaps using debts from past exchanges	
	7. To indicate superior bargaining position: For example, having the only copy of a book in the library checked out to you; demonstrating a skill in a technique or knowledge needed by the group	
	8. To make unique and valuable contributions in return for status: Presenting knowledge which is superior to that given by other members of the group; taking more responsibility than other members	
	9. To develop or clarify group goals: Action to ascertain that group member is certain of group goals	
	10. To facilitate attainment of group goals: Structuring the group; keeping the group to goal-directed behavior	

PREDICTING GROUP PERFORMANCE

Fiedler (1967) developed a model that would predict group or team effectiveness based on leadership style, group variables, and task variables. He found that three main factors within a situation affect group performance:

- Leader position power, or the actual power to hire and fire
- Leader-member relations, or how well individuals get along
- Task structure, or clearness of task (e.g., Can it be written down?)

On the subject of the task structure variable, Fiedler further described four ways a task might be judged clear or unclear:

1. Using an impartial measure, determine whether or not a decision can be "proved" correct. For example, do statistics or other quantitative or measurable behaviors support the decision? This is called decision verifiability.
2. Determine if the group members understand the requirements of the task.
3. Determine if more than one procedure can be used to accomplish the task.
4. Determine if the problem has more than one correct solution. For example, the task of educating young children (or of all children, for that matter) is not a clear task—there are several effective ways to do it and several correct solutions to most problems.

If a task is unclear, as in steps 3 and 4 of the list, then further steps should be taken to agree on one procedure or one solution, such as agreeing on the philosophy in an early childhood program. Any tools that can add clearness to the task are helpful, such as the materials provided in Appendices A, B, and C.

Fiedler (1967) found that any group that exhibited two out of three of the major factors listed earlier (positive leader-member relations, clear task structure, and a powerful leader position) would probably be effective. Taking this discovery into account, when working in the field of education where the task is unclear, one can see that positive leader-member relations and leader position power become essential. Conversely, anything that can be done to make the task more clear (such as producing written goal statements, developing curriculum, using checklists, providing handbooks for the Executive Board or staff members) will help a small group become more effective in the field of education and in many fields.

Examples of Different Group Factors

Leader Position Power

A parent committee provides an appropriate illustration of a situation in which there is no leader position power. For example, let us say that the members and the chairperson of a parent committee are asked to design a flyer for a parent education meeting. Since there is no leader with hiring or firing power (i.e., leader position power) in any volunteer group, including this one, the other two factors become very important. Let us assume this particular group has good interpersonal relationships, or leader-member relations, and we already know that they have a clear task. When something like a written draft for a flyer is requested (a clear task), it enables an appropriate committee (presumably a Parent Education committee) to confirm all of the details involved—such as time, place, topic, theme, refreshment plans, costs, and schedule for the meeting—before writing it down in the form of a flyer. When the two factors of a clear task and positive leader-member relations are present, a group is able to successfully complete its task, in this case, producing an effective flyer. A second level of this task might be to ask the committee to write a recommended list of 20 parent education topics from which the whole parent group can select 10. This type of group interaction is diagrammed in Figure 4.2.

Unclear Task

A different combination of factors can be seen in a staff meeting in which a Director is meeting with teachers to update the curriculum in art and science. Updating curriculum is an unclear task, but the Director does have leader position power. If the group members get along well (leader-member relations), invariably they will succeed at this task. The first step an observer will see in such a situation, however, will be numerous efforts to clarify the task. For example, they perhaps will divide into two subgroups, one for art and one for science, according to their interests. Attempts to list major headings will come next. A leader also might bring in sample curricula dealing with these content areas. Anything that can be done to clarify the task from the beginning will help the group work more effectively. Figure 4.3 provides a diagram of this type of group.

FIGURE 4.2
No Leader Position Power

Leader–member relations	Task structure	Hiring–firing power
+	+	0

FIGURE 4.3
Unclear Task

Leader–member relations	Task structure	Hiring–firing power
+	0	+

Leader-Member Relations

A third type of interaction might be seen when a Director meets with staff to compose a letter to the parents on the topic "How the staff and Director feel about discipline," with the intention of placing this letter in the front of both the parent handbook and the staff handbook. This is a specific task. When it has been completed, a written document will be the result. Even though the task is specific, however, it is not easy; it touches on the purposes and means of discipline, a very fuzzy topic at best. If this group gets along well with each other, and with the Director, so much the better. If they do not (poor leader-member or interpersonal relations), the Director may want to ask each person to write an individual draft. The Director can then compile them into one or two versions before presenting them to the group as a whole. Figure 4.4 provides a diagram of this type of group interaction.

FIGURE 4.4
Poor Interpersonal Relations

Leader–member relations	Task structure	Hiring–firing power
0	+	+

TEAM LEARNING AND SHARED VISION

Now that some of the dynamics of small groups have been analyzed and understood, a better understanding of "team learning" is possible. As was mentioned previously, as a team becomes more aligned, a shared vision and philosophy emerges, and individual energies harmonize (Senge, 1990). A jazz ensemble is an example of this same cohesiveness, or synergy, in which the whole becomes greater than the sum of its parts.

Educational organizations that emphasize continued learning on the part of staff (team learning) can work together with shared energy and enthusiasm. According to Senge (1990), such organizations need people who continually expand their capabilities; this leads to greater understanding of the complexities of the task, to clearer vision, and to an improved sharing of mental models, whether these are mental models for curriculum or scenarios for the center and the parents (see Chapter 8 on planning). For those aspiring to build such a team, being responsible for the learning opportunities of children, adults, and one's self is a first step. Senge (1990) sees leaders as designers, stewards, and teachers, and notes that while learning disabilities are tragic in children, they are fatal in organizations.

THOUGHTS ON TEAM BUILDING

Coming together is a beginning; helping together is progress; working together is success.

Henry Ford (1863–1947)
American Industrialist

People acting together as a group can accomplish things which no individual acting alone could ever hope to bring about.

Franklin Delano Roosevelt (1882–1945)
Thirty-second U.S. President

There is nothing good or bad per se about a group. A group can be a roadblock to progress, enforcing "group think" and conformity upon its members, paralyzing decision-making processes, and smothering individual initiative. Under other conditions, a group can be a powerful synergism of talents, strengthening its members, speeding up the decision-making process, and embracing individual and personal growth.

Rensis Likert (1930–1981)
Director of the Institute of Social Research, University of Michigan

In assessing a child-care center's team and "teamness," consider constructing appropriate rating scales (Eitington, 1984, pp. 361–364). Figure 4.5 shows an assessment scale that provides a list of characteristics describing "teamness"; the person using this tool is asked to use a scale from 1 to 5 to rate how well each characteristic applies to the group. The completed assessment provides not only a measure of the group's present effectiveness, but also establishes a goal to strive for. Such a rating scale can be given out as an exercise at a staff meeting. Small groups could then divide up the five top selections (and perhaps the five bottom selections also) and discuss implementation strategies. Then the whole group can reconvene to discuss the ideas.

Another rating scale can be constructed that assesses team communication. The scale, similar to Figure 4.6, can be constructed with 8 or 10 statements describing communication when it is at its best.

A rating scale that assesses team problem-solving and creativity might show statements about group problem-solving, similar to the scale shown in Fig. 4.7.

FIGURE 4.5
"Teamness" Assessment Rating

Please rank from 1 (doesn't apply) to 5 (strongly applies)

_____	Cohesion	_____	Cooperation
_____	Pride	_____	Communication
_____	Decision-making	_____	Goal setting
_____	Openness	_____	Creativity
_____	Trust	_____	Conflict
_____	Team self-assessment	_____	Support
_____	Team membership identification	_____	Mutual respect
_____	Leadership	_____	Commitment
_____	Feedback to leader	_____	Atmosphere

Once these scales are developed and adapted for the center, they can be distributed to staff for self-assessment. These measures can be used as a springboard for discussion at a staff meeting, and they can be especially useful as an occasion for praise and recognition of a staff that is really working well together.

FIGURE 4.6
A Rating Scale to Assess Team Communication

Please rank from 1 (strongly disagree) to 5 (strongly agree)

_____ 1. Members listen to each other.

_____ 2. The leader listens to all team members.

_____ 3. There is freedom to be candid with each other.

_____ 4. Constructive feedback is freely interchanged to improve the group.

_____ 5. Members all participate at meetings.

_____ 6. Members double-check with each other before taking action.

_____ 7. "Air-time" is shared fairly at meetings.

_____ 8. Resources are available for information needed by the team.

_____ 9. Information is shared willingly and not withheld, including information on new policies, projects, and pay.

_____ 10. Members are not afraid to tell the leader "bad news."

_____ 11. The leader is candid about performance so that there are no surprises at personnel evaluation time.

_____ 12. The team communicates well with other groups in the organization.

FIGURE 4.7
Assessing Team Problem-Solving and Creativity

> **Please rank from 1 (terrible) to 5 (great)**
>
> _____ 1. Meets problems "head-on."
>
> _____ 2. Regards problems as challenges.
>
> _____ 3. Striving for innovation and creativity are important to the team.
>
> _____ 4. Participating is important for all team members.
>
> _____ 5. Rather than attacking new ideas, the team is concerned with the big picture for the team.
>
> _____ 6. Utilizes conflict or disagreement to enhance learning and idea generation. (Shows creative use of conflict.)
>
> _____ 7. Delegates to enhance innovation.
>
> _____ 8. Viewed by outsiders as a constructive problem-solving force.
>
> _____ 9. Solves problems with total team consensus, when appropriate.
>
> _____ 10. Presents and discusses ideas rather than defends them.

SUMMARY

A small group exists when two or more people have a unifying relationship, such as common goals or physical proximity. Utilizing the characteristics of groups is an important skill of leadership, and understanding their dynamics as described by Fiedler or other theorists can be useful. Characteristics of groups include norms, which are standards of behavior expected by group members, and individual roles, which can consist of a person's total pattern of expected behavior or of behavior during certain situations.

An informal group is defined as two or more people associated with one another in ways different from the formal organizational structure. Informal group leaders can be powerful and may be chosen by consensus, or to fill a leadership vacuum, but they are usually trusted. As such, an informal group leader is a good person for a formal leader to have on his or her side, and often is able to explain things to the community. Informal leaders are sometimes called "opinion leaders" in sociology. The synergism and energy that teams and small groups can provide are a beneficial force for accomplishing an organization's objectives.

BIBLIOGRAPHY

Argyris, C. (1962). *Interpersonal competence and organizational effectiveness.* Homewood, IL: Dorsey Press.

Argyris, C. (1985). *Strategy, change and defensive routines.* Boston: Pittman.

Beach, D. S. (1980). *Managing people at work: Readings in personnel.* New York: Wiley.

Bonner, H. (1968). *Group dynamics: Principles and applications.* New York: Harper and Row.

Cartwright, D. (Ed.). (1968). *Group dynamics, research and theory.* New York: Harper and Row.

Eitington, J. E. (1984). *The winning trainer.* Houston: Gulf Publishing House.

Fiedler, F. E. (1967). *A theory of leadership effectiveness.* New York: McGraw Hill.

Jacobs, T. O. (1970). *Leadership and exchange in formal organizations.* Alexandria, VA: Human Resources Research Organization.

Jaffee, C. L., & Lucas, R. L. (1969). Effect of rates of talking and correctness of decisions on leader choice in small groups. *Journal of Social Psychology, 79,* 247–254.

Kiefer, C., & Stroh, P. (1984). A new paradigm for developing organizations. In J. Adams (Ed.), *Transforming work.* Alexandria, VA: Miles Riler Press.

Schon, D. (1983). *The reflective practitioner: How professionals think in action.* New York: Basic Books.

Senge, P. M. (1990). *The fifth discipline: The art and practice of the learning organization.* New York: Doubleday.

Strata, R. (1989, Spring). Organizational learning—the key to management innovation. *Sloan Management Review,* pp. 63–64.

Motivating Staff, Parents, and Children

The best administrators and managers of all kinds agree on one thing: People support what they help to create (Senge, 1990). This idea also applies to the process of understanding and building vision, goals, and strategies within an organization. When people are involved in thinking through the philosophical components of an organization, a task structure is more likely to evolve that will capitalize on the natural motivation inherent in all people. Everyone is motivated by something, so the Director's task is to set up a supportive climate with high performance goals to try to access this natural motivation

(Senge, 1990). This will promote a self-fulfilling prophecy—that of an excellent center where excellent people work. By encouraging people to take responsibility and by constantly checking one's own assumptions about people, being wary of multicultural or gender filters, a Director is well on the way to having a center where people motivate themselves.

Two theories of motivation give new insights into how actions on the behalf of employees produce certain effects. The first is a two-factor motivation theory, developed by Herzberg, Mausner, and Snyderman (1959). The second theory discussed here is that developed by Maslow (1970), which can be viewed as a one-factor motivation theory. Maslow's theory of motivation looks at individuals, and is based on the assumption that things that are absent will satisfy when they are present. Herzberg's theory, on the other hand, looks at motivation within organizations. Of the many theories of motivation, these two are particularly useful in administering early childhood programs.

TWO-FACTOR MOTIVATION THEORY

"What would motivate my teachers to really work towards the goal of enabling children to be happy and competent?" wonders a Director. "I wish I had more money to pay them. Maybe I'll give Sue a small raise—that's only a few dollars a week more. Then I think I'll ask Mary if she'd like to attend that all-day conference next month. It costs $30, but it's only a one-time expense." What will be the results of these two "trial balloons"? In this case, the teacher who got the raise asked for another raise in three months; the teacher who received the training, however, was able to use those new skills for several years.

In two-factor motivation theory, as outlined by Herzberg, Mausner, and Snyderman (1959) and diagrammed in Figure 5.1, two types of factors are needed to motivate employees. The first type of factors are termed the dissatisfaction or "hygiene" factors, and are shown in the left-hand column of Figure 5.1. The second type of factors, shown in the right-hand column, are called motivator factors. The vignette in the previous paragraph about Mary and Sue illustrates this theory, in part.

Dissatisfaction or Hygiene Factors

The words *hygiene factors* used along with the term *dissatisfaction factors* really denote the extrinsic or outside factors of a facility—the things in a child-care center that a Director can do something about. Dissatisfaction factors are group-oriented factors that are all around a person at work, and they set the tone of the working atmosphere. Dissatisfaction factors include salary, working conditions, interpersonal relations, policy, hours, status, security, and quality

FIGURE 5.1
Herzberg Two-Factor Motivation Theory

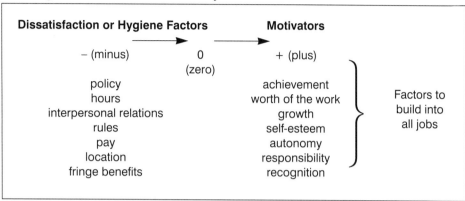

of supervision (which can be measured by observing whether the Director follows staff around and is nosy, or whether the Director trusts the staff). These factors are the ones usually chosen to improve when an administrator wants to strengthen motivation in an organization. For example, if morale is low, many administrators think that they should increase the pay, improve the hours, have more staff parties (improve interpersonal relations), or improve on some other hygiene factors. However, Herzberg found that even if all of these factors are excellent, this excellence will merely prevent employees from being dissatisfied. In Figure 5.1, this situation is illustrated by the arrows, which show the employee moving from a minus position up to a zero position. In other words, employees may not complain as much, but they are still not motivated to do their best work.

Although studies have shown that by improving hygiene factors, increased motivation does not necessarily follow, they are still very important. If a person is too dissatisfied, he or she will not even be interested in the motivating factors. It is important to realize that even in the best organizations, one or two of the hygiene factors may be beyond the administrator's control. In child-care situations, for example, the hours and the wages are somewhat controlled by outside factors. The two-factor theory of motivation is still particularly applicable in these situations, however, because all of the motivator factors can be implemented within a given program while costing the child-care center nothing or very little.

Motivator Factors

According to Herzberg, motivator factors are the second type of factors needed to inspire employees to do their best. These factors, shown in the right-hand column of Figure 5.1, are successful in motivating people because they are internal. It has been found that when motivation comes from within rather than from outside circumstances, people are happier and more able to successfully fulfill their responsibilities. Administrators, then, need to build motivators into the structure that can become internalized. For example, feelings of job satisfaction are internal motivators that are likely to come from the work itself. These feelings include a sense of achievement, a sense of responsibility, and a sense that the work itself is worthwhile.

In early childhood education, there can be a tremendous benefit gained from internal motivators, because working with children is inherently worthwhile. The work done by teachers or parents (i.e., working with children) is known as a "psychologically draining" job; teachers and parents are on duty long hours, and they must deal with repeated crises. On the other hand, working with children is an important life's work, because the consequences are far-reaching (Hamburg 1987). Persons active in early childhood work have a part in shaping the future of the country. It is important to remind workers (parents and teachers) of this often, and to say, "Thank you; what you are doing is *important* work."

In contrast to the importance and reward of careers involving work with young children are jobs that workers feel are unimportant and unrewarding. For example, most persons who work in factories, turning three bolts or inserting three computer chips all day, everyday, will have to find motivators other than job satisfaction, since the work itself will never be as inherently interesting and as far-reaching as working with young children. Factory owners know that they have this problem, so they pay assembly line workers high wages and just assume that morale problems are inherent to the business.

Even though job satisfaction may be more difficult to find in some jobs than in others, motivator factors *can* be developed by any administrator, allowing employees to feel a real sense of satisfaction in their work, not just an absence of dissatisfaction. Other motivators besides job satisfaction include building employees' self-esteem, encouraging them to grow and learn, giving them opportunities for professional growth and advancement, and providing them with some autonomy. Giving people autonomy means allowing them to work on their own; in the child-care field, this means giving opportunities for independence to aides, parents, children, and teachers.

Studies have found that people will stay in a job longer if the work really satisfies (or motivates) them, even though it may not pay well. Some people say, "If I only earned more, I wouldn't care what I did." This generally is not true, however. Earning more in an unrewarding job may please a person for a year or two, but burnout soon occurs. Finding really satisfying work is one of the finest qualities one can seek in life.

Recognition is another important motivator for all ages, adults or children. Everyone likes to be recognized for something: for a bright smile, for a job well done, for having a special hobby, and for their own unique qualities, whether job related or not.

Such motivating factors are the variables that really cause people to be motivated and happy in their work. Hygiene factors are important; in fact, they build job commitment. But when motivating factors are also present, *organizational commitment* is built along with job commitment. *Organizational commitment* is a commitment to the goals of a particular organization. In early childhood education, these goals may be providing the best quality child care in town, or developing happy, competent children. Every child-care center has some overriding goals beyond just barely keeping the center going. One such overall goal might be for the parents to have a sense of pride in having their children enrolled in such a fine program. Whatever goals are chosen, however, all of the staff needs to be committed to them. Developing motivator factors within the working conditions of an educational program really helps to secure this needed commitment of staff and parents.

Knowing the two-factor motivation theory can help in finding the right job. In fact, one interviewee uses this motivation theory as a criterion for selecting a job. When she goes for an interview, she asks the other people working there, "What do you like about working here?" If the replies are mostly, "The pay is regular" or "The hours are good" (hygiene factors), she doesn't take the job. On the other hand, if the employees reply, "They let you try out your own ideas" or "They'll support you when you get going in a project" (motivator factors), she will usually take the job, even if it pays a little less than another job with plenty of positive hygiene factors.

More time should be spent in working more motivators into child-care job settings; as stated before, these motivators are not only important, but they are also free, or at least easily affordable. When determining how best to incorporate motivators into a center, however, remember that the goal is job enrichment, not job enlargement. Motivators should not add so much extra work and challenge that the job becomes overwhelming. When motivators are effectively used, the payoff in commitment and motivation on the part of the staff provides a benefit for the center and encourages maximum effort much of the time. (Minimum effort, in contrast, is the minimum amount of work an employee must do to avoid getting fired. See Chapter 7 for more on this subject.)

The goal in integrating motivators into the program is to help people realize their potential. For example, if there is an aide in the center who is very creative, give him or her more opportunity to design bulletin boards, to produce newsletter illustrations, or to use that talent of creativity in any other way that helps him or her to grow and that benefits the center. When an organization realizes its obligation to recognize the potential in people, both individuals and the organization profit. If the center believes in people, these same people will reward the center by being motivated to expend more effort on the center than on something else. Many organizations are wasting a lot of valuable talent because they fail to motivate people. This results in not only an economic loss, but also a loss in human happiness. While hygiene factors can recharge a person, motivator factors allow a person to become his or her own generator.

CLOSING THE EXPECTATIONS GAP

The two-factor theory of motivation parallels what early childhood educators believe in: the importance of building a child's self-esteem and of helping a child reach his or her potential. Good theory about people can apply to any age, whether child or adult. Just as children respond to those who believe in them and who recognize their potential, so do adults. Adults, just like children, like to be helped to create and achieve, to be responsible and to grow. Within each person, however, there is often an expectations gap between what a person does and what he or she is capable of doing (Figure 5.2). A person who is encouraged to create and achieve will be using more of his potential, whether he or she perceives that potential or not. For example, in early childhood programs, encouraging aides to reach their potential can be done in many ways. Renaming the job of aide to perhaps program assistant or associate teacher, which reflects more expectations and abilities, might be one step. Then, enlist these people in any task that needs creativity: Have them help create a section of a morning curriculum activity; ask them to think up a song with children's names in it; encourage them to create new endings for stories; or invite them to develop new activities for rhythm and movement. The more an organization can help to close the gap between a person's actions and a person's abilities, the more of a sense of commitment its workers will feel towards the organization's goals.

In helping people realize their potential, they need to be trained to handle more *responsibility*; however, they have to find satisfaction in it. Along with taking on more commitments, people need to build a sense of competence and confidence, as well as a sense of growth. It is not wise to just lay on a "ton" of responsibility and then say, "Aren't you happy?"

When training people to manage more responsibility, it might be useful to set aside a small section of each day during which one member of the staff who is familiar with a particular task can train another person in that same task. For example, the staff member usually in charge of story hour may want to teach an aide to take over this task. In the same way, parents and/or volunteers can be trained to take responsibility for specific tasks, such as reading stories, supervising the finger painting corner, or working in the puzzle corner with children. Such a method of delegation builds a sense of achievement into the job, as well as creating a sense of responsibility.

Emphasizing the *value of the work* is another way to help workers reach their potential. The value of child-care work is one of the easiest things to reinforce, but often it is not done. Remind people of the center's philosophy regularly—in the newsletter, in the center's bylaws, and on bulletin boards. Con-

FIGURE 5.2
Expectations Gap

What one does ⟶ What one is capable of, or what one is expected to do

dense your goals into a simple sentence, such as, "We believe in having a good program for children—respecting children, respecting materials, and respecting adults." Repeat this sentence often in the hearing of the center's staff. Consider varying the goals every year, to keep interest in them high.

Recognition is also easy to give, and reinforces the attempts people make to reach their potential. For staff, have a "Teacher of the Month" (or Week) bulletin board. For this display, show a picture of the teacher and list his or her birthday, hobbies, favorite jokes, pets, and the names of his or her children. Make sure it is in a location in which parents can see it as they come in, so they can feel more at ease with and can better greet the teacher. Remember, anything that gives the staff a lift just naturally helps them to be nicer to the children.

Directors need a lift, too, and it is important for them to attend workshops, conferences, or courses to gain new ideas and to receive some recognition for what can be a lonely and isolated job. Since there are many problems a Director cannot complain about or share with his or her staff, it is important to get involved in a program where people have similar problems.

Encouraging professional *growth* is an important means of helping people close the expectations gap. Assisting people in this growth by paying a parent or teacher's way to an inexpensive local or regional conference, or by offering regular staff and parent training at the center, can reap great rewards. Even if only two or three people seem to be getting something out of training programs provided at the center, offering such education on a regular basis is an opportunity for growth. College courses fall under this category also. Tell the staff, "We want you to grow professionally, so you can apply for an even better job in the future." People need to feel that they are getting something back from working for your organization. If they feel they are growing, they will benefit from and appreciate one of the best things a program can offer.

In a field in which people are asked to give all day, centers have to give staff something in return—refill them—so that they in turn can be warm and loving to the children. Studies on stress show that people can only give out so much before they burn out. As a general rule, the more an administrator can support staff, help them feel good about themselves and their personal worth, and help them feel that what they are doing is really worthwhile, then the more they will have confidence in and a better feeling about themselves.

The Director can personally encourage staff to realize their importance to the center, to the children, and to the parents. People like to feel good about themselves. It is a real human need. Helping people feel good about themselves is something that is not very hard to do. Sometimes, though, there is a natural tendency for an administrator who feels discouraged to think, "How come *they* get to feel good about themselves when I've got this budget problem?" This is dead-end reasoning, however. If the center can give the staff something for their efforts (recognition, self-esteem), it is likely that the fruits of this appreciation will eventually benefit the center and cheer up the Director, too.

The questionnaire shown in Figure 5.3 and its accompanying key (Figure 5.4) can help centers find out just how their staff feels and in what areas motivating factors might be increased.

FIGURE 5.3
"Analysis of Staff Motivation" Questionnaire

Question	Fantastic	Pretty Good	Just Okay	Not So Good
1. How do you like the work you do?	Highly exciting; it's the work you always wanted	Promising; better than average; somewhat gratifying	Average; so-so; worthwhile	Routine; dull and confining; meaningless
	SCORE: **3**	SCORE: **2**	SCORE: **1**	SCORE: **0**
2. How much control do you have over the way you do your job?	You're the captain of your ship, and do it your own way	You decide what to do and have your plan approved by supervisor	You and Director decide what you are to do (together)	You do as you're told
	SCORE: **3**	SCORE: **2**	SCORE: **1**	SCORE: **0**
3. What kind of relationship do you have with your supervisor?	Effective; he/she really does understand you	More often effective than not	Effective sometimes and ineffective others	Ineffective relationship
	SCORE: **3**	SCORE: **2**	SCORE: **1**	SCORE: **0**
4. What kind of relationship do you have with your coworkers?	Great group; they're your kind of people	Some likeable	Pleasant, but "dull"	"Wet cement"
	SCORE: **3**	SCORE: **2**	SCORE: **1**	SCORE: **0**
5. How do you feel about the progress you've made over the past year?	Involved in new and more difficult tasks	Have some new job tasks not previously handled	New tasks, but they are small, routine duties	Not going anywhere; same old thing
	SCORE: **3**	SCORE: **2**	SCORE: **1**	SCORE: **0**
6. To what extent do you participate in decision-making?	In most cases, opinions are asked for and used constructively	Ideas are asked for	Not involved in decision-making, but informed of matters necessary to know about	Not informed of job-related matters
	SCORE: **3**	SCORE: **2**	SCORE: **1**	SCORE: **0**

Question	Fantastic	Pretty Good	Just Okay	Not So Good
7. Are you given opportunities to attend conferences, in-service classes, or workshops in your area of specialization or interest?	Regularly SCORE: **3**	Occasionally SCORE: **2**	Rarely SCORE: **1**	Never heard of those SCORE: **0**
8. Have you been given a raise in salary, promotion, or a better work location recently?	Every 6 months SCORE: **3**	Once a year SCORE: **2**	Over 18 months SCORE: **1**	Never SCORE: **0**
9. All in all, how do you feel about your pay?	Earning top dollar; likely to be rich in 10 years SCORE: **3**	Generous; can make a good living SCORE: **2**	Average; ordinary SCORE: **1**	Miserly pay, little hope for the future SCORE: **0**
10. In the past year, have you received any awards or acknowledgments for a job well done??	Every time you turn around SCORE: **3**	Occasional pat on the back SCORE: **2**	Almost never SCORE: **1**	Don't even know you're alive SCORE: **0**
11. Do you feel sure of steady employment?	Very sure SCORE: **3**	More sure than unsure SCORE: **2**	More unsure than sure SCORE: **1**	Don't know what tomorrow holds SCORE: **0**
12. Do you like where your job is located?	Ideal SCORE: **3**	Sub-ideal SCORE: **2**	Could be closer SCORE: **1**	It's an overnight trip on the freeway home SCORE: **0**

Question	Fantastic	Pretty Good	Just Okay	Not So Good
13. What is your work setting like?	Luxurious facility; tons of resources and equipment	Comfortable; nice place; sufficient resources and equipment	Run down	Dismal; cockroach carnival
	SCORE: **3**	SCORE: **2**	SCORE: **1**	SCORE: **0**
14. What kinds of fringe benefits do you receive?	Long vacation, tuition aid, pension paid, life and medical insurance	Most of these	Some of these	Few of these
	SCORE: **3**	SCORE: **2**	SCORE: **1**	SCORE: **0**
15. Does your supervisor call you ___?	By your first name, or name you prefer			Avoid calling you by your name
	SCORE: **3**			SCORE: **0**
16. Who evaluates your progress?	You evaluate your own	Cooperate in evaluation with supervisor	You are given a chance to review and discuss the evaluation given you	Given an evaluation
	SCORE: **3**	SCORE: **2**	SCORE: **1**	SCORE: **0**
17. Does your job role or status give you authority over others?	To a high degree	Somewhat	Very little	Not at all
	SCORE: **3**	SCORE: **2**	SCORE: **1**	SCORE: **0**
18. How much time and freedom does your job allow?	Your time is your own; freedom to come and go	Some free time (1 hour or more per day)	Little or no relief (10 minutes or less)	Slave driven
	SCORE: **3**	SCORE: **2**	SCORE: **1**	SCORE: **0**
19. What kind of guidance do you receive on the job?	Well-planned with individual attention	Periods of no guidance	Once in a while; vague	Poor; little or no attention
	SCORE: **3**	SCORE: **2**	SCORE: **1**	SCORE: **0**

FIGURE 5.4
Key to Motivation Questionnaire

Total: 13 factors
           (7 hygiene) + (6 motivators)

Score: hygiene   = 21 points (50%)
           motivator = 36 points (50%)

Questions:

Hygiene Factors   **Motivators**

Salary—#9   Autonomy—#18, 16, 2
Supervisor—#3   Worth of work—#1
Coworkers—#4   Recognition + Achievement—#10, 15
Location— # 12   Growth needs— # 19, 7
Fringe benefits—# 14   Advancement— # 5, 8
Working conditions—# 13   Responsibility—# 6, 17
Security—# 11

Incorporating Motivator Factors into a Child-Care Program

It is an interesting exercise to take the list of motivator factors and then brain-storm ways in which more of these motivators can be written into the job description of an aide, a parent and/or volunteer, a teacher, a Director, or into the plans for children. The following groups of motivators were developed to help parents become more involved since that is a key part of a good child care program. They were gathered from two sources: a "staff meeting" role-play group organized during a motivation segment of a college credit child-care management course, and a 1993 teacher-directors conference. The Motivator Activities provided in Appendix E also show some ways of "building in" moti-vators for staff, parents, and children.

Responsibility

1. Train parents to hold offices on the center's Advisory Board.
2. Train parents to be classroom volunteers, then provide opportunities one or two hours a week or every two weeks. For example, some opportunities might include breakfast helpers, late afternoon helpers, or Saturday yard clean-up helpers. Such a program gives parents a sense of "ownership" in the center and in their children's education.
3. Invite creative parents to make instructional materials for teachers to use in their classrooms. One center had an "International Week" in which a different country was the topic of each day, and parents provided input on snacks, stories, activities, and crafts.

The Value of the Work

1. Send home "happygrams"—flyers that have a smile face on them— describing something the child did well today. (Run off a group of blank forms on a copier.) Send "happygrams" to the staff and parents for their efforts, also.

2. Send home ideas of ways in which parents can help the center, or send home lists of items the center can use and that parents can contribute.

3. Send home ideas for learning activities that parents can do with their children. Often emphasize to parents that they are their child's most important teacher. (See the Home Learning Enablers in Appendix A.)

4. Invite a parent to participate in a children's class or a staff meeting as a guest speaker. Ask the person to tell about his or her own job/career; for example, children might be interested in hearing a dentist talk about his or her career. Staff might enjoy hearing from a person with a career in music, art, or dance.

5. Share good ideas on parenting issues or tips on single parenting in brainstorming sessions, and then publish the best ideas in a newsletter.

6. Praise parents in the newsletter or in person when they build a support network for each other, such as by picking up the children of a parent who is sick.

Recognition

1. At a parent gathering, give a certificate with a gold seal on it to a parent for her or his *first* contribution to a center. Have a "warm fuzzy" note pad and send home one or two notes a day to parents for their contributions.

2. In each month's newsletter, mention names of those who have helped the center in some way.

3. Give "thank-you" corsages at the end of the year to parents who have volunteered 10 hours (or some other attainable goal) of time over the course of the year. On a chart in the hall (where all can see), keep track of the hours given. Give a more elaborate "thank-you" gift at the end of the year to parents who help 25 hours, and a still more elaborate gift to those who help 40 or 50 hours. Have the Parent Advisory Board decide what the gifts should be, and perhaps hold a fundraiser to earn money to pay for the gifts. One center calls these gifts the "Above and Beyond Awards."

4. Create a "Parent of the Week" display on a bulletin board or in a newsletter. Describe the featured parent's hobbies, interests, job, family news, and so forth. List compliments given that person, or have the person's children write "I love my mommy (or daddy) because . . ." sentences. Do the same for other family members, such as grandparents. Post pictures of children new to the center and of their parents so all can get to know them.

5. Acknowledge and implement parents' ideas whenever possible. At meetings, validate their input for solutions that are useful.

6. Praise parents in front of their children. Reinforce and complement parents' positive interactions with children.

7. Display a toy a parent has made or a craft done by a parent. At a potluck supper, give out recipes that parents have developed, with the cook's name written on the cards.

8. In the newsletter, write paragraphs about one or two parents a month.

9. Involve children in drawing pictures for parent recognition and thank-you notes.

Growth

1. Invite parents to attend workshops and conferences.

2. Train parents to advance to responsible volunteer positions and then allow them to attend selected teacher's meetings. Develop a "theme for the year," such as fitness or music, to add focus to these meetings.

3. Help parents with their own jobs/careers. Put out a listing of local jobs available; have a meeting on résumé writing. Share information about adult stages of human development and about supports adults need at different stages in their lives.

4. Send home some Home Learning Enablers, which are one-page activities that describe a 5- or 10-minute activity parents can do with their child. (Some example activities include counting steps, stacking soda or soup cans, and making instant pudding. For more examples, see Appendix A.)

5. Tell/share information about resources in the community.

6. Encourage parents to read library books on different topics, both child-related and adult-related, and then have a meeting in which parents and staff vote on books to give their "seal of approval." Develop a parent library to allow parents access to these resources.

7. Invite parents to attend early childhood conferences.

8. Share child development information frequently.

ONE-FACTOR MOTIVATION

Abraham Maslow (1970) is quite well-known in the field of psychology, and his work on the hierarchy of human needs is also used in management. This theory states that the bottom level of needs in the triangle or hierarchy (shown in Figure 5.5) must be met before an individual can or will want to move on to the next level. A person therefore is motivated by one factor: whether or not his or her needs are met on his or her particular level of the hierarchy. This theory, when applied as a motivation theory, assumes that by meeting a person's needs on a particular level, the person will be *motivated* to go on to the next level. When a specific need is filled, the person is satisfied and ready to move on.

As was stated before when comparing the two-factor and one-factor theories of motivation, Maslow's theory looks at individuals, whereas Herzberg's theory looks at motivation within organizations. Maslow's hierarchy of needs is based on the assumption that those things absent will satisfy when they are present. In this context, in order to motivate people, you need to meet them on the level where they are and then help them move forward to the next level. Of course, it is difficult to correctly estimate another person's level of need. Some suggestions to increase the accuracy of estimating someone's level of need include finding out more about the person's background, discovering the person's place in her family as she was growing up (birth order), and learning about the person's general situation at present. Fulfilling this list can be very difficult, since many times important pieces of information are not known even by the individual. Knowledge about birth order is particularly helpful, however.

Physiological Needs

Humans tend to concentrate on meeting physiological needs before being concerned with higher level needs. However, when the needs at this level are partially satisfied, other needs emerge. The classic example of this is of the early missionaries who attempted to preach to people who were starving. Starving people have to eat before they can hear any message being brought to them.

FIGURE 5.5
Maslow's Hierarchy of Needs

Anxiety, Safety, and Security Needs

One can see the effect anxiety, safety, and security needs have on an individual's personality by observing elderly people who live in big cities, who worry about being mugged, and have 12 locks on their doors. This fear and worry (need) is so great, and with good cause, that the higher level needs do not concern them. An individual at a higher level may also experience this anxiety, safety, and security level after a traumatic experience, such as an auto accident, occurs. For several months following the accident, the person might be quite fearful and worried about safety while driving or riding in a car. According to Maslow's theory, then, it is important to "meet people where they are."

Love, Affection, and Belonging Needs

Maslow believes that most of America is at this level. The need for love, affection, and a sense of belonging often can be seen in children.

Self-Esteem Needs

If a person feels loved, is not really feeling threatened or unsafe, and is not really hungry or in need of rest, then, according to Maslow, that person would not mind increasing self-esteem in some way, perhaps by taking on additional responsibilities or becoming chairperson of a committee. A person with pressing needs in another area, however, does not need or want status responsibilities on top of their other worries.

Self-Actualization Needs

The highest level needs, which are self-actualization needs, are satisfied only after needs at the four lower levels have been met. At this fifth level, the individual is concerned with the development of his or her potential. This person has peak experiences of insight or understanding. The person at this stage, which many people never reach, has a better perception of reality, accepts self and others, is more creative, and is better able to become completely human in the realization and development of his or her full potential. Truth, goodness, beauty, and meaningfulness are recognized and enjoyed by this person.

Some theorists say that only older people can reach the self-actualization level; however, this writer has met many people in the field of early childhood education at this level who periodically have had peak experiences—times of feeling really good about their work with young children of all ages. For example, a Director who has planned a good staff training program and can see that it has really helped the staff may experience the self-actualization level. It is important to take time to value this feeling, since it is a "pay-off" of a kind for the effort expended. A Director might take a moment to think, "I worked hard on that, and it really seems to be benefiting the center." Similarly, people must learn to value the insights that come to them about what they might do next. Perhaps such insights can be written down and reviewed until the time is right to put them onto a long-range or short-range goals list.

APPLYING ONE-FACTOR MOTIVATION

The previous section discussed some practical ways of motivating adults by using the one-factor theory. This section will apply the theory to children and their needs. Some time will also be devoted to identifying the need levels of adults as well, since the same ideas for motivating children also can be used with adults.

The first step in motivating children is to think of different behaviors or problems a child might show based on each level of Maslow's hierarchy of needs. For instance, a child who is a discipline problem could be exhibiting any of the five levels of needs on the hierarchy.

- What physiological needs might cause a child to be a discipline problem?

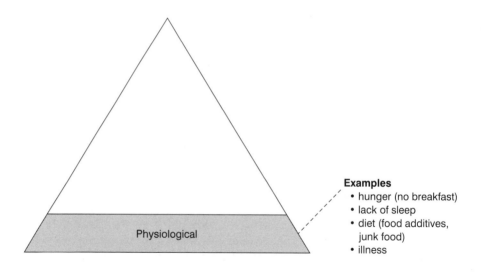

Examples
- hunger (no breakfast)
- lack of sleep
- diet (food additives, junk food)
- illness

Physiological

- What safety concerns, fears, or anxieties might result in a discipline problem?

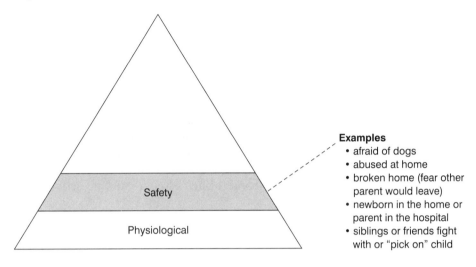

- What love, affection, and belonging needs could cause a child to be a discipline problem?

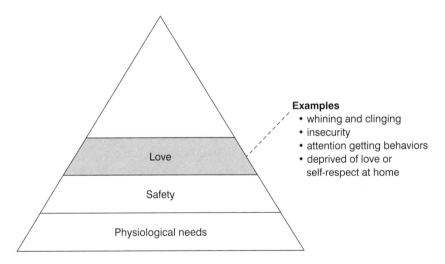

One idea for motivating children who exhibit love, affection, and belonging needs is to implement a "Child of the Week" activity. One center took a picture (or a picture could be drawn) of a different child each week, mounted the picture in the middle of a large piece of construction paper, and had all the children say one nice thing about the child. For example, the comments children made about Tommy included such things as: "I like his shoes," "He shared the green truck with me," and "He tells good jokes." These comments were written down all around the picture, then this "Child of the Week" poster was sent home. Tommy's family loved the poster and sent it to his grandparents after posting it on their own refrigerator for the month. This is self-worth and self-esteem building in action.

This "Child of the Week" activity is good not only for the child receiving the attention that particular week, but also for all the children, because they learn what it sounds like to hear and to say nice things about another child. The put-down-for-a-laugh shows have become so popular on television, and this behavior has become so accepted as children get older, that learning to say positive things about one another becomes doubly valuable and needed when children are young. More credit and reinforcement are needed for saying good things about people. Similar activities, such as choosing a "King" or "Queen" for the day, also build self-esteem. (Have two or three crowns on hand for emergencies.) Even adults respond to such esteem-building activities.

- What self-esteem needs would cause a child to be a discipline problem?

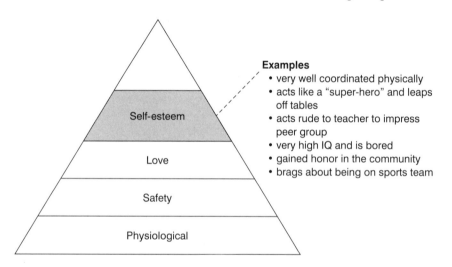

Examples
- very well coordinated physically
- acts like a "super-hero" and leaps off tables
- acts rude to teacher to impress peer group
- very high IQ and is bored
- gained honor in the community
- brags about being on sports team

From this discussion, one can see that children (or adults) might act the same way for many different reasons. For example, in one child-care situation, a boy came to school each morning and pinched every child. The teacher realized that this action was the boy's way of saying "hello." She then was able to teach him better ways of greeting the other children. This child's discipline problem was an outward sign of his love, affection, and belonging need. However, another child could act the same way (pinching her classmates) because she feels threatened by the other children (anxiety, safety, and security need) or because she wants to impress her peer group (self-esteem need). Clearly, the Director's or teacher's analysis of what level a child is on, therefore, must be on target. Seeking more training on this topic can be very helpful in sharpening one's analytical skills, since selecting a particular child's level is hard to do.

As a teacher, for example, it might be easy to look at a child who is a discipline problem—who is loud, fidgety, and punches his neighbor—and say, "I'll give you some attention in a moment. Stop bothering me." If that child is really hungry, however, more attention will not help him or her much.

Similar problems come up when applying the one-factor theory of motivation to adults. If someone has specific needs at one level, solutions based on another level of need will not be effective motivators. For example, a teacher who had grown up in a large family and never had a room of her own was having trouble sharing cupboard space with other teachers. By assigning her some cupboard space of her own in which to keep her materials, the Director met the teacher's deep-seated need to protect her "stuff" and to have her own space. This solution was more effective in meeting this teacher's need than perhaps sending her to a workshop on efficient use of storage space might have been.

An administrator must try to think about each employee, decide if he or she has a pressing need, identify it, and then try to work with the employee on that level. The level of physiological needs should not be ignored; adults can be operating on this level when they come to work without breakfast or after having too little sleep. One center actually voted to come in early each day for their coffee break and used this time for an exchange. Staff members took turns preparing coffee and providing food, and everyone's day got off to a better start.

Some other problems or needs that can lead to applications of Maslow's theory in terms of understanding more about the level an adult might be on, in addition to the *physiological level* discussed previously, might be:

Anxiety, Safety, and Security Level
- worried about a health problem
- worried about financial problems
- spouse lost job
- sudden divorce
- spouse abuse

Love, Affection, and Belonging Level
- single parent
- conflict with spouse

Self-Esteem Level
- loss of job or spouse

Self-Actualization Level
- not enough opportunities to use talents, skills, and abilities

Obviously a center's Director or Executive Board is not usually equipped to deal with many of these problems, but acknowledging their existence and helping employees find referrals to an appropriate community resource or resources might be a first step. Encouraging all adults involved with the center to treat others with support and kindness also builds a positive climate in the workplace.

Occasionally an administrator may have an employee with such a strong need that he or she really should not work in a child-care situation. One example is that of a teacher, a very good teacher up to this point, who was having tremendous problems at home with an alcoholic husband and an ensuing divorce. Although the administrator did not know all the circumstances, the entire staff had noticed that the teacher had started yelling at the children and even hitting them. The administrator realized that there was no way the center could meet this teacher's pressing needs, and encouraged the teacher to find another kind of work, for a year or two, and then to come back. Not all jobs require perfect patience all day long; other jobs are available for people who cannot reasonably be expected to change their behavior during certain circumstances.

Maslow's theory encourages one to look carefully at an individual, try to identify his or her level (or one's own) correctly, and then try to work towards solutions based on this level. It is helpful to draw out the hierarchy triangle chart, and brainstorm (even alone) some of the possible causes for a person's behavior at each level. This exercise will help prevent identifying the wrong level in a particular situation and then going down a blind alley.

Encouraging staff, parents, and children to do their best, to reach for their full potential, and to feel good about themselves is a valuable life's work. This encouragement will reap tremendous returns for the organization and for the individuals who provide this motivation.

SUMMARY

Certain themes run throughout this chapter (and this book) that are known to facilitate any organization and are particularly appropriate in early childhood programs. One of these themes includes providing a supportive workplace rather than a defensive one; a supportive atmosphere allows for the openness, caring, and good morale so needed by all adults who work with young children. In a supportive workplace there is empathy and a realistic concern for the needs and development of others, as well as a positive regard for the self-esteem of all persons involved (children and adults). Spontaneity, creativity, and a willingness to try new things (risk-taking) are valued in both children and adults. Providing the opportunity for all concerned to take part in problem-solving, regardless of rank or status, is another hallmark of the workplace climate needed in an open, caring early childhood program. Focus should be on problems to be solved rather than on interpersonal fault-finding, and on the use of technical expertise and training to solve issues. This leads to finding ways to "do it better," with concern given to mutual learning and the development of strategies to improve the way things are done. In short, a supportive climate includes the following characteristics:

1. descriptive (of behavior)
2. solution-oriented
3. vision driven
4. empathetic
5. collegial (friendship among equals)
6. experimental

With this theme in mind, many of the chapters, in addition to this one, mention ways to involve many persons in the planning and implementation of programs for young children. This approach is the most professional one, as developed in the following chapters.

BIBLIOGRAPHY

Adler, N. J. (1991). *International dimensions of organizational behavior*. Boston: PWS-Kent Publishing.

Barley, J. E. (1986, September). Personnel scheduling with flex-shift: A win-win scenario. *Personnel*, p. 63.

Bass, B. M. (1985). *Leadership and performance beyond expectations*. New York: The Free Press.

Bass, B. M., & Stogdill, R. M. (1989). *The handbook of leadership* (3rd ed.). New York: The Free Press.

Beach, D. S. (1975). *Readings in personnel*. New York: Wiley.

Bennis, W. (1989). *Why leaders can't lead: The unconscious conspiracy*. San Francisco: Jossey Bass.

Bennis, W., & Nanus, B. (1985). *Leaders*. New York: Harper and Row.

Birch, D., & Veroff, J. (1968). *Motivation: A study of action*. California: Brooks/Cole.

Blake, R., & Mouton, J. S. (1964). *The managerial grid*. Houston: Gulf Publishing.

Click, P. M., & Click, D. W. (1990). *Administration of schools for young children*. New York: Delmar.

Cone, W. F. (1974). *Supervising employees effectively*. Don Mills, Ontario: Addison-Wesley.

Conger, J. A. (1989). *The charismatic leader: Behind the mystique of exceptional leadership*. San Francisco: Jossey Bass.

Cook, C. W. (1980, April). Guidelines on managing motivation. *Business Horizons*, p. 23.

Decker, C. A., & Decker, J. R. (1988). *Planning and administering early childhood programs*. Columbus, OH: Merrill.

Driver, M. J. (1979). Individual decision making and creativity. In S. Kerr (Ed.), *Organizational behavior*. Columbus, OH: Grid Publishing.

Drucker, P. F. (1977). *People and performance: The best of Peter Drucker on management*. New York: Harper's College Press.

Eiselen, S. S. (1992). *The human side of child care administration: A how to manual*. Washington, D.C.: National Association for the Education of Young Children.

Eysenck, H. J. (1964). *Experiments in motivation*. New York: Macmillan.

Fuller, J. L. (1962). *Motivation: A biological perspective*. New York: Random House.

Gellerman, S. W. (1963). *Motivation and productivity*. New York: American Management Association.

Hamachek, D. E. (1968). *Motivation in teaching and learning*. Washington, D.C.: National Education Association.

Hamburg, D. A. (1987). *Fundamental building blocks of early life*. New York: Carnegie Corporation.

Hammer, W. C. (1979). Motivation theories and work applications. In S. Kerr (Ed.), *Organizational behavior*. Columbus, OH: Grid Publishing.

Hannaford, E. (1967). *Supervisor's guide to human relations*. Chicago: National Safety Council

Harvis, P. R., & Moran, R. T. (1990). *Managing cultural differences*. Houston: Gulf Publishing.

Hersey, P., & Blanchard, K. H. (1988). *Management of organizational behavior: Utilizing human resources*. Englewood Cliffs, NJ: Prentice-Hall.

Herzberg, F. (1982). *The managerial choice: To be efficient and to be human* (2nd ed.). Salt Lake City, UT: Olympus Publishing.

Herzberg, F. P., Mausner, B., and Snyderman, B. (1959). *The motivation to work*. New York: Wiley.

Jongeward, D. (1973). *Everybody wins: Transactional analysis applied to organizations*. Reading, MA: Addison Wesley.

Jorde-Bloom, P. (1988). *A great place to work: Improving conditions for staff in young children's programs*. Washington, D.C.: National Association for the Education of Young Children.

Klein, S. M., & Ritti, R. R. (1984). *Understanding organizational behavior*. Boston: Kent Publishing.

Klimoski, R. J., & Hayes, N. J. (1980, Autumn). Leader behavior and subordinate motivation. *Personnel Psychology*, p. 33.

Kotter, J. (1988). *The leadership factor*. New York: Free Press.

Lawler, E. E. (1973). *Motivation in work organizations*. Monterey, CA: Brooks/Cole Publishing.

Maslow, A. H. (1970). *Motivation and personality* (2nd ed.). New York: Harper and Row.

Mason, R. H., & Spick, R. S. (1987). *Management: An international perspective*. Homewood, IL: Richard Irwin.

McClelland, D. C., & Burnham, D. H. (1976, March). Power is the great motivator. *Harvard Business Review*, p. 54.

McGregor, D. (1960). *The human side of enterprise*. New York: McGraw-Hill.

Murray, E. J. (1964). *Motivation and emotion*. Englewood Cliffs, NJ: Prentice-Hall.

Quick, J. C. (1979, July). Dyadic goal setting within organizations: Role-making and motivational considerations. *Academy of Management Review*, p. 4.

Rosenthal, R. (1973, September). The Pygmalion effect lives. *Psychology Today*.

Senge, P. M. (1990). *The fifth discipline: The art and practice of the learning organization*. New York: Doubleday.

Stahl, M. J. (1983, Winter). Achievement, power and managerial motivation: Selecting managerial talent with the job choice exercise. *Personnel Psychology*.

Taylor, B. J. (1989). *Early childhood program management*. Columbus, OH: Merrill.

Terry, G. R. (1974). *Supervisory management*. Homewood, IL: Richard Irwin.

Wagel, W. H. (1986, April). Opening the door to employee participation. *Personnel*, p. 63.

CHAPTER SIX

Professionalism: More Than Meets the Eye

After World War II, the U.S. workforce began to hear the word *professional* used almost interchangeably with the words *experienced* or *trained*, such as when referring to a doctor or a lawyer. The Industrial Age, which Toffler (1980) calls "the Second Wave," put experts on a towering pedestal. One of the basic rules of this period, according to Toffler, was "specialize to succeed" (p. 262). In the late 1970s, the word *professional* referred to a specialist in a general field; for example, a special education teacher or a dental hygienist fit into the definition of *professional*. The 1980s brought the term *professional*

into the affective domain by characterizing the word as a mental focus or an attitude. A professional was a total package, a complete entity. This affective attitude came at a good time for those in the child-care industry, because during the 1988 and 1992 presidential elections, child care became a national political issue as well as a state and local one. Also by that time, the field of early childhood had evolved into a true profession, which currently encompasses early childhood education, child development, preschool, and child care. Each of these aspects also has its own subfields related to the umbrella profession.

The educational reform movements of the 1980s and 1990s also influenced the professionalization of the early childhood field. As the nation focused on issues such as quality education, developmentally appropriate curriculum and practice, and better teacher training, those who were part of the early childhood field had legitimate data to present. Currently, education is facing even more reforms, and the early childhood field has an even stronger role in building a solid educational foundation. David Elkind (1990) said,

> I am not an economist. But I can do simple arithmetic. When I subtract the cost of psychological and educational remediation at later age levels (from the cost of developmental child care), I come up with a huge surplus. From that simple-minded calculation, I argue that money spent on insuring quality child care is a wise investment that in the long run will save the nation both money and anguish. (p. 28)

In a discussion of why teacher professionalism is important at all levels—nursery through grade 12 (or N–12)—Michael Fullan (1993b) states that teaching and teacher development are fundamental to the future of society. He calls for action that links initial teacher development with continuous teacher development, even if this means restructuring universities and schools and their relationship to each other. Since child-care personnel are frequently called "teachers," and in fact are teachers, child-care centers should be included in this restructuring as well. These centers deal with children in the formative first four or five years of life.

Systems such as the N–12 education system do not change by themselves; it is the actions of individuals and small groups working on new concepts and approaches that produce the breakthroughs. One of these breakthroughs is the new paradigm for teacher professionalism, which covers all elements of children's programs for all ages of children (Fullan, 1993b, p. 17).

PROFESSIONALISM: A NEW PERSPECTIVE

It is helpful to look at the attributes of all professions when discussing the early childhood profession and the adult professionals who work in programs for young children. The attributes of a profession include:

1. Specialized knowledge;

2. Agreed upon principles and ethics;

3. Knowledge that is based on the practical rather than the academic (e.g., the precedents in law versus those in philosophy);

4. Theoretical knowledge that is not known to lay persons;

5. Membership in professional associations or in societies that publish journals, give conferences, and promote continuing education;

6. Prolonged specialized training required by all professions;

7. "Standards of Practice" are adopted by a profession;

8. A code of ethics is adopted and shared by a profession as the client is in a "lower power" position;

9. Work is performed with autonomous practice. Members of a profession work with some autonomy with respect to the client (e.g., they do not dictate to the client) and with respect to the employer (the employer does not dictate the practice and values of the profession); and

10. An altruistic mission or vision. A profession sees itself as altruistic, that is, doing work that is essential to society. Professionals identify their goals with the good of humanity. This altruism can mean working longer hours on occasion and inhibits professionals from slipping into customer/sales language. (Katz, 1987)

Child-care professionals provide education, care, nurturing, safety, and security to young children, but the service of providing child care is given to the parents or guardians of those children, rather than to the children themselves. These parents and guardians perceive child-care providers as being service-givers, whether in the public sector or the private sector. Therefore, a look at the history of public servants is warranted.

In his discussion of the evolution of the American public service, Frederick Mosher (1968) outlined the chronology of public servants, as shown in Table 6.1.

TABLE 6.1
Chronology of Public Servants

From *Democracy and the Public Service* by F. Mosher, 1968, New York: Oxford Press. Copyright 1968 by Oxford Press. Reprinted by permission.

1789–1829	Government by the Gentleman
1829–1883	Government by the Common Man
1883–1906	Government by the Good
1906–1937	Government by the Efficient
1937–1960	Government by the Administrator
1960–2000	Government by the Professionals

Government by the Gentleman

When the United States Constitution was ratified, a great many of those in influential positions in the new government were landed gentry (wealthy landowners) who were loyal to the new government and showed great fitness of character. These men were veterans or supporters of the War for Independence, and as such, were thought to have proven their loyalty, and their service was viewed as a personal investment in the new government. These positioned gentlemen held high ideals about the new democracy, and contributed much to this new form of government " . . . of the people, by the people, for the people. . . ."

Government by the Common Man

The election of Andrew Jackson in 1828 ushered in the "Era of the Common Man." Jackson was the first candidate to appeal to and depend on voters to elect him to office rather than on the backing of a particular political machine. Beginning with this election, the ordinary citizen began to participate in the workings of the government. Entry into the process was through the "spoils system," that is, government appointments in return for political support. Although Thomas Jefferson, president from 1801 to 1809, was probably the first to make use of the spoils system by refusing to appoint Federalists to political office after his Democratic-Republican party was established, it was during Jackson's presidency that the phrase "to the victor belong the spoils" was introduced and openly practiced.

While the spoils system did much to increase loyalty to particular candidates and political parties, this arrangement also proved to be a breeding ground for corruption, incompetence, and nepotism. A classic example of this system gone awry was the Tammany Hall establishment in New York City. The Society of Tammany, which was originally begun to further the ideals of independence, liberty, and federal union of the country, soon turned to political activities. Many scandals are associated with the Society of Tammany as its power as a Democratic political machine overstepped its bounds. Another example of the spoils system under Andrew Jackson that brought this process closer to home was the political appointment of local postmasters.

Government by the Good

The Pendleton Act, or the Civil Service Act of 1883, ushered into public service the concepts of merit pay and promotion, and gave rise to moral crusades like child labor laws. President Woodrow Wilson called for the separation of administration and workers, and public servants were asked to remain politically neutral. To this day, *neutral competence* is the watchword of public servants as administrations change.

Government by the Efficient

In the late 1940s, Frederick Taylor's scientific management theories became popular. Using scientific methods, Taylor studied and measured the problems of the workplace. Time and energy management and specialization of tools, machines, and people were some of the concepts he introduced. He emphasized rationality, quantitative measurements, specialization, standardization, and efficiency; in other words, "maximum output, minimum upkeep" (Taylor, 1947). Currently, some bureaucracies who look backward to the Industrial Age rather than forward to the Information Age still aspire to this goal. Some even confuse machines with people when it comes to the expectations made of personnel.

Government by the Administrator

Because of the great economic and social problems that occurred during the Great Depression era, the federal government assumed a much larger role in the everyday life of the U.S. citizen. Franklin Roosevelt, whose administrative effectiveness ranks him as one of the United States' most innovative Presidents, created many new government agencies to deal with the problems the country faced. In fact, so many new organizations were created that Roosevelt felt the need to establish a committee to recommend solutions for the new administrative tangles all these agencies brought about. One recommendation made by this new committee, called the Brownlow Committee, was that the Civil Service Commission become a federal agency headed by a single administrator who would report directly to the President. The committee also recommended that personnel management be integrated with general management. In doing so, personnel functions were decentralized, allowing middle and lower management greater input into the decision-making processes.

In 1949, the Classification Act was passed, which formally outlined the responsibility of government agencies to provide job descriptions, performance evaluations, and promotions. Principles of Management, sometimes known as POSDCORB (Plan, Organize, Staff, Develop, Coordinate, Operate, Review, Budget), became a teachable discipline. Other similar strategies and theories became popular as well.

Government by the Professionals

Currently, 1 out of every 3 public servants is a professional; that is, they have formal training, a license or certification, and belong to a professional organization. Expertise is power, and knowledge is the most flexible, versatile, and basic kind of power (Toffler, 1990, p. 474).

The Civil Service Reform Act of 1978 eliminated the bipartisan Civil Service Commission, and in its place established the Office of Personnel Management (OPM), the Merit System Protection Board, and the Federal Labor Relations Board. Each of these organizations have leadership who have professional credentials, even if they are politically appointed.

Unionization of public employees has accelerated during the last two decades. Although unions have existed in the American workplace for many years, it was President Kennedy, through an executive order, who allowed government employees to organize into unions or to engage in collective bargaining (Moore, 1985), thus allowing professionals more decision-making input.

PROFESSIONAL WORK: SOME CHARACTERISTICS

In Lester Bittel's book *What Every Supervisor Should Know* (1985) the author outlines four unique characteristics that separate professional work from other types of work. These characteristics are complementary to, but different from, those qualities described by Lillian Katz at the beginning of this chapter.

1. *Professional work is investigative in nature.*   Assignments that are approached from a professional point of view are done so with observation skills, record keeping, analysis, and follow-through. Conclusions and problem-solving done any other way are more or less haphazard.

2. *Professional work requires individual contributions.*   In an organization where all team members have a common goal of excellence, each professionally minded person will make a personal commitment and contribution to the goal.

3. *Professional work is not routine or repetitive.*   This may seem an odd characteristic when thinking about the child-care field, but looking at each child creatively is far from routine and repetitive. Professional people look for creative, enriching ways to go about everyday tasks and view children as unique and individual.

4. *Professional work increases in importance and difficulty, but the increase does not occur in discrete stages.*   Just as children do not all develop in the same way and at the same time, neither does a job well-done. There are wide ranges between the simple and the complex in the field of child care and in the administration of programs, but as administrators and staff capitalize on their strengths and work on their weaknesses, the program as a whole becomes more productive.

Bittel also answers the question, "How can I, the supervisor, learn to modify my approach when dealing with each individual employee's perception of professional work?"

1. *Realize that professional employees want to be recognized as members of a profession.*   Truly professional employees are more often career-oriented than company- or center-oriented. They are usually individualists who are constantly evaluating themselves. They dislike regimentation and compulsion.

2. *Ensure credit and recognition from top management and parents is given to employees for outstanding work and unusual accomplishments.* Generally speaking, professional employees guard their own ideas and do not appreciate it when someone else, especially a supervisor, takes credit for their ideas.

3. *Give proper dignity to the title of each position held by each employee.* Job titles are as important as the job itself.

4. *Adopt liberal policies with respect to time off for personal reasons.* Professional employees enjoy a work environment where rigid control of the time clock and the policy manual are the exception rather than the rule. People respond positively to "being treated like a professional."

5. *Encourage knowledgeable workers to take part in the activities of their professional societies.*   Networking with other child-care professionals can validate an employee's work.

TEACHER/DIRECTOR BURNOUT AND FATIGUE

Katz (1975), in listing the principles of teaching teachers, suggests that teachers will interact with children in the way that they themselves have been taught. If respect is shown to teachers and their self-image is valued, they are more likely to pass this respect on to other adults and to the children with whom they will be dealing. Human development research reports that employees in the service fields need to experience basic fulfillment in order to do their best jobs helping others, whether children or adults. In fact, the degree to which these workers feel fulfilled will be reflected in the degree to which they give of themselves.

Consider the very real problem of teachers in role conflict. According to Katz (1975) and Fuller and Brown (1975), this conflict is especially felt in the first year of teaching. Teachers and child-care administrators often see themselves divided into two contradictory roles: the executive, who is directive, supervisory, and critical; and the counselor, who is supportive and oriented toward the pursuit of knowledge. The constant tension between these two roles, plus the stress caused by insufficient time for extraneous (or required) duties, takes a toll on the personality. Sometimes, no matter what reforms are made, teachers leave their building each day discouraged, angry, and depleted. These consequences are detrimental to teacher morale and effectiveness, and many teachers resign or become ultra critical.

The concern in teacher education and administration for the feelings and self-concept of teachers is perhaps the result of this perception of the "psychological drain" that occurs in helping professions such as teaching children. Teacher and Director burnout and fatigue can develop if these concerns are not addressed. It is generally being recognized that teachers learn by doing, just as children do (Jones, 1973), and that active involvement in the learning process is the most likely method of developing and changing feelings, beliefs, attitudes, and understanding in teachers. In other words, by providing teachers with opportunities to learn, burnout and fatigue can be avoided or lessened.

College courses and staff development programs can be a great asset to administrators of early childhood programs. Those who have participated in such sessions have listed problem-solving activities and "the feeling of support gained from finding out that others share the same dilemmas" as the most valued experiences in these programs. Other comments found in program evaluations by early childhood Directors include: "It's nice to know of others with the same problems"; "This is the kind of 're-charging' I need after a year and a half of solo work"; "I feel better about everything now"; "I'm changing my priorities to support teachers more now"; "This was an inspiration to tackle many of the things I've put off—I've bogged down in day-to-day busy work." Topics felt to be of particular value were staff relationships, home learning activity enablers, newsletter writing, brainstorming techniques, incorporation procedures, and budgeting time. Experiencing the feeling that "we are all working together" and that there are many different solutions to similar problems is a valuable benefit to administrators in the thick of day-to-day child-care operations.

Administrators can help bolster teachers by realizing that effective administration of programs for children requires that warmth and sincere support be given to the teachers, who are directly involved with the children. Helping teachers find rewards and job satisfaction in daily encounters with children and adults, and seeking and providing training in all aspects of a program from budget to curriculum to the building of satisfactory interpersonal relationships, seem reasonable goals. The teacher must be respected, cared for, and fulfilled.

To handle the many stresses of the early childhood field, it is essential to learn coping mechanisms, one of which is developing self-management skills. Other strategies might include seeking knowledge of group dynamics and motivation theory; seeking skills relevant to, and awareness of, one's own personal style; seeking knowledge of alternative ways of presenting curriculum content; and sharing problems and solutions with peers. Suggestions for mechanisms include: selecting a goal, recording the quantity and circumstances of behavior, changing the settings for events, establishing effective consequences, and focusing on environmental contingencies.

Teachers and administrators need to develop the ability to self-encourage, so that they can sustain their efforts when others are not around to provide support. Taking part in self-management training programs can help teachers maintain their enthusiasm rather than becoming discouraged when personal difficulties and frustrations are encountered. Winklestein (1976) suggests that the usability, availability, and continuity of such training are basic considerations in helping teachers maintain professionalism and avoid burnout and fatigue. Katz (1975) recommends that the time of training be shifted so that more training is available to the teacher *on* the job rather than *before* it. Many teachers say that their preservice education has had only a minor influence on what they do day-to-day in their classrooms, which suggests that strategies and techniques learned before employment will often not be used in the actual job situation.

According to Katz (1975) and as implied by Winklestein's (1976) requirements for the availability and continuity of training, timing or pacing of teacher training is important for early childhood education teachers as well as for teachers of children of all ages. Research is pointing to "developmental stages" that occur during teaching, with special needs marking each stage. Katz (1972) gives one listing of these stages as survival, consolidation, renewal, and maturity, each of which lasts about one year. In writing about how teachers' feelings affect the way teachers deal with children, Katz develops the viewpoint that the way administrators treat the teachers is the way the teachers treat the children. By thinking of teachers as being in developmental stages, it is easier to determine the right, and therefore most useful, timing of possible training offerings.

Wade (1977) found, in a review of teacher education research, that teachers valued mutual support and encouragement; pooling ideas and resources; and the chance to reflect and develop judgments by comparing individual responses to the same experiences. Child-care Directors and early childhood teachers particularly benefit from these components when they are incorporated into teacher training. These items could be set as goals for methodology in the early childhood teacher training curriculum.

Incorporating a methodology concerned with the basic needs of teachers into the curriculum, and timing the presentation of staff development and workshop offerings so that on-the-job adults can participate, are ideas supported in the research as well as in some successful programs currently offered.

PROFESSIONALISM: REALISTIC GOALS FOR CHILD-CARE ADMINISTRATORS

When considered realistically, professionalism is not a trait with which one is born. It is an attitude to develop, and it takes time, experience, and a solid knowledge base to acquire true professionalism. Some goals for which a professional child-care administrator should strive are:

- A solid knowledge base of the varied fields of early childhood education and of basic, good administration principles
- Appropriate practice based on that knowledge base
- Strategic planning, in which short-term and long-term goals are set and achieved (see Chapters 7 and 8)
- Networking within professional organizations such as the National Education Association (NEA), National Association for the Education of Young Children (NAEYC), state and local Associations for Young Children (AYCs), Child Care Information Exchange, and local professional business organizations
- Providing meaningful inservice training and participatory decision-making for center employees, which conveys a message of professionalism to the staff (See Chapter 9 for a discussion of decision-making.)

PROFESSIONALS IN A GROWING PROFESSION

As child-care professionals identify new needs in their field, more models of effective child-care centers are required. One method of envisioning ways to develop new or additional centers (or organizations) is described by Toffler (1990). In the context of what he calls a "flex-firm," smaller units are able to draw information, people, and money from one another or from other outside organizations. This concept might be particularly useful for professional child-care administrators who wish to develop more child-care slots and additional centers under one umbrella. Within the flex-firm, the units may be next door to one another—as in California where centers purchase one, two, or more residential homes and convert them to child-care centers—or across town, across the state, even across continents. With a computer, a telephone, and a facsimile machine, these units can enjoy a free, fast flow of information. Unit functions may overlap or be divided logically (such as preschool and school-age children in separate units), geographically, or financially. Individual units can choose to either use or adapt central services provided by headquarters. People can thus trade ideas, data, hints, insights, facts, strategies, kindly gestures, and smiles that are essential to an efficient organization (Toffler, 1990, p. 187).

Connecting the right people with the right information is the key for effecting change at every level. With the need for child care tripling and quadrupling while the number of child-care centers is only doubling (Hamburg, 1990), the need for excellent, professional child-care programs to expand in one way or another is evident. Research reports that centers of 60 children or fewer are ideal for children (Spodek and Saracho, 1990), but more centers are needed. The flex-firm umbrella concept, along with modern technology and child-care software programs, enables this effort.

Future Needs for Early Childhood Professionals

Since there are a variety of settings for early childhood professionals as well as a variety of programs, many competencies and a broad knowledge base are needed. Spodek and Saracho (1990) list 12 predictions regarding the profession of early childhood.

1. The field of early childhood education will continue to expand and there will be an increasing need for early childhood practitioners.
2. The children enrolled in early childhood programs will continue to be more diverse (and younger and younger), making teaching a more complex task.
3. The role of the early childhood teacher will expand to become increasingly responsible for out-of-class activities. (These activities will include parent education components as well as health, nutrition, and social services elements.)
4. A distinction between the care and the education of young children will continue to be made, as will a distinction between the practitioners who provide those services.
5. There will continue to be distinct levels of professionalism among early childhood practitioners, as well as varied ways of entering the field.
6. Practitioners will continue to enter the field with a wide range of levels of preparation.
7. The move toward better educated and better prepared certified teachers of young children will continue, which will include more teacher preparation programs that go beyond a four-year degree.
8. Early childhood personnel training programs will continue to expand at the vocational and community college level.
9. Use of electronic media will be expanded in the preparation of teachers. (Note: This is true for many disciplines.)
10. While the older ideas of competency-based and field-based teacher education programs will continue to decline, new approaches to field-based programs will be elaborated with the creation of university-related professional development centers.
11. Professional associations will continue to press for higher standards of practice and higher standards for entrance into the field of early childhood education.
12. The knowledge base of early childhood education will continue to expand both through research and through contributions from such fields as sociology and anthropology.

As Saracho and Spodek point out, these are predictions, not inevitabilities; however, in a field as diverse and fast growing as early childhood education, they are helpful.

SUMMARY

As a society moves into the information or knowledge age, relationships between classes, races, genders, professions, nations, and other social groupings change, according to Toffler in his book *Powershift* (1990). These groupings are altered by shifts in population, ecology, technology, culture, and other factors. The profession of early childhood education is at just such a juncture. It could well rise to the status and visibility it deserves, as the importance of a far more heterogenous workforce and population is realized. A solid education is required to help citizens develop a strong self-esteem and the competencies necessary to cope with the changes that will occur as the information age moves forward.

As the country works to protect and invest more in its future, as evidenced by its concern with the national debt and its involvement with environmental issues, investment in young children, who are the country's future citizens, is also wise. In discussing early childhood education and other national issues, Charles Bowsher, Comptroller General of the United States from 1981–1996, stated that consumer attitudes, so popular in the 1980s and part of the 1990s, will perhaps give way to needed "investment attitudes" (1993). The importance of the early childhood education profession and the reasons for its importance in shaping the future of the world will therefore receive increasing attention as a valuable investment.

BIBLIOGRAPHY

Ade, W. (1982). Professionalism and its implications for the field of early childhood education. *Young Children, 37*(3), 25–32.

Alschuler, A. S. (Ed.). (1982). *Teacher burnout.* Washington, DC: National Education Association.

Benham, N., Miller, T., & Kontos, S. (1988). Pinpointing staff training needs in child care centers. *Young Children, 43*(4), 9–16.

Bittel, L. (1985). *What every supervisor should know.* New York: McGraw Hill.

Bowsher, C. A. (1993, May). *Major issues facing congress and the new administration.* Speech given at the American Society for the Public Administration, Washington, DC.

Bredekamp, S. (Ed.). (1987). *Developmentally appropriate practice in early childhood programs serving children from birth through age 8.* Washington, DC: National Association for the Education of Young Children.

Bredekamp, S., & Shepard, L. (1989). How best to protect children from inappropriate school expectations, practices and policies. *Young Children, 44*(3), 14–24.

Caldwell, B. (1983). How can we educate the American public about the child care profession? *Young Children, 38*(3), 11–17.

Cedoline, A. J. (1982). *Job burnout in public education.* New York: Teachers College Press.

Dresden, J., & Myers, B. K. (1989, January).

Early childhood professionals: Toward self definition. *Young Children, 44*(2), 62–66.

Elkind, D. (1990, April). Headshakers and mindbinders. *Child Care Information Exchange*, p. 28.

Feeny, S., & Chun, R. (1985). Effective teachers of young children. *Young Children, 41*(1), 47–52.

Fullan, M. (1993a). *Change forces: Probing the depths of educational reform*. London: Falmer Press.

Fullan, M. (1993b, March). Why teachers must become change agents. *Educational Leadership, 50*(6), 12–17.

Fuller, F. F., & Brown, O. H. (1975). Becoming a teacher. In K. Ryan (Ed.), *Teacher education* (pp. 25–52). Chicago: University of Chicago Press.

Greenberg, G. F. (1984). *Managing stress*. Dubuque, IA: William C. Brown.

Hamburg, D. A. (1990). *A decent start: Promoting healthy child development in the first three years of life*. New York: Carnegie Corp.

Hostetler, L., & Klugman, E. (1982). Early childhood job titles: One step toward professional status. *Young Children, 37*(6), 13–22.

Jones, E. (1973). *Dimensions of teaching-learning environments: Handbook for teachers*. Pasadena, CA: Pacific Oaks College.

Jones, E. (1990). Creating environments where teachers, like children, learn through play. In *Developing staff skills* (reprint collection no. 7), pp. 3–6. Redmond, WA: Child Care Information Exchange.

Jorde, P. (1986). Early childhood education: Issues and trends. *The Educational Forum, 50*(2), 171–181.

Jorde-Bloom, P. (1998). Assess the climate of your center: Use the early childhood work environment survey. *Day Care and Early Education, 15*(4), 9–11.

Kamii, C. (1985). Leading primary education toward excellence. *Young Children, 40*(5), 3–9.

Katz, L. (1984). The education of preprimary teachers. In L. Katz (Ed.), *Current topics in early childhood education*, (Vol. 5, pp. 209–228). Norwood, NJ: Ablex.

Katz, L. (1987). The nature of professions: Where is early childhood education? In L. Katz & K. Steiner (Eds.), *Current topics in early childhood education* (Vol. 7, pp. 1–16). Norwood, NJ: Ablex.

Katz, L. G. (1972a). Condition with caution. *Young Children, 27*(5), 277–280.

Katz, L. G. (1972b). Developmental states of preschool teachers. *The Elementary School Journal, 23*(1), 50–54.

Katz, L. G. (1975, October). Some generic principles of teaching. *Second collection of papers for teachers*. Urbana, IL: Univ. of Illinois, College of Education. (ERIC Document Reproduction Service No. 119 807)

Moore, P. (1985). *Public personnel management: A contingency approach* (Chapter 2). Lexington, MA: DC, Heath.

Mosher, F. (1968). *Democracy and the public service*. New York: Oxford Press.

Naisbitt, J., & Aburdene, P. (1983). *Megatrends*. New York: William Morrow.

Naisbitt, J., & Aburdene, P. (1990). *Megatrends 2000*. New York: William Morrow.

National Association for the Education of Young Children. (1982). *Early childhood teacher education guidelines for four- and five-year programs*. Washington, DC: Author.

Raquepaw, J., & deHass, P. A. (1984). *Factors influencing teacher burnout* (Report No. CG 018 202). Chicago: Paper presented at the annual meeting of the Midwestern Psychological Association. (ERIC Document Reproduction No. ED 256 980)

Seefeldt, C. (1988). Teacher certification and program accreditation in early childhood education. *Elementary School Journal, 89*(2), 241–251.

Southern Association on Children Under Six. (1985). *Position statement on quality four year old programs in public schools*. Little Rock, AR: Author. (ERIC/ECE Document Reproduction Service No. ED 272 272)

Southern Association on Children Under Six. (1986a). *Position statement on supporting parents*. Little Rock, AR: Author. (ERIC/ECE Document Reproduction Service No. ED 272 272)

Southern Association on Children Under Six. (1986b). *Position statement on quality child care*. Little Rock, AR: Author. (ERIC/ECE Document Reproduction Service No. ED 272 272)

Spodek, B., & Saracho, O. N. (1990). Professionalism in early childhood education. In B. Spodek, O. N. Saracho, & D. L. Peters (Eds.), *Professionalism and the early childhood practitioner* (pp. 59–74). New York: Teachers College Press.

Swick, K. J. (1989). *Stress and teaching*. Washington, DC: National Education Association.

Taylor, F. W. (1947). *Scientific management*. New York: Harper and Row.

Toffler, A. (1980). *The third wave*. New York: Bantam.

Toffler, A. (1990). *Powershift*. New York: Bantam.

Wade, B. (1977). Initial teacher education and school experience. *Education Review*, pp. 58–66.

Winklestein, E., and others. (1976, June). *In-service training models for early childhood education programs* (Report No. PS 008647). Urbana, IL: Univ. of Illinois, College of Education. (ERIC/ECE Reproduction Service No. ED 125 754)

PART THREE

The Role of the Director

Leadership, planning, decision-making, and problem-solving are some of the main components that make up the role of the Director. These functions are the foundations of the administrative and management structures of a center and if they do not form a strong foundation, the structure is not as steady or secure as it might be. Building on an attitude of excellence in personnel hiring and training, team building, motivation, and professionalism, a center can move forward with the tasks of implementation, operation, and evaluation. Time management and good assistance are important as well. Assistance can be supplied by technology (such as computers), as well as by experienced people (such as a good administrative assistant).

As a center becomes larger, the Director needs to be increasingly aware that one third or more of his or her time should go to parent relations and community outreach. A Director should assess the percentage of time spent on

1. functions, such as talking on the phone, doing paperwork, working with people one-on-one or in groups; and
2. the categories of people with whom this time is spent, such as with children, staff, parents, and/or community.

More categories can be added to these assessments to accommodate unique situations. Pie charts showing these percentages of time spent, such as those shown in the figure on page 120, can reveal rewarding insights.

Director's Time Analysis (Sample)

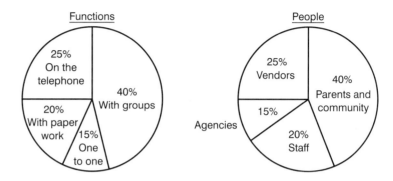

Functions
- 25% On the telephone
- 40% With groups
- 20% With paper work
- 15% One to one

People
- 25% Vendors
- 40% Parents and community
- 15% Agencies
- 20% Staff

When planning for assistance, in addition to the use of one or more computers along with useful child-care software packages, adequate human resources will be needed. As a center grows from 25 to 50 children, a head teacher or education director may need to be added. A full-time administrative assistant may replace a secretary and take over more of the administrative duties. However, the Director is still in charge of overall policy-making, budgeting, personnel development, and any activities that might take him or her out of the center.

As a center grows from 25 to 50 children, classes might grow in number. For example, the center may expand from two classes to four classes, accommodating the younger children in the smaller classes. The Director continues to handle parent admissions activities, and the teachers handle routine daily parent contacts. The administrative assistant deals with fee collection. As a center reaches about 50 students, the Director usually is freed from in-center activities. Fund-raising, making agency contacts, and more admissions work are required. Meetings and planning become slightly more formal; many of the ideas given in the next four chapters may be even more useful and necessary.

As a center grows to serving 75 children, many of the Director's activities stay the same, but due to growth, they become more complex and require more time and effort to perform. The Director is still the overall administrator, and deals with policy-making, budgets, hiring and dismissals, and staff salaries, as well as plans with the staff and the Board to determine long-range goals. He or she remains the chief link to outside agencies for resources and sponsorship. An assistant Director may take on the short-term staff training and many administrative duties, such as purchasing (using the Director's guidelines). The advisory capacity of the assistant's position is mostly in the areas of child care and teaching. The secretary/bookkeeper handles the administration that can be delegated, assists with scheduling, and answers the telephone. A center of this size might have six classes of children, so age, maturity, and special needs can be addressed in even more discrete ways.

An analysis of how much time the Director spends on functions and categories of people becomes even more important as the center grows. If one feels that "doing paperwork" is the most important part of the job (or is the largest part of the job), some changes may need to be made to involve other members of the staff more. Directors report that they work between 40 and 60 hours a week, but as the number of hours approaches 55 and 60 hours per week, the likelihood of burnout increases and the individual may leave the field. Assessment of management functions needs to be continuous, and many of the ideas in Chapter 10 for individual problem-solving can be used to analyze and break down tasks and projects into manageable parts. Facilitating the group of adults who are involved in a center—staff, Board, and parents—to move toward center goals requires an understanding of leadership and the use of power, which are presented in the next chapters.

CHAPTER SEVEN

Understanding Leadership and the Use of Power

An awareness of sound leadership principles can offer new insights to those responsible for providing well-run, quality programs for children. Leadership includes the ability to create a vision and develop strategies, along with the management tasks of planning, implementing, operating, and evaluating. Because working with young children is one of the most important occupations to which a person can devote his or her life, excellence should be the goal of all aspects of child care, especially the leadership aspect.

LEADERSHIP

Leadership in early childhood education administration means planning for change, then implementing, putting into operation, and evaluating those plans. Leadership functions are designed to accomplish change for the improvement of the organization, and not just for change's sake. Administrative functions and responsibilities, as well as leadership functions and responsibilities, may be carried out by the same person; however, administrative roles and leadership roles are different. Administrative duties focus on just keeping things going, such as committees, policies, and regulations. Administration alone is not leadership; instead, it is the activity of using old processes to obtain old or ongoing goals. Leadership, on the other hand, uses new processes to achieve ongoing goals, or new processes to reach new goals (Figure 7.1).

For example, in a child-care or preschool situation, a leader might be called upon to uphold an ongoing, tried-and-true goal of developing happy, competent children. The leader might decide to use a new process to help reach this goal, such as having the staff brainstorm types of training they want or need, and then, with the staff's help, planning four to eight training sessions from this list.

A new goal for a child-care center might be that of opening another branch of the center in a new location; the leader could use "old" processes, such as the same administrative foundations and sequence of steps that were used to open the first center, to accomplish this new goal. An example of a new goal that might be accomplished through a new process might be that of adding a parent workshop series to the center's offerings, with topics planned by parents during brainstorming sessions and with parent chairpersons to run the workshop series. The possibilities are endless.

How does a Director or leader make significant changes that will achieve better quality results? Usually this goal involves long-term changes, which may take one or two years to plan, and then two to three years to implement. This process requires leadership. Under the terms of social exchange, which bases leadership on successful interactions and the ability to persuade others toward group goals (rather than on force), leadership is an interaction between persons in which the first person presents information in such a way that the second person is convinced that the benefits to him/herself will be greater than

FIGURE 7.1
Leadership vs. Administration

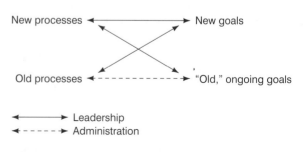

the benefits to the first person (cost-benefits improved); because of this, the interaction avoids direct confrontation and moves the persons or groups toward goals without making status or power differentials obvious (Jacobs, 1971, p. 237).

A good example of this can be found in the story of a Director of a large midwestern child-care center. Her center was in a small town in the middle of flat, hot, dusty farmland. Even so, she always managed to hire extremely able assistant Directors, who were competent, productive people. How did she do this? She told them that if they would do their best work for her for four years, she would then write a persuasive letter of recommendation to any of the biggest child-care systems in the country that they chose. (They could see their cost-benefits improving.) The Director made it clear that she didn't expect these assistants to stay with her forever, just for four years. Without this leadership gesture, which provided young professionals the chance to see the direct benefits of giving their boss their best efforts, this Director might have had assistants quitting in one year. She also might have had a hard time enticing able people to her locality at all.

Obviously this type of leadership requires interpersonal interaction skills in persuading other people. Some employees prefer an *authoritarian* (autocratic) type of leadership and some followers or employees prefer a *humanitarian* (friendly or kindly) type of leader. The choice will depend on the situation, the leader, and/or the followers.

SOURCES OF POWER

There are different *sources of power* described in management theory; by combining two or three of these sources, an administrator can "widen" his or her power base." Remember, *power is the ability to influence others,* and, according to this definition, is always granted from below. The following sources of power, therefore, are ways leaders can seek to influence others' behavior.

Reward Power

Reward power is derived from one person's capacity to reward another person in exchange for his compliance with desired behavior. This compliance is expected to happen without supervision, and works best when the person's acceptance of direction and evidence of providing effort (results) *can be seen*. If a Director sees good teaching or good relationships between a teacher and children, it is important to give praise or a smile right then. So much of what is important in early childhood is not tangible and cannot easily be seen at just any time. If a positive action or situation has been reinforced at the time of occurrence, then it easily can be referred to later when the Director is considering the person for a raise, or selecting a "Teacher of the Month" to be featured on a bulletin board.

Coercive Power

Coercive power is not the result of merely withholding rewards; it is the capacity to actually inflict something negative on a person, such as reducing her hours or dismissing her. The outcome of using this kind of power is not good—it tends to cause workers to "cover up," to lie, to turn in false reports, and in general to sabotage the goals of the organization. In early childhood education, coercive power is particularly undesirable since physical punishment is prohibited with the children; if it is used, it may cause these undesirable results in children also.

Legitimate Power

Legitimate power is just that: Because the Director is the Director (holds that job), people *expect* him or her to lead and delegate responsibility by asking others to do things. However, the leader's efforts to make changes must appear to be "reasonable and correct" to the group, or else the leader will need to make his or her position clear by informing the group of his or her point of view or by helping them understand more about his or her responsibility. Elected officials have this type of "legitimate power."

Referent Power

The source of referent power is that people find the leader so attractive, competent, and understanding that they want to *identify* with her. They wish to please the Director by seeking to do as she asks. This is the kind of leader who "inspires" people, and often those being led have no idea of the power this leader has over them. Referent power is one of the most effective sources of power and is a valuable one for all early childhood administrators, since it is important for staff and administrators to model ways to inspire the parents and children.

When people model their behavior after a leader, it allows the leader great influence. In such a situation, people do things because they like the leader, they want to do something the leader might like, and they want to be like the leader. People have different areas in their lives, or groups of reference, that might involve different referent people; for example, work life, social life, family life, and religious life are all groups of reference.

Expert Power

Expert power lies in the workers' view that the administrator has more knowledge and ability in a given area. This is an easy power source for a leader to maintain and increase by updating her knowledge with workshops and courses, keeping up with professional reading, *and talking about it*, whether in staff training meetings or informally. Employees will be supportive and will follow directions without supervision in relationship to how expert they think the leader is.

Those who are experts should remember that when dealing with other peoples' ideas, work, or property, one should always maximize the person's self-esteem, and give credit at the end of a project when it is successful. If a project is unsuccessful, the "idea person" will be grateful to be saved from the embarrassment of criticism.

SOCIAL EXCHANGE: HOW TO MAKE INTERACTIONS WORK FOR YOU

In applying the basic concept of social exchange to leadership, one can compare it to a checking account. A leader can have a plus or minus balance of "credit," and he or she can add to this or subtract from it.

In social exchange theory, the central question is *why* a group member subordinates himself to someone of higher status. The answer lies in the type of "balance" a leader builds, whether it be positive or negative. When a leader starts out, he or she usually has a neutral balance. From that point on,

1. everything the leader says builds plus or minus credit;
2. the leader's follow-up on what he says builds plus or minus credit; for example, if the leader gets resources as promised, a plus credit is built; and
3. plus or minus credit is built by the reward or punishment the leader gives to those who do well or poorly in relationship to organizational goals.

Usually a new leader starts off with a slight plus credit, because she is "the leader," unless the leader or Director before her has done an unusually poor job. In the latter case, a leader starts off with a slight minus credit, and must allow a longer time to "build trust" according to the three suggestions just given.

When a leader begins his job, the organization can put a publicity item in the newsletter to help give him a "plus credit" start. Even if the previous leader left with a minus credit, however, there is only a limited carry-over effect, since credit is mostly based on the new individual, and what he does. A new leader also earns a small plus credit because people assume he has access to resources.

Making a good change is often a slow and deliberate process. To make a positive change, a new Director must have the group's support, or at least their indifference, rather than their opposition. If the group doubts the leader, the cohesiveness of the group may be split. Some individuals in a group work slowly and cautiously to split the staff. This, of course, ruins the organization. In order to prevent this, the leader has to make the proposed rewards great enough to keep people quiet and working; she also shouldn't promise anything she can't deliver.

A leader can always earn more credit if she has a plus to begin with, but as credit grows, so also does the blame when plans do not succeed. Directors should decide if they want this accountability and if they have the competency for it. Maybe a given individual has other competencies rather than leadership.

Idiosyncrasy Credit

The term *idiosyncrasy credit* refers to the number of peculiarities, or idiosyncrasies, the Director or new leader is "allowed" to have. Idiosyncrasy credit, sometimes called personality credit, develops slowly, over time. In the beginning, then, it is best for a leader to present only one or two idiosyncrasies until credit is well established.

A new Director or principal usually comes into a program and sees lots of things she wants to change. Writing all these good ideas in a notebook will be useful later, since after a while the fresh perspective wears off and the needs of the program may not be identified as clearly. After making a list, the Director should choose only two ideas and decide how to implement them in the next six months. Two more ideas can be focused on in the following six months. One Director reveals this plan in a letter to the staff, which she includes as the first page in her staff notebook. (The staff notebook is a resource given to each staff member, and includes schedules, policies, rules, a calendar, etc.) In this letter, the Director states her philosophy, either generally or for the specific upcoming year:

> Our philosophy this year will emphasize *respect*—respect for children, respect for adults, respect for materials, and respect for new ideas.

or

> Our philosophy this year will emphasize physical fitness, which will include the addition of a new piece of playground equipment and serving more nutritious snacks.

Following the paragraph on philosophical topics, the Director includes a paragraph describing her two idiosyncrasies.

I would like to remind you that I am more upset than I am comfortable when I see someone discipline a child for wetting or dirtying his pants. I'd like to ask you all to refrain from this type of discipline out of respect for me. Also this year, I'd particularly like to have a special emphasis on having the children sing more during the day.

Thanks for being such a great staff. This center wouldn't be the best center in town if it weren't for each person's special efforts. I want you to know how much I appreciate them.

Sincerely,
Sue Smith, Director

The idea here is that the Director gets to have two idiosyncrasies—even if they are a little unusual—just because she *is* the Director. This acceptance of her idiosyncracies, or her idiosyncracy credit, builds with time and with her abilities in social exchange and interactions. Generally, leaders have a greater positive balance of idiosyncrasy credit than do followers.

Studies show over and over again that workers at least want a fair exchange in their work situations, and that they prefer getting more back in return for their efforts. If they feel they gain self-esteem and status from working in a good center where their extra efforts are especially valued, they will begin to feel that they are getting a fair exchange. This in turn earns the leader more credit.

The amount of credit a leader gets is based on the *perceptions* of the group members relative to the accomplishment of group goals. A leader, therefore, should let the group know when the center is praised or when group goals are met in a way in which the staff may not be aware.

In summary, to gather credit, a leader must:

1. facilitate group attainments, and the group has to know it (The leader can't tell them, however; they must get their perceptions through interactions.)

2. resolve conflicts

3. increase resources

Since a leader's credit is partially built as a result of his or her ability in social exchange, it is important to realize that social exchange is popularity-based. Mostly it is based on workers *liking* to be with the leader, because the leader makes people feel good about themselves. The followers feel that they provide a service to this kind of leader, and like being helpful to him or her (referent power).

Popular leaders can tolerate, accept, and appreciate a wide range of values—they are not dogmatic. Of course, a leader can never know exactly how employees will interpret his or her behavior, or what they will do in response. Leaders can hope for the best, though. Most groups within an establishment develop fairly strong informal organizations. The leader's goal should be to have the purpose of this network be the same as the purpose of the center, such as having the best center in town.

Minimum Effort vs. Maximum Effort

Usually when an employee begins work, there is a written or unwritten "employment contract" stating that the employee will accept direction and will provide effort without question. This requirement is called a *minimum effort*, which is basically what an employee must do unless he or she wants to risk getting fired.

One goal of leadership is to obtain, at least part of the time, individual effort from employees that far surpasses this minimum. To obtain this greater effort, there must be some sort of process that leads individuals to be concerned about the achievement of organizational objectives for reasons other than just their pay and fringe benefits. The employees must be genuinely concerned about the welfare of the center itself, either by identifying with it, or by feeling that the goals themselves are right and proper. Either attitude will lead to superior efforts. Such employees take pride in saying, "I work for the best center in town."

Perhaps the most important aspect of the interaction between adults and a child-care center is that the interaction must reflect to the adult that the center considers him important, thus providing him with a feeling of personal worth. Each person has a strong need to feel accepted and appreciated by others. To the extent that a center communicates a feeling of worth and support to an individual, whether staff or parent, that individual will feel rewarded; *in exchange*, that person will feel motivated to repay the center through greater cooperation and through encouragement they give to other adults and the children. This exchange happens best when adults know they will get even more respect if their behavior is continued and improved upon.

One large system of child-care centers in Philadelphia has a wonderful program of gradually improving rewards. Hourly records are kept of how much time each parent "gives" the center; this time might be spent attending parent-officers meetings, going along on field trips, providing classroom assistance, checking out library books for the center's use, painting or repairing equipment, or any of the other myriad ways parents can help. These volunteer parents write in their hours on a chart posted in the hall near their child's room. At the end of the year, the Director provides rewards such as corsages for parents who provide 10 to 15 hours of help, a large gift selected by the Board to the parent who provides the most number of hours of help, and smaller gifts to the runner(s) up for the most hours given. Each year the parents' committee votes for new "prizes," and then earns the money to pay for them as part of their fund-raising events.

When looking for ways to maximize the effort given by the adults involved in a particular center, the leader should remember that commitment is very slow to build, but very easy to destroy! It is precious, and something to be nurtured.

Organizational Variables

In his two books *New Patterns of Management* (1961) and *The Human Organization* (1967), Rensis Likert found that organizations have three sets of variables, as illustrated in Figure 7.2. If long-term change is the goal, the leader must provide input into the first set, which then affects the second set, and then the third set. These variables are as follows:

1. *Causal variables*   The organization has some control over these, which include policies, rules and regulations, salary, fringe benefits, interpersonal relations, and hours.

2. *Intervening variables*   These include perceptions, attitudes, and loyalty, which are built on the causal variables.

3. *End variables*   These result from the attitudes and loyalty of a center, and include as an end goal happy, competent children (our definition of productivity for the early childhood world) and cooperative staff or parents. On the negative side, end variables may include waste, pilfering, turnover of staff, lateness, and absenteeism.

Most of Likert's research is based on *perceptions*; although perceptions may not reflect what is really going on, *perceptions are what count*, because they affect the end variables. If undesirable behaviors are noted in the end variables column of the chart in Figure 7.2 when it is applied to a specific center, plans

FIGURE 7.2
Likert Model

VARIABLES		
Causal	**Intervening**	**End**
Policy	Perceptions	Happy, competent children (productivity)
Rules	Attitudes	Cooperative staff/parents
Salary	Loyalty	
Fringe benefits		Waste, pilfering, lateness, staff
Interpersonal relations		turnover, absenteeism
Hours		
	6 months–2 years	6 months–2 years

Note: Remember to consider the *time factor* in the above process. For the variables in each column to effect a change in the next column, the time or "organizational lag" needed between sets of variables is six months to two years.

can be made to make changes in causal variables. Perhaps it is time to ask the staff as a group to review and update staff policy. Although salary is often a problem in the early childhood work world, almost all of the other causal variables can be changed easily to better benefit or accommodate the staff, which in turn creates better feelings and more loyalty. Salary, of course, can be changed also, but external as well as internal factors are involved in making such a change. Appendix F provides some Leadership Enablers that give a few ideas for possible changes in causal variables as these are the only variables that can be changed directly.

The following story of Mary, an aide, illustrates how a simple change in causal variables can affect other variables.

> Mary was always 20 to 30 minutes late for work each morning, which upset the staff-child ratio during those 20 to 30 minutes. The Director had spoken to Mary several times, but no change in Mary's lateness had occurred. Finally, in a one-to-one conference, the Director learned that Mary had a six-year-old child who left for school at 8:15 a.m. Mary's bus to the center left at 8:00 a.m., and she usually missed it. This Director quickly saw that a tender-hearted person like Mary wasn't about to leave a crying six-year-old for the sake of any job. So she adjusted Mary's work schedule to start and end half an hour later. Mary was very grateful (intervening variable) for this understanding attitude on the Director's part, and was loyal to the center and kind to the children for the rest of the time she was employed there (several years).

The time lag in Mary's change of perception—from feeling that this was just a job with inconvenient hours to a feeling of gratitude—occurred considerably faster than the six months shown on the chart, but then this was a small change.

Unfortunately, this chart works in reverse, too. Where there is waste, absenteeism, staff turnover, and unhappy children, a Director or an observer might find disloyal staff who perceive the policies and regulations as harsh and unfair or who have other complaints (whether justified or not). This is a larger problem, and the full two years might be needed after some of the causal variables have been changed for attitudes to change as well. Output changes, and really happy, competent children, might take two *more* years after the attitudes change.

Because of this time lag, it is important never to judge a program, and perhaps drop it, after only one year. As was mentioned earlier, when a new Director comes in, he often sees many things that he might want to change. Since this initial time is a "building trust" time, the changes should come gradually. After a year, the Director may look at the four areas he has chosen to work on (two every six months), and find it hard to see noticeable improvement. The Likert model suggests the benefits of waiting another year before dropping these efforts, since attitudes and perceptions change slowly, but are well worth waiting for.

CHARACTERISTICS OF SUCCESSFUL LEADERS

While studying large companies with many branches, Likert (1953) compared the 30 most successful managers with the 30 least successful managers in the same company. He found that the major differences between the two groups fall into five categories:

1. *Providing social support for workers and groups.*   This factor was found to be the most important characteristic; it is a causal variable that a leader can control to build good attitudes.
2. *Providing high task orientation.*   Successful leaders always clarify the overall goals of the organization and remind workers of their importance.
3. *Providing a high degree of technical expertise.*   Successful leaders know their fields. They take courses and workshops to keep up professionally, and thus are able to be problem-solvers and help train their workers.
4. *Maintaining a high degree of role differentiation.*   While successful leaders are friendly with their staffs, they do not "go out drinking with the boys" or share details about their recent divorce. By being sure to do the things that only a leader can do (set goals, resolve conflicts, increase resources), and avoiding the temptation of "pitching in" with everyone, leaders serve their organizations better. This is not to say that leaders should not pitch in sometimes (such as when the fish tank breaks!), but they must reserve time for planning and keeping up with professional reading.
5. *Providing general supervision.*   In contrast to providing "nosy" and specific supervision, successful leaders meet with groups of people in a *general* way. General training and direction can be offered at staff meetings, for example. The concept here is that workers are hired because they are competent, and are trusted to do a good job. It was found that specific, close supervision makes people feel mistrusted. Even praise that is too intrusive can "hem people in." People who feel mistrusted immediately develop attitudes of disloyalty and nonsupport for the organizational goals.

In a child-care situation, adhering to these five conditions creates a climate that leads to happy, competent children as well as to other positive results.

People want a leader who can be a focal point. It is much easier to follow a leader who gets supplies (increases resources), provides goal orientation and facilitates group attainments, and resolves conflicts between people.

Leaders also characterize the organization that they lead. For example, Likert (1961) divides organizations into four types, as illustrated in Figure 7.3, based on the management style of the leader(s):

System 1: exploitative authoritative

System 2: benevolent authoritative

System 3: consultative

System 4: participative group

In extensive and numerous (300 to 400) studies, Likert found that when organizations change from System One to System Four management, their income changes from 15 to 20 percent *below* their projected budget to 15 to 20 percent *above* their projected budget. This benefit of a System Four management style—which is characterized by extensive, friendly interaction with people—reflects the fact that the most valuable asset of any organization is its people. When a Director gets overly task-oriented, she is selling short her most valuable asset—people. In fact, when leaders operate under the philosophies of "let's run a tight ship," "clean it up," and "let's have less noise," the most productive employees leave first, since they get better offers elsewhere.

A System One organization in which workers are afraid to talk to management usually enforces norms very harshly; for example, job threats are a frequent occurrence. Quite often there is something being "covered up" at higher levels of management, which restricts the professional employee's desire for free-flowing information. In one such instance, a Director took a nap in the broom closet every afternoon, and this was the "forbidden secret." This partic-

FIGURE 7.3
Likert's Four Systems of Management

System 1: Exploitative authoritative	System 2: Benevolent authoritative	System 3: Consultative	System 4: Participative group
Workers afraid to talk to management	Workers less afraid to talk	Workers fairly free to talk	• Extensive, friendly interaction: People really are working with you • Productive, problem-solving atmosphere; not win-lose • Management knows what workers' problems are

ular Director's center was clearly a System One center, and employees were disciplined for questioning the leadership. This is a true example, and is only recorded here to show how peculiar these indiscretions might be. Other more usual "secrets" may include excessive drinking or misuse of funds. Suffice it to say, System One is often a "deficit model," with the leader feeling easily threatened.

A System Two management style, in which employees are less afraid to talk, often comes into being when a new Director replaces a System One Director, and the employees cannot quite believe the improvement. The six months needed to build trust, as described earlier in this chapter, will be the minimum in this case, since 18 to 24 months may be necessary to allow for "institutional lag."

System Three represents the reality in many well-run child-care programs that have Directors who were "socialized" under System One and Two organizations themselves, but who are trying for a more open and participative style that harmonizes better with the early childhood field. However, people tend to manage in the way *they* were managed as employees; first managers can be strong models, whether positive or negative ones.

System Four Directors usually have experienced, and have been greatly helped by, this particular style in other situations. They are believers in the extra power, creativity, and motivation that a System Four style can unleash. Role-play practice of each of these management styles can demonstrate to observers the strengths of System Four and the weaknesses of other styles, since real-life observations are not usually possible.

Treasurers and Executive Boards often do not have the vision to build toward a System Four management style, and often suggest some short-term, budget-oriented solutions to problems instead. The specifics of how to apply System Four management goals will vary with the individual organization, but it must be remembered that people have to be treated well in order to want to put any extra effort into changes. This boils down to the fact that leaders need to respect each individual's human dignity within that person's *own* framework.

If a Director or supervisor would like to find out what type of management system his program appears to be, he can ask any employee the questions provided in the staff questionnaire shown in Figure 5.3, along with, or instead of, the question, "How much confidence and trust do you feel your superior has in you?" When reviewing the results of such a questionnaire, keep in mind that the formula for a successful organization is supportive relationships (including opportunities to advance), plus high performance goals, plus technical competence.

Supportive Relationships + High Performance Goals + Technical
      Competence = Successful Organization

When one first starts to work at building positive attitudes, loyalty, and perceptions, "productivity" may decline in the first six months. This is because, before undertaking this new goal, *all* resources were put into productivity, whereas now some resources are divided.

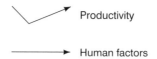

Some people in the organization may have been "just waiting" to let the leader know their problems, only now bringing their many needs to the leader's attention. To survive this phase of "building attitudes," the leader can find other ways to maintain productivity, such as:

1. using up inventory
2. borrowing
3. cutting back in other ways

In the long run, a worker who feels respected will be much more willing to give "the best center in town" his or her maximum effort. Such effort leads to the realization of the goal—the center really *does* become the best in town, and everyone associated with it takes pride in providing really excellent care for young children. This is true productivity.

THE USE OF POWER

Sometimes power is erroneously defined as negative and coercive. The positive aspects of power, however, already have been discussed in the context of leadership. For the purposes of this discussion, the following definitions of power and authority will be used:

* *Power* is the ability to influence another's behaviors. This influence is always granted from below, that is, by the people over whom it is exercised. Therefore, power is not guaranteed; some people would rather die than change for someone else.
* *Authority* is the vested right to try to influence others. This right is always granted from above.

In the context of these definitions, power has to be earned, whereas authority is given.

Power actually increases when it is given away, since more workers, and thus more ideas, become involved. The graph in Figure 7.4 shows this relationship. Some people think the more power they give away, the less they have. (A few elementary-school principals demonstrate this belief.)

FIGURE 7.4
Perceptions of Power

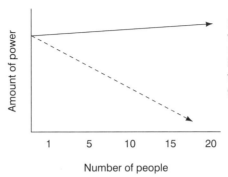

Power actually increases when you give it away. (More ideas and workers are involved.) But some people think the more power they give away, the less they have.

For example, suppose Director Smith approaches her Executive Board and says, "We need to have a fund raiser this spring, and I think Mrs. Williams and Mrs. Adams could co-chair it." What happens? Mrs. Williams and Mrs. Adams suddenly find that they are much too busy to help out this spring, and they are *so* sorry. However, if Director Smith turns the power of deciding how to solve their fund-raising problems over to the Board, she may find she winds up with *three* fund raisers: a "no-bake" sale, a fair, and a center-wide picnic. Since each person is confident about the success of her project and likes the idea so well, she is ready to work on it, and the center benefits. The total amount of "power" is multiplied.

However, there *are* times when a Director needs to take the lead and be "in charge." For example, when there is an emergency, clear leadership is needed. Another example in which a leader should take charge would be in implementing the ideas resulting from planning-group discussions such as those described in Chapter 8, such as facilitating the discussion of a scenario and then putting into action a plan to build more of a physical fitness theme (or other theme) into the center day. Clear leadership and modeling may be needed to get started.

Two things determine whether or not attempts to make changes will work: The potential costs and consequences of the change the leader is initiating, and the workers' view of the Director's responsibility. When contemplating a change, the Director needs to consider the workers' views and, if necessary, change them by providing more information about the responsibilities of the Director. This is a good time to develop joint goals to solve the problems that created the need for changes.

Working as a group to develop joint goals implies positive potential consequences of the change being initiated; the staff sees that the leader values their input and ideas. Naturally, this helps to offset any potential costs of the change being initiated, large or small, such as having to rearrange schedules, classrooms, or coffee breaks.

If the staff forms a coalition in the leader's favor, they will accept many more of the leader's ideas. To facilitate this, a Director should talk one-to-one with staff members. It is hoped that such a coalition would include the entire staff, but if the majority, or even a few workers, understand the change and have had time to make suggestions during informal chats, the coalition will help the leader reduce his or her costs. Although a coalition risks costs to the leader, more often it will help the leader to avoid costs (that is, the costs involved with presenting an idea and having it turned down).

SUMMARY

Social exchange behaviors for *leadership* are partly learned in early childhood. The children who learn these behaviors build high self-esteem and a strong self-concept at an early age. They learn that they are desired, loved, and popular. This knowledge helps them to take risks and to make decisions, and because these children are popular, they are asked to make decisions or to take risks.

Adults leaders as well as children can learn to value the payoffs that result from risk-taking (such as asking the staff to implement a change). Both adults and children also can learn to accept failures that may result from risk-taking. By learning from their mistakes, leaders can say, "I won't make the same mistake twice" or "I can usually do *something* to help correct a wrong decision." It is important to remember, however, that it is difficult to change behavior and to maintain this change over a long period of time. In stress situations, a person's behavior will not change much; instead, it will remain fairly consistent with that person's most comfortable style, whether this style is "human-oriented" or "task-oriented."

Some leaders realize how others perceive them, and some leaders do not. The leader who does not learn to read others' perceptions keeps going out on a limb and then finds that she has no support. To read others' perceptions, leaders must learn to read behavior and "body language." They need to be sensitive to the emotions and actions of others. If a leader doesn't feel she has support, it is better *not* to take a stand; instead, she should discuss the issue more ahead of time, informally, in one-to-one conversations, thus building trust. Since stress can block some of this discussion, arranging a more relaxed situation, such as having a meeting over coffee or food of some kind, might be in order.

The more valuable the leader is perceived as being, the greater the credits, rewards, and salary he or she receives. Just as directing one child-care center can help families and improve the quality of life for their children, directing three child-care centers, or even adding 20 more openings in one center, can help an increased number of families or children.

BIBLIOGRAPHY

Ackoff, R. L. (1970). *A concept of corporate planning*. Philadelphia: Wiley.

Allen, R. W., Madison, D. L., Porter, L. W., Renwick, P. A., & Mayes, B. T. (1979, Fall). Organizational politics: Tactics and characteristics of its actors. *California Management Review, 22*(4), 77–83.

Banfield, E. C. (1961). *Political influence*. New York: The Free Press.

Bass, B. (1981). *Stogill's handbook of leadership*. New York: The Free Press.

Beach, D. S. (1975). *Managing people at work: Readings in personnel*. New York: Wiley.

Blake, R. R., and others. (1964, Nov./Dec.). Breakthrough in organizational development. *Harvard Business Review*.

Blau, P. M. (1964). *Exchange and power in social life*. New York: Wiley.

Boyatzis, R. (1982). *The competent manager*. New York: Wiley.

Brearley, A. (1976). The changing role of the chief executive. *Journal of General Management, 3*(4), 62–71.

California Council of Parent Participation Nursery Schools, Inc. (1968). *Pointers for participating parents*. San Francisco: Author.

Child Care Information Exchange. (1990). *On being a leader: Reprint collection # 5*. Redmond, WA: Author.

Decker, C. A., & Decker, J. (1990). *Planning and administering early childhood programs*. Columbus, OH: Merrill.

Drucker, P. (1967). *The effective executive*. New York: Harper & Row.

Drucker, P. (1974). *Management*. New York: Harper & Row.

Fiedler, F. E. (1967). *A theory of leadership effectiveness*. New York: McGraw-Hill.

Fiedler, F. E. (1971). *Leadership*. New York: General Learning Press.

Herzberg, F., Mausner, B., & Snyderman, B. (1959). *The motivation to work*. New York: Wiley.

Jacobs, T. O. (1971). *Leadership and exchange in formal organizations*. Alexandria, VA: Human Resources Research Organizations.

Kotter, J. P. (1973). The psychological contract: Managing the joining up process. *California Management Review, 15*(3), pp. 91–99.

Kotter, J. P. (1977, July/August). Power, dependence, and effective management. *Harvard Business Review*, pp. 125–136.

Kotter, J. P. (1978). *Organizational dynamics: Diagnosis and intervention*. Reading, MA: Addison-Wesley.

Kotter, J. P. (1979a). Managing external dependence. *Academy of Management Review 1979, 4*(1), 87–92.

Kotter, J. P. (1979b). *Power in management*. New York: AMACOM.

Kotter, J. P. (1982). *The general managers*. New York: The Free Press.

Kotter, J. P., Faux, V. A., & McArthur, C. C. (1979). *Self-assessment and career development*. Englewood Cliffs, NJ: Prentice-Hall.

Likert, R. (1953). Findings of research on management and leadership. *Proceedings: Pacific Coast Gas Association, 43*.

Likert, R. (1961). *New patterns of management*. New York: McGraw-Hill.

Likert, R. (1967). *The human organization*. New York: McGraw-Hill.

Lorsch, J., & Allen, S. A. (1973). *Managing diversity and interdependence*. Cambridge, MA: Harvard University Press.

McClelland, D. C. (1970). Two faces of power. *Journal of International Affairs, 24*(1), 29–47.

McClelland, D. C. (1975). *Power: The inner experience*. New York: Irvington.

McGregor, D. (1960). *The human side of enterprise*. New York: McGraw-Hill.

Miles, R. H. (1980). *Macro organizational behavior*. Santa Monica, CA: Goodyear.

Nichel, W. G. (1982). *Marketing principles* (2nd ed.). Englewood Cliffs, NJ: Prentice-Hall.

Pascale, R. T., & Athos, A. G. (1981). *The art of Japanese management*. New York: Simon and Schuster.

Peters, T. (1978, Fall). Symbols, patterns, and settings. *Organizational dynamics*, pp. 3–23.

Pettigrew, A. (1973). *The politics of organizational decision making*. London: Tavistock.

Pfeffer, J. (1981). *Power in organizations*. Marshfield, MA: Pitman.

Presthus, R. (1962). *The organizational society*. New York: Vintage.

Rickarts, T. (1975). *Problem solving through creative analysis*. Epping, England: Gower Press.

Rumelt, R. P. (1974). *Strategy, structure, and economic performance*. Cambridge, MA: Harvard University Press.

Salancik, G., & Pfeffer, J. (1977, Winter). Who gets power and how they hold on to it: A strategic contingency model of power. *Organizational dynamics*, pp. 3–21

Sayles, L. (1964). *Managerial behavior*. New York: McGraw-Hill.

Sonnenfeld, J., & Kotter, J. P. (1982). The maturation of career theory. *Human Relation, 35*(1), 19–46.

Tannenbaum, R., & Schmidt, W. H. (1973, May/June). How to choose a leadership pattern. *Harvard Business Review*.

Vroom, V. & Yetton, P. W. *Leadership and interpersonal behavior*. New York: Holt, Rinehart and Winston.

CHAPTER EIGHT

Planning

Good planning is the key to a smoothly running program for young children. Planning can help educators anticipate decisions that must be made; it can help leaders manage interdependent decisions; and it can provide a process by which staff and parents can have input and so "buy into" the goals and strategies of the organization.

Some people claim that the main value of planning does not lie in the actual plans produced, but in the process of producing them. In this context, the main benefit of planning comes from the interaction of people and ideas as they think about mid-range and long-range goals for a program or center. Therefore, planning cannot be done *for* a group, but must be done *by* the group.

Many of the best ideas of employees may surface in such planning sessions, and can be suitably adapted onto a time line along with other "best ideas." Implementing every step of the plan is less important than developing the habit of sharing good ideas and planning for the future, especially when this interaction occurs within a framework that is structured enough to allow good ideas to be captured and thought through. As with children and the curriculum, the process of learning is more important than the product of learning.

During the planning process, both the program being planned for and its environment can change, so it is nearly impossible to consider all the variables at the outset. Therefore, as a plan is carried out, it is necessary to continuously update the plan, both individually and as a group. To prevent being "sandbagged" by change, it is important to try to understand the environment systematically on at least five levels: global, national, community, workplace, and individual. (See Figure 8.7 for specific examples of each of these levels.) When changes in each of these levels are considered in relation to the impact(s) they might have on a program for young children, new insights emerge and actions and contingency plans can be developed. In addition, planners can also

1. try to alter the course of the change,
2. decide how to capitalize on the advantages of the change, or
3. plan to resist the change.

Anticipating change and predicting it helps an organization and its people feel more "on top of things" and therefore maintains morale. Long-range planning that affects many functions of the organization and that is hard to reverse should be considered carefully. For example, opening another center across town is a long-range decision that could require a lot of the center's resources in terms of money, person-hours, and equipment or materials. On the other hand, planning next week's lunch menu is a short-range decision; it is hoped that this type of decision-making can be delegated to another person or group, along with most other considerations of short-range planning. (For a discussion of techniques for decision-making, see Chapter 9.)

THREE PHILOSOPHIES OF PLANNING

There are many philosophies of planning, of course, but the three that will be discussed here include satisficing, optimizing, and adaptivizing (Ackoff, 1970).

Satisficing is arriving at one solution that meets objectives and goals that are feasible and desirable. It implies "being satisfied." The satisficing planner sets a few simple goals and is happy to satisfy them. This outlook harbors the danger of not being long-range enough, or of not considering the outside environment enough, but for some problems it is an appropriate approach. An additional danger of satisficing is that sometimes at the end of a long meeting, when time is a factor, a single solution can look more and more attractive even when it is not the best or the most appropriate solution.

Optimizing is similar to the rational approach taught in business schools. The goal in optimizing is to do as well as possible, and in this context, many, many alternatives can be generated. Unfortunately, generating all these options takes more time than is always available. In the rational approach, criteria are developed after the problem is defined, then three to five alternatives are considered against these criteria. When weighing the alternatives, some variables can surface that then may be combined in yet a new way. Some variables cannot be controlled, such as weather, economic conditions, the competition, technological developments, and preferences of parents. Unfortunately, the optimizer sometimes ignores these variables, and often ignores goals that cannot be quantified. For example, an optimizer might consider the financial bottom line to be more important than the "happiness" of the children.

Adaptivizing is the name given to planning that adapts, or "gets outside the box," and considers solutions from a very different perspective than does satisficing or optimizing. Often this type of planning happens when the problem is redefined and looked at in new ways. Chapter 10, which discusses problem-solving, suggests a number of ways to do this.

Adaptivizing provides for five different sets of plans:

1. commitment planning
2. contingency planning for better conditions
3. contingency planning for worse conditions
4. responsiveness planning for better conditions
5. responsiveness planning for worse conditions

These different plans are based on knowledge of the future, which can be certain, uncertain, or completely unknown. Planning for a future that is fairly certain is called *commitment planning*; the center's budget might be an example of this.

Planning for an uncertain future that could be a little better or a little worse than the present situation is called *contingency planning*. Such planning requires two approaches (contingencies): one for somewhat better conditions, and one for less good or somewhat worse conditions.

Planning for a future that cannot be anticipated, or that is unknown, also requires two sets of plans: one for much better conditions and one for much worse conditions. This type of planning is called *responsiveness planning*, and it is frequently overlooked. It's labeled *responsive* because this planning builds responsiveness and flexibility into an organization. The plan shown in Figure 10.1, which includes a suggestion for conducting a computer camp on Saturdays if computers are bought, rented, or given to the center, shows how responsiveness planning might be done for a favorable situation. A responsiveness plan for unfavorable conditions (such as a major industrial plant or military base closing near the center) might list financial emergency measures, such as plans to rent out one or two classrooms for other uses or for small business incubators. Another emergency measure might be to eliminate the most expensive and least used part of your program, such as a breakfast-before-school program.

The adaptive planner tries to change the system or the structure so that efficiency is the result. Organizations that plan this way tend to use their employees' best potential and therefore are very effective.

MANAGING CHANGE: OBJECTIVES AND SCENARIOS

Commitment planning, or planning for a fairly certain future, can also be called *reference projection,* because it essentially involves predictions that can be made if nothing new is done. What one would *like* to do can be referred to as a *wishful projection;* the difference between the two (reference projection and wishful projection) defines the gap that can be filled by planning and setting objectives onto a time line. Directors usually have many aspirations for their organizations, and most of these fall under the category of wishful projections. The steps that can take a center from its reference projection to a wishful projection are called *planned projections.* To make these steps more efficient, a time schedule can be attached to each step or objective in the planned projection.

Sometimes it is difficult to discover the aspirations, or wishful projections, of those involved in an organization, and to learn people's answer to the question: "What kind of center do you want this to be?" An effective way to uncover these aspirations is through the use of scenarios that focus on different topics. In the motion picture industry, a scenario describes what people will do when acting out a story. Scenarios in management planning describe different models of what people will do or what must or might happen to reach different goals. In this context, scenarios allow for various areas of wishful thinking to be quantified so that decisions regarding possible goals can be made. Scenarios also help determine any possible goal conflicts. By identifying and resolving goal conflicts early on, and thus reducing conflicts and encouraging useful discussions, any project can be further enhanced.

Scenarios can be developed around policies, programs, procedures, practices, and courses of action. In each case, the person developing the scenario makes a pictorial model of the existing policy, course of action, or other item that needs to be examined. (See Figure 8.2 for an example of a scenario model.) The developer puts a box around each existing step listed in the model. Then, alternatives for each step in the model can be discussed by either a group or an individual. As the four or five (or more) boxes are reviewed and brainstorming occurs, a scenario begins to emerge. Although some of the ideas that emerge may be inappropriate for the particular situation under discussion, they can lead to other, more plausible, suggestions.

Developing a Philosophy

When identifying problems and solutions for a child-care center, it is helpful to be clear on the style or values of the center. Discussing the philosophy of the center with both the staff and the parent group will help to define the philosophy more clearly. This discussion, which can take the form of a brainstorming session, should first occur during a staff meeting, followed by having the staff vote on the 5 or 10 most important elements in the philosophy. This list of important elements can then be taken to a parents' meeting (perhaps displayed on a flip chart or large poster) and parents can use these ideas to brainstorm *their* ideas about philosophy. After parents have taken a vote on the most important items in their list, the staff list and the parent list can be combined; usually an impressive philosophy statement results. This statement can be added to the bylaws, the publicity brochures, the bulletin boards, and wherever else information on good child care is needed. A sample philosophy is given in Figure 8.1.

Voting on which elements of the philosophy are most important gives parents a true feeling of involvement and can be repeated every fall during an orientation period. One center added the idea of "physical fitness" to its philosophy one year, then emphasized "respect for children, adults, and equipment" another year. During parent planning meetings, parents get the opportunity to hear the many expectations other parents have for child-care centers; after voting, parents can find out which elements are favored by the majority, thus

FIGURE 8.1
Philosophy

The philosophy of the Children's Education Child–Care Center is based on the belief that children are individuals who are learning and growing. Within a child-size world, the focus of the center will be:

1. to provide programs which, in balance, enhance a child's development socially, emotionally, physically, and intellectually.

2. to provide individualized attention within the context of a group setting.

3. to foster an acceptance of self and of the differences in others.

4. to develop a sense of respect and a caring attitude that comes from freedom within limits.

5. to learn actively through play.

6. to work with parents as active partners in their child's learning.

discovering that not all wishes can be met. For example, if a parent feels strongly that her child should be taught French, but that same ideal is not held by the majority, the parent may wish to look for another center. On the other hand, after seeing that French cannot be worked into the program, the parent might decide to provide for outside lessons while allowing her child to remain at the center. Whichever option the parent chooses, the Director and teacher can be saved a year of complaints and unhappiness on the part of the parent.

Developing Scenarios

After the philosophy is in place, the "style" of your center will be clear; then possible ideas for improvement of one aspect or another can be generated. The Director can begin translating into goals these ideas and the values given in the philosophy. At this point, it is important to develop a schedule for attaining these goals. While a Director's list of goals may look quite different from the philosophy, they still remain relevant. These goals might include:

- To remain financially afloat by increasing the center's income
- To build quality into the program by focusing on specifics in the philosophy
- To improve safety throughout the center
- To build staff morale

An effective way of working toward achieving these goals is to develop a scenario for one or more of them. Again, a scenario is a description of what an organization might look like at some specified time in the future. It is a description rather than a financial plan. The use of scenarios is based on the idea that what a center becomes depends more on what it does than on what is done to it. It builds on the idea of making the future happen rather than on letting events occur and then asking, "What happened?" A center can design almost any kind of future it wants for itself, given careful planning and involvement of staff and parents. A scenario allows room for wishful thinking for the future. Several scenarios have been developed here as examples.

The first step in developing a scenario, as we discussed previously, is to draw a model of the activities done throughout the day in a center. See Figure 8.2.

FIGURE 8.2
A Model of Child-Care Activities

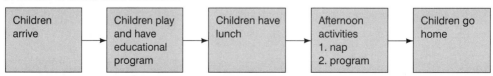

The second step in developing a scenario for a particular goal is to brainstorm alone or perhaps with a group about ways that particular goal could be implemented; for each box in the model, two or three ways of implementing the goal can be listed. For instance, for the goal of increasing a center's income, the scenario might look like the one shown in Figure 8.3.

After this step is completed, the Director has lots of ideas from which to choose several logical projects that might increase the center's income. Sometimes ideas are not volunteered during the development of the scenario, but these ideas may stay in the back of people's minds, and the Director may hear more about these possibilities next year, as well as hearing some modifications of ideas already used this year.

Another scenario, this one focusing on building quality into the program according to the philosophy given in Figure 8.1, and that also works toward building staff morale, might look like the one shown in Figure 8.4.

FIGURE 8.3
Increasing a Center's Income

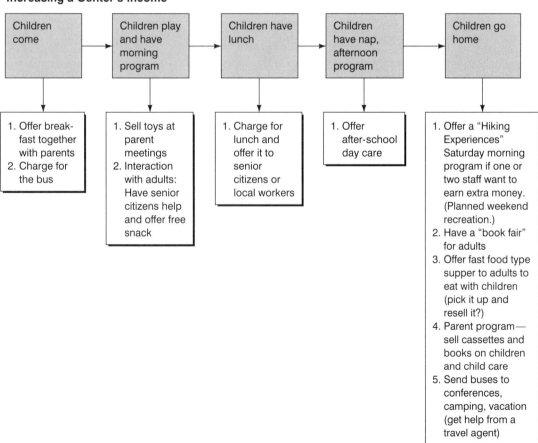

FIGURE 8.4
Building Quality and Staff Morale

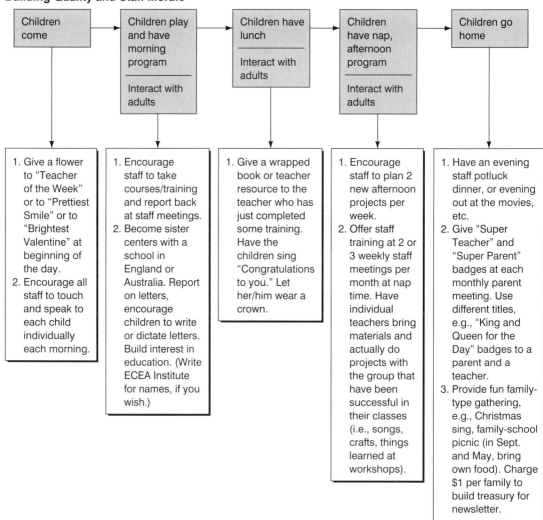

Space in the day's activities model does not permit listing all the ideas that can be generated from item 1 in the philosophy (Figure 8.1). When physical fitness is the focus of the year, for example, purchasing more outdoor equipment, finding more imaginative ways to use what is there, and inviting a speaker to come to a staff-parent workshop on Movement Education are a few ideas that could be explored. The possibilities are limitless, and generating them makes a good exercise for beginning-of-the-school-year staff training meetings. If the staff can help choose two or three goals for staff training for the year, then the improvement of quality and morale have a good start.

Use the decision-making tree described in Chapter 9 to help decide which projects the Director might invite the group to become involved in planning.

Since some ideas would benefit from outside funding, or might require permission from another group, a section on writing proposals has been included in Chapter 12.

STRATEGIC PLANNING

Strategic planning is the name given to the process of looking first, in an organized way, at outside environmental opportunities and risks, and then focusing on the center's strengths and weaknesses (i.e., its available resources). It is better for a center to develop plans and opportunities, not just to respond when outside events have an impact. At the very least, strategic planning has the effect of adding some predictability to outside impacts.

When arranging a planning session, a first step might be for the group to think of two or three significant events in society that will impact child-care centers and schools. It is not necessary to agree on these events, but as the leader/facilitator collects each person's list, some consensus usually emerges. This first step is called *external analysis,* and is shown in Figure 8.5. Responses might include such things as the changing multicultural demographics and society's move into the information age.

After discussing some of the events that might affect child-care, a "visioning" exercise of some type might be useful. To begin such an exercise, simply

FIGURE 8.5
Strategic Planning Steps

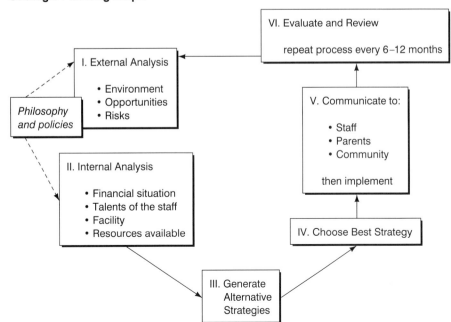

ask people what they envision telling people about the center in five years, or use the scenarios approach just described. Once this information is recorded, review the mission or philosophy statement for the center. At this point, the statement might need to be rewritten or need some policies added to it. This done, the group can review the external analysis done earlier, and then review the internal strengths and weaknesses of the center to develop the *internal analysis,* shown in Figure 8.5. An example of an internal weakness might include debt, which would not allow the center to expand. On the other hand, a strong line of credit could be considered a strength, since this would allow for expansion. The depth of professional and managerial talent also must be considered when developing an internal analysis.

As with the external analysis, it isn't necessary to reach a consensus on the internal analysis. However, with the combined lists of strengths and weaknesses, it is easier to set priorities and then write objectives for the next three to five years, which should be done when the internal analysis is complete. Then the group is ready to write strategies for new programs and processes.

Generating alternative strategies (Step III in Figure 8.5) can be done alone or in a group brainstorming session; however, choosing and implementing a strategy requires group involvement and outward communication to be most effective. Steps IV, V, and VI in Figure 8.5 model this process. This planning time can be the most valuable that a Director spends because it prevents management by default. Failure to plan can result in ineffective, undirected action. (This situation has also been described as planning to fail from failing to plan.)

Once several strategies are generated for accomplishing priorities, the best strategy can be agreed upon. (It is important to keep a record of all the strategies generated, even those not chosen, since they may become useful when outside events change.) The strategy chosen as the best should then be communicated to head teachers, to staff, to parents, and to the public, as appropriate (see Step V in Figure 8.5). It is hoped that all but the general public will have been involved in one way or another before this juncture. The last step taken after these plans become operational, and which may begin next year's or next quarter's planning session, is to evaluate and review the chosen strategy and the accompanying choices against the knowledge of what actually happened, thus building improved strategies and choices for the future (see Step VI in Figure 8.5). The whole process, then, is a continuous circle, as shown in Figure 8.6.

FIGURE 8.6
The Management/Planning Circle

Strategic Planning and Sources and Impacts of Change

Since programs for young children are affected by outside trends, including demographic and economic changes, planning for the future becomes essential. Figure 8.7 shows the results of a brainstorming session on the topic "Sources and Impacts of Change in Programs for Young Children." The results demonstrate how even national and global concerns can affect the workplace, and how individuals must manage the impact of such changes.

Formulating such data makes an interesting exercise for staff or Board meetings, since the information or ideas in the boxes may change every few months. Scheduling such a brainstorming session also could be a first step in a strategic planning exercise during which all levels of environment are to be considered for their potential impact. A second meeting, in which Figure 8.7 might be used as a handout, could include more of the strategic planning steps, such as considering the opportunities and risks of each change, perhaps beginning with impacts at the national and community level. The staff might choose one category—such as social, physical, or technological—to develop more fully in terms of the workplace or of the individuals who work there.

After considering possible alternatives such as the ones listed in the last two rows of Figure 8.7, as well as other alternatives suggested by those assembled, the group can vote on one or two of best alternatives to pursue. Once the alternatives have been chosen, communicate this first to the staff, then to the public and parents. For example, using bulletin boards and the newsletter as a medium, inform parents that the center is having a unit on other countries, or will be inviting legislators to a picnic. Different committees might work on each alternative. More ambitious plans that will use more resources, such as opening a center across town, could be tested using the scenario process, which helps a group (or individual) to simulate possibilities and probabilities for the new idea.

SUMMARY

The excitement and friendly interaction that occurs when generating ideas in a brainstorming session helps teachers (and/or Board members) "learn through play" (Jones, 1990). It also creates in the participants a feeling of being stronger, more helpful, and more "empowered" (Berlew, 1990). Designing situations in which people can succeed, such as these brainstorming sessions for considering hypothetical scenarios and strategies, unlocks creativity and puts some of the joy and energy back into the sometimes taxing work of being an adult involved with a child care-center. As people come up with ideas, they will be more likely to offer help. Innovation is attractive and new ideas are inter-

FIGURE 8.7
Sources and Impacts of Change in Programs for Young Children

Impacts	Political	Economic	Social	Physical	Technological
Global	Changes in Eastern Europe have caused cutbacks in the U.S. military and in defense industry spending.	Economic globalization: Pacific Rim countries will be doing more business with the U.S.	Families will be moving and relocating.	Families and children travel, fly more easily to distant places.	Computers and the information age are transcending national barriers.
National	Families caught in sudden transition will be short of money while at least one spouse looks for new work.	There is a national upsurge in East/West fashion, food, curricula, etc.	Even more women with children will enter the work force.	Feature national trips and international trips in classroom learning opportunities.	Public schools are getting more and more computers for children's use.
Community	Offices of economic development may look to child care centers to provide jobs.	Some communities have high numbers of "new" minorities, e.g., Asians.	More and better child care will be needed on all economic levels: deluxe to basic.	Families may move across town to follow new businesses.	Have a community fundraiser to buy the center one or more computers.
Child Care Program (workplace).	Can encourage local legislators to support child care legislation.	Offer learning units about Asia and other countries.	Consider adding some deluxe services to help offset a sliding fee scale.	Share information about trips and where children have moved from.	Make plans for children and staff to use (play with) computers, learning through play.
Individual	Invite legislators to a center picnic or other function. Take their picture and write an article for the paper.	Encourage Asian and other ethnic families to bring in food or share "show and tell" with their children.	Encourage parents to build up their child's self-esteem and competence by doing things with them at home.	Have staff/parent bulletin board with news of trips or places people have moved from, so all can learn.	Encourage staff to take individual computer classes.

esting and draw support. As was stated in the chapter on leadership, Chapter 7, if things have been discouraging for a while, two or three idea sessions may be needed to get useful planning under way.

If a center insists that its innovations be high quality, it will be ahead of the game when standards go up (Foster, 1986). The center will also earn great word-of-mouth publicity and will probably have happier children attending the center. It might be necessary to have Saturday programs for children to help pay for some innovations, but feeling more in control of the center's future will be worth it.

BIBLIOGRAPHY

Ackoff, R. L. (1970). *A concept of corporate planning.* New York: Wiley.

Ackoff, R. L. (1974). *Redesigning the future: A systems approach to societal problems.* New York: Wiley.

Argyris, C., & Schon, D. (1974). *Theory in practice: Increasing professional effectiveness.* San Francisco: Jossey-Bass.

Bennis, W., & Nanus, B. (1985). *Leaders: The strategies for taking charge.* New York: Harper and Row.

Berlew, D. E. (1990). Effective leaders make others feel stronger. In *On being a leader* (reprint no. 5), pp. 13–16. Redmond, WA: Child Care Information Exchange Press.

Berlew, D. E. (1974, Winter). Leadership and organizational excitement. *California Management Review.*

Bradford, D. L., & Cohen, A. R. (1984). *Managing for excellence: The guide to developing high performance in contemporary organizations.* New York: Wiley.

Foster, R. (1986). *Innovation: The attackers advantage.* New York: Summit Books.

Jones, E. (1990). On creating environments where teachers, like children, learn through play. In *Developing Staff Skills* (reprint no. 7), pp. 3–6. Redmond, WA: Child Care Information Exchange Press.

Kanter, R. (1983). *The change masters: The innovation for productivity in the American corporation.* New York: Simon and Schuster.

Kelly, C. M. (1987). The interrelation of ethics and power in today's organizations. *Organizational Dynamics, 16*(1), 4–18.

Kelly, C. M. (1988). *The destructive achiever.* Reading, MA: Addison-Wesley.

Koontz, H., & O'Donnell, C. (1972). *Principles of management* (3rd ed.). New York: McGraw-Hill.

Lindbloom, C. E. (1980). The science of muddling through. In H. J. Leavitt & L. Pondy (Eds.), *Readings in managerial psychology.* Chicago: University of Chicago Press.

McGregor, D. (1960). *The human side of enterprise.* New York: McGraw-Hill.

Naisbitt, J., & Aburdene, P. (1990). *Megatrends 2000.* New York: William Morrow.

Peters, T. J. (1987). *Thriving on chaos: Handbook for managing revolution.* New York: Knopf.

Peters, T. J., & Austin, N. (1985). *A passion for excellence: The leadership difference.* New York: Random House.

Peters, T. J., & Waterman, R. H. (1982). *In search of excellence: Lessons from America's best-run companies.* New York: Harper and Row.

Rogers, C. (1977). *On personal power.* New York: Dell.

Vaill, P. B. (1989). *Managing as a performing art: New ideas for a world of chaotic change.* San Francisco: Jossey-Bass.

Wack, P. (1985, September/October). Scenarios: Uncharted waters ahead. *Harvard Business Review,* p. 72.

Weisbord, M. R. (1978). *Organizational diagnosis: A workbook of theory and practice.* Reading, MA: Addison Wesley.

Weisbord, M. R. (1987). *Productive workplaces: Organizing and managing for dignity, meaning and community.* San Francisco: Jossey-Bass.

CHAPTER NINE

Decision-Making for Administrators

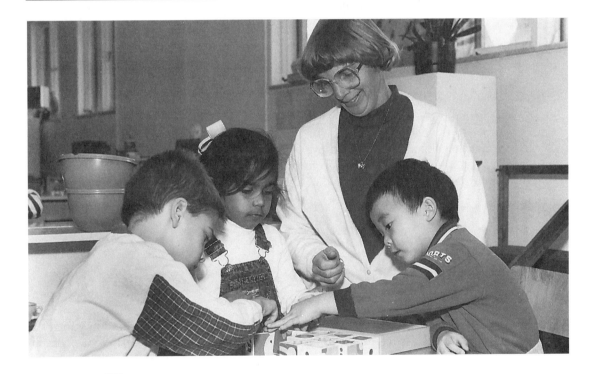

Leadership involves decision-making. To lead effectively, one needs to plan changes that will improve the organization. Enacting these changes may involve using old processes to achieve new goals, using new processes to continue working towards ongoing goals, or using new processes to aim for new goals. Planning should be a continuous process as new resources, goals, policies, or needs arise. If a plan is looked upon as an interim report, as it should be, it is essential that the planners get together at regular meetings to adapt and improve plans that have been made, and to generate new plans. Research has shown that any time the leader involves staff, parents, or the Board in planning and decision-making, the leader builds commitment. But how can the leader do this? And when?

The Greek word for administration is *kuberneseis*, which refers to the work of ships' pilots who steer the ships through rocks and shoals to the harbor. All administrators have days when they say, "The fog is too thick!" "Where is the harbor?" "Why are there so many rocks?" In the midst of these questions, though, administrators of all kinds need to have wisdom, because if the administration of an organization is not well run, the organization itself will not be able to meet its goals. Administrators also need to promote encouragement, confidence, and commitment on the part of staff, parents, and the Board of Directors if an outstanding center is the goal. Throughout the daily struggle of navigating through the fog and avoiding the rocks, it is rewarding to be a part of an organization about which staff and parents can be proud and enthusiastic.

Again, having an outstanding center requires leadership and decision-making skills. Throughout this book, and especially in the chapters on leadership and motivation, the end-of-chapter bibliographies list many early childhood education administration materials that discuss the ideas behind effective leadership. One of these basic premises behind leadership is that the more power a leader gives away—by involving others in decision-making, coordination, or supervision—the more total shared power a leader has. Not all decisions are appropriate for group involvement, however, so further analysis of the decisions to be made and of the decision-making process is needed.

EASY DECISIONS

When making a decision that has only two possible outcomes, and in which the leader has no preference, he or she can flip a coin. For slightly more complicated decisions, however, a decision-making strategy is useful, such as listing the pros and cons of a decision in separate columns on a piece of paper. The benefit of this and other decision-making strategies is that they help the decision-maker look at a problem in a more systematic way, and they often reveal relevant questions that may not at first have been apparent.

In a well-run organization, most "easy" decisions can be delegated to an appropriate staff member, after parameters have been set by the leader. For example, deciding where to hold the end-of-the-year picnic might be done by vote, or by a committee, or by asking Mrs. Smith to choose this year, and so forth. Much has been written about the benefits of delegating such decisions to the lowest feasible level, which builds commitment all through a staff's organizational system. For example, "This year the aides will decide at which park we will have the picnic."

HARDER DECISIONS

A *decision tree* is a useful tool for making decisions that are somewhat complex. A decision tree can be generated during meetings with staff, parents, or the Board, and can be a helpful method of providing information and encouraging discussion before a vote is taken. A simple tree also can be used by individuals to solve personal problems, such as whether to buy a new car, repair the old one, or buy a used car.

To continue with our picnic example, a simple decision tree could be developed to decide whether lunch will be barbecued or whether parents will supply potluck items. The tree might start out like this:

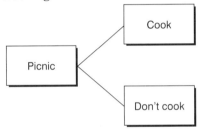

The next step is discussion (or information-gathering), which might focus on whether or not the parks under consideration have facilities for cooking, what hours the parks are available, how much advance notice is necessary, and so forth. The tree begins to look like this:

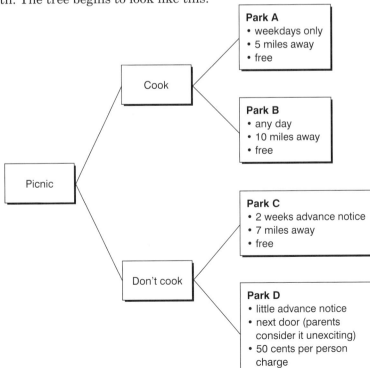

This tree could have additional branches placed to the right as more details are considered, such as the possibility of swimming at the parks, available amusements, or car pool arrangements. Once the tree is completed, it is ready to be used; the group or the decision-maker first considers the items the farthest to the right. One way to start the decision-making process is to rank all the considerations on a preference scale of 1 to 10 or –1 to –10, as shown in the following example:

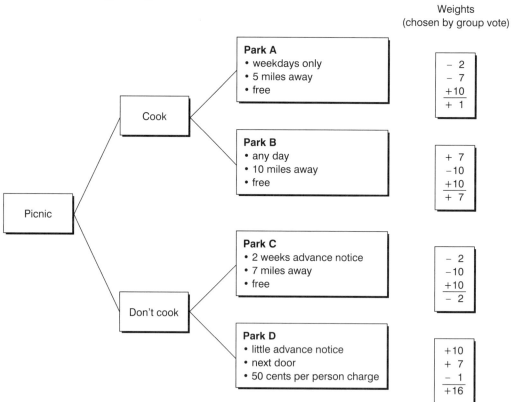

Weights
(chosen by group vote)

Park A
• weekdays only
• 5 miles away
• free

– 2
– 7
+10
+ 1

Park B
• any day
• 10 miles away
• free

+ 7
–10
+10
+ 7

Cook

Park C
• 2 weeks advance notice
• 7 miles away
• free

– 2
–10
+10
– 2

Picnic

Park D
• little advance notice
• next door
• 50 cents per person charge

+10
+ 7
– 1
+16

Don't cook

When this ranking system is used, Park D becomes the favorite if parents do not mind providing unheated food. If the group would rather cook, Park B seems better. The question could now be presented at the parents' meeting with a choice between Park B and the cooking option or Park D with no cooking. When parents are given the opportunity to discuss the options, the factor of whether parents consider Park D exciting or not, or whether that is even important to the parents, would surface.

Using a simple tree of this sort is helpful in making other group decisions, either with staff or parents. This method also gets people interested and often they will go out and research other options and bring in new information for next year's activity. This type of decision-making, then, benefits the organization in the long run because it builds commitment and interest. The remaining question for an administrator, however, is how many people should be involved in a given decision? And how does the administrator involve them?

VROOM'S DECISION-MAKING TREE

Victor Vroom and Philip Yetton, in their book *Leadership and Decision-Making* (1973), suggest that a series of questions be asked about a decision to decide how many people to involve in the process. These questions appear across the top of Figure 9.1, but we will discuss them first for clarification.

Is there a quality requirement such that one solution is likely to be more logical than another?

This first question assigns a very special meaning to the word *quality*. A decision is categorized as a "quality decision" if a large percent of an organization's money, materials, people, and/or time are to be used. Since "people time" is a very scarce resource in early childhood programs, the amount of time a Director or teacher would have to devote to a project is always a consideration. Other characteristics that must be considered in a quality decision—in addition to the percent of money, man/woman power, or materials—are whether or not the decision uses scarce resources, and whether or not the decision is easily reversible. Examples of quality decisions might include opening a new center across town (this would use a lot of money and time), changing a major part of the curriculum, or changing in a major way the process the center uses to relate to its parents.

Do I have sufficient information to make a high-quality decision?

Often the administrator does not have sufficient information to decide on an issue, but knowing that much is a start. For example, if a leader knows she wants to start another center across town, but also realizes she does not know what steps are necessary to carry out this dream, she can start reading books and asking people for more information. If she has gone through the Vroom decision-making tree and has decided to involve her staff at this point, she might invite to staff meetings guest speakers who have successfully started second centers. She might also ask the staff to start researching this problem that "the center is looking into," without necessarily stating that the center plans to open a second branch.

Is the problem structured?

The meaning behind this question is: Does the leader know exactly what information is needed, who possesses it, and how to collect it? In terms of starting a new center, the answer would probably be "no." If the question under consideration were, "What is the jungle gym with the lowest price?", the answer would probably be "yes," because the leader would at least know *how to get* that information.

FIGURE 9.1

Decision-Process Flow Chart for Both Individual and Group Problems

A. Is there a quality requirement such that one solution is likely to be more rational than another?
B. Do I have sufficient info to make a high quality decision?
C. Is the problem structured?
D. Is acceptance of decision by subordinates critical to effective implementation?
E. If I were to make the decision by myself, is it reasonably certain that it would be accepted by my subordinates?
F. Do subordinates share the organizational goals to be attained in solving this problem?
G. Is conflict among subordinates likely in preferred solutions? (This question is irrelevant to individual problems.)
H. Do subordinates have sufficient info to make a high quality decision?

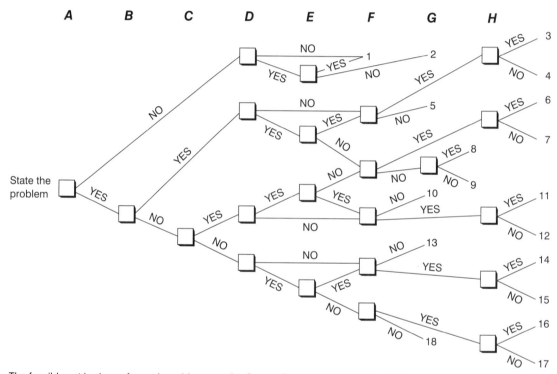

The feasible set is shown for each problem type for Group (G) and Individual (I) problems.

1 { G: AI, AII, CI, CII, GII
    I: AI, DI, AII, CI, GI

2 { G: GII
    I: DI, GI

3 { G: AI, AII, CI, CII, GII
    I: AI, DI, AII, CI, GI

4 { G: AI, AII, CI, CII, GII
    I: AI, AII, CI, GI

5 { G: AI, AII, CI, CII
    I: AI, AII, CI

6 { G: GII
    I: DI, GI

7 { G: GII
    I: GI

8 { G: CII
    I: CI

9 { G: CI, CII
    I: CI

10 { G: AII, CI, CII
     I: AII, CI

11 { G: AII, CI, CII, GII
     I: DI, AII, CI, GI

12 { G: AII, CI, CII, GII
     I: AII, CI, GI

13 { G: CII
     I: CI

14 { G: CII, GII
     I: DI, CI, GI

15 { G: CII, GII
     I: CI, GI

16 { G: GII
     I: DI, GI

17 { G: GII
     I: GI

18 { G: CII
     I: CI

Source: From *Leadership and Decision-Making* (p. 13) by V. H. Vroom and P. W. Yetton, 1973, Pittsburgh: University of Pittsburgh Press. Copyright 1973 by the University of Pittsburgh Press. Reprinted by permission.

Is acceptance of the decision by subordinates critical to effective implementation?

This question is a very important one to ask in connection with many decisions. If subordinates will be the ones carrying out a decision (such as implementing a new curriculum or a new parent-relations program), then giving the subordinates enough information and a range of choices to gain their acceptance will be the key to success or failure. In the question of opening a center across town, needing subordinate support would depend on whether a totally new staff would be sought, or whether several top teachers would be asked to transfer for one or two years.

If I were to make the decision myself, is it reasonably certain that it would be accepted by my subordinates?

This question relates to the previous question, obviously, but serves as a reminder to a leader who might be tempted to go out on a limb. It is always better to allow more time for understanding and discussion if it is apparent that the limb could be sawed off. It also helps the leader to assess the emotional climate surrounding a given issue.

Do subordinates share the organizational goals to be attained in solving this problem?

It is hoped that in an early childhood organization, the answer to this question would be "yes"; the whole staff should be working toward the goal of happy, competent children participating in their program. However, sometimes people take a job just to earn some money, and if that describes the majority of a staff, then staff training, motivation helps, and perhaps some selective hiring and firing are needed. On the other hand, if the majority of the staff does identify with the goal of having the best center in town (or any goal that benefits children and parents and is agreed upon by all or most), then involving the staff in decision-making will enhance staff commitment and the organization. When subordinates share the organization's goals, the group can look together for solutions that are in the best interests of the organization.

Is conflict among subordinates likely in preferred solutions?

This question can be skipped on the decision tree if subordinates share the center's goals, but if subordinates do not share organizational goals, it is important to preplan how to handle possible conflict or to decide if the preferred solution is worth the risk of conflict.

Do subordinates have sufficient information to make a high-quality decision?

Often subordinates do not have enough information, and this leads to a natural opportunity for staff training on a given topic. Board members can be invited to attend the staff training too, if that is appropriate. In discussion, or ahead of time, the leader can identify the problem more clearly and, by using the Vroom tree, decide which solution and degree of staff involvement is appropriate.

After working through the tree, the leader can use Figure 9.2 to examine possible decision methods for group or individual problems. The codes at the bottom of Figure 9.1, such as AI, AII, CI, CII, and GII, correspond to the possibilities given in Figure 9.2. Where several codes or "feasible sets" are listed in Figure 9.1, the code listed farthest to the left is the fastest method for solving the particular problem being worked through. In these figures, *A* refers to autonomous methods, *C* refers to cooperative methods, and *G* refers to group methods.

Deciding the Degree of Group Involvement

As the solutions progress from AI to GII in Figure 9.2, the more ways it becomes possible to involve the group. In AI the leader makes the decision himself by using the information available at the time. When considering a problem such as whether or not to open another center across town, a leader often chooses this method of decision-making.

If the leader needs more information to make a decision, solution AII suggests that she obtain the necessary information from subordinates, but still make the decision on her own. For example, the leader could gather information by asking staff and parents, "Do you think this town could use another child-care center? Where would be a good location? What special programs might be an asset?" Depending on the situation, the leader may or may not tell others about her plans. Either way, other people serve only as information-providers; they do not participate in the decision-making.

In the next solution, CI, the leader talks one-to-one with staff and parents, but does not meet with them as a group. These discussions can be done informally, such as at a social gathering, and can occur over time or in a number of ways. After the leader gathers the necessary input, he makes the decision on his own, perhaps taking others' views into account or perhaps not.

The next solution, CII, is similar to CI in that the leader finally decides alone, perhaps not even using the subordinates' advice, but this time the subordinates are gathered together in a group to give their suggestions. This arrangement allows everyone to be familiar with the question and also provides a situation in which people can build on one another's ideas. If the leader should decide later that she does need help, at least her subordinates will know

FIGURE 9.2
Decision Methods for Group and Individual Problems

Group Problems	Individual Problems
AI You solve the problem or make the decision yourself, using information available to you at the time.	AI You solve the problem or make the decision yourself using information available to you at the time.
AII You obtain the necessary information from your subordinates, then decide the solution to the problem yourself. You may or may not tell your subordinates what the problem is in getting the information from them. The role played by your subordinates in making the decision is clearly one of providing the necessary information to you, rather than generating or evaluating alternative solutions.	AII You obtain the necessary information from your subordinate, then decide on the solution to the problem yourself. You may or may not tell the subordinate what the problem is in getting the information from him. His role in making the decision is clearly one of providing the necessary information to you, rather than generating or evaluating alternative solutions.
CI You share the problem with the relevant subordinates individually, getting their ideas and suggestions without bringing them together as a group. Then **you** make the decision, which may or may not reflect your subordinates' influence.	CI You share the problem with your subordinate, getting his ideas and suggestions. Then you make the decision, which may or may not reflect his influence.
CII You share the problem with your subordinates as a group, obtaining their collective ideas and suggestions. Then you make the decision, which may or may not reflect your subordinates' influence.	GI You share the problem with your subordinate, and together you analyze the problem and arrive at a mutually agreeable solution.
GII You share the problem with your subordinates as a group. Together you generate and evaluate alternatives and attempt to reach agreement (consensus) on a solution. Your role is much like that of chairman. You do not try to influence the group to adopt "your" solution, and you are willing to accept and implement any solution which has the support of the entire group.	DI You delegate the problem to your subordinate, providing him with any relevant information that you possess, but giving him responsibility for solving the problem by himself. You may or may not request him to tell you what solution he has reached.

Source: From *Leadership and Decision-Making* (p. 195) by V. H. Vroom and P. W. Yetton, 1973, Pittsburgh: University of Pittsburgh Press. Copyright 1973 by University of Pittsburgh Press. Reprinted by permission.

what it is she needs help with. Of course, if the leader does follow a particular line of advice, either deliberately or by straw vote, she should let the appropriate person or group know and show appreciation for the help. If the leader does not use the advice, and if an explanation is appropriate or needed, she can explain that circumstances were such that another solution seemed better at the time.

In solution GII, the decision-maker shares the problem with the group and then acts as a discussion leader while everyone generates as many solutions as possible. Then the group votes to decide which solution is best. Whichever solution is chosen by the majority is the one the leader is willing to adopt and implement, and, of course, this solution has the support of the entire group. This method might be very helpful if the leader knows he or she wants to start a new center across town, but is not sure where to locate it. The leader would probably want to have the center in a fairly convenient location for new enrollees. It also may be that one, two, or three teachers will *volunteer* to work at the new center when they hear that they will have a say in the new location and the new equipment.

This GII solution is especially useful when the leader knows that he or she wants to do something big, but doesn't know how to go about doing it or even where to learn how. By opening the problem to the group, more resources and more ideas can flow. The group may decide they want to know more about the problem; guest speakers can be invited and literature provided as everyone learns more and has time to ask friends and acquaintances. Interesting problems *attract* able people, and the leader will find all sorts of resources becoming available. Also allowing some time to find a solution gives "the grapevine" time to work; for example, an aide might ask a competitor's brother, or some other informal network person, some key "how-to-do-it" questions that would be inappropriate to ask at higher levels.

The list of solutions for individual problems follow the same pattern as those for group problems, but are appropriate for one-to-one problems. An additional code, DI, is involved in this list, and indicates delegating the problem and its responsibility to a subordinate. As usual, politeness in seeking information or asking advice is essential.

USING THE DECISION TREE

The following section contains several case studies of actual decision-making situations. Practice using the decision-making tree as you consider the situations and the decisions that were made. Figure 9.3 provides a decision-making worksheet that contains abbreviated questions and boxes for decision points. As you use a pencil to trace through the tree, if a question is unclear, go back to Figure 9.1 to study the longer version of the tree and read the accompanying explanation in the text. Figure 9.4 shows the decision tree simplified even more.

FIGURE 9.3
Vroom's Decision Tree—Simplified

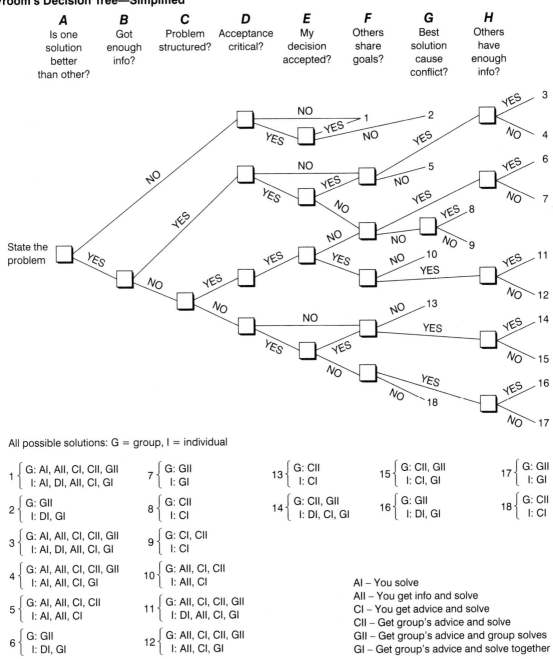

All possible solutions: G = group, I = individual

1 { G: AI, AII, CI, CII, GII
    I: AI, DI, AII, CI, GI

2 { G: GII
    I: DI, GI

3 { G: AI, AII, CI, CII, GII
    I: AI, DI, AII, CI, GI

4 { G: AI, AII, CI, CII, GII
    I: AI, AII, CI, GI

5 { G: AI, AII, CI, CII
    I: AI, AII, CI

6 { G: GII
    I: DI, GI

7 { G: GII
    I: GI

8 { G: CII
    I: CI

9 { G: CI, CII
    I: CI

10 { G: AII, CI, CII
     I: AII, CI

11 { G: AII, CI, CII, GII
     I: DI, AII, CI, GI

12 { G: AII, CI, CII, GII
     I: AII, CI, GI

13 { G: CII
     I: CI

14 { G: CII, GII
     I: DI, CI, GI

15 { G: CII, GII
     I: CI, GI

16 { G: GII
     I: DI, GI

17 { G: GII
     I: GI

18 { G: CII
     I: CI

AI – You solve
AII – You get info and solve
CI – You get advice and solve
CII – Get group's advice and solve
GII – Get group's advice and group solves
GI – Get group's advice and solve together

165

FIGURE 9.4
"Banana" Decision Tree

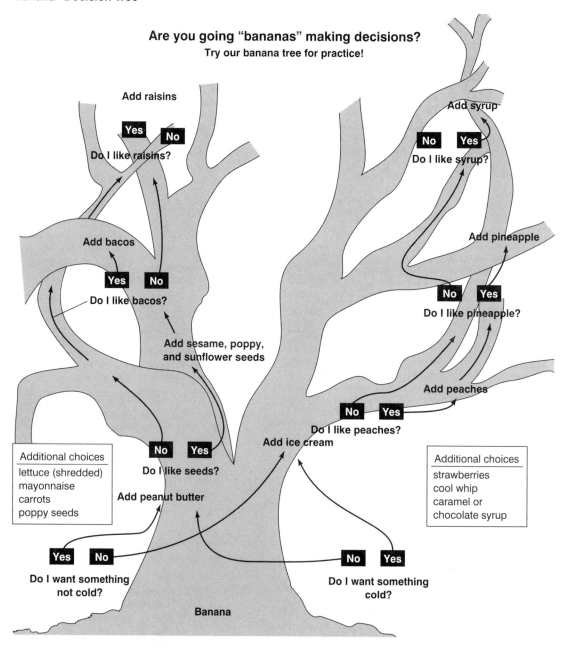

Are you going "bananas" making decisions?
Try our banana tree for practice!

Add raisins

Yes   No

Do I like raisins?

Add syrup

No   Yes

Do I like syrup?

Add bacos

Yes   No

Do I like bacos?

Add pineapple

No   Yes

Do I like pineapple?

Add sesame, poppy,
and sunflower seeds

Add peaches

No   Yes

Do I like peaches?

Add ice cream

No   Yes

Do I like seeds?

Additional choices
lettuce (shredded)
mayonnaise
carrots
poppy seeds

Add peanut butter

Additional choices
strawberries
cool whip
caramel or
chocolate syrup

Yes   No

Do I want something
not cold?

No   Yes

Do I want something
cold?

Banana

Case Study: Unpaid Tuition

The Director had trouble collecting tuition from one family and abruptly told them that their child's enrollment was terminated at the center. Other parents were horrified because they knew that this family was a particularly needy one. The father was out of work, the mother was recovering from an auto accident, and they had a new baby in addition to the child enrolled at the center. The Director's decision caused a lot of talk and complaint. Staff morale dropped to a new low because they viewed the action taken with this family as harsh and unkind.

Using the Decision Tree

Follow these points on the tree in Figure 9.1.

1. *Is this a quality decision?*   Perhaps the answer to this question appeared to be "no" to the Director, but actually it should have been "yes," because ultimately the problem took up a very high percentage of Director, staff, and parent time.

2. *Did the Director have sufficient information to make a quality decision?*   Apparently not, since the only information she took into account was that the center needed to stay afloat financially.

3. *Is the problem structured?*   Yes, because the Director knew where to get more information.

4. *Is the acceptance of the decision by staff and parents critical to effective implementation?*   Since the Director can decide anything she wants if she owns the center or is sole manager of it, the key word here may well be *effective*. Creating a lot of gossip among the staff and community is time-consuming and worrisome. The answer to this question should have been "yes."

5. *If I decided myself, would staff and parents accept it?*   As we know from hindsight, the answer is "no."

6. *Do staff and parents share the organizational goals to be attained in solving this problem?*   Apparently the answer here was "yes," because the adults involved wanted to be helpful to this family. The family had been upstanding members of the community before their string of misfortunes.

7. *Is conflict among subordinates likely?*   This question is skipped on the branch of the tree we have traveled so far.

8. *Do subordinates have sufficient information to make a high-quality decision?*   The answer here could be mixed, since the subordinates knew of the family's needs, but perhaps didn't know about the center's budget problems.

9. *Result.*   Interestingly enough, GII is recommended as the *fastest* solution, whether the answer is "yes" or "no." Taking the decision to the parent/staff Board turns out to be the solution to try first. This action would allow the Director to present her budget problems as well as her hard-and-fast rule that tuition must always be paid on time. The Board could vote as to whether this particular situation was a "special exception" for which they could use scholarship funds. If no scholarship funds existed, the Board might resolve to develop such a revolving fund by setting up some fund raisers, although they would not be able to help this particular needy family at this time. If the Director had shared the problem *before* taking action, however, subordinates could have become aware of the factors involved and could have taken positive steps to help now, or if not now, at least in the future. Months or even years of gossip and complaint could have been averted.

10. *What actually did happen?*   The problem was handled as originally described. A staff member brought it up in a class a year later because she was still upset about it, and the class took it through the decision tree as a learning exercise.

Case Study: Should a Values/Morals Statement Appear in the Center Philosophy?

The Director of a new center couldn't decide whether to include into the center's statement of philosophy any mention of teaching enrollees values and morals.

Using the Decision Tree

1. *Is this a quality decision?*   While implementing this decision might not use a large percent of money, people, or materials, the decision itself might be hard to reverse. If the answer here is "no," the Director might decide to include the statement but have parameters put around it (such as, "Don't name a particular church"), and then hand the wording over to a Board or parent group to iron out. If the answer is "yes," we can proceed through the tree.

2. *Does the Director have sufficient information to make a quality decision?*   In this case, the Director did not know what the majority of the parents preferred, or whether there was a strong feeling either way.

3. *Is the problem structured?*   Yes, because the Director did know from which group she could get more information.

4. *Is the acceptance of the decision by staff and parents critical to effective implementation?*   Yes, because a philosophy that causes conflict is not representative of the program.

5. *If I decided by myself, would staff and parents accept the decision?*   Since the Director really didn't know how others would respond, she decided to say "no."

6. *Do the staff and parents share the organizational goal of having a top-quality center?*   The Director answered "yes" to this question.

7. *Is conflict among subordinates likely?*   Again, this question is skipped.

8. *Do subordinates have sufficient information to make a high-quality decision?*   Yes, because they know how they feel about this issue.

9. *Result.*   The solution that was recommended by the tree as the fastest way to solve this problem was GII.

10. *What actually happened?*   The Director took the problem to the parent group since within the staff, one member wanted the values statement and several members were neutral. The parents voted to include a phrase in their philosophy about teaching children values and morals, so there was no problem after all. The parents were pleased to be asked about something they cared about.

Case Study: Late Pick-Up of Children

The center was plagued with a few parents who were habitually arriving from 6:10 p.m. to 6:25 p.m. for their children, when the center was due to close at 6:00 p.m.

Using the Decision Tree

1. *Is this a quality decision?*   The Director decided that this was a quality decision because the parents would be very unhappy if the penalty for lateness was made too stiff or if the center did not allow for genuine emergencies. On the other hand, the staff was really grumbling about having to stay late for the sake of a few parents.

2. *Did the Director have sufficient information to make a quality decision?*   The Director felt that she needed more information.

3. *Is the problem structured?*   Yes. The Director decided to ask the Executive Board of the parent group to make a recommendation.

4. *Is acceptance of the decision by subordinates critical to effective implementation?*   Yes. If the problem continued, staff members would probably quit.

5. *If I decided myself, would staff and parents accept the decision?*   The Director was unsure of the support she would receive if she made a decision that subordinates did not agree with.

6. *Do staff and parents share the organizational goals to be attained in solving this problem?*   The Director answered "no" to this question, based on her perceptions of subordinates' attitudes. (The answer to this question is always based on the "gut feel" of the client or person with the problem.)

7. *Is conflict among subordinates likely in preferred solutions?*   Yes.

8. *Result.*   On the tree, the solution at which the Director arrived was CII, which says to share the problem with the group, get their suggestions, and then make the decision alone.

9. *What actually happened?*   The Director did ask the Executive Board of the parent group for ideas and suggestions on this problem. The group felt it was a very severe problem, because if one parent took advantage, others would also be tempted to do so. The suggestions ranged from charging $1 per minute for lateness, to $5 per 15 minutes, to sending the child by taxi to an emergency neighbor's house, to requiring the offending parent to paint equipment on a Saturday. The Director settled on charging $1 per minute and announced the decision at the parent group meeting with the support of the Executive Board. Lateness has dropped off dramatically at this center. The lateness policy is also clearly communicated so that everyone knows about the rule.

SUMMARY

Decision-making is indeed key in leadership processes; however, the ability to structure decisions and then break them down into manageable parts is necessary in decision-making, and these skills can be learned. Sometimes making a decision one's self can be the *slowest* way to a resolution when group support is needed and group involvement would be better (and faster). Taking three to six months to involve the Board, the staff, and the parents is often the fastest decision approach possible when a large decision is involved and when an individual decision might result in years of controversy. This chapter broke down some of the parameters to consider when approaching a decision, and the following chapter on problem-solving provides additional tools that may be useful.

BIBLIOGRAPHY

Alber, H. H. (1961). *Organized executive action: Decision making, communication, and leadership*. New York: Wiley.

Anderson, J. G. (1968). *Bureaucracy in education*. Baltimore: Johns Hopkins Press.

Argyris, C. (1985). *Strategy, change and defensive routines*. Boston: Pittman.

Beach, D. S. (1975). *Managing people at work*. New York: Wiley.

Blake, R. R., & Mouton, J. S. (1964). *The managerial grid*. Houston, TX: Gulf Publishing.

Chambers, G. S. (1971). *Day care—resources for decisions*. Washington, DC: Government Printing Office.

Dale, E. *Management: Theory and practice*. New York: McGraw Hill.

Decker, C. A., & Decker, J. (1992). *Planning and administering early childhood education*. Columbus, OH: Merrill.

Drucker, P. F. (1967). *The effective executive*. New York: Harper and Row.

Fiedler, F. E. (1958). *Leader attitude and group effectiveness*. Urbana, IL: University of Illinois Press.

Fishburn, P. C. (1973). *The theory of social choice*. Princeton, NJ: Princeton University Press.

Goldman, T. A. (1967). *Cost effectiveness and analysis: New approaches in decision making*. New York: Praeger.

Horowitz, I. (1970). *Decision-making and the theory of the firm*. New York: Holt, Rinehart and Winston.

Lakein, A. (1973). *How to get control of your time and your life*. New York: Signet.

Millett, J. D. (1968). *Decision making and administration in higher education*. Kent, OH: Kent State University Press.

Paine, F. T. (1975). *Organizational strategy and policy*. Philadelphia: Saundus.

Senge, P. (1990). *The fifth discipline: The art and practice of the learning organization*. New York: Doubleday.

Stata, R. (1989, Spring). Organizational learning—the key to management innovation. *Sloan Management Review*, pp. 63–64.

Shirley, R. C. (1976). *Strategy and policy formation: A multi-functional orientation*. New York: Wiley.

Stodgill, R. M. (1974). *Handbook of leadership*. New York: The Free Press.

Vroom, V. H. (1967). *Methods of organizational research*. Pittsburgh: University of Pittsburgh Press.

Vroom, V. H. (1973). *Leadership and decision-making*. Pittsburgh: University of Pittsburgh Press.

CHAPTER TEN

Creative and Analytical Problem-Solving

A director's problems are often made up of a group of subproblems or activities. Breaking down these larger problems into parts can be helpful, but a Director also needs a feel for the total situation. When beginning to solve a problem, it is helpful to state the problem in as open-ended a way as possible; then a selection can be made from any or all of the problem-solving techniques that might be appropriate.

STEPS IN PROBLEM-SOLVING

The first step in problem-solving is to ask the initial question: *Is the problem within the problem-solver's (Director's) sphere of influence?* If it is, then using individual problem-solving techniques to solve the problem may be enough. If the problem is not within the Director's/administrator's sphere of influence, then group techniques are a must. It is helpful at this point to identify key persons and involve them in whichever group techniques are chosen. Several aids to decision-making exist, such as the decision tree discussed in Chapter 9, and brainstorming and synectics, which are group techniques that will be discussed later in this chapter.

The next step in problem-solving is to ask: *Are time and change important?* Problems can be further divided into those for which time and/or change are important, and those for which time and/or change are less important. For example, planning a new curriculum for next year would fall into the second, or static, category (not changing rapidly, under less time pressure); on the other hand, meeting a proposal deadline this month would fall into the first, or more dynamic, category (with high time pressure and the promise of possible change). Obviously, there will be situations that fit both categories, since time and change are both important.

INDIVIDUAL TECHNIQUES

The individual analytical techniques described in the following section should be quite familiar, since they are often used in everyday situations. The section that follows analytical techniques, which describes individual creative techniques, lists many procedures that also can be used for group problem-solving. An administrator can first "walk through" the technique alone, or he or she might want to gather group ideas first.

Individual Analytical Techniques

Many of the techniques used when making individual decisions are analytical in nature. For example, checklists are a familiar analytical problem-solving aid, as are lists of "pros" and "cons" that relate to a specific decision or problem. Using a scale of 1 to 10 to weigh ideas on a checklist or list of pros and cons (that is, rating ideas from 1 to 10 or –1 to –10 according to the problem-solver's feelings or some particular criteria for weighting) also helps clarify priorities and is an individual analytical technique. An attribute list, which is described in the creative techniques section, can also be used as an analytical technique. The decision tree used in Chapter 9 is analytical in nature, and can be used by individuals or by a group.

Another analytical technique could be called the "Six-Question Approach." To demonstrate this, let us use the example of deciding to purchase a new piece of playground equipment. First, gather catalogs (or other reference materials appropriate to a given problem). These resource materials help "warm up" an individual or a group and serve as a springboard into discussion. Then, as possibilities are chosen, ask these six questions:

What is it?

What must it do?

What *does* it do?

What will it cost?

What else might do the job?

What will that cost?

Individually thinking through these questions sharpens one's thinking and clarifies the issues involved.

Computer-Aided Problem-Solving

Another aid to individual decision-making and analytical problem-solving is the several computer software systems designed specifically for child-care center management. There are three types of software that are useful for centers: planning software (that is, software that aids in making projections, establishing long-range plans, and setting up cash flow patterns and budgets); communications and printing software; and record-keeping software.

The planning software also can be used to develop scenarios (possible plans for the future) as a Director considers the five outlooks discussed in Chapter 8:

- Things will go as expected.
- The situation will get a little better.
- The situation will get a little worse.
- The situation will get much better.
- The situation will get much worse.

Simulating the numbers, budgets, and other factors of a one-year, five-year, and ten-year plan can help a Director take a "dry run" through a likely scenario. These "pilot program views" are subject to error, of course, since the future *is* uncertain and computers are famous for only projecting the known or linear possibilities that have been entered into it. However, uncovering hidden possibilities or predicting problems is worth the effort involved (Senge, 1990).

Individual Creative Techniques

Morphological Analysis

Morphological analysis is a comprehensive way to list and examine all of the possible solutions to a problem, as well as combinations of these solutions. It is a technique that can be done individually or with a group. The steps of this method are

1. Define the problem broadly.
2. List the interdependent variables.
3. Enter the variables on the horizontal axis of a chart.
4. Select the most promising alternatives and list them on the vertical axis of the chart.

The object of morphological analysis is to review all possible solution combinations. Figure 10.1 illustrates this technique; in this example, the broad problem is how to expand a center's services so that the center's income will increase.

FIGURE 10.1
Morphological Analysis: How to Expand Services and Increase Income

Variables	Old Population	Some New Population	New Population
Old product	Child-care center	Advertise for school-age/after-school program	Advertise summer day camp to the geographic area
Some new product	Offer Saturday games and hiking program	Have older children also come to the games and hiking program (with their parents for some events)	Have separate Saturday program of games, hiking, and other enrichments for school-age children
New product	Offer summer or Saturday computer camp	Offer computer camp to older children	Advertise summer computer day camp—Offer it to teenagers 12–15 also

Figure 10.1 shows a gradual progression of goals and objectives that can be applied to future years. In this example, lack of floor space and expertise might be problems, but using the extra space available during the summer might be planned, or hiring teachers who are trained in both computers and child development might be tried. When first considering changes, an organization should try building on old strengths of either the population served at present or of the product (present services); that way, an organization does not get too far out on a limb when trying new things. It has been found that *starting* changes by instigating a new service for a new population is the least feasible alternative. It is easier to start by providing a familiar service to a new population or by providing a new service to a familiar population.

Morphological analysis can also be done with a group in a brainstorming session to gain more ideas and add details to concepts already suggested. A staff training session might be greatly enlivened by such an exercise. In general, this whole analysis process is designed to generate ideas. The combining and recombining of functions and possible alternatives provides numerous opportunities to look at a problem and develop fresh, novel solutions.

Attribute Lists

A specialized form of morphological analysis is the *attribute list*. This type of analysis is done by listing attributes of the functions desired (or not desired) on one side of a matrix, and then listing possible forms across the other side of the matrix. In this manner, form and function are separated and new insights emerge. The advantage of using the matrix is that each function can be considered as it would appear in each form. Also, elements within each function can be considered.

FIGURE 10.2
Attribute List

Dimensions of the problem	Elements within the dimension
Rudeness	Of administrative assistant to professionals, parents, visitors
Incompetence	Late work, lost work, surliness about complaints
Programs threatened	Income and prestige loss, relationship with community agencies threatened
Wants all requests to be made in writing	Delays work, creates rigidity, violates norms of informality
Filed grievance citing sexism and racism as reasons for the behavior described above	Involves legal language and delays, learning about parameters involved; can work to the benefit of management or the employee

Figure 10.2 is an example of an attribute list of this type. In this particular case, the list was used to better understand a difficult personnel problem involving a grievance that was filed by an administrative assistant. This problem was resolved when the person took three months medical leave without pay, and while on leave, actually took a new job. In looking back at the circumstances of her hiring, it was found that her references had not been checked closely; if they had, it would have been discovered that she had shown this behavior in the past. Her grievances against a large number of people in this organization (17 out of 23) were found to be unsubstantiated.

Attribute lists are also intended to help generate ideas about a service, situation, or product under consideration. In these types of situations, the list is generated and then analyzed to find items that would improve the situation, service, or product (happy, competent children in the case of early childhood programs). For example, an individual or a group (staff or Board) might want to improve the outdoor area around the center while minimizing any hazards. A list of attributes or features could be developed similar to Figure 10.2a.

Checklists can be developed for each item and then forced relationships can be developed next or later. (A forced relationship develops when participants are given a new word, concept, phrase, or object and asked to relate it to the problem being studied. The idea is to find new stimuli to "force" creativity.) When this activity is done in a group setting, the leader or facilitator can introduce a new word, concept, phrase, or subject relating to the main task, and then, before coming back to the main task, the group can brainstorm ideas that stem from the new subject. For example, to help a group brainstorm ideas relating to the main task of improving the outdoor area, the facilitator might introduce the phrase "playing in a garden." This phrase generates thoughts of integrating *beauty* into the children's play area. Ideas might include allowing children to plant seeds in the beds (zinnias, carrots, and radishes, for example). For centers with almost no outside area, container gardens could be used and then brought indoors during the winter.

For the subject "picnic/snack area," subtopics such as "benches," "tables," and "trash cans" can be generated and discussed. The same procedure can be used with any other topic; finding comparisons among other lists can help enhance this problem-solving method, because it is an interim step in the main problem-solving task.

In the outdoor play area example, when the facilitator uses a word like "beauty," it creates forced relationships and generates new ideas in one direction. Introducing the phrase "physical fitness" initiates a whole new group of relationships and steers ideas in another direction. Adding another column

FIGURE 10.2a
Attribute List with Forced Relationships

Item	Beauty Attributes	Physical Fitness Attributes
Lawn	Adds to beauty	Used as a running area and for large muscle exercise
Beds—flowers	Add to beauty	Do not add to fitness since they cannot be walked in or touched
Beds—nonflowering (e.g., ivy)	Add to beauty (Is sturdy and harder to damage)	Do not add to fitness
Fences	Can be attractive	Required to make safe areas for outdoor fitness
Flowering trees	Add to beauty (Cannot easily be damaged at the tree trunk level, once mature)	Do not add to fitness
Other shade trees	Add to beauty (Lend shade and comfort for outdoor activities)	Do not add to fitness
Shrubs	Add to beauty	Do not add to fitness
Hedges	Add to beauty	Do not add to fitness
Walks, tricycle paths	Can be attractive	Used for many large muscle activities
Stone walls	Can be attractive	Can be a safety hazard near outdoor play
Picnic/snack areas	Can be attractive	Add to ambiance and variety of outdoor play
Signs	Can be attractive	Add to safety of outdoor play
Outdoor play equipment (as listed in Chapter 11)	Can be attractive	Required for children's fitness

(entitled "Expense") to the attribute list also could help clarify certain situations. For example, when expense is considered, the cost of building a stone wall might be too high, but if a stone wall already exists, the cost of making it safe and usable might be manageable.

Problem Redefinition

Whether creative problem-solving is done by an individual or a group, *redefinition of the problem* may be needed. There are many redefinitional techniques, but only a few will be reviewed in this chapter. Since persons in programs for young children are usually quite creative, applying these skills to administration problems in this setting can be very useful. The book *Applied Imagination* by Alex Osborn (1960) is filled with additional ideas.

- Questioning is always a favorite redefinition technique. Some example questions might include: What would happen if I made it (the center, the program, etc.) larger? What if I made it smaller? What would happen if we turned it upside down (e.g., ran it all night instead of all day)? What if we put it on the top floor instead of the bottom floor? (Or the bottom floor instead of the top floor?) What if we rearrange it in another way?

- Restating the problem by using key beginning phrases is another helpful redefinition technique:

  What would I do if I had three wishes?

  You could also define the problem as . . .

  The main point of the problem is . . .

  The problem, put in another way, is like . . .

  Another, even stranger, way of looking at it is . . .

  The worst thing that could happen is . . .

- Another creative redefinition approach is the "List Ten Ways This Can Be Done" method (or "List Ten Ways This Might Look," or some other similar phrasing that helps generate ten aspects of a problem).

- Another redefinition technique is to ask the question "How does a similar event occur in nature?" This tactic is sometimes called the Bionic Approach. An example of this method might be: If a mighty oak grows from a little acorn, maybe a system of child-care centers can be grown from an acorn of an idea.

Boundary Examinations

To do a boundary examination, another type of problem-solving technique, first write the problem. Then underline the nouns, verbs, and adjectives. Using a dictionary or thesaurus, find two or three substitutes for each underlined word.

This technique produces new ways to define a problem and thus can yield new solutions. For example:

> **PROBLEM:**
>
> | Angry | mothers take up too much of the teacher's |
> |---|---|
> | (upset) | (caretakers)   (counselor's) |
> | (frustrated) | (relatives)   (administrator's) |
>
> | time at the | beginning of the morning. |
> |---|---|
> | (hours) | (mid-morning) |
> | (minutes) | (lunch time) |
> | (attention) | (evening) |

Solutions that pop up from this particular boundary examination include setting aside time for parents during the lunch hour, or scheduling evening meetings to offer parents education that might help them with frustrations in their lives. This education might include child-raising helps, career strategies, and methods for understanding and resolving conflicts with children or the center.

Wishful Thinking

Wishful thinking, another creative problem-solving technique, can make a valuable contribution to formal problem-solving situations. To get started, have participants complete the sentence: "If I could break all the constraints, I would . . ." For example, experts who conduct budgeting seminars always advise organizations to design an "ideal budget," or one that is based on what is really needed and wanted, and then to work backwards to tailor the budget to what can be afforded. Beginning this way rather than starting out with an "actual budget," or one that is based on the present dollar amount, allows a record to be made of the organization's priorities and goals, so that when money does become available, it can be better used. In child-care situations, often one of a center's dreams becomes the latest trend in programs that receive government grants. One center posted a long sheet of shelf paper inside the Director's office door. As people thought of ideas, they jotted them on this "wish list." When requests for proposals came from the state or federal government, the center checked the list to find any topics that matched. One year, for example, programs helping the elderly and programs focusing on reading were the "grant-getters of the year," so the center developed a proposal and subsequently received funding for an "Adoptive Grandparents" program that featured older adults who volunteered in the classroom. These volunteers read to the children, cuddled them, and helped them with crafts activities.

Many kinds of restraints can be ignored in wishful thinking. The size of the building, the salary of workers, or the training budget are only a few examples. This wishful thinking device sets up new thinking patterns. The next phase is to return to the practical realm with statements such as: "I can't really do that, but I *can* . . ."

Analogies and Metaphors

Devices often found in early childhood storybooks—analogies and metaphors—can also be used in administration. An *analogy* is a direct comparison between two objects or ideas that have similar characteristics. In contrast, a *metaphor* is a figure of speech in which one word or phrase is used in place of another object or idea to show the similarity between the two. For example, "the ship of state" is a metaphor, as is referring to old age as "the evening of life."

Both analogies and metaphors are useful in problem-solving because they generate data and help to produce ideas about or solutions to a problem. Metaphors are more powerful because they demand a greater change of perspective, but both devices help participants see new principles. For example, when considering the metaphor "evening of life," the images called to mind include softening light, singing birds, and quietness. Other common metaphors include "quiet leadership," "bear hug," "paper shuffler," or even "brainstorming." An analogy that many women who own small businesses use to describe their feelings about their enterprise is that of "bearing a child and watching it grow." To them, this analogy captures the great joy of creating something where before there had been nothing.

A discussion that involves analogies can be a useful lead-in to a group creative problem-solving session in which participants will be using brainstorming or synectics techniques. A current discussion topic in education is the role of child-care personnel. One analogy is that child-care personnel serve as "architects," helping the parent develop the child according to the parent's goals. An opposing view is that of the child-care staff serving as "physicians," diagnosing ills and prescribing cures. When deciding which role your center supports, both analogies generate a whole cluster of concepts and thus make good springboards for discussion at either staff or parent meetings. Another possible analogy is that of the Director as a "nurturing parent," since both Directors and parents are concerned with the growth of those for whom they have responsibility.

Direct analogy, which can be denoted by the words "as if," might be used in certain situations to the benefit of everyone. For example, suggest to the child-care staff that they think about rude parents "as if" these parents had a terrible tragedy in the past. This builds compassion and patience in the listener before the parent even starts talking and may even be true but unknown.

Drawing a Model

Several problem-solving approaches suggest drawing a situation model of the problem to show the relationships involved. The model could use boxes or circles, much like the models for scenarios shown in Chapter 8 on planning. As shown in Figure 10.3, the situation model's developer can expand this basic outline of the problem or situation by drawing boxes that show elements that are outside of the problem but that are closely related to it. Lines are used to connect these "outside" elements to the main problem. This method of expansion can uncover the possible causes of or factors in a problem and can encourage decision-making or planning.

GROUP TECHNIQUES

Individual analytical techniques, such as creating a checklist or listing pros and cons, can also be done effectively in a group. Decision aids can be processed individually or in a group as well. (More suggestions about decision

FIGURE 10.3
Factors Outside of the Situation Model

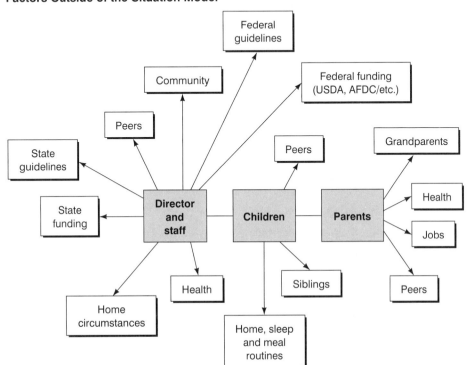

aids can be found in Chapter 9 on decision-making.) One of the best methods for group problem-solving might be to address the following five questions:

What is the problem?

Who needs to be involved?

What more do we need to know?

What would an ideal solution be?

What would be the first step(s) in realizing a solution?

Using these questions to begin a group discussion can "break open" a problem and result in some answers, which can be written on a chalkboard or flip chart for later consideration.

The creative group techniques that will be discussed in this section include brainstorming and synectics. Brainstorming during a problem-solving session produces a large number of ideas but does not necessarily bring about a deeper level of insight into the overall problem. Synectics, unlike brainstorming, requires someone to play the part of the client who has the problem. This method produces fewer, but more in-depth, solutions.

Brainstorming

Whether using the brainstorming technique at a parent or staff meeting, this approach works best when there has been some sort of warm-up on the topic to be discussed. This warm-up may be as simple as a detailed description of the issues to be considered. The five questions listed in the previous section provide a good warm-up for many problems. After using this particular warm-up, the group can brainstorm about possible first steps. Before the group time begins, an individual warm-up might be to ask each person to write down three or more ideas about the topic or to suggest three possible solutions.

The brainstorming procedure is divided into two parts. The first part is idea generation, and there are some set rules for this stage:

1. All ideas are given equal respect.
2. There is no criticism of any suggestion, no matter how wild.
3. All ideas are written down on a chalkboard or flip chart that can be seen by the group. This allows people to see the ideas and build on other members' suggestions.

Writing the ideas sets the stage for the second part of brainstorming in which the ideas are ranked or given priority. One approach to ranking is to give every group member 3 to 7 votes (depending on the total number of ideas that will be ranked). By allowing 3 to 7 votes per person rather than just one, greater nuances within a solution are revealed. As voting occurs, a natural ranking appears. If the client or person with the problem is present, it should always be made clear that he or she may choose among *all* the solutions generated by the group, and need not follow the solutions ranked high by the group. The client, after all, knows the problem most intimately; he or she may have received new insights during the idea-generation session and might prefer to use one of these discoveries instead of the ideas voted on by the group.

Reverse brainstorming is also a useful technique. To approach the problem using this method, ask: "What are all the possibilities of ways things could go wrong?" In other words, reverse brainstorming is a way of looking at the problem from the reverse side of the discussion question.

Synectics

Synectics is a Greek word that means "joining together different and apparently irrelevant elements." In this context, synectics is a group problem-solving technique that joins together different people and their different ideas. It requires a leader to serve as a facilitator and also requires a "client." The client has the ultimate say as to whether a solution will work or not, and he or she "owns" the problem. The client also can decide what might correct a factor that blocks a particular solution's usability. The group's role is to act as a "think tank" for the client. While the client is the evaluator in this technique, other group members can hear the ideas generated and can see them written on a flip chart or chalkboard and are thus free to use them in their own way.

After providing a suitable warm-up for the group, staff, or Board during which time the situation is described, the facilitator writes out the problem, defined in an open-ended way, for all to see. Then solutions are generated by the group and are written in columns below the problem, as shown in Figure 10.4. After this step is completed, the client is asked to respond to the solutions and give them a plus or minus rating. If a solution is given a minus sign, a comment about why the solution would not work is written on the visual aid. The minus responses are then addressed by asking "How to avoid" questions, and new solutions are generated. This procedure is shown in Figure 10.5 in which the broad current problem of how to have a U.S. policy on child care is the subject, and which was addressed by a graduate public administration class in policy analysis. This topic is a good discussion springboard for a professional association meeting or other similar group.

SUMMARY

Since problem-solving is a continuing component of administering and managing programs for young children, applying creativity to problem-solving can give educators a lift as well as uncover new ideas. Early childhood educators

FIGURE 10.4
Synectics Model

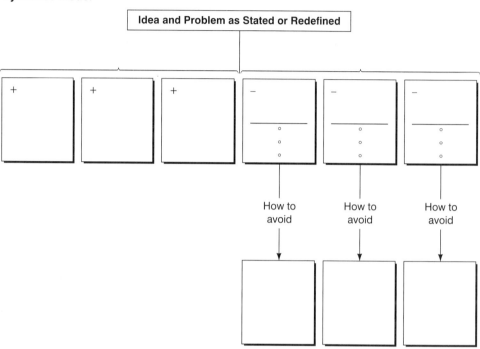

know that creativity builds children's self-esteem; it also builds adults' self-esteem and feelings of competence. Reading through this chapter and trying some of the ideas, perhaps starting with a small sphere of influence before branching out to a larger sphere, can give educators that extra supply of energy that is needed in work with young children. Figure 10.6 gives a useful overview of the techniques discussed in this chapter and categorizes them as individual or group techniques and as creative or analytic approaches. Many of the creative approaches listed under individual techniques also make interesting and useful exercises for groups or classes.

Decision-making, as opposed to problem-solving, is usually future-oriented because it is concerned with future consequences and the probability of success. According to Peter Drucker (1977), problem-solving often looks back at a particular situation. That is, when a problem is solved, a decision is no longer needed because things are restored to "normal," or to a "steady state." On the other hand, decisions lead to change and to changed circumstances, so that problem-solving often is needed again.

When Directors see change as opportunity, they are more inclined, when small problems occur, to practice problem-solving techniques ahead of time, whether alone or in groups. Thus these Directors are better equipped to make decisions that focus on the future and that create a new optimal stage for their

FIGURE 10.5
How to Have a U.S. Policy on Child Care (Synectics Problem-Solving Example)

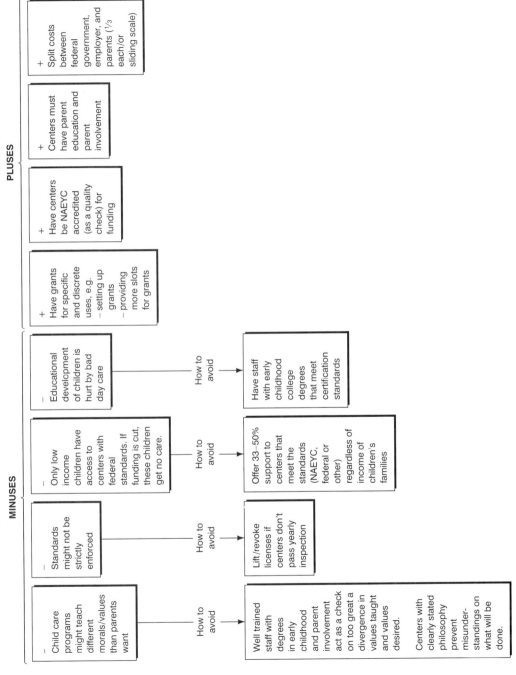

*As brainstormed by a graduate-level college class.

FIGURE 10.6
Creative and Analytical, Individual and Group Problem-Solving Techniques

INDIVIDUAL	EITHER	GROUP
Creative	*Analytic*	*Creative*
1. Morphological analysis and attribute lists	1. Checklists and attribute lists	1. Brainstorming
2. Redefining the problem	2. Decision trees and other aids	2. Synectics
3. Reversals	3. Six-question approach	
4. How is it done in nature?	4. Computer-aided projections and scenarios	
5. Boundary examinations		
6. Drawing a model		
7. Wishful thinking, big dream, inspired approach		
8. Analogy and metaphor		
9. Questioning		
10. Ten ways this can be done		

centers. Effective follow-up to problem-solving sessions—both to assess growth after using various techniques and to identify the adequacy of these techniques—can occur in the form of three-month, six-month, and twelve-month check-ups with staff members. Taking the time to look back on a particular problem and to reflect on the chosen solution, or to build upon the solution at the present time, is a useful exercise and is an essential part of evaluation and reflection in practice. Large corporations use this method to follow up with managers after six and twelve months to assess adaptation, growth, and change, and child-care programs could also benefit from this reflection process.

Several analytical approaches can be used in the prediction of success. These can include:

1. Asking "What will guarantee success? What will guarantee failure?"
2. Listing "Our Expectations" and "Our Concerns," in separate columns, to facilitate analysis.

3. Listing "Anticipated Risks" and "Ways of Overcoming Risks," in separate columns, in a device similar to synectics.

It would be ignoring the "real world" to disregard some of the negative questions that are likely to be asked when a new plan is being considered. Using these analytical approaches to sharpen the issues, and facilitating the analysis by thinking through both positive and negative aspects, helps prepare the Director and/or staff for their new optimal stage or plan.

One final list of some common "do's and don'ts" in problem-solving might include the following:

- Try to identify the real problem, not just symptoms of the problem.
- Identify the "owner" of the problem if possible. If the wrong group is asked to solve the problem, the results can be resentment, noncooperation, and even charges of meddling.
- Try to identify all the possible alternatives, since high-quality problem-solving and decision-making require a good look at all the choices.
- Develop a written plan for implementation. No solution is better than the plan to activate it. This means getting consensus on who does what, how, and when.
- Monitor the implementation. Appoint a monitor, coordinator, or trouble-shooter who can use time and staffing charts developed jointly. Using flip charts, rough drafts of these can be developed at consensus meetings and then later refined. This avoids bottlenecks, frustrations, finger-pointing, and slippages. One center even organized a "problem-solving committee" with representatives from each classroom that met once a month to share ideas on how to improve working conditions in ways large or small. They acknowledged the problem, came up with practical solutions, and monitored the implementation.

The best problem-solving situation supports and facilitates decision-making and helps programs move to a more optimal stage or condition. Using problem-solving techniques helps the Director and the group move smoothly through each of the following stages: generating ideas, making a decision, planning a course of action, considering alternatives, planning, implementing, operating, and evaluating. A trained facilitator even can be brought in to help with big problems or big decisions that will affect a large percent of the program's resources.

Problem-solving often uncovers the need for more resources or better operational systems, so the next section deals with ongoing issues in operations such as facilities, equipment, room arrangement, scheduling, finances, and proposal development.

BIBLIOGRAPHY

Ackoff, R. L. (1987). *The art of problem solving.* New York: Wiley.

Blake, R. R., & Mouton, J. S. (1969). *Building a dynamic corporation through grid organization development.* Reading, MA: Addison-Wesley.

Cartwright, D., & Zander, A. (1960). *Group dynamics.* New York: Harper and Row.

Chase, S., & Chase, M. T. (1951). *Roads to agreement.* New York: Harper and Row.

Cummings, P. W. (1988). *Open management.* New York: American Management Associations.

Drucker, P. F. (1954). *The practice of management.* New York: Harper and Row.

Drucker, P. F. (1977, March-April). Peter Drucker on the manager and the organization. *Bulletin on Training,* p. 4.

Dyer, W. G. (1978). When is a problem a problem? *The Personnel Administrator,* pp. 66–71.

Eitington, J. E. (1984). *The winning trainer.* Houston, TX: Gulf Publishing.

Fisher, B. A. (1974). *Small group decision making: Communication and the group process.* New York: McGraw-Hill.

Gannon, M. J. (1977). *Management: An organizational perspective.* Boston: Little, Brown.

Harrison, E. F. (1975). *The managerial decision-making process.* Boston: Houghton Mifflin.

Hyman, R. T. (1975). *School administrator's handbook of teacher supervision and evaluation methods.* Englewood Cliffs, NJ: Prentice-Hall.

Lee, I. J. (1952). *How to talk with people.* New York: Harper and Row.

Likert, R. (1961). *New patterns of management.* New York: McGraw-Hill.

Likert, R. (1967). *The human organization: Its management and value.* New York: McGraw-Hill.

Marrow, A. J. (1972). *The failure of success.* New York: American Management Association.

McGregor, D. (1960). *The human side of enterprise.* New York: McGraw-Hill.

Miller, D., & Starr, M. (1967). *The structure of human decisions.* Englewood Cliffs, NJ: Prentice-Hall.

Murnighan, J. K. (1981, February). Group decision making: What strategies should you use? *Management Review,* pp. 55–62.

Osborn, A. (1960). *Applied imagination.* New York: Scribner's.

Parent Cooperative Preschools International. (1984). *Leadership development: A facilitator's handbook.* Indianapolis: Author.

Parnes, S. J., Noller, R. B., & Biondi, A. M. (1976). *Creative actionbook.* New York: Scribner's.

Parnes, S. J., Noller, R. B., & Biondi, A. M. (1977). *Guide to creative action.* New York: Scribner's.

Rawlinson, J. G. (1981). *Creative thinking and brainstorming.* New York: Wiley.

Rich, D., & Jones-Shoemaker, C. (1978). *The three R's plus: Teaming families and schools for student achievement.* Washington, DC: The Home and School Institute.

Senge, P. (1990). *The fifth discipline: The art and practice of a learning organization.* New York: Doubleday.

Simon, H. (1976). *Administrative behavior.* New York: The Free Press.

Ulschak, F. L., Nathanson, L., and Gillan, P. G. (1981). *Small group problem solving: An aid to organizational effectiveness.* Reading, MA: Addison-Wesley.

VanDersal, W. R. (1974). *The successful supervisor in government and business.* New York: Harper and Row.

Wiles, K., & Lovell, J. (1975). *Supervision for better schools.* Englewood Cliffs, NJ: Prentice-Hall.

PART FOUR

Operational Issues

Operational issues are ongoing, but their efficient implementation depends on leadership, planning, decision-making, and problem-solving. All of these processes, when used well by the human resources team, benefit the motivation level, the team building efforts, and the skills of the entire staff. They also lead to a feeling of professionalism throughout the center. As parents receive parent education and become knowledgeable about what a good early childhood program includes, involving them in a center's operation can help a program meet the challenges facing early childhood education and young children.

Issues such as facility usage, room arrangement, and scheduling all allow opportunities for discussion as to why a center does things in a certain way and how this philosophy benefits children. Rethinking these areas every year or so during parent-staff orientation meetings keeps the program fresh and up-to-date. One center that had tolerated an awkwardly placed closet for years found that by sharing the problem, a committee of parents and community volunteers rebuilt it, adding to it a deck and an interesting play space on top. Fresh thinking yields many more ideas than can be used at first, but by keeping a list of all of them on a bulletin board or other central location, as circumstances change, the list will seed thinking about possible solutions.

Finances, record-keeping, and proposal writing also lend themselves to sharing the load and sharing the power; thus, as seen in Chapter 7 on leadership, the total power of the program increases. As problems in these areas are shared with a specific committee that is devoted to that particular topic, more ideas and expertise are brought to bear and better solutions emerge. For example, a parent who feels less-than-expert in dealing with his or her toddler may have expertise in the management information systems of the center or the center's administration. By participating in this area, the parent can gain a sense of esteem for having helped the center. By having parents participate in pricing or budgeting for equipment and supplies, parents can learn what equipment and supplies are good for children.

Finally, recognition for a job well done is rare in many job situations, and volunteers value it as well as staff. Successful child-care centers make sure to recognize participants' efforts.

CHAPTER ELEVEN

Facilities, Equipment, Room Arrangement, and Scheduling

W hen visiting different child-care programs, one can see many similarities and variations in programs, some of which are very good and some of which are not as good. All good programs, however, have the common goal of providing growing experiences for children.

Children's growing experiences require a sound underlying philosophy of early childhood education, upon which teachers and parents agree. From this foundation follows a better understanding of children's needs, good programming, and good relationships among the center staff and with parents. When considering early childhood programming, key issues, in addition to curriculum choices, are facilities and the use of space, equipment and room arrangement, and scheduling.

FACILITIES AND THE USE OF SPACE

It is essential for children to be physically active in mastering their world. They become mentally alert as they develop the ability to move with purpose. The facilities chosen to house a particular center, then, need to allow this type of activity—providing opportunities for indoor and outdoor large-muscle play as well as meeting the local fire and zoning regulations. When beginning a new center, it should be remembered that to a certain extent, the layout of an existing facility dictates its usage. The situation can be very different when a Director and Board have an opportunity to design and build a new space in a housing area, office complex, or shopping area.

Daily surroundings are very important; a well-planned child-care environment can be one of a child's most valuable teachers. The environment introduces the child to the colors, shapes, smells, and sounds of the world. Infants and toddlers grow and learn by interacting with their environment, so the environment must be one that is safe and interesting. Indoor and outdoor areas need to be free of dangerous conditions or hazardous materials. The playground equipment must be checked often to ensure its safety. A first-aid kit also must be kept and staff should be well-trained in administering first aid during an emergency. In addition, the child-care setting should accommodate the needs of the caregiver as well as the infants, toddlers, and preschoolers (Lally & Stewart, 1990).

When setting up a child-care environment, there are eight concepts to remember (Lally & Stewart, 1990, pp. 7–16). The ideal infant/toddler/preschooler care-giving environment should

1. ensure safety
2. promote health
3. provide comfort
4. be convenient
5. be child-sized
6. maximize flexibility
7. encourage movement
8. allow for choice

Because space requirements are calculated on a per-child basis, the number of children that will be in a group or classroom has important implications for facility design. The best-planned indoor and outdoor physical environment fosters optimal growth and development through opportunities for exploration and learning.

Outdoor Play

Play facilities for children must provide room for two things: action and contemplation (Stone, 1970). The proof of a good outdoor play yard is in its use. Will children have room to move and the opportunity to affect their environment—feel it and mold it? Can they put together a playhouse or clubhouse or at least improve on one that already exists? Can they try out new ideas, make rules, discuss possibilities, experience success and failure, learn to try again? Is there room for water play? For sand play? One center met the children's need to use their hands to shape, mold, and feel a medium by setting up a water table on wheels, so it could be used indoors or rolled outdoors for warm-weather play. A similar table could be used as a mobile sand table, or the water table could double as a sand table during a different week.

Even large pieces of equipment can be moved and set up in new places to give an outdoor space a new look. Slides can be added to a jungle gym or a path for tricycles built to extend children's play in new ways. Good equipment invites departures from routine; for example, it can make possible a morning snack out-of-doors (Stone, 1970).

Children learn and relearn as they play with common materials such as water, sand, and even mud (provided in some sort of container, perhaps). Children are discovering and learning when they have the opportunity to control this small piece of their environment. Outdoor equipment and structures should be selected to allow creative expression and imaginative interpretation by children. If possible, the outdoors should be an extension of indoor space; doors that are readily accessible and windows that allow plenty of outside views are ideal.

A child needs to be able to react more energetically and quickly to his or her environment than does an adult. Discovering space—distance, height, width, level and inclined planes, and how one's body fits into and around space—is part of the physical development of childhood (U.S. Dept. of Health, Education and Welfare, 1969). Outdoor space may be large or small, flat or hilly, grassy or paved, shaded or unshaded. A brook is nice, but a hose or buckets of water will do in the summer. Whatever the available space offers, imagination can be used, just as it is indoors, to provide the active play children need and must have: running, jumping, climbing, and throwing. Providing for outdoor activity and children's large muscle development makes it less likely that this energy will all be expended indoors in ways that are wearing on the staff and that the staff is less-equipped to handle.

Age Grouping

Traditional age-grouped classes, such as those for toddlers, three-year-olds, four-year-olds, and five-year-olds, are found in most programs for young children. This allows for grouping equipment and materials according to the same developmental level or, as in the case of chairs and tables, the same size. For example, two-year-olds need different-sized chairs than do five-year-olds.

A further benefit of traditional age grouping is that teachers need only be expert with a particular age, or at least be highly focused on one age group each year. Of course, even children who are the same age will present a range of abilities, from the youngest in the group to those who are more advanced than average, so a wide knowledge of child development will always be needed. However, age grouping is more suitable for beginning teachers or for centers that have a relatively inexperienced staff or that have staff members involved in on-the-job training.

Activity Grouping and Multi-age Groups

Some centers must work with a particular space that dictates that the large muscle room, the creative activities room, and the story/quiet room be dedicated exclusively to these kinds of activities. In such a situation, use of the rooms by mixed-age groups results. Some programs choose a multi-age group approach for many reasons other than space, and public schools use this approach on occasion, establishing grades like K–1, 1–2, or 5–6.

The educational benefits of mixed-age grouping have been discussed by reformers such as Montessori, Pestolozzi, and Dewey. Since the 1930s, educators have become increasingly aware of the limitations of a rigidly age-grouped system. Educators have found, in contrast, that nongraded organizational systems can allow for recognizing and planning for a wide range of child abilities. It also allows for differential rates of progress and makes it easier for the teacher to adjust to individual emotional and social needs.

What, then, is multi-age grouping? This particular philosophy opposes the restriction of individual age-grouped levels and instead offers flexible groupings that encompass a two- to four-year span, allowing movement between levels for those children ready to advance or needing more help. The multi-age classroom concept is based on vertical grouping, meaning that children can have the same teacher or teaching team for more than one year. Also, mixed-age grouping compels educators to organize learning activities and curriculum so that individuals and small groups of children can work on different tasks together. The benefits of mixed-age groupings include:

- Children have a wide selection of models from whom they can learn; it provides older children with leadership opportunities and younger ones with more complex pretend play opportunities.

- Mixed-age grouping seems to result in greater cooperation and less competitive pressure and therefore seems to lead to fewer discipline problems.
- Mixed-age grouping can be an effective strategy for dealing with different levels of cognitive maturity so intellectual growth is stimulated.

The disadvantages of mixed-age grouping include:

- Same-age, same-sex children may have difficulty in developing friendships, if the group is small.
- Older children often have fewer challenges than do younger children.
- Younger children, especially if they are very competitive, may be frustrated by the perceived gap between their work and that of older children.
- Scheduling special enrichments or field trips can be difficult.
- Teachers are required to do more planning for a wider range of children, and therefore an experienced teacher is needed (Lodish, 1992).

The external organization of age-grouped or multi-age classrooms is less significant than is the quality of the classroom environment and the learning opportunities made available. Because children respond differently to different situations, it is important to have some choices in possible groupings and to operate with flexibility.

Architectural and Legal Requirements

The architectural design of a child-care facility should be in keeping with the program's philosophy. For example, a teacher-directed philosophy may require less space than would an interaction-with-the-environment or learning-through-play philosophy. Room to move about and provision for physical and psychological comfort are needed.

When planning for direct or indirect federal assistance of any kind, programs must be accessible to disabled children and employees. Section 504 of P.L. 93-112 describes the requirements of making programs accessible to the disabled. Money in the form of grants may be awarded by Congress to pay for all or part of the costs for remodeling buildings to eliminate barriers for disabled children; this funding is authorized in P.L. 94-142, and is dependent upon Congress's determination of appropriateness for funding this part of the law (Decker & Decker, 1992). With full inclusion of all children being required by federal legislation, all programs serving all families will need to be well-informed and ready to serve the physically challenged population.

States vary in their requirements for indoor and outdoor space per child. Some states do not even have an outdoor space requirement. Thirty-five square feet per child for indoor space is an average, but some states require less; as children get older, providing more space per child is more appropriate. Poor arrangement can reduce the usefulness of large amounts of square footage per child, so careful planning and attention need to be addressed to indoor and outdoor space layout and equipment layout.

Lighting

Lighting affects physical well-being; seasonal affective disorder (SAD), a condition that occurs when there is less daylight during the shortened winter days, affects some adults and may also affect children. Making the best use of available light, then, is very important. The brightness and attractiveness of centers can be increased by using local or spotlight lighting, and reflective surfaces in the room can greatly increase the efficiency of the lighting that is chosen. Light-colored walls, light-colored tables and countertops, and even light-colored floors can add brightness and cheerfulness to rooms. Glare can be controlled by using blinds, louvers, curtains, and flat finishes. Ideally, the window area should be about 20 percent of the floor area, and windows should be low enough so that children can see out.

Heating/Cooling

A comfortable temperature of around 68° to 72°, whether through heating or cooling, needs to be maintained at the *children's* level. Thermometers that are placed low on the walls, or even a thermostat placed at the children's level, can monitor this zone for temperature. Good ventilation is also a requirement, and it is important not to close spaces in and reduce ventilation when air conditioning is installed in child-care centers. If there is no humidifier installed, humidity can be added to the rooms through open fish tanks or a water table.

Acoustical Control

Since young children make noise, attention to acoustical control and sound absorption is important. Rugs are the least expensive approach to acoustical absorption, and centers can ask parents or the community for donations. Rugs must be kept clean, so placement must be a consideration. Some centers may use rugs or carpets only for certain areas, such as the block area and the story area. Long flat walls reflect sound; to counteract such a design, decorations, bulletin boards, and children's pictures might be hung on clotheslines to help break up wall space and sound waves as they hit the walls. Padding on furniture legs can also reduce noise.

Legal Requirements and Agency Regulations

Licensing in most areas is handled by local and state agencies who inspect nursery schools, preschools, and child-care centers. Although licensing takes time, an interim permit is often issued to allow the program to get under way while awaiting health, fire, and safety inspections. A center may need to alter buildings if they fall short of any requirements necessary for licensing. (One example of a necessary alteration is the need to install fire doors.) The cost of many alterations may be covered by specific grants or funds, or they might be shared with the landlord in some instances.

It may be necessary to deal with regulations or standards in any or all of the following areas:

- Zoning
- Business licensing
- Safety issues, including fire extinguishers, smoke alarms, fire alarms, exits, and escape plans
- Educational standards, including teacher/pupil ratio; indoor space/child ratio; outdoor space/child ratio; staff qualifications; and health requirements
- Equipment
- Parking
- Building codes, including those for electricity, plumbing, heating capacity, and access, as well as environmental requirements, such as whether or not lead paint or asbestos is present
- Health regulations, including food preparation, food storage, number of bathrooms, lighting, and ventilation
- Transportation regulations or licenses

Most high-quality early childhood programs establish educational standards that far exceed any regulations that may be required by legislation. When beginning a new center, a valuable early step in considering architectural and legal requirements is to visit several similar early childhood programs and observe their different housing arrangements. Interview teachers and administrators regarding the regulations they must meet in their city, county, state, or province. It might also be helpful to consider the information in the *Early Childhood Environmental Rating Scale* (Harms & Clifford, 1980). To aid in such information gathering, many national early childhood conferences provide opportunities to visit excellent early childhood programs that have interesting layouts.

Outdoor Space

Since outdoor space and indoor space flow together in a developmental program, many of the same considerations should be used when setting up both areas. There should be time to use and explore the space; it should demonstrate flexibility and adaptability; and it should be safe and secure for children, day and night.

Playground and Layout

Many states and licensing authorities have requirements about the amount of average outdoor space available to each child, with suggested space ranging from 75 to 250 square feet per child. In general, more is better, as long as supervision can be carefully accomplished. Fencing with gates is required, and enclosing outdoor play areas is one of the first major expenses for a center that is just starting up.

Many wonderful materials are available on the subject of playgrounds and playground layout, as well as catalogs from different equipment suppliers. Some programs earmark their initial registration fees to go to a "large muscle equipment fund," since the necessary large playground equipment can include expensive items, such as a jungle gym, that are difficult to acquire on a tight budget. Researching the selection of large muscle equipment is a wonderful task to delegate to a committee made up of parents, since much parent education can occur while the committee pours over catalogs (which the Director can provide), and checks and compares prices, delivery options, and set-up plans.

The playground can include a tricycle path, an area for sand play, an area for water play, and even a garden. Lovell and Harms (1985) developed a rating scale that can serve as a useful checklist for designing or improving an outdoor play space.

Outdoor Storage

Outdoor storage is essential to a rich and varied outdoor play program, because it enables the housing of tricycles, movable equipment, and seasonal items. A wide door and a ramp to the outside of the storage building (perhaps removable) allows children to come in and help bring out the equipment. Whether the storage building is a shed or an outbuilding attached to the main building, or just a garage, it can serve as a windbreak for the children's play space. Raised flooring in the storage room is a must to prevent dampness and rust. Some programs even fence the roof of a storage building, if the roof is flat, and allow the children to use it as a "tree house," perhaps attaching a slide and cargo net. Imaginative use of, and changes to, the outdoor play area are as important as they are for indoor play area(s).

EQUIPMENT AND ROOM ARRANGEMENT

Because all children have a great deal of potential and because there is such an infinite variety of individual differences among children, it is important that a child-care center offer to its children rich and varied opportunities through its curricula and equipment so that the needs of each child will be met.

Even the most inspired and experienced staff members have limited time and energy. Requirements of the staff can be eased if the spaces for children are

carefully planned and arranged. In spaces properly designed for child development, the doors, walls, windows, floors, furnishings, and fixtures can motivate a
child's curiosity, encourage the potential for learning, and provide assistance to
the staff. When the staff can focus on the children's activities rather than on
the deficits in the indoor or outdoor spaces, a better program results.

Equipment

Activities and moods can shift rapidly in a program for young children. Indoor
spaces that promote quiet, perhaps equipped with soft items such as large pillows on the floor, are just as important as the block corner and the truck run
area. Making use of movable shelving units, rolling storage bins for blocks and
small toys, and worktables and painting easels that can be used in new locations at different seasons all help provide the adaptability and flexibility that
enhance a program. Materials or items that are in a clutter, or are stored in
such a way that a child must always ask for them, are frustrating for children
and for adults.

Too much single-purpose furniture can also restrict activities and the use of
imagination. There should be room for the unexpected: a grocery-box train, a
large box made into a house, and frequent changes in the dramatic play area.
The scene changes in the dramatic play area can range far and wide: a veterinar-
ian's office, a dentist's office, a library, a styling salon, a pizza restaurant, a gas
station, and whatever else the children propose and agree upon. Stocking these
play areas with receipt pads, note pads, and writing tools can encourage a print-
rich environment for older preschool children, and also adds realism to their
play. Joining related play areas, such as the block area and the housekeeping
corner, can expand children's play as they find ways to combine the materials
from both areas (Dodge, 1988; Seefeldt & Barbour, 1990; Trawick-Smith, 1992).

Adults are aware of the need for privacy at one time or another, but often
there is a tendency to overlook this same need in young children. A classroom
is an extraordinarily stimulating place, so children will frequently wish to take
a break, catch their breath, and enjoy solitude in a quiet area. This private
space should be respected by both the teacher and other children (Cherry,
1976; Miller, 1990; Seefeldt & Barbour, 1990; Trawick-Smith, 1992).

The "ambiance" of the classroom includes such elements as lighting, texture, and noise. Each of these features affects play in various ways.

Lighting

A sunny, naturally lighted room is considered vital to the development and
health of young children as mentioned earlier. A room brightened by sunshine
provides the opportunity to observe the daily passage of time and to see objects
at different stages of daylight (Trawick-Smith, 1992). Therefore, having large,
uncovered (but coverable) windows is the ideal arrangement, with full-spectrum
lighting used in the absence of windows (Cherry, 1976; Trawick-Smith, 1992).

Texture

A variety of textures tends to promote more frequent and varied use. Providing rugs, quilts, pillows, bean bag chairs, and cushions gives the room a "soft" feel. Trawick-Smith concludes from Weinstein's (1979) study that a "soft and warm environment creates security and comfort and reduces stress in young children" (Trawick-Smith, 1982, p. 27). Other textures may include messy, manipulative items such as sand, finger paint, shaving cream, water, grits, rice, oatmeal, cornstarch, clay, play dough, carpet squares, sheepskin, and tile (Dodge, 1988; Miller, 1990).

Throughout the years, one of the most effective ways teachers have provided for play is through the use of *learning centers*, which usually occupy separate areas within the classroom. Some of the most common learning centers used are areas for a library (books), woodworking, art, music, sand/water, blocks, manipulatives/table toys, and dramatic play (Cherry, 1976; Dodge, 1988; Miller, 1990; Seefeldt & Barbour, 1990; Trawick-Smith, 1992).

The library/book area is a quiet, cozy spot where children can retreat and read a favorite book or look at pictures. Books are displayed in an interesting and accessible manner, with the covers visible. Old magazines, parts of a newspaper, and catalogs can also be included. By providing comfortable chairs, pillows, and bean bag chairs, the teacher creates a very inviting atmosphere. Obviously, this area should be situated away from noisier activities in order to minimize distractions.

Woodworking can be an extremely popular activity, especially for those children who have never had such opportunities before, and the benefits abound (Cherry, 1976). As children manipulate materials, improved eye-hand coordination occurs; both imagination and memory are exercised as children construct different objects; children also can practice measuring and approximating distance as they build objects. The teacher can stock the woodworking center with such items as glue, toothpicks, styrofoam, pipe cleaners, tape, glitter, wood scraps, and paper strips. When more sophisticated materials (such as hammers, nails, and saws) are introduced, an adult must supervise the activity closely, and goggles may be required when certain materials are in use. Because of the nature of this center and to minimize danger, a limit should be placed on the number of children who may participate at the same time (Seefeldt & Barbour, 1990).

Art is another popular activity. Typically, children of all ages love to explore and create with different types of media and materials. By providing a well-planned art center, the teacher demonstrates awareness of the cognitive importance of art. The use of open-ended art activities, not patterns, promotes creativity and instills pride in achievement. The manipulation of the media allows children to develop small motor skills as well as eye-hand coordination. The art area should be located close to a water source for cleanup, and might include easels and tables as work areas (Dodge, 1988; Miller, 1990; Seefeldt & Barbour, 1990).

Children enjoy music enormously, yet too frequently it is offered only at certain times of the day. It is important to allow children opportunities to experiment with instruments and recordings on their own. A music center, which allows such exploration, could be located in a quiet part of the room or in a noisier area, depending on the teacher's expectations (Seefeldt & Barbour, 1990). In either case, limits should be set as to how loud the instruments and music can be played. Tape recording the songs children naturally make up and sing adds interest for the children. (These tapes can also be shared with parents.)

Often sand and water are ignored as learning tools because they are messy, but many mathematical concepts, such as measuring and comparing, can be learned through the use of these materials. Children can use these substances to observe cause and effect and to practice problem-solving. Sand and water areas are another type of learning center where eye-hand coordination and small motor skills are strengthened. The sand and water area should be in a quiet, secluded place and children should be encouraged to keep the materials in the appropriate containers (Dodge, 1988).

Manipulatives and table toys include such items as Legos™, Lincoln Logs™, Bristle Blocks™, snap beads, and other similar hands-on materials. They can be used on the floor or on a table, by one child or by several. Table toys can be categorized as self-correcting, open-ended, or collectible (Dodge, 1988). Self-correcting toys are ones that fit together in one particular manner, such as puzzles, lotto games, nesting boxes, and self-help skill frames. Open-ended toys can be put together in many creative ways and include Legos™, colored cubes, Lincoln Logs™, and attribute blocks. Collectibles consist of groups of similar items, such as buttons, seeds, rocks, and shells. By using all of these different types of table toys, children practice fine motor skills and eye-hand coordination. They learn about relationships as they practice sorting and classifying objects. This type of learning center usually works best in a quiet area where children can concentrate, but if some manipulatives are occasionally placed close to the unit blocks, children can combine materials from the two areas (Dodge, 1988; Miller, 1990; Seefeldt & Barbour, 1990).

Blocks are some of the most valuable teaching tools, as well as some of the most forgotten. Teachers rarely incorporate blocks beyond first grade, yet there are many developmental benefits when they are used in later years. Children can acquire numerous mathematical concepts, including shape, size, length, height, weight, and balance. Children can create with blocks, developing eye-hand coordination and small motor control as they do so. They can take pride in their constructions and experience a sense of accomplishment. When children are working as a group on blocks, many social skills are practiced, such as sharing and cooperating (Dodge, 1988; Seefeldt & Barbour, 1990).

Dramatic play areas are usually very lively. Teachers can provide props related to specific themes, such as a fast-food restaurant, a hospital, or other community establishments as mentioned previously. Housekeeping and dress-up equipment might also be kept in this area; children can create wonderful dramatic play situations with such materials. By changing the materials occasionally, as was mentioned earlier, the teacher will encourage use of the area (Miller, 1990). A fast-food chain or other community service organization might donate materials that could be used in the dramatic play area.

Noise

Controlled acoustics and comfortable surfaces promote quiet play. The environment for any classroom needs to provide for noisy group activities as well as for quiet individual pursuits. When a classroom is basically box-shaped—with a flat ceiling and a flat floor—then color, texture, and lighting, in addition to acoustical controls, need to be employed to provide the best possible environment for children. Too small a space can interact with noise in such a way that children may react by withdrawing or by increasing physical aggression (Weinstein, 1979).

Equipment Summary

In equipping a child-care center, it is necessary to be clear about its aims. If the center is to emphasize the development and self-fulfillment of the whole child socially, emotionally, physically, and intellectually, this goal will be seen in the center's choice of equipment. Some suggestions include:

Equipment to provide for emotional release
- Messy: finger paint, clay, sand, water, mud
- Creative: paints, posters, scissors, glue
- Pets

Equipment to provide for social development
- Dramatic play and housekeeping corner
- Adequate quantity and kinds of items in high demand, such as telephones, doll buggies, irons, wagons, tricycles

Equipment to provide for physical development
- Large muscle equipment
- Materials that promote sensory experiences
- Facilities for meeting bodily needs

Equipment to provide for intellectual development and stimulation (This category includes all of the above plus some activities specifically aimed at challenging mental growth.)
- Books, puzzles, lotto games
- Puppets, dolls, trucks, blocks
- Science and other subject materials appropriate for early childhood

Room Arrangement

In arranging rooms for children, it is important to remember that children are small, and because in general the world seems just too large to manage, they want to feel stronger, bigger, and more competent. Through imagination and make-believe, children create situations that they can control. A child's problem-solving and creative planning sometimes come from the ability to imagine the idea and to imagine the possible steps to achieving goals. Children need opportunities to think about and weigh the consequences of their actions. To provide for all of these diverse requirements, room arrangement should accommodate the following:

1. Housekeeping/dramatic play
2. Table activities
3. Paints
4. Blocks
5. Equipment for indoor large muscle activity
6. Music
7. Books
8. Science

SCHEDULING

Scheduling to meet the main objectives of the program and its philosophy helps to provide continuity of development and is the backbone, along with planning, of any child development program. Some of the overall considerations to keep in mind include:

- Does the program include large blocks of time for self-directed play?
- Are there only a few times when all the children will be doing the same things at the same time?
- Are there provisions made for children who do not want to listen to a story or participate in music or science activities?
- Are the transitions from one activity to another accomplished smoothly?
- Is the atmosphere relaxed and unhurried?
- Is there a good relationship between the teacher, the aides, and the parents?
- Is there respect for the teacher as the leader?

- Is support provided for the child who needs help with a puzzle? Who needs more suggestions in the block area? Who needs a role in the housekeeping/dramatic play corner? Who needs help sharing and taking turns? Who needs help with the hammer or saw?

Sample Schedules

Child-Care Centers

Child-care centers, which often must plan for a day that begins at 6:30 or 7:00 a.m. and does not end until 6:00 or 6:30 p.m., can benefit from a flexible schedule at the beginning and end of the day. Children often arrive and depart at different times during these flexible transition periods. A possible sample day is shown in Figure 11.1.

Infant and Toddler Programs

With infants and toddlers, it is especially important that a secure attachment bond be allowed to form with one caregiver and that the bond not be ignored or harmed by routinely rotating caregivers. The scheduling may have to be adjusted to accommodate this arrangement. When setting up a schedule, keep in mind that in general, infants set their own schedule and pace; toddlers can follow the all-day sample format shown in Figure 11.1, with provisions for morning and afternoon naps as needed individually. The secure bond that is formed at this particular age lasts a lifetime (Erickson, 1963) and also yields immediate benefits in the child's well-being throughout the year and in the caregiver's retention at the center (Honig, 1993).

Half-Day and Preschool Programs

The traditional preschool half-day program, as shown in the sample schedule in Figure 11.2, does not include a nap, unless an "extended day" program is offered on two or three days a week. In an extended day program, children bring their lunch, have a nap, and participate in additional indoor and outdoor supervised play.

Kindergarten

Kindergarten programs follow a schedule similar to the one for a half-day program, with variations due to the curriculum in the particular school system. Usually an opening group time begins the day. All-day kindergartens sometimes use two classrooms (alternating two groups), setting one room up with subject matter and other centers, and the other room with choosing-time centers (see Figures 11.3 and 11.4). The room arrangements shown in Figures 11.3 and 11.4 contain many useful ideas for other age groups as well.

FIGURE 11.1
Child-Care Sample Schedule

6:30–9:00 a.m.	Welcome time, breakfast, free choice time in the center areas. Provision is made for children who want sleeping time.
9:00–11:30 a.m.	Active play and free choice time including finger plays, stories, songs, and art activities. Toileting and snack provided mid-morning integrated with the activities.
11:30 a.m.–12:00 p.m.	Quieter activities and preparation for lunch (toileting and hand washing).
12:00–1:00 p.m.	Lunch
1:00–3:00 p.m.	Nap and quiet playtime for children who do not take naps or who take short naps.
3:00–3:45 p.m.	Mid-afternoon snack and toileting time.
3:45–6:00 or 6:30 p.m.	Indoor and outdoor supervised play until departure.

FIGURE 11.2
Half-Day Program

9:00–9:30 a.m.	Welcome time, free choice activities with a collage table and a science table in addition to centers as children gather.
9:30–10:30 a.m.	Indoor play with child-selected activities and a teacher-organized art or craft activity (finger painting, making play dough, etc.). Discussions about the theme of the day (week or unit). Toileting begins at the end of this period and clean-up time.
10:30–11:00 a.m.	Snack time with finger plays and conversations. Discussions about food and recent experiences.
11:00–11:45 a.m.	Outdoor play.
11:45 a.m.–12:00 p.m.	Return indoors for story time and preparation to go home. Clean up, reflect on the day's learnings, plan for tomorrow.
12:00 p.m.	Departure time.

FIGURE 11.3
Center-time Room

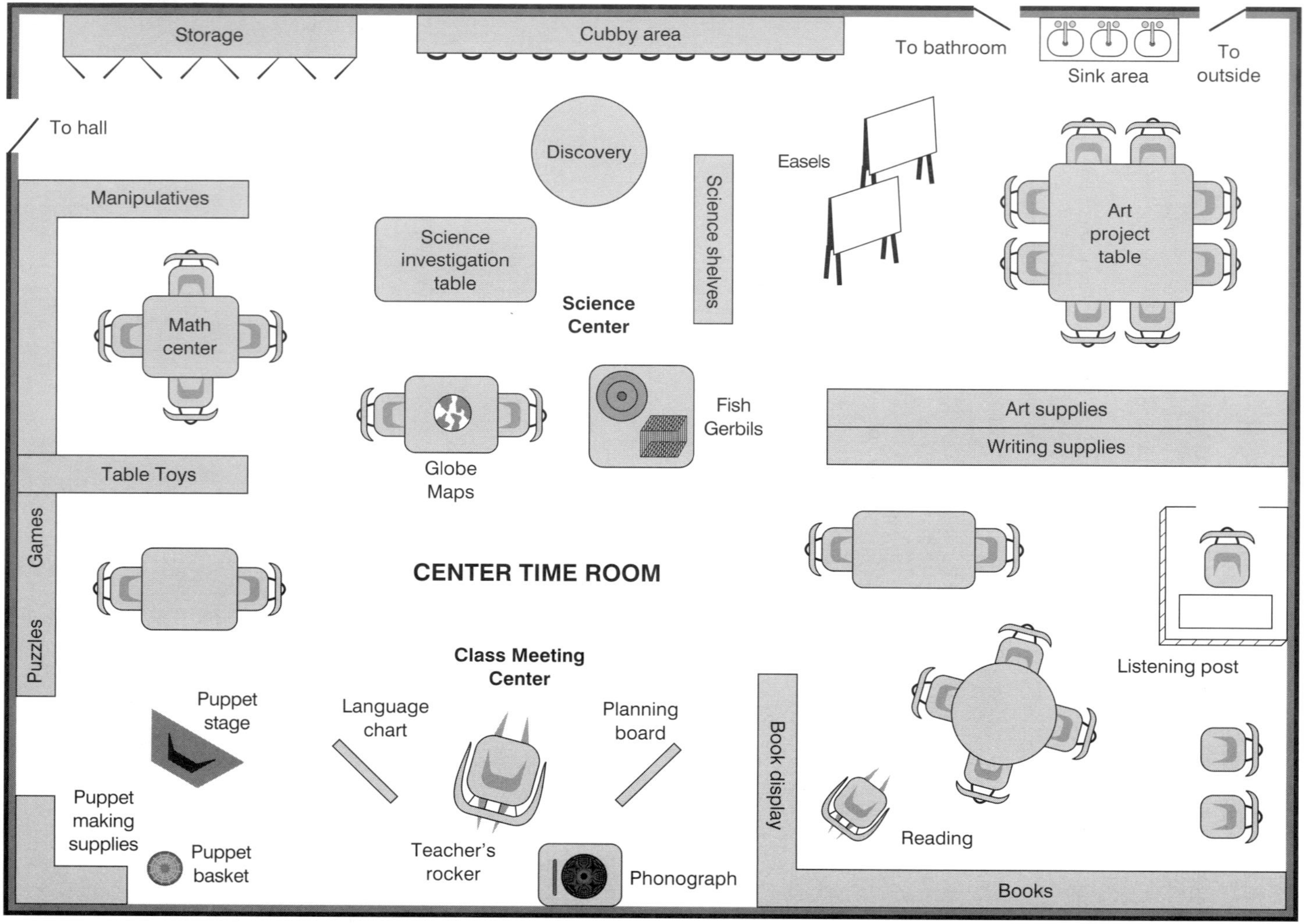

Courtesy of Harriet Hougland.

FIGURE 11.4
Choosing-time Room

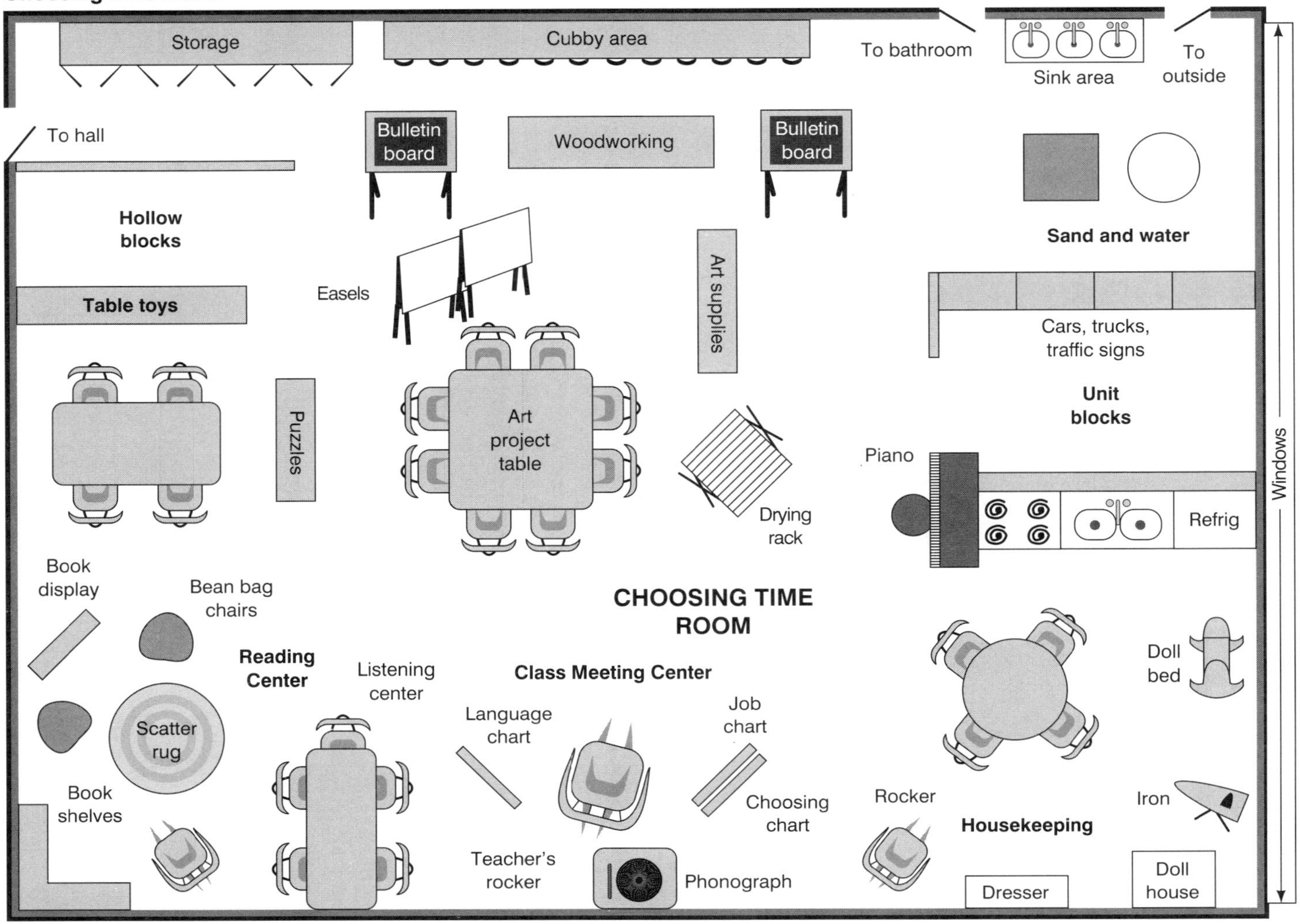

Windows

To outside

Sink area

Sand and water

Cars, trucks, traffic signs

Unit blocks

Refrig

Doll bed

Iron

Doll house

Housekeeping

Dresser

Rocker

Piano

To bathroom

Bulletin board

Drying rack

Art supplies

Woodworking

Cubby area

Easels

Bulletin board

Art project table

CHOOSING TIME ROOM

Job chart

Choosing chart

Class Meeting Center

Language chart

Teacher's rocker

Phonograph

Storage

To hall

Hollow blocks

Table toys

Puzzles

Bean bag chairs

Reading Center

Book display

Scatter rug

Book shelves

Listening center

Courtesy of Harriet Hougland.

209

SUMMARY

How facility spaces, equipment, room arrangement, and scheduling are used is an important subject of discussion with early childhood educators. A program staff may need to discuss several issues related to their particular situation or plans for expansion, such as age grouping versus multi-age grouping, activity grouping versus space available, as well as other issues. As these concerns are discussed among the staff, Board, and parents, a practical (concrete) springboard is developed for learning about what excellent programs for young children might and can include.

As mentioned earlier, the adaptations used to make space, equipment, room arrangement, and schedules work for a particular center can vary over time. Adapting spaces and routines to a particular facility and demographic area creates uniqueness and pride of achievement. As children are nurtured, and so grow and develop, so will a well-run center that is nurtured then grow and develop. To help create a well-run center, the next chapter deals more fully with operational issues such as finances, record keeping, and proposal writing.

BIBLIOGRAPHY

Bingham-Newman, A. M., & Saunders, R. A. (1977). Take a new look at your classroom with Piaget as a guide. *Young Children, 32*(4), 62–72.

Bredekamp, S. (1987). *Developmentally appropriate practice in early childhood programs serving children from birth through age 8*. Washington, DC: National Association for the Education of Young Children.

Cherry, C. (1976). *Creative play for the developing child*. Belmont, CA: David S. Lake.

Christie, J. F., & Wardle, F. (1992). How much time is needed for play? *Young Children, 47*(3), 28–32.

Decker, C. A., & Decker, J. R. (1992). *Planning and administering early childhood programs*. Columbus, OH: Merrill.

Dodge, D. T. (1988). *The creative curriculum for early childhood*. Washington, DC: Teaching Strategies.

Dodge, D. T., & Colker, L. J. (1992). *The creative curriculum for early childhood*. Washington, DC: Teaching Strategies.

Eddowes, E. A. (1991). The benefits of solitary play. *Dimensions, 20*(1), 31–33.

Eisenberg, J., & Jalongo, M. (1993). *Creative expression and play in early childhood education*. New York: Macmillan.

Eisenberg, J., & Quisenberry, N. L. (1988). Play: A necessity for all children. A position paper of the Association for Childhood Education International. *Childhood Education, 64*(3), 138–145.

Elkind, D. (1987). *Miseducation*. New York: Knopf.

Elkind, D. (1989). Developmentally appropriate practice: Philosophical and practical implications. *Phi Delta Kappan, 71*(2), 113–117.

Elliott, S. (1986). The role of the teacher in children's play. In J. S. McKee (Ed.), *Play: Working partner of growth*, pp. 42–46. Wheaton, MD: Association for Childhood Education International.

Erickson, E. H. (1963). *Childhood and society* (2nd ed.). New York: Norton.

Fein, G., & Rivkin, M. (Eds.). (1986). *The young child at play: Reviews of research* (Vol. 4). Washington, DC: National Association for the Education of Young Children.

Harms, T., & Clifford, R. M. (1980). *Early childhood environment rating scale*. New York: Teachers College Press.

Honig, A. S. (1993). Mental health for babies: What do theory and research teach us? *Young Children, 45*(6), 30–35.

Lally, J. R., & Stewart, J. (1990). *A guide to setting up environments*. Sacramento, CA: California Department of Education.

Lodish, R. (1992, May). The pros and cons of mixed-age grouping. *Principal, 71*, 20–22.

Loughlin, C. E., & Suina, J. H. (1982). *The learning environment: An instructional strategy*. New York: Teachers College Press.

Lovell, P., & Harms, T. (1985). How can playgrounds be improved? A rating scale, *Young Children, 40*, 3–8.

McKee, J. S. (1986). Play materials and activities for children birth to 10 years: People, play, props and purposeful development. In J. S. McKee (Ed.), *Play: Working partner of growth*, pp. 15–28. Wheaton, MD: Association for Childhood Education International.

Miller, K. (1990). *More things to do with toddlers and twos*. Chelsea, MA: TelShare Publishing.

Morrison, G. S. (1991). *Early childhood education today*. New York: Macmillan.

Myers, B. K., & Maurer, K. (1987). Teaching with less talking: Learning centers in the kindergarten. *Young Children, 42*(5), 20–27.

Papalia, D. E., & Olds, S. W. (1990). *A child's world: Infancy through adolescence*. New York: McGraw-Hill.

Pattillo, J., & Vaughan, E. (1992). *Learning centers for child-centered classrooms*. Washington, DC: National Education Association of the United States.

Rogers, C. S., & Sawyers, J. K. (1988). *Play in the lives of children*. Washington, DC: National Association for the Education of Young Children.

Rubin, K. H. (1977). Play behaviors of young children. *Young Children, 32*(6), 16–23.

Rubin, K. H., & Howe, N. (1986). Social play and perspective taking. In G. Fein & M. Rivkin (Eds.), *The young child at play. Reviews of research* (Vol. 4), 113–125.

Seefeldt, C., & Barbour, N. (1990). *Early childhood education: An introduction*. New York: Macmillan.

Seifert, K. L., & Hoffnung, R. J. (1991). *Child and adolescent development*. Boston: Houghton Mifflin.

Sherman, G. (1977). *Restructuring a kindergarten classroom to include more developmentally appropriate activities*. (Ed. Dept. Practicum Report). Ft. Lauderdale, FL: NOVA University. (ERIC Document Reproduction Service No. ED 350 097)

Singer, D. G. (1986). Make-believe play and learning. In J. S. McKee (Ed.), *Play: Working partner of growth*, pp. 8–14. Wheaton, MD: Association for Childhood Education International.

Smilansky, S. (1971). Can adults facilitate play in children?: Theoretical and practice considerations. In G. Engstrom (Ed.), *Play: The child strives toward self-realization*, pp. 39–50. Washington, DC: National Association for the Education of Young Children.

Spodek, B., Saracho, O. N., & Davis, M. D. (1987). *Foundations of early childhood education: Teaching three-, four-, and five-year old children*. Englewood Cliffs, NJ: Prentice-Hall.

Stone, J. G. (1970). *Play and playgrounds*. Washington, DC: National Association for the Education of Young Children.

Travers, P. D., & Reborne, R. W. (1990). *Foundations of education: Becoming a teacher*. Englewood Cliffs, NJ: Prentice-Hall.

Trawick-Smith, J. (1992). The classroom environment affects children's play and development. *Dimensions, 20*(2), 27–30, 40.

U.S. Department of Health, Education and Welfare. (1969). *Designing the child development center*. Washington, DC: Author.

Weinstein, C. S. (1979). The physical environment of the school: A review of research. *Review of Educational Research, 35*(49), 577–611.

CHAPTER TWELVE

Finances, Record-Keeping, and Proposal Writing

Much of running a center and keeping its budget "in the black" requires good management practices. In part, good management results from paying close attention to the financial aspects of a center, the record-keeping processes, and any plans for future income that may necessitate proposal writing. Since child-care is essentially a service, qualified personnel is key to a successful center, and more attention is given elsewhere in this book to training and performance objectives for child-care staff. In addition to overseeing the training and performance of staff, however, budgets and records need to be kept, and all these tasks need to be done well. If the responsibilities of maintaining the budget and records are not given to the Director, then a person should be hired especially because he or she has these capabilities. To understand the foundation for the financial part of center operations, this chapter will begin with a start-up plan. A center that is already in operation can adapt the following activities as seems appropriate.

STARTING UP: DEVELOPING A MANAGEMENT PLAN

Many publications and free materials are available to help persons develop a management plan. Local bookstores and the United States Small Business Administration (Washington, D.C., 20416) have these materials. Generally, new businesses are advised to allow at least 6 to 12 months for planning for a start-up. This time provides a chance to meet with interested parents and to form working committees, as described in Chapter 1, for the following areas:

Developing the program philosophy

Setting up bylaws and filing incorporation papers

Purchasing equipment and supplies

Planning for the hiring of teachers/Director

Planning marketing and public relations strategies

Checking on licensing and zoning regulations

External Review

Any start-up plan should carefully review at least three other centers and place the findings on a matrix, as shown in Figure 12.1. Within the matrix, rank each item as better or worse than your own plan, and then note any good ideas or new possibilities that this exercise might yield.

Setting Goals and Establishing a Time Line

Once the external review is complete, there are other important steps that must be taken in a start-up plan: developing a time line to chart beginning and ending dates for various tasks; developing measurable goals and subgoals; establishing an action plan; making allowances for obstacles; and providing for review and resetting of goals. The time line and philosophy for a university child-care center is shown in Appendix D. Most centers, in planning for the 12

FIGURE 12.1
Comparison Matrix

	Equipment	Location	Staff competence and attitudes	Layout
Center A				
Center B				
Center C				
Our center				

months before opening day, will have a time line similar to this one developed by a committee. The time line for 24 to 12 months prior to opening day, which in this case was spent in getting university approvals, would vary with the parent organization and with zoning and other regulations that must be met.

INCOME ISSUES

Much of a center's success in staying "in the black" will depend on how well the organization sets tuition fees and develops the plan for income. If the cost per child is figured so low that the margin of income does not even cover expenses, the center will not be able to build up a surplus for future growth or to cover emergencies. If the cost per child is set too high, in all likelihood the enrollment will fail to meet the income projections. It is hoped that before the center opens, the tuition and other sources of income will have been decided upon, so that the average cost per child that the center expects to maintain will be clear, with adjustments for inflation as needed.

Does the center expect to provide deluxe child care, good-quality child care, or the best possible low-budget child care? Determining which goal the center should aim for will help to decide the best possible location for the center, and will pinpoint which corporate personnel offices should receive information, or where flyers and fact sheets should be distributed. It will also determine, to some extent, the quality of services to be offered, within approved accreditation ranges. Extra programs in a foreign language or a Saturday computer camp may not be desirable for a low-budget program, but may be very appropriate for a deluxe service program. Ideas for this type of program planning are discussed in the chapter on problem-solving.

Additional income from federal, state, or local grants should be planned at this point, always remembering the basic rule: "Don't put all your eggs in one basket." In other words, do not rely on only one grant or even on only a few grants. Grants need to be renewed, and they do get cancelled, so having several funding sources is always wise. To help in applying for grants, a section on proposal writing is included in this chapter. Sending proposals to corporations to suggest educational partnerships is also useful. If a center is to be housed within a corporation, the outline presented in this chapter will give a thorough presentation format for decision-makers in the corporation.

After establishing a tuition and income policy that is synchronized with the program's philosophy and overall developmental goals, the Director must look at the amount of income and the number of enrollees needed to cover expenses and to build a surplus. If the center has been operating for a year or longer, decision-makers can analyze past records and find out the percentage of income needed for operating expenses and the resulting net surplus. This surplus should be in addition to the amount needed to pay off loans taken to start the center. Surplus funds are a necessity for unexpected price increases in supplies and materials, for adding classrooms or teachers, for increasing the hours of operation, or for building more centers.

If the center has just opened, decision-makers will have to estimate the costs and income carefully. A good rule of thumb is to figure the number of enrollees at 10 to 15 percent less than the maximum possible. This underestimating will allow for a surplus in income in good times, and will provide coverage in case of a sudden drop in enrollment. Costs for administration, bookkeeping, tax services, and publicity costs (that is, all of the overhead) should already have been figured into the cost per child on a percentage basis. This planning will help the Director know how many available child-care slots must be filled for the program to maintain a surplus or contingency fund balance.

Not all child-care slots need to have the overhead percentage attached to them, however. A sliding scale is possible if some slots have a higher percentage and some a lower percentage for overhead. If the income is figured too low, though, the resulting additional children may cost more than the center can support. If this occurs and the center does not have substantial outside grants, raising other center prices should be considered. Decision-makers should keep in mind the overall "mark-up" for tuition and the above-cost percentage needed to pay for overhead and to build a surplus, in addition to knowing what competing centers' prices are.

PURCHASING

It may not seem that child-care programs must buy a lot, since they are a service provider, but a great deal must be purchased to keep a center operating for long hours. Keeping a well-stocked supply of equipment, food, and classroom supplies, as well as keeping up with maintenance services such as housekeeping, depend on a buying schedule. This takes careful research into who and where the best vendors are, including how prices and benefits compare.

When to buy deserves attention, as well. Are there preschool and child-care buying cooperatives in the area, or should the center start one in the next five years? Normally, it is better to avoid speculative buying because it interferes with the normal operations of the center's business. (In other words, don't stock up on green paper unless the amount needed for the year is clear!) Speculative buying can lead to losses and storage problems. As soon as enough time has passed to judge, the center can determine how much of a certain material to buy by checking the center's records. Obviously it is important not to overbuy, but it is just as important not to underbuy. If the center does not buy enough food or supplies, these items will not be there when they are needed. To help with these problems of estimating, some records for inventory control are needed. The goal is to keep the inventory in balance—neither too large or too small. There should be a proper proportion and variety both of supplies and food.

While some organizations keep a dollar control system showing the amount of money invested in each category, a unit control record-keeping system is more appropriate for child-care programs. The unit control system tells how much of each item is in the inventory, from whom the items were bought, when orders were placed and when reorders must be made, how much the items cost (receipts), and when the items will be used. These records guide the center in determining what, from whom, when, and how much to buy. A computer spread-sheet software program greatly facilitates this type of record-keeping.

RECORD-KEEPING

Center failures can often be attributed to inadequate records. Every Director needs to be able to foresee impending disaster in time to take corrective action; to develop this kind of foresight, it is important to have records that show trends and highlight possible problems. By keeping up-to-date records, the Director can avoid problems that make it difficult to see in advance the direction in which a center might be headed. It may require extra work to keep adequate records, but this work will be well worth the effort and expense to any center. Many record-keeping tasks can be delegated to an administrative assistant.

When developing a record-keeping system, it is very important to keep records to substantiate the following:

1. Returns filed under federal and state tax laws, including income tax and social security laws;

2. Requests for credit from equipment manufacturers or for bank loans; and

3. Claims about the center, should it become necessary to transfer ownership.

In addition to these records, and perhaps most important, are records that plan for, and outline the distribution of, surplus funds allocated for growth and improvement.

With an adequate yet simple record-keeping system, questions such as the following can be answered:

1. How much are the income and expenses?

2. What are the expenses? Which expenses appear to be too high?

3. What is the center's gross surplus margin; the net surplus?

4. How much are we collecting on our delayed billings (if any)?

5. What is the condition of the working capital?

6. How much cash is on hand and in the bank?

7. How much is owed suppliers?

8. What is the net worth of the center; that is, what is the value of the center when liabilities are subtracted from assets?

9. What are the trends in receipts, expenses, surplus, and net worth?

10. Is the center's financial position improving or growing worse?

11. How do the assets compare with debts owed? What is the percentage of return on the original investment?

12. How many cents out of each dollar of income are net surplus? (Metcalfe, 1973)

By preparing and studying balance sheets and profit-and-loss statements, and by keeping this information in sufficient detail and in an orderly fashion, these and other questions can be answered. The following is a list of records grouped according to their use. Every center will not need every record; perhaps only a few records will be necessary for a particular center. However, these lists may call attention to some records that can be used to great advantage. When deciding which records to use, one should first answer the questions: How will this record be used? How important is the information kept likely to be? Is the information available elsewhere in an equally accessible form?

Inventory and Purchasing Records (These records provide facts to help with buying and selling.)

Inventory control record

Item/unit perpetual inventory record

Out-of-stock sheet

Open-to-buy record

Purchase order file

Supplier file

Accounts payable ledger

Income Records (These records reveal facts to determine income trends.)

Record of monthly/weekly tuition receipts

Summary of monthly/weekly tuition receipts (also quarterly summary and half-year summary)

Promotion plan and plan for dissemination of center information and publicity (to increase income)

Cash Records (These records show what is happening to cash.)

Daily cash reconciliation (tuition receipts and other income)

Cash receipts journal

Cash disbursements journal

Bank reconciliation

Accounts Receivable Records (These records keep track of who owes the center and whether payments are made on time.)

Accounts receivable ledger

Accounts receivable aging list

Employees' Records (These records maintain information legally required and are helpful in the efficient management of personnel.)

Record of employee earnings and amounts withheld

Employees's withholding exemption certificate (Form W-4)

Record of hours worked

Record of expense allowance

Employment applications

Record of changes in rate of pay

Record of reasons for termination of employment

Record of employee benefits

Job descriptions

Crucial incidents records

Fixtures and Property Records (These keep facts needed for taking depreciation allowances and for insurance coverage and claims.)

Equipment records

Insurance register

Bookkeeping Records (These records, in addition to some of those listed previously, are needed if you use a double-entry bookkeeping system.)

General journal

General ledger

For efficient operation, a center needs information from records to watch trends and for tax purposes. Furthermore, centers should use records to plan. With a well-thought-out plan as a guide, chances for success are strengthened. A budget is a record that shows the statistics of such a plan. Working up a budget helps to determine just how much increase in surplus is reasonably within reach. The budget will answer such questions as: What income will be needed to achieve the desired surplus? What fixed expenses will be necessary to support this income? What variable expenses will be incurred? A good budget enables administrators to set goals and then determine what steps to take to reach those goals.

Of course, administrators periodically should compare budget projections with actual operations. Using contingency planning and responsiveness planning (described in Chapter 8) at least quarterly or every six months is also a good idea. With effective records, one can do these comparisons. Then, when discrepancies show up, corrective action may be taken before it is too late. Choosing the right corrective action will depend upon knowledge of management techniques in buying, setting tuition, selecting and training personnel, and handling other management problems as described throughout this text. In addition, the Budget Priorities Worksheet in Figure 12.2 can be a useful staff workshop/orientation tool, or a mid-spring yearly planning tool, to help integrate good ideas with goal development.

PROPOSALS TO HELP YOUR CENTER GROW

Since presenting proposals for many reasons (funding, grants, support) is frequently asked of nonprofit and service organizations, it is hoped that this section will serve as a useful outline. A positive attitude and careful attention to detail are two key ingredients for successful proposal writing.

A well-written proposal describing an idea that will help one's center improve and/or serve more children can be written by following a few guide-

FIGURE 12.2
Budget Priorities Worksheet

Please list all items you would like to see in the budget next fiscal year. This is not a guarantee it will come to pass, but it will help us to give priorities to certain items. Try to give an estimated dollar amount. Thank you.

Item	Price

lines. The first step is to write a letter introducing the idea. As a first submission, most groups or foundations usually want a two- to four-page letter introducing an idea. This letter should cover all the areas of concern that will be addressed at greater length in a later, longer version of the proposal. Other funding sources may require a brief summary as well as the complete proposal or application at the time of submission.

For either length document, at a minimum the following main points must be covered:

1. Why the project should be undertaken. (Why should this organization be awarded funds to do it?)

2. How you will carry out the project's implementation. (What steps will it entail? How will these steps be organized?)

3. How the project will be managed. (What is the staffing? What are the qualifications of staff members? How will they be managed? How will the time line be followed to ensure all intended activities take place?)

4. How the project would fit into what the organization is already doing. (What are the institutional qualifications for doing it? How will other ongoing program activities make for a better project result by serving as (no-cost) resources? This is another way of underscoring the question in number 1.)

In addition to these topics, of course, is the budget. This item must be treated separately because of the many different situations of grantees and grantors. Suffice it to say that it should indeed be included and should match the other items in the document in proportion. For example, with a three-page proposal, a half-page of budget information should be enough to give the reader the general categories of expenditure envisioned, the total amount involved, and some sense of whether the estimates seem reasonable. With a longer proposal, substantially more detail will probably be required.

Why Should the Project be Undertaken?

Regardless of how much administrators know about a potential funding source's interest areas—whether through explicit statements in application guidelines or other means—it is important to lay some general groundwork for establishing the value of the proposed work. This first section of a proposal also serves to introduce the organization making the proposal. By showing an awareness of the context in which it operates, the organization lets the funding source assess its credibility and also, therefore, the project's.

This section of the proposal is often called "Understanding the Problem." This implies that an understanding of the problem or need must be reached, and that this understanding must be mutual. After establishing an understanding of the problem, this section then includes a description of the situation that the proposed project will address. This section might also be titled "Background Statement" or even "Introduction."

At this point, the proposal might include statistics on the number of children in the city and other relevant facts that in concert establish the need for continued provision of the services offered (such as mentioning recent cutbacks in local public programs). If the project proposed involves any improvements in the way services are presently provided, note here the problems that exist, and how the project would resolve them.

To show what the organization's role has been in services to date, it is necessary to describe the organization somewhat in this section. This is the first opportunity to show the reader how important the organization's services have been and thus how important it is that they continue and expand. Note that this is different from the *description* of the organization, which comes later.

In concluding this section, the most effective way to lead the reader into the next section, which describes the project, is to end on a note that brings together the problem described and the organization's ability to address it now. In other words, describe why this organization should be funded to carry out this particular program; let the reader know that this organization can do the job better than anyone else, whatever that job may be. The point to get across, although this language may be too strong, is: "And thus it is clear that our organization is ideally situated to address this pressing need." The final sentence in this section then carries the eager reader into the proposal: "The following section describes exactly how we will carry out this important project."

Description of the Project:
How the Project Will Be Carried Out

This section establishes in the reader's mind whether or not the applicant *should* be allowed to carry out this project. In other words, is the planning sound? Does the project really address the need identified earlier? Has the project been thought through step by step, and described in enough detail to make it clear that the applicant already has some idea of how to cope with problems, should they arise?

Writing this section of the proposal is actually an organization's chance to do this planning. While the idea of the project should be clear before one starts writing, the opportunity presented here to think through the details allows the writer to make it clear to the reader that the applicant can manage the project, and that the project makes sense. This goal is accomplished by the following components:

1. an introductory section that briefly states what the project is, and, if appropriate, describes the theory behind the project;

2. the nuts-and-bolts section (i.e., the rest of this section of the proposal), which shows how this organization will *do* the project; and

3. the descriptions of the elements of the project that are left for more terse presentation in the management plan, which will be discussed in the following section.

There are two basic ways to present how you will *do* the project, and they can be used separately or together. Both require a presentation of some sort of time line for the project—how long the project is expected to last, what important steps happen at what points in the time line, when results (such as reports) can be expected, and so forth. (Some summary of this time line should go in the introduction to this section as well.) The two presentation techniques are 1) by task or activity (or month), and 2) by job or function (e.g., staff positions). Which technique is used depends on the nature of the project. If an organization is seeking funds for ongoing operations, with no major events occurring during the proposed time period, a description of staff activities might best describe the project. It is important that the work be quantified in this section, however—the number of children served by each staff member per month, the number of homes visited, the number of meals served—whatever the project concerns. This permits the reader to get a "feel" for the project and its impact relative to the size of the problem.

The other technique for describing activities is basically chronological—what will happen first, what will happen next, and so forth. This method of description is useful when there are activities that cannot begin until earlier project steps have been completed, such as selecting teaching/testing materials, seeking enrollments through community outreach, and so forth. Planning in this manner is invaluable to the applicant because it helps him or her foresee potential problems if things do not get done in time for other things to start. With this foresight, it becomes possible to develop approaches around these problems, and to adjust the project plan at this stage or to modify one's thinking so that these problems will never arise (or if they do, the applicant can be prepared for them).

Because this element alone does more than any other part of a proposal to convince the reader that an organization knows what it is talking about and that the funding group can have confidence that the organization funded will spend their money wisely, even if the "function" method of describing the project is chosen, the applicant should give examples of possible situations that may arise, or demonstrate how the different staff functions will interrelate. For example, illustrate how outreach and health workers will visit the same families at the same time, or how meetings and parent-home visits will occur in a certain sequence, or whatever. If the proposed project is designed to continue an ongoing service but on an expanded scale, the proposal writer probably should chose the chronological approach of presentation to demonstrate how each new element required will be put in place before services are needed, such as preparing food, expanding space, hiring aides, buying materials, and upgrading record-keeping. Expanding an established center might include adding more slots, hiring senior citizens or teenagers as aides, adding slots for handicapped children, adding a component of the Head Start program in a geographic area previously unserved, or opening a second center across town.

Building the reader's confidence in the applicant's planning ability aids the successful reception of the proposal. It also underscores the applicant organization's value in furthering the funding organization's own objectives. By noting in this section past projects that have been executed by the applicant organization and by mentioning related activities that demonstrate similar management requirements as those now being proposed, the organization can show its suitability for carrying out the proposed project. By providing such examples, the applicant is saying to the reader, "We will do this well because we have a record of doing such things well, and we will continue to do so in the future, whether with your funding or not." This confident attitude tells the reader that this is an organization of merit and stability (Cavenaugh, 1993).

Management Plan

Those who award grants need to have some sense of how a potential recipient is going to spend the money it is given. One way this information can be presented, which reinforces both the plans for project activities and the detailed budget, is in the form of a discussion of management controls. This need not be pages of detailed charts and graphs, but should contain at least the following:

1. A section on staffing, which includes an organizational chart for the project, a brief statement explaining how the project fits into the larger organization administratively, and, for each staff position, a description of the duties of the position. For professional staff, enclose a description of the person you plan to hire to fill each position. Resumés should also be included, appended to the end of this section.

2. A project time line (if appropriate). Here a chart similar to the one shown in Figure 12.3 might be helpful. In this chart, months are listed across the top and activities are listed down the side. Horizontal lines of appropriate length are used to indicate when each activity occurs and how long it is expected to last.

FIGURE 12.3
Project Time Line Example

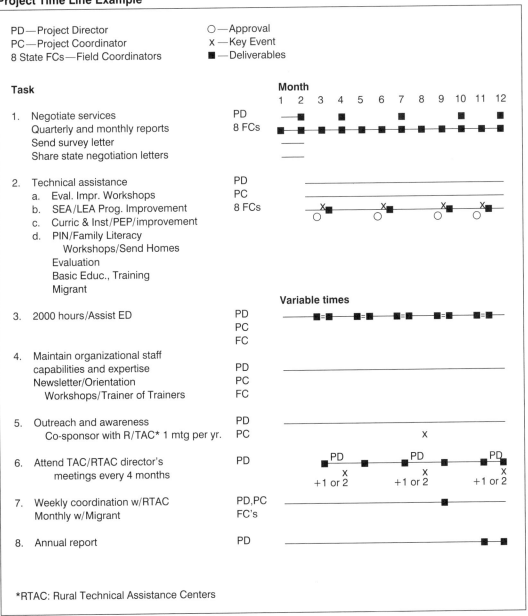

3. A second section on staffing that describes when different staff positions begin and end, if these time frames are different from the start and end of the project period. Also indicate which positions are part-time and which are full-time. This staffing section also can be shown in chart form, with months across the top, positions down the side, and horizontal lines depicting the active periods of each position. This type of visual planning can help in arranging short-term services, such as the hiring of testing consultants, and can, when used with the earlier project activities time line, give you a better idea of which months will be your busiest! (At this point, for example, you can begin saying, "Oh, that falls too close to the Christmas holidays; let's change it." Other conflicts and time pressures become apparent when using this tool to consider how the project fits in with the world going on around it.)

Institutional Qualifications

The last section of a proposal presents a fuller description of the applicant's organization, and is less specifically oriented to the particular project being proposed than is any other section. This section might be similar in a number of proposals. Here the applicant might

1. give a brief history of the organization, citing its growth in the number of services provided since it was formed;
2. mention significant qualifications of staff members other than those who will be working on the proposed project directly, pointing out their value as resources to the project;
3. describe other areas of work the organization is involved in, whether related to the proposed project or not; and
4. list some specific past projects, including, where appropriate, the funding agencies and the names and phone numbers of contact people within those agencies who documented the work. Depending on your organization's size and scope, this could be a lengthy list; while it need not be exhaustive, it should provide several different references that can be contacted—three to eight independent sources connected to an organization's more recent projects is sufficient.

SUMMARY

If a funding application covers all four areas discussed in this chapter, a potential supporter will gain a good idea of who an organization is, what it wants to do, why the project should be done, and how the organization proposes to do it. After such a proposal has been compressed into a three-page letter, along with the all-important budget—the heart of the matter, the only thing left is to close with, "We await your early reply and are eager to begin this important project. Thank you for your consideration. Sincerely yours," etc. The proposal format given in this chapter, including the materials listed and in the appropriate sequence, almost ends on this note automatically, with or without the final reminder.

When planning to prepare an application for funding, allow enough time (working backward from the due date to the time you *should* start and the time you *must* start) to cover all of the points described in this chapter. Very few funding applications are successful, and most of those rejected are done so because they lack completeness. There is no reason to suffer this fate, especially considering that in choosing to prepare such an application, time must be invested that takes time away from one's other duties and responsibilities. To justify the time spent, the proposal should therefore at least be complete.

A shorthand way of keeping all of these proposal sections in mind, and of remembering that one is competing for money against other organizations so that one must persuasively argue one's case, is the following:

I.   Understanding the Problem

We know all about this.

II.   Description of the Project

We will do this project exactly like successful ones should be done, only better, because we know so much about the problem. (See section I.)

III.   Management Plan

We'll plan; we'll manage.

IV.   Institutional Qualifications

We have been doing this for years. (See section I.)

Of these reminder comments, only the one under section III should be taken as tongue-in-cheek: It seems to say merely that "we'll get by," and foundations and agencies certainly do not want to fund that sort of casualness! View this comment instead as a reminder that there *must* be planning and management control evident in and discussed in your application.

The process of making group decisions involving one's staff and parents, and of then writing down the ideas and illustrating them with a time line (preferably also in a group situation), is a useful planning device even if no funding source is involved. The budget and record-keeping sections at the beginning of this chapter further facilitate this planning. Many of the ideas provided in the scenario section in Chapter 8 will generate income on their own. However, if there are national, state, or community funding sources that might be interested in the project or in part of it, add Steps I and IV from the previous outline to develop a more complete proposal. The following Proposal Development Guide is offered as a further aid. Both sets of guidelines were developed by persons who have separately been awarded several million dollars for their organizations in early childhood, education, and human services fields.

Proposal Development Guide

This guide has been prepared to assist in preparing technically valid, fundable proposals.

Answer all questions that apply to the program.

Include all supportive and illustrative materials available.

Anyone who reads the proposal should clearly understand the program purpose, the plan to operate, what the objectives are, and what will occur on a day-to-day basis.

A. *TITLE*
   Name of the program.

B. *SPONSOR*
   1. Name of the sponsoring agency, organization, or group.
   2. Name and title of responsible person.
   3. Brief outline of sponsor's background as to type of agency, organization, or group; include any activities sponsor may now participate in or programs currently operated by sponsor.

C. *BACKGROUND AND OVERVIEW* (including needs assessment)
   Support the request for funds for the program being applied for.

D. *CHARACTERISTICS OF POPULATION TO BE SERVED*
   1. Who is this program expected to reach?
   2. Outline eligibility requirements (if any).
   3. How many persons will be served during the first year of operation?

E. *PROGRAM MISSION* (Purpose)
   What is the purpose of the program?

F. *STATEMENT OF THE PROBLEM*
   Why is the program needed? Be sure to state specific problems involved.

G. *PROGRAM OBJECTIVES* (Planned activities to fulfill mission)
   What are the specific objectives of the program? (What is it you are trying to do?)

H. *LOCATION* (include map)
   1. What are the geographical boundaries of the total area to be served?
   2. Indicate the census tracts.
   3. Indicate on a map prospective site(s) where program is expected to operate (include addresses when possible).

I. *PROGRAM OPERATION*
   Describe in detail how the program will operate. The following questions will assist you.

How will the program operate?

How is the operation related to the objectives of the program?

How will the program work in relation to staff members?

How will the program work for the population to be served?

How will the program work in relation to the other activities, if any, of the sponsor?

J. *RESIDENT PARTICIPATION*
1. What part do residents play in the operation of your present organization? Parents? Parent-Residents?
2. What part did residents have in developing the plans for this program?
3. Describe other ways in which local residents will be involved (subcommittees, local corporations, etc.).

K. *ADMINISTRATION*
1. How is this program administered?
Briefly describe the staff structure and the role of the policy-making and advisory boards involved in running the program.
2. How will the program be connected to other community programs operated in the same neighborhood(s)?
3. Include two organizational charts, each of which clearly illustrates the supervisory relationships (1) of the staff and (2) of the policy-making and advisory boards.

L. *PERSONNEL*
1. List each staff position and furnish a detailed job description for each job title (include non-professionals, aides, volunteers, etc.). Be as specific and complete as possible.
Follow this outline:
a. Job title:
b. Reports to:
c. Supervises:
d. Duties and responsibilities
e. She/he would work closely with:
f. Qualifications necessary for the job:
2. Volunteers—Give the following information:
a. Title of staff persons who will be assigned to supervise volunteers. (This responsibility should be included in the position description for this person.)
b. Title of staff person who is assigned responsibility for the administrative collecting and reporting of volunteer time. (This responsibility should be included in the position description for this person.)

    c.   Approximate number of volunteers and volunteer hours planned, per month, for this program.

    d.   What responsibilities and duties, and in what components of your program, will volunteers be assigned?

    e.   How do volunteer activities implement your program operation and objectives?

3.   Guidelines for training:

In preparing proposals for programs to be funded, you should be aware that most proposal readers, in reviewing requests for funding, will consider whether an adequate program of staff training will be conducted during the grant period.

Therefore, include in proposals a brief outline of plans for an in-service training program. This training program should be designed to:

a.   improve the ability of staff to relate; and

b.   increase the technical skills needed by staff to work at maximum capacity.

As part of the process of developing an in-service training program, an in-service training committee should be established. This committee should be broadly representative of staff, including both professional and non-professional employees.

In the proposal, training plans for the following three groups should be discussed separately:

a.   Office and clerical workers;

b.   Non-professional employees; and

c.   Professional staff.

Please indicate also the resources on which you plan to rely for training (e.g., your own professional staff, consultants).

Training plans that comprise only routine supervision or weekly staff meetings will not be acceptable. Training time need not necessarily be extended evenly throughout the grant period. If desirable, it may be concentrated within a relatively short period, e.g., daily for several weeks. College courses and requirements for taking them can be listed in this section.

M. *BUDGET*

Use the worksheet in Appendix D (p. 474) in preparing the budget for this program. Special things to look for are the following:

1.   In "Personnel," *fringe benefits* should be computed. Breakdown percentages of fringe components (FICA, health insurance, etc.).

2.   In "Travel," local travel should be based on actual *need*; any out-of-town travel must be justified in a budgetary footnote.

3. In "Space costs and rentals," write in the actual cost and actual square footage wherever possible.
4. In "Consumable supplies:"
   a. *Office supplies*—budget on a per person, per annum formula based on actual cost.
   b. Postage.
   c. *Publications*—to be kept to an absolute minimum.
   d. *Non-federal share* (for federal funding)—The amount of non-federal share to support the proposed program must be at least 20% of the total program cost. This 20% may be in the form of cash (to pay for some specific budget item, e.g., personnel, equipment, consultant services, etc.), or use of volunteers, donations of free use of space, equipment, etc. All non-federal share items must be itemized in the budget and become a part of the total program costs.
5. In "Equipment," determination on the basis of anticipated need:
   a. determine what equipment is owned;
   b. determine what equipment is rented, the monthly rental, and the feasibility of purchasing; and
   c. estimate the cost of servicing machines.
6. In "Other costs:"
   a. *Telephone:* Cost should be estimated on a per person formula based on actual cost experience.

N. *EVALUATION*
   1. How will this program be evaluated?
   2. Who will conduct the evaluation?
   3. What type of information will be gathered?
   4. How do you expect program evaluation to affect program operation?

O. *PLANS FOR NEXT YEAR* (usually used for refunding)
   1. What modifications will be made in the present programming and operation?
   2. What new methods, approaches, or components will be added to help achieve program objectives?
   3. What old methods, approaches, or components will be discontinued? Why?
   4. What staff changes, if any, will be needed because of program change or modification? (Fowler, 1982)

BIBLIOGRAPHY

Assistance with child care expenses. (1990, May). *Employees Benefit Plan Review*, pp. 21–22.

Auerback, J. D. (1988). *In the business of child care*. New York: Praeger.

Ballenger, J., & Franklin, G. M. (1991). Perceptions of rural small business owners and managers toward child care assistance. *Proceedings Small Business Institute Directors Association*, pp. 148–153.

Berney, K. (1988, May). Child care by consortium. *Nation's Business*, p. 23.

Bredekamp, S. (Ed.). (1987). *Developmentally appropriate practice in early childhood programs serving children from birth through age 8*. Washington, DC: National Association for the Education of Young Children.

Cavenaugh, D. N. (1993). *Personal interview*. Washington, DC: National Association of Community Health Centers.

Cherry, C., Harkness, B., & Kuzma, K. (1987). *Nursery school & day care center management guide*. Belmont, CA: Fearon Teacher Aids (a division of David S. Lake Publishers).

Clay, J. M. (1989, September). The child care issue: Benefits required by a changing workforce. *Employee Benefits Journal*, pp. 32–34.

Early childhood teacher education: Traditions and trends. (1988). *Young Children, 44*(1), 53–57.

Fowler, A. (1982). *How to write a proposal*. Speech given at the Administering Day Care and Preschool Seminar, July 14, 1982, Trinity College, Washington, DC.

Galinsky, E. (1989). The staffing crisis. *Young Children, 44*(2), 1–4.

Galinsky, E., & Friedman, D. (1986). *Investing in quality child care: A report to AT&T*. Basking Ridge, NJ: AT&T.

Gotts, E. E. (1988). The right to quality child care. *Childhood Education, 64*, 268–275.

Hildebrand, V. (1984). *Management of child development centers*. New York: Macmillan.

Huth, S. A. (1989, September). Corporations provide variety of child care options. *Employee Benefit Plan Review*, pp. 49–51.

Leavitt, R. L., & Krause-Eheart, B. (1985). Maintaining quality and cost effectiveness through staffing patterns. *Child Care Information Exchange, 45*, 31–35.

Levin, R. (1989, January). Child care: Inching up the corporate agenda. *Management Review*, pp. 49–51.

Metcalfe, W. O. (1973). Starting and managing a small business. In *Starting and Managing Series* (Vol. I). Washington, DC: U. S. Small Business Administration.

Morgan, G. (1987). *The national state of child care regulations*. Watertown, MA: Work Family Directions.

Morgan, G. G. (1982). *Managing the day care dollars: A financial handbook*. Cambridge, MA: Steam Press.

National Association of State Boards of Education. (1988). *Right from the start: The report of the NASBE task force on early childhood education*. Alexandria, VA: Author.

Need for child care. (1988, August). *Supervision*, pp. 10–11.

Overman, S. (1990, August). Plant workers, families find not all time created equal. *HR Magazine*, p. 38.

Overman, S. (1990, August). Wizards program work-family solutions. *HR Magazine*, pp. 40–41.

Overman, S. (1990, August). Workers, families cope with retail's irregular schedules. *HR Magazine*, p. 44.

Peters, T. J., & Waterman, R. H. (1982). *In search of excellence*. New York: Harper & Row.

Ritter, A. (1990, March). Dependent care proves profitable. *Personnel*, pp. 12–16.

Schweinhart, L. J., Koshel, J. J., & Bridgman, A. (1987). Policy options for preschool program. *Phi Delta Kappan, 68*, 534–530.

Snow, C. (1983, November). *As the twig is bent: A review of research on the consequences of day care with implications for caregiving.* Paper presented at the Annual Conference of the National Association for the Education of Young Children, Atlanta, GA.

Travis, N., & Perreault, J. (1981). *Day care financial management: Considerations in starting a for-profit or not-for-profit program.* Atlanta, GA: Child Care Support Center.

Home Learning Enablers

This 14-week supply of activities is ideal for building parent involvement. All activities utilize common household items if any materials are needed. These Home Learning Enablers will help parents learn, with a minimum of effort, new ways of talking and interacting with their children; in addition, parents can learn these skills with little guidance from teachers. The activities are specific, sequenced from less difficult to more difficult, and related to the curriculum: three factors found to be of top importance in maintaining the gains early childhood programs work so hard to achieve. The activities can be sent home with children and feedback sheets can be returned to the center in the same way. Teachers then can review returned feedback sheets to see which areas of learning might need further emphasis, and to review parents' comments.

Parent Involvement

In a review of 28 studies, it was found that in order to *maintain* the gains young children made in early childhood programs, parent involvement was a must. It was also found that if parents were given specific, curriculum-related activities in a sequence, these gains were maintained the most effectively. The following Home Learning Enabler (HLE) activities will help you provide just such a service to your parents (and your children), and also will help to ensure that the efforts made at your center to really help children will have a lasting effect.

The following five features were evident in the 28 programs that showed immediate and lasting gains for children due to parent involvement:

1. The importance of the teacher-to-parent instruction phase in building trust.
2. The curricular emphasis in materials used for home teaching.

3. The ratio of parent to teacher for instruction in home teaching activities (one-to-one was best).

4. The structure (or sequence) of the home teaching activities, from easier to harder, was found to be of top importance for the most stable gains.

5. The specificity or detail and definition of the home teaching activities.

The Home Learning Enabler series involves numbers two, four, and five of these features that help guarantee lasting effectiveness. Building trust in one-to-one situations also occurs in most good centers.

We are particularly proud of the Home Learning Enablers Set I; in a recent study of 127 three-year-old children (60 treatment children and 67 control children), the Home Learning Enablers were linked to significant IQ increases for those children who used them compared to those who did not, at the 95 percent confidence level. Our research showed gains of 1 to 36 IQ points for children using Home Learning Enablers Set I. The Stanford Binet IQ test was given to all of the 127 children before and after the 14-week period, during which time the treatment children received the HLE activities. We found that children gained in IQ scores if the parents only did a few of the activities. We are projecting similar gains for children who use HLE Set II, which is meant for four- and five-year-olds, and similar but less dramatic gains for children in kindergarten, first, and second grades. These activities can be used as "send-homes" in school-age child-care programs, as well as by schools.

The Home Learning Enablers are an attempt to encourage home learning by providing instructional materials in the homes of children to prepare them for later school achievement. This goal is an outgrowth of studies done by Levenstein (1975), which suggested that if mothers were given an attractive, relatively simple tool to help their children learn, these mothers in turn assumed some responsibility for their preschool children's verbal growth.[1] A relatively inexpensive form of encouraging parents' interaction with their own children is sending home, weekly, one-page Home Learning Enabler activities that suggest brief, enjoyable parent-child interactions in the home. Learning then occurs in the reciprocal process between parent and child, which is the heart of this program.

There is obviously a need for bridging the gap between the formalized learning that occurs in educational program settings and the informal learning opportunities that parents can take advantage of at home. If educators need instructional materials, it is reasonable to assume that parents need materials too. Additionally, there seems to be a need to encourage more parent-child interaction and verbal communication. Thus, the home learning activities described in this appendix are designed to encourage verbal responses between parent and child.

---

1. Levenstein, P. (1975). *The Mother-Child Home Program*. New York: Carnegie Corp.

Home Learning Enablers: Set I

After Home Learning Enabler activities were developed, they were tested weekly by parents and their children who were enrolled in federally funded day-care centers in Maryland. As a result, the parents became actively involved with their children, and returned feedback sheets even in centers that previously did not have a strong parent involvement program. The following is a copy of one of the feedback sheets received from a parent. It is designed so that parents can tear off the form along the perforation and return it to their child's teacher.

- -

For: ___*Kimberly Peters*___
(Child's Name)

1. Did you or someone else do the activity with the child?   Yes ____ No ____

   If yes,

2. How many times did you do the activity?   Once ___   More than once _*2*_

3. How much time did the activity take?   - - - - - _✓_ - - - - - - -
                                              0   15 mins.   More
                                                                         than
                                                                         30 mins.

4. Did you enjoy this activity with your child?   Yes _✓_ No ____

5. Do you feel your child understood it?   Yes _✓_ No ____

6. Do you feel your child needs more help in this area?   Yes ____ No _✓_

7. Please share any adaptation you may have of this activity, or describe a new activity. (Write on the back, if necessary.)
   Thanks for cooperating!

___*Julia A. Griffith*___   ___*Mrs. Hall*___
Signature   Teacher's Name

Kim especially enjoyed the game.
Especially when played to the tune
of the "Mulberry Bush."

As mentioned before, the activities in HLE Set I are appropriate for children who are older two-year-olds or young three-year-olds through age four and a half. Set II is developed for young four-year-olds through age five and a half. This appendix includes a complete set of activities for ages three through second grade. Feedback sheets similar to the one shown should be included on the back of every activity sent home. (See p. 284 for a blank copy.)

The step-by-step Home Learning Enablers are unique in that they utilize household objects as systematic instructional materials. This has proven to be an easy, inexpensive mechanism for involving parents. Although this program was pilot tested in Maryland, it easily could be applied nationwide.

A distinct sequence is followed in each activity. First, the *name* of the activity gives the parent a hint as to the content, and is usually colloquial if at all possible. The *"Reason"* section tells the objective or purpose of the activity and provides a line or two of explanation about what the activity teaches. An attempt is made here to be as specific as possible without using educational jargon, long words, or long sentences. Activities have been purposefully written at an eighth-grade reading level.

The *"What You Need"* section lists needed materials. These lists are meant to suggest items that are simple, inexpensive, and already available in the home. Another unique feature of these Enablers is the *"Time Needed"* section, in which the time requirement is always shown clearly; beginning activities, especially, are kept short, about 3 to 10 minutes each. Parents are tired after a day's work, and three-, four-, five-, six-, and seven-year-olds have short attention spans. The activities have been timed, so they are as close in approximation to the time listed as possible.

The *"What To Do"* section gives a simple step-by-step approach to the activity. An effort is made to be brief and clear in this section. The *"Did It Work?"* section provides the parent with some evaluation information by describing observable signs of the success of the Enabler activity. Finally, the *"Easier and Harder Ideas"* section provides ways to adapt the activity by making fairly minor changes. An easier adaptation for younger children is provided in number 1, and a harder adaptation for older or more able children is given in number 2. These ideas also encourage parents and children to creatively adapt Enabler activities and then share these suggestions with the teacher.

Sending Home HLEs

Classroom teachers should send home with every child an HLE each week, along with a cover letter/feedback sheet, perhaps using a safety pin to fasten the activity to the child's clothing. The parents will have seven days to do the activity with their children, one or more times, before returning the feedback sheet and receiving another activity. Participation each week, as well as the degree of participation, is entirely voluntary on the part of parents.

Return of the Feedback Sheets

Children will return the tear-off feedback sheet to their classroom teacher. If the original copy is lost, parents can complete another copy of the feedback sheet either at home or in the classroom. Teachers then review the feedback sheets to see which areas of learning might need further emphasis. Centers that have used the Enablers have found that many parents take pride in checking the blank stating that their child does NOT need more help in that particular area. Parents also write in other interesting and useful comments that build the communication link between parent and teacher.

My Homework

Reason

To help your child understand that many things can be red

What You Need

Anything red in your home or outside

Time Needed

3 to 5 minutes any time

What To Do

1. Talk about 3 or 4 things that are red: a toothbrush, a stop sign, a plastic toy, a book, etc.
2. Ask your child which things are red. Tell the child that this is his or her "red" homework.
3. Do this for several days until the child can always correctly tell you what is red. Then go on to "green" homework.

Age of Child

2, 3, 4

Did It Work?

Can your child name things that are red, even if they are quite different, for example, a bowl and a chair? If not, do "red" homework some more.

Easier and Harder Ideas

1. Go on to do other colors, but always do just one color at a time.
2. Ask your child to point out the color red in storybook pictures or magazines. Have your child look for red in the American flag, in other flags, or in cars or trucks.
3. Give your child a red object to keep.

"red!"

Stacking Cans

Reason

To help your child develop eye-hand coordination

What You Need

2 groups of 3 matching cans: soup cans, tuna fish cans, soda cans, or any cans that are not too heavy

Time Needed

3 to 5 minutes

What to Do

1. Put all the cans in front of the child.
2. Build a bridge with three of the cans. Then say, "Look, I made a bridge."
3. Ask your child to make a bridge. If you have more sets of cans, he or she can make towers on top of the bridge if he or she wants.
4. Make bridges out of other matching items, such as throw pillows, cereal boxes, pudding boxes, or empty milk cartons.

Age of Child

2, 3, 4

Did It Work?

Does the bridge hold up or fall down?

Easier and Harder Ideas

1. Make a set of blocks for your child from empty milk cartons that have been washed out. Stuff them with crumpled newspaper and tape the pointed ends down flat. Perhaps a brother or sister might help by doing a few each week. Keep the blocks in a box or a paper bag.
2. Let your child glue grocery boxes together for a permanent "bridge," and then run cars or have dolls walk over it.

Flower Power

Reason

To help children use words to describe things they see and smell

What You Need

Flowers in a garden, a supermarket, or a floral shop

Time Needed

5 minutes

What to Do

1. Ask your child to choose a flower to smell.
2. Ask her to put her nose close to the flower, close her eyes, and smell the flower.
3. Ask your child to tell you what it smells like. (Like Grandma? Like perfume? Is there no smell?)
4. Ask your child to compare the smells of two different flowers. Talk about the colors of the flowers. Are any yellow? Red? etc.
5. Talk to your child about why people give flowers to each other: To show love and caring, to celebrate special events, etc.

Age of Child

3, 4

Did It Work?

Can your child use more and more words to tell you about flower smells or other smells?

Easier and Harder Ideas

1. Help your child gather a bunch of real flowers to give to a friend, neighbor, or relative. (Dandelions are fine.) Let her draw a flower picture for the gift if no flowers are available. Flower pictures from magazines could also be used. Paste them on cardboard or paper.
2. Help your child decorate cookies to look like flowers. Smell things in the kitchen and talk about what the smells remind you of. Does mustard remind you of hot dogs and picnics?

Outdoor Fun Bag

Reason

To help your child learn by using the senses to touch and feel and talk about nature items found outdoors

What You Need

Paper lunch bags or grocery bags

Time Needed

5 to 10 minutes

What to Do

1. Explain that together you will collect rocks, leaves, and sticks.
2. Go for a walk and fill the bags. Talk about the trees from which leaves have come.
3. Talk about other things you see outside. Does an airplane fly over? Do you hear a truck? Talk about these and other things you see and hear.

Age of Child

3, 4, 5

Did It Work?

Could the child tell you the names of leaves, sticks, and rocks (that is, call a leaf a "leaf," a stick a "stick," and a rock a "rock")?

Easier and Harder Ideas

1. Did you see any animals on your walk? Talk about them.
2. Go for another walk and look for different nature items: acorns, smooth rocks, weeds.
3. Make a collage by gluing the nature items on a piece of paper. Give it as a gift to someone special.

Jump, Hop, Skip

Reason

To help your child listen more carefully

What You Need

Nothing

Time Needed

3 to 5 minutes

What to Do

1. Tell your child you are going to play a game. Ask him to listen carefully while you (or another child) hop on one foot, then jump on two feet.
2. Ask him to close his eyes. Then you (or the other child) hop or jump a second time. Ask him to tell you if he heard hopping or jumping.
3. Ask him to hop and jump while you have your eyes closed. Tell him what he is doing.
4. Add a skip for a third sound for him to name.
5. Ask him to close his eyes while you make other sounds for him to describe. Then reverse roles and let him do this for you.

Age of Child

3, 4

Did It Work?

Can your child tell you correctly what motion you are making?

Easier and Harder Ideas

1. While you are in your car, ask your child to close his eyes. Then tap on the steering wheel. Ask him to guess what you did. Tell him the words for noises he can't describe. At home tap a spoon on a glass or plate to play the same game.
2. Jump or clap several times and have your child tell you the number of times you jumped or clapped. Or, jump or hop to demonstrate an addition problem for him to solve (for example, 2 + 2). Let him do one for you.

Circle Time

Reason

To help children recognize the basic shapes of a circle or square

What You Need

2 grocery bags, crayon or marker

Time Needed

5 to 10 minutes

What to Do

1. Lay out the grocery bag. Draw a circle on it.
2. Ask your child to draw a circle on her grocery bag. Ask the child to draw more circles.
3. Talk about which circles are big and which are small.
4. Talk about other things in the room that are in the shape of circles, such as plates, glasses, or cans.
5. Draw a square on your bag. Ask her to draw a square too. Use a new bag, or turn over the circle bag if needed.
6. Talk about other squares, such as a table, a box, or a piece of paper. Which squares are big? Which are small?

Age of Child

3

Did It Work?

Can the child make a mark that looks anything like a circle? A square? Can she identify and talk about objects that are these shapes?

Easier and Harder Ideas

1. Buy crackers shaped like circles, squares, and triangles. Let the child spread peanut butter, jam, or butter on them. Play a matching game with the shapes to make sandwiches. Use cut up bread if crackers are not available.
2. Cut shapes out of paper and ask your child to match them. Start with circles and squares. Then add triangles and rectangles.

Learning from Water

Reason

To help your child learn math words and phrases such as *how much*, *too much*, *half full*, *part full*, *needs more*, and *full*

What You Need

Tub of bath water or kitchen sink with 2 or 3 inches of water in it;
5 or 10 plastic cups, bottles, and measuring cups

Time Needed

5 or 10 minutes

What to Do

1. Gather plastic cups, bottles, measuring cups, and a plastic pitcher if you have one.
2. Ask your child to pour water from one cup into another until the second cup is *full*.
3. If water spills out of the container, explain that it was *too much* water. If he fills it *part full* or *half full*, tell him that.
4. Ask your child *how much* water is in another cup. Then ask if it *needs more* to be *full*.
5. Do these steps as many times as your child wants to.

Age of Child

2, 3

Did It Work?

Can your child tell you when a cup is *full*? When there is *too much*?

Easier and Harder Ideas

1. Ask your child to tell you which bottles are large and which bottles are small.
2. Using measuring cups, ask your child how many 1/4 cups it takes to fill 1 cup. (With spilling, it may take more than 4, but the process is still fun.) How many 1/2 cups to fill 1 cup?

"Put Away" Words

Reason

To help your child match words with objects

What You Need

Bag of grocery items

Time Needed

3 to 5 minutes

What to Do

1. Tell your child that together you are going to put the groceries away while using words to tell about the items.
2. Describe an item to your child; for example, "find a can with red on it," or "find a big box of soap." Ask your child to bring the item to you *while* describing it; for example, "this is a can of chicken soup," or "this soap is for washing clothes."
3. Repeat the activity for other items.
4. Ask your child to group together items that look alike. Then identify the grouped items for your child: "Oh, I see you have two cans of beans."

Age of Child

3

Did It Work?

Can your child tell you the names of more grocery items than before?

Easier and Harder Ideas

1. Let your child tell you items to put away.
2. At mealtime, talk about the foods that are being served. Talk about who likes them, and whether you use a fork or knife or spoon to eat them.

Laundry Lotto

Reason

To help your child notice when things are alike or different

What You Need

Laundry that needs sorting

Time Needed

5 or 10 minutes

What to Do

1. Explain how to match two laundry items such as two towels.
2. Let your child match other laundry items, such as tee shirts, handkerchiefs, underwear, or socks.
3. Ask your child to match some laundry items by color.
4. Ask your child to make a separate pile of clothes for each member of the family.

Age of Child

3

Did It Work?

Can your child match some laundry items correctly?

Easier and Harder Ideas

1. Put out sets of objects such as two forks and a spoon or table knife; two plates and a cup; or two sticks and a rock. Talk about which things are alike and which are different in each set. Ask your child to hand you the item that is different.
2. Let your child sort and match some nickels, pennies, and dimes. Buttons can also be used by letting your child sort colored buttons from white buttons.

Stairs and Chairs

Reason

To help your child learn the meanings of some new words and to help your child learn to follow and give directions

What You Need

Some stairs, either indoors or out; a chair; an object, such as a rock or a stick or toy, to place on the stairs or on the chair

Time Needed

5 to 10 minutes

What to Do

1. Ask your child to go *up* the stairs.
2. Ask your child to go *down* the stairs.
3. Ask your child to walk *across* one stair.
4. Ask your child to stand *in front of* the stairs.
5. Ask your child to place an object *on top of* a stair.
6. Now use the chair and ask your child to sit *on* the chair and then get *under* the chair. Next, ask your child to put an object *in back of* the chair and then walk *around* the chair.

Age of Child

2, 3

Did It Work?

Can your child follow the directions at least part of the time?

Easier and Harder Ideas

1. Trade places with your child and let him direct you.
2. Ask an older child to count the stairs. When the child can do that, give him more difficult directions, such as "go up four steps and come back down two"; "go up one step, walk across it, and then go up three more"; etc. Place a small reward on the stairs.

The Three Bears

Reason

To help your child learn new words; to help her tell a story; to help her enjoy doing things with an adult

What You Need

Any story book that repeats words a lot, such as "Goldilocks and the Three Bears," "The Three Little Pigs," "The Three Billy Goats Gruff," or others

Time Needed

5 or 10 minutes

What to Do

1. Read one of the stories to your child. Stop before the most familiar lines and let the child say the words with you: "Someone's been eating my porridge!" "Who's been sleeping in my bed?"

2. Say the words in different tones of voice. For example, use a deep voice for the father, a squeaky and high voice for the baby. Let your child say the words in the same voice that you use.

3. Stop more frequently while reading the story. As you stop, let your child repeat the line with you.

4. When your child knows the words alone, let her say them alone.

Age of Child

3, 4, 5

Did It Work?

Does your child ask to have the stories read over and over? Can she say some of the words with you?

Easier and Harder Ideas

1. Read other books with your child. Always have your child "help" with the reading. Ask him or her to make up a new ending.

2. Talk about the pictures with a young child. Don't worry if you only cover about two or three pages.

3. Let your child put together his or her own book. Glue pictures (either magazine pictures or ones your child has drawn) on paper. Bread wire twists can be used to hold the pages together. Make a cover.

With or Without Mittens

Reason

To help your child learn to describe how things feel; to help your child learn about texture

What You Need

A pair of your child's mittens; some objects to feel such as a marble, a quarter, a cookie, a magazine, and a chair

Time Needed

3 to 5 minutes anytime

What to Do

1. Ask your child to put on his mittens and then touch different objects. Ask him to describe how these things feel. For instance, he might describe them as "lumpy," "flat," or "warm."
2. Then have him take off the mittens and describe how the same items feel. For example, he may say, "Lumpy in some places, smooth in others."
3. Set out five different items at a time. Put on your gloves or mittens and let your child ask you to describe how some items feel.
4. This activity can be done anywhere; in the car is especially good. Have your child feel the seat, the window handle, etc.

Age of Child

3, 4

Did It Work?

Does your child use more words to describe the items when he is not wearing his mittens? Does he use more and more words the longer you play the game?

Easier and Harder Ideas

1. Using several pairs of mittens or gloves, play a matching game.
2. Ask your child to tell you what he can do with his mittens on and his mittens off.
3. Display several pairs of mittens. Ask your child to tell you what is alike about them and what is different about them.

Pick a Toy

Reason

To help your child learn names for objects

What You Need

Bag of small toys, or other small items found in the home

Time Needed

5 minutes

What to Do

1. Pick an item out of the bag and name it.
2. Ask your child to name the object. If she can name it, allow her to keep it; if not, have her return it to the "picking bag."

Age of Child

2, 3, 4

Did It Work?

Can your child name all the items? When she can, start a new "picking bag" that contains different items.

Easier and Harder Ideas

1. Use magazine pictures for this activity too. The pictures last longer when glued to cardboard. Pictures of animals are very good for this activity.
2. Cut into two or four pieces a picture that has been glued to cardboard so that it becomes a puzzle. Keep the picture-puzzles in an envelope.

HOME LEARNING ENABLER (#1)

PRE-READING

New Titles for Stories

Reason

To help your child use a few key words to tell about things

What You Need

Nothing

Time Needed

3 to 5 minutes

What to Do

1. Tell or read a familiar nursery story to your child. Ask him what another good title might be for this story.
2. Show your child a picture that seems to tell a story.
3. Ask your child:

- What is happening?
- What happened before this time in the story?
- What will happen next?
- What sounds will the people and the animals make?
- How do you think this story will end?

Age of Child

4, 5

Did It Work?

Does your child think up new titles for other stories? Can he tell you new endings for stories? Can he make sounds for the stories?

Easier and Harder Ideas

1. Let your child have fun with names. Ask: "What's a good name for someone who is always happy? Or for a baby who cries a lot?"
2. Take turns telling a story that you start. Then have your child add a sentence; then you add a sentence, and so forth until you both like the ending.

My Grocery List

Reason

To help your child observe carefully and to match pictures and objects

What You Need

A piece of cardboard, magazine pictures of grocery items, scissors, glue

Time Needed

10 minutes to prepare the list, plus the time needed to complete a regular shopping trip

What to Do

1. Talk with your child about the things you plan to buy at the grocery store.
2. Look through magazines or grocery store flyers for pictures of four or five of these items. For example, find a picture of your particular brand of soup, cereal, and soda.
3. Together with your child, cut out these pictures and ask her to glue them onto a piece of cardboard.
4. Tell her, "This is your grocery list." When you get to the store, let her find those items and place them in the cart. The list can be used every week if these are items you buy regularly.

Age of Child

2, 3, 4, 5

Did It Work?

Did your child select the correct items pictured on his or her "grocery list"? Did your child enjoy the shopping trip more?

Easier and Harder Ideas

1. Have a young child start with only two or three items that you glue onto the cardboard for him or her.
2. For an older child, print the name of each item, and perhaps the price, under each picture. An older child can work with eight or nine items and then work up to a separate list made for different categories of food. For example, one list might be for fruits and vegetables: lettuce, carrots, potatoes, and apples. Another category might be dairy products: milk, eggs, cheese, and margarine.

Math Notes

Reason

To help your child recognize numbers; to help your child know "how many" for each number

What You Need

Small scraps of paper, pencil

Time Needed

3 minutes

What to Do

1. Tell your child you will play a game together. Write a number on a piece of paper and have him or her jump or step that many times.
2. Write the number *2* on a piece of paper and hand it to your child. Ask him or her to step forward *2* times.
3. Write the number *3* on another piece of paper and hand it to your child. Ask him or her to step backward *3* times. Write the number *1* on another piece of paper and ask your child to jump *1* time.
4. Stick to the numbers your child knows for sure. Move up to the numbers *4* and *5* after the first week. This activity is ideal to fill time while waiting for appointments.

Age of Child

3, 4, 5

Did It Work?

Can your child step or hop the correct number of times? Does he enjoy the game?

Easier and Harder Ideas

1. Ask your child to bounce a ball *x* number of times.
2. Use a ball to bounce an addition problem for him: Bounce the ball two times, pause, then bounce the ball one time. Ask your child how many times the ball was bounced.
3. Trade places and let your child bounce an addition problem for you to solve.

Whip It Up

Reason

To help your child learn some basic math concepts; to help your child develop eye-hand coordination

What You Need

Egg beater, instant pudding, milk

Time Needed

10 minutes

What to Do

1. Pour the milk into a bowl according to the directions on the box. Tell your child you are measuring 2 cups of milk (or whatever amount the directions call for). Add the pudding to the milk in the bowl. Start beating.

2. Have your child do most of the beating.

3. When the pudding has been beaten one minute, help your child pour it into bowls. Talk about the concepts of *half full*, *not too full*, *needs more*, and *too full*.

4. After the pudding sets (about 5 minutes), let your child eat some and enjoy her efforts.

Age of Child

2, 3, 4

Did It Work?

Could your child work the egg beater? Is your child beginning to recognize the meanings of the words *full*, *half full*, etc.? Would your child like to make pudding again?

Easier and Harder Ideas

1. Let your child use a baked frozen pie shell and make a pie using the pudding. Talk about the different amount of milk that is needed to make the pie filling (if this amount is different from the regular pudding recipe). Encourage the whole family to praise the completed pie.

2. Let your child play with a mechanical egg beater (not electric!) in the bathtub or in a sink filled with soap suds. Have her wear a plastic apron at the sink, or perhaps a trash bag tied at her waist. Your child may also want to use pudding as finger paint. Vanilla pudding makes yummy paint and is less messy than chocolate.

My House

Reason

To help your child learn to group and organize items, a skill needed in reading

What You Need

Grocery bags; magazines, catalogs, or the magazine section of newspapers; scissors; glue; marker or crayon

Time Needed

15 minutes

What to Do

1. Cut open a grocery bag to make a large sheet of paper.
2. Ask your child what room in the house he would like to choose furniture for.
3. Write the name of the room on the bag.
4. Let the child find pictures of furniture to go in the room. For example, a sofa for the living room, a stove for the kitchen, or a bed for the bedroom.
5. Help your child cut out the magazine pictures and glue them on the flattened bag.
6. Do other rooms on other days.

Age of Child

4

Did It Work?

Can your child find at least four items for each room? Can he find them in magazines, name them, and put them in the correct room?

Easier and Harder Ideas

1. With your child, glue pictures of rooms on separate grocery bags and label the bags with the name of the room. Ask your child to place pictures of furniture that belong in each of these rooms in the correct bag. When there is time, cut open the bags and glue down the pictures as in the original activity.

2. Make labels for the furniture in one or more of the rooms in your home. Let your child place the labels on the floor in front of the corresponding pieces of furniture.

Why Do You Like _____?

Reason

To give your child the chance to present her own reasons and thinking; to help your child understand that there are reasons for events

What You Need

Nothing

Time Needed

5 minutes

What to Do

1. Ask your child why she likes a certain story. Sometimes you may have to help by saying, for example, "Because Goldilocks ate pancakes?" The child will often say, "Oh, no," and then tell her own reasons.
2. Ask your child why she likes her favorite color. Why does she like her favorite toy?
3. Ask your child what she likes about school and about home. Ask how she would change things if she could.

Age of Child

4

Did It Work?

Can your child give more and more reasons why she likes something? Does your child enjoy this activity and smile while doing it? Does she ask other children for reasons?

Easier and Harder Ideas

1. Ask your child why she should do something and why she should not do something. Make it into a game and call it "Yes I should; No I shouldn't." For example, let her tell you why she should or should not be allowed to watch certain TV shows.
2. Ask your child why she should or should not go to bed at a certain hour.
3. Try not to disagree with your child; instead, listen to see if she understands two sides to an issue. Ask why she should or should not eat nutritious meals. Together think up more topics to discuss.

My Telephone Book

Reason

To help your child practice letter and number recognition; to help your child learn to read numbers in left-to-right order

What You Need

A piece of cardboard, crayon or magic marker

Time Needed

4 minutes

What to Do

1. Ask your child the names of friends and important people he would like to have in his "telephone book."
2. Have him dictate the names of his friends to you while you print them on cardboard. Print the names in letters about one inch tall.
3. By each person's name, print his or her telephone number. Add parents' work phone numbers, the phone numbers of grandparents and neighbors, and the numbers of the fire department and police station.
4. Keep the cardboard "telephone book" by the phone. Add any other needed numbers.
5. If your child asks, "What shall I do next?", suggest that he call a friend and invite him to come and play. (That's why his or her friends come first on the list.)

Age of Child

4, 5, 6

Did It Work?

Can your child make a call using the numbers on his list?

Easier and Harder Ideas

1. Keep a list of two or three friends and one emergency number for a younger child. Or, take pictures of friends and family and paste the pictures on the cardboard next to their phone numbers. This helps the child match the right number with the right person.
2. Help an older child write the names and numbers on the card himself. Use two pieces of cardboard if he prints large letters.

Comparing

Reason

To help your child learn how things are alike and how they are different; this is a needed skill in both language and math

What You Need

Old magazines

Time Needed

3 to 5 minutes at any time

What to Do

1. Cut out magazine pictures of the following items to compare. Each day, ask your child to compare one of these sets and discuss the differences.
   - a bird and an airplane
   - a sunny day and a rainy day
   - a slipper and a boat
   - something wood and something glass
2. Ask your child to compare the character of Father Bear in "Goldilocks and the Three Bears" with another bear in another story.
3. Ask your child to compare your work with your spouse's work. Then let her ask you how they are alike and how they are different.
4. Ask your child to compare clothes hung in a warm place with clothes hung in a cooler place.

Age of Child

4

Did It Work?

How many ways does your child compare things? Does the number increase?

Easier and Harder Ideas

1. Put a dish of water in the freezer compartment of your refrigerator. Ask your child to compare this with a dish of water from the tap.
2. Ask your child to compare cooked food with the same food uncooked. Try an egg, a dessert, apples, carrots, or hamburger.

Play Store

Reason

To help your child learn about money and simple addition

What You Need

Four different items from your kitchen cupboard such as a cereal box, a pudding box, and 2 cans; 20 pennies

Time Needed

5 to 10 minutes

What to Do

1. Play store with your child. Put the four grocery items in front of your child.
2. Make a 5¢ price tag for each item.
3. Ask your child to give you the right number of pennies to "buy" an item.
4. Let your child "buy" all four items; have him count the pennies he has left after each "purchase."
5. Let him sell the boxes back to you now.

Age of Child

4, 5, 6

Did It Work?

Can your child count out the right number of pennies? Does he have enough left to buy the last item? Does he enjoy the game?

Easier and Harder Ideas

1. For a younger child, make a 2¢ price tag for each item and give him 8 pennies.
2. Show your child 4 nickels and explain that they are worth the same as the 20 pennies. Have your child "buy" items with the nickels.
3. For an older child, provide more items and use dimes, nickels, and pennies. Keep the prices at 5¢ each until he understands the right coins to use.

Learning New Words

Reason

To help your child learn new words

What You Need

Two or three old shoe boxes and an assortment of objects:

cotton	a spoon
sandpaper	a book
a bell	a whistle
a stone	a marble
a child's block	a key
a piece of crumpled paper	

Time Needed

3 to 5 minutes

What to Do

1. Fill each box with some of the objects.
2. Blindfold your child and let her handle the objects. Ask her to tell you what they are or what they feel like. Encourage her to use new words.
3. Ask her what words each object reminds her of. For example, does the spoon remind her of ice cream? Does the whistle remind her of a policeman? Let the child blindfold you and then you tell her what the objects feel like. Try to use words she has not heard before.

Age of Child

3, 4, 5, 6

Did It Work?

Does your child suggest new items to add to the box? Does she gather her own collection? Is your child able to tell you more things that each object reminds her of?

Easier and Harder Ideas

1. Blow the whistle, ring the bell, and rattle the crumpled paper out of sight (perhaps in a paper bag). Let your child tell you what she hears.

2. Assemble a "smell box" with mustard, cinnamon, and some vinegar. Blindfold your child. Ask your child what these smells remind her of.

3. Assemble a "taste box" with salt, pepper, a piece of candy, a piece of cheese, and a piece of cold cereal. Blindfold your child. Ask her about how these things taste.

What's It Made Of?

Reason

To help your child learn the words for materials that houses and buildings might be made from

What You Need

Pictures of houses; copy of the story "The Three Little Pigs" (either your own copy or a copy from the library)

Time Needed

5 or 6 minutes

What to Do

1. Read the story of the three pigs to your child.
2. Talk to him about the materials they used to build their houses. Which material lasted the best?
3. Talk to your child about materials used to build real houses. What are windows made of? Doors? Show him pictures of houses.
4. On another day, talk with your child about materials other things are made of. For example, ask, "What are books made of? Magazines? Cars? This activity can be done while riding in the car. Show your child pictures of the objects or the actual objects when you get home if he does not see one during the trip.

Age of Child

3, 4, 5, 6

Did It Work?

Can the child talk about what things are made of? For example, can he name the materials in houses, windows, and books?

Easier and Harder Ideas

1. Ask a younger child to huff and puff with you when the wolf is blowing the houses down in the story.

2. Ask an older child what things are made of while you are out in the neighborhood. For example, what are sidewalks, buildings, tires, and toys made of?

My Map

Reason

To help your child learn his or her home address

What You Need

A large grocery bag; crayon or magic marker; old picture magazines; scissors; glue, stapler, or tape; photograph of your home, if possible

Time Needed

10 to 15 minutes

What to Do

1. Help your child cut open a grocery bag so that it will lie flat.
2. Ask your child to draw or glue a picture of your home in the center of the grocery paper.
3. Draw your street and have your child watch as you write the name of the street. Help your child print the number of your home. Together, sing your address to the tune of "Twinkle, Twinkle, Little Star." (For example, "1234 Main Street, St. Louis, Missouri.")
4. Draw an "X" on this map to mark the home of your child's best friend or of a helpful neighbor.
5. Add another important place and its name each day. For example:
   - your child's school or child-care center
   - the home of the nearest relative
   - the nearest fire or police station

Age of Child

4, 5, 6

Did It Work?

Does your child know her home address?

Easier and Harder Ideas

1. Talk with your child about which place on your map is nearest your home and which is farthest away. Mark and label those two locations. Make guesses as to how far the distances are between these places and your home (don't worry about exact distances).

2. Use a phone book to discover street names and addresses of places you wish to add to the map. Write this information in big, bold print on the grocery bag. Then have your child draw or paste a picture of these places on the map.

3. Add the nearest library, your favorite supermarket, the nearest drugstore, the neighborhood post office, and the nearest gas station. Staple or tape another flattened grocery bag to the first one if you need more space.

4. Tape the map to the refrigerator, the washing machine, or a window in your home. Let everyone look at it and use it.

Opposites

Reason

To help increase your child's vocabulary; to help him or her better understand the idea of opposites

What You Need

Nothing

Time Needed

3 to 5 minutes

What to Do

1. Tell your child that you are going to play a game. Ask him to supply the missing words in what you say.
2. Say, "A father is a man; a mother is a _____." (Accept *girl*, *lady*, and *woman* as correct answers.)
3. Then say:

   "One rock is big; the other rock is _____."

   "A brother is a boy; a sister is a _____."

   "Soup is hot; ice is _____."
4. Stop and discuss any missing word that he supplies incorrectly. Wait to play the game again until tomorrow.

Age of Child

4, 5, 6

Did It Work?

Does the child answer with reasonably correct answers? Progress to having your child ask you some opposites.

Easier and Harder Ideas

1. When talking with a younger child about opposites, place two objects in front of her. For example, use a rock and a piece of cotton and talk about "hard" and "soft." Or use a long stick and a short stick and talk about "long" and "short." Other opposites might be high and low, black and white.

2. Ask an older child to supply some harder opposites:

   "An inch is short; a mile is _____."

   "A rock is hard; a pillow is _____."

Reading Stop Signs

Reason

To help your child recognize letters and words in the community around him

What You Need

Nothing

Time Needed

3 to 5 minutes

What to Do

1. Take your child on a walk.
2. When you come to a STOP sign, hold your child up and have him trace the letters with his finger.
3. Tell him the name of each letter as he traces it. Then when he's finished tracing, tell him the word is *STOP*.
4. Follow this procedure with other signs that he can reach, perhaps those found in a shopping center.
5. Talk about the color of the signs.

Age of Child

4, 5

Did It Work?

Can your child recognize STOP signs? Praise him for "reading" them to you. Does he take an interest in the letters on other signs?

Easier and Harder Ideas

1. Ask your child to tell you the color of the STOP sign. Find other signs and ask him to identify at least one color on each.
2. Talk about the shapes of street signs; for example, YIELD signs are triangular in shape, and other signs are round or square. Ask your child to tell you the shape of the signs you pass. Then, you tell him what they stand for or say.

HOME LEARNING ENABLER (#1)

Telephone Number Song

Reason

To help your child recognize and match numbers, and to help her learn her phone number

What You Need

Telephone, seven pieces of paper the same size

Time Needed

10 minutes

What to Do

1. While showing your child the telephone, talk about your phone number. Write out your phone number and use tape to attach it to your phone if the number is not there already.
2. Sing the first part of "Twinkle, Twinkle, Little Star," substituting the numbers of your telephone number for the words of the song. For example: "7 6 2 - 4 1 0 4, now I know my phone number."
3. Write the individual numbers of your phone number on separate pieces of paper. Ask your child to line them up in order to match her phone number.
4. Mix up the pieces of paper and ask your child to line them up again.
5. Let your child mix them up for you to put in order.

Age of Child

4, 5, 6

Did It Work?

Can your child put the numbers in order? Can she sing her phone number?

Easier and Harder Ideas

1. Write the phone numbers of a relative and three friends on a piece of cardboard for your child. She can use this for her "phone book."
2. Sing the alphabet song, substituting the number and street name of your home address. End the song with "now I know my home address."

Making a Chart

Reason

To help your child remember to do things daily; to match what he does with pictures

What You Need

Crayons or markers, a piece of paper large enough for a chart (8½" × 11" or larger), magazines, scissors, and tape

Time Needed

10 minutes

What to Do

1. Cut out pictures of things you want your child to use everyday or of the activities you want him to take responsibility for. For example, find a picture of a toothbrush, soap, and a hairbrush or comb; or, find a picture of clean white teeth, some clean hands and a face, and some nicely combed hair.
2. Draw a chart with 8 spaces across and 5 or 6 spaces down.
3. Paste the cut-out pictures down the left column. Across the top seven spaces, write the days of the week.
4. Each day when your child brushes his teeth, washes his hands, or combs his hair, allow him to make a check mark or place a sticker in the box for that day.

Age of Child

5, 6

Did It Work?

Does your child enjoy marking his achievements on the chart each day? Does it help him remember to wash his hands and face? Brush his teeth? Comb or brush his hair?

Easier and Harder Ideas

1. Have only two lines for a younger child, perhaps using a picture of a toothbrush and a picture of soap.

2. Add other chores to the chart for an older child. Cut out pictures of silverware for setting the table, a picture of a bed for making his bed, and a picture of a toy box for putting away toys.

Paper Bag Fun

Reason

To help your child learn the meanings of prepositions (the little words that tell where things are)

What You Need

A large paper grocery bag

Time Needed

10 minutes

What to Do

1. Stand a grocery bag up on the floor. Ask your child to stand *beside* the bag.
2. Ask your child to stand *in front of* the bag. Now direct her to stand *in back of* the bag.
3. Ask your child to walk *around* the bag.
4. Ask her to put the bag *under* a chair. Then have her place the bag *on top of* the chair, then *beside* the chair.
5. Let your child give you directions to follow with the bag.

Age of Child

4, 5, 6

Did It Work?

Can your child follow the directions, at least part of the time?

Easier and Harder Ideas

1. A younger child can, with help, open out the bag flat and lie down *upon* it.
2. An older child can cut open the bag to be flat, and use it to draw a map of the neighborhood or at least of her street.

Rhythm Clapping

Reason

To help your child listen carefully; to provide him with practice in using words about numbers

What You Need

A radio or tape player

Time Needed

5 minutes

What to Do

1. Clap your hands and count in a rhythm, such as 3 fast claps and 2 slow claps.
2. Ask your child to copy you. Do other sequences and clap in lots of different ways, letting your child copy you each time.
3. Turn on the radio or tape player. Clap to the music. Count your claps to the music.
4. Ask your child to clap and you copy him.

Age of Child

4, 5, 6

Did It Work?

Can your child copy you? Can he count, at least up to five?

Easier and Harder Ideas

1. Even a two-year-old enjoys keeping time to music. Have him jump or bounce to the rhythm.
2. Use other sounds to count: tap on the table, cough, snap your fingers. Ask your child to take turns copying you or another child.

Describing Objects

Reason

To help your child learn to talk about how things feel; to help her learn about texture

What You Need

Shoebox-sized box, key, steel wool, a coin, small sponge, scrap of material, crunched up paper, a cookie, and other common objects

Time Needed

5 to 10 minutes

What to Do

1. Ask your child to help you put several objects in a box. Talk about how they feel when you put them in. Are they smooth? Rough? Soft? Hard?
2. Close your eyes and ask your child to close hers. Ask her to pick up an object and tell you what it is. See if you can guess what it is. Take turns. Eat the cookie as a treat.
3. Do this activity using other objects in the house.

Age of Child

3, 4, 5, 6

Did It Work?

Does your child use more words to describe the items? Does she use more and more words the longer you play the game?

Easier and Harder Ideas

1. Talk about other objects in your home. The floor is hard. The mirror is smooth. Sandpaper or a nail file is rough.
2. Ask an older child to find and name three things that are hard, three things that are smooth, and three things that are soft.

Alike or Different?

Reason

To help your child notice and talk about likenesses or differences

What You Need

Several sets of three objects each, with two alike and one different in each set; for example, three coffee cups (two alike and one different), three buttons, two pennies and a nickel, or three socks

Time Needed

5 to 10 minutes

What to Do

1. Place a set of objects in front of your child. Ask him to pick up the two items that are exactly alike.
2. Ask him to tell you one or two ways they are alike.
3. Ask him to tell you one or two ways they are different from the third object.
4. Pick up the third object that is different and tell your child one or two more things about it.
5. Do this with the other sets of objects.

Age of Child

4, 5, 6

Did It Work?

Can your child tell you one or two ways the objects are alike or different?

Easier and Harder Ideas

1. Ask a younger child to help you match pieces of laundry, such as socks, underwear, or shirts.
2. Ask an older child to tell you three or four ways objects are alike or different.

Number Clips

Reason

To help your child see that a written number stands for an actual number of items

What You Need

five clothespins or five hairclips, a magic marker, magazines or newspapers, scissors

Time Needed

10 minutes

What to Do

1. Write the numbers one to five on the five clothespins or hairclips. On the back of the clip, draw the number of dots that represent that number.
2. Look through the newspapers and magazines for pictures of groups of items, such as cars, clothes, or food items.
3. Cut out the pictures. Have your child clip each picture with the clip that has the matching number of dots.
4. Turn the clip over so your child can see the matching number.

Age of Child

4, 5, 6

Did It Work?

Can your child clip the correct number of pictured items with the matching number clip, at least part of the time?

Easier and Harder Ideas

1. Ask a younger child to count to five as she touches individual items. Have her count stairs as she climbs, cans as you put away groceries, fruit as you make a salad, or any other household things.
2. Have an older child make clips representing the numbers 1 to 10, then have her match larger groups of items.

Everyday Shapes

Reason

To help your child recognize shapes; to help him realize that shapes are all around him

What You Need

Paper, pencil or markers

Time Needed

10 minutes

What to Do

1. Draw and talk about different shapes: a square, a circle, a rectangle, and an oval.
2. Talk about the differences between the shapes. Which have corners? Which are smooth?
3. Ask your child to look together with you for shapes in your home. For example, point out the squares in the floor tile, the circles in the top and bottom of a lampshade, the oval kitchen spoons, and the rectangles in the windows.

Age of Child

4, 5, 6

Did It Work?

Can your child identify some of the shapes correctly?

Easier and Harder Ideas

1. Look for shapes wherever you go. For example, point out to your child the shapes in lights, road signs, store windows, and gas stations.
2. Cut out several shapes and ask an older child to combine the shapes to make a house, a wagon, a snowman, and other objects.

Identifying Sounds

Reason

To help your child understand that words begin with sounds and that alphabet letters represent those sounds

What You Need

Shopping bags filled with various items from a recent shopping trip

Time Needed

5 to 10 minutes

What to Do

1. Ask your child to help you put away the items you bought at the store.
2. Have your child pick out an item that starts with a sound she knows; for example, if your child knows the sound of *m*, ask her to find the milk in the grocery bag. Repeat the sound, then ask your child to bring you other *m* items, such as meat or mushroom soup. Draw an *m* on a piece of paper and explain to your child that this letter stands for the sound she hears at the beginning of *milk, meat,* and *mushroom.*
3. Name other purchases. Ask your child to repeat the name and then bring the item to you. Talk about the beginning sound of the item's name, and write that letter on another piece of paper. Give the paper to your child and have her keep a "book" of letters she knows.
4. Take turns putting away purchases by letting your child ask you for items.

Age of Child

5, 6

Did It Work?

Can your child match sounds and letters for one or two letters? Is her "letter book" getting thicker?

Easier and Harder Ideas

1. At mealtime, ask your child to tell you the sounds each food begins with. Say the sound and the letter, and then write it for her.

2. At bedtime, name the furniture in the room and talk about the sounds the names begin with. Name the letter for your child.

Helping Wash Dishes

Reason

To help your child see that some things sink and some float; to encourage your child to make predictions and then see if he is right

What You Need

Soapy water in the sink or bathtub, apron (plastic if you have it)

Time Needed

5 to 10 minutes

What to Do

1. When you are washing dishes, give your child an apron and ask him to help. If some dishes are plastic, show him how the lighter ones will float.
2. Show him how the heavy things sink.
3. Give him some plastic containers or lids and have him guess which ones will float. Then ask him to test each one to see if it floats.
4. Give him some heavier items such as a metal spoon or a coin. Ask him to guess if it will float or sink, then have him test it to find out.
5. Let him ask you if you think something will float or sink.

Age of Child

4, 5, 6

Did It Work?

Does your child guess correctly that one or two items will float or sink?

Easier and Harder Ideas

1. A younger child can do this in the bathtub with bathtub toys. Add some heavier items that will be "sinkers."
2. An older child can gather up 5 or 10 items he thinks will float or sink and then test them.

_____
(Date)

Dear Parent:

Did you know that you are your child's most important teacher? Would you take 5 minutes this week and do the following activity with your child? Please fill in the sheet below with your ideas and comments, then tear it off and send it back to the center. Thank you.

_____
(Teacher's Name)

(Tear Off)

- -

Feedback Sheet

For:_____
(Child's Name, Grade)

1. Did you or someone else do the activity with the child? Me _____ Other _____
2. How many times did you do the activity? Once _____ More than once _____
3. How much time did the activity take?   _____ 15 minutes or less
                                           _____ 30 minutes or less
                                           _____ More than 30 minutes
4. Did you enjoy this activity with your child?   Yes _____ No _____
5. Do you feel your child understood it?   Yes _____ No _____
6. Do you feel your child needs more help in this area? Yes _____ No _____
7. Please share any adaptation you may have of this activity, or describe a new activity. (Write on the back, if necessary.) Thanks for cooperating!

_____   _____
Signature   Teacher's Name

_____
(Activity name, grade, and number)

Parent Letter/Feedback Sheet
(This form is to be sent home with each activity)

HOME LEARNING ENABLER (#1)

Listening to the Weather

Reason

To help your child notice the weather and build listening skills; to help her keep track of the weather for a week

What You Need

Radio (the car radio is fine), pencil, paper

Time Needed

5 minutes

What to Do

1. Ask your child to listen to the weather forecast with you. Talk about what the forecast means and what clothes she should wear to be prepared for the weather.
2. On a piece of paper, keep track of sunny days, rainy days, hot days, or cold days.
3. Ask your child to keep track of weather announcement changes from day to day. Ask her if she notices whether or not predictions differ with different weather forecasters.

Age of Child

5, 6, 7

Did It Work?

Does your child notice the weather more? Does she choose the right kinds of clothes to wear for the weather?

Easier and Harder Ideas

1. Read the newspaper's weather prediction to your child.
2. Mount an outdoor thermometer outside a window. Read the temperature together, and see if it differs from the temperature predicted for the day.

Teaching Sorting Skills

Reason

To help your child notice when things are alike or different; to help him classify things

What You Need

Sewing kit, tool box, gadget drawer, or jewelry box

Time Needed

10 minutes

What to Do

1. Ask your child to find all the things that are round in your tool box or jewelry box.
2. Ask your child to find all the long things or all the short things.
3. If you are using sewing supplies, ask him to sort the buttons from largest to smallest.
4. Have your child pick something for you to sort. Have your child choose the categories you must sort the objects into.

Age of Child

5, 6, 7

Did It Work?

Can your child group together correctly things that are similar, such as things that are round? Can he correctly separate things by category?

Easier and Harder Ideas

1. Have a younger child sort buttons by color.
2. Ask an older child to sort things by sounds, perhaps using a toolbox full of objects. For example, what sound does a nail make when it's dropped? Does it sound the same as or different from a screw that is dropped? From a bolt?

Telling a Story

Reason

To help your child learn about sequence, that is, what comes before or after something else

What You Need

Nothing (This is a good activity to do in a car.)

Time Needed

5 minutes

What to Do

1. Begin a story and ask your child to finish it.
2. Ask her to begin a story and then you complete it.
3. Take turns telling parts of a story that you think up together.
4. Write down your child's story or ask a visitor or family member to write it down. These written stories are fun to read later.

Age of Child

5, 6, 7

Did It Work?

Can your child complete a story you start? Does she ask to do the activity again?

Easier and Harder Ideas

1. Ask other family members to take turns telling a story with the two of you. Stories about family history are good subjects for this activity.
2. When reading a story or a picture book to your child, stop and ask your child to guess what happens next.

Playing Store

Reason

To help your child learn about money; to help him practice adding and subtracting

What You Need

20 pennies, 4 nickels, 2 dimes, 4 objects from the kitchen, slips of paper, and a pencil

Time Needed

10 to 15 minutes

What to Do

1. Talk about the concept of 5 pennies being worth one nickel. Put these coins in front of your child.
2. Talk about 10 pennies being worth a dime. Put these coins in front of your child.
3. Write the words *5 cents* and *10 cents* on separate pieces of paper. Put each piece of paper near its respective number of pennies. Tell your child that the paper shows the value of each set of pennies.
4. Put out four objects and then place the *5 cents* and *10 cents* slips of paper ("price tags") beside two of the items. Ask your child to buy one of the objects from you by paying for it with either the dime, the nickel, or the correct number of pennies.

Age of Child

5, 6, 7

Did It Work?

Can your child count out the correct coins for his "purchases" at least some of the time?

Easier and Harder Ideas

1. Ask your child to choose four food items and then tell you the price of each. Write, or have your child write, each price tag and then play store.

2. Use price tags totalling less than 20 cents for all four objects. Ask your child to count out the correct change to buy the objects. Provide more coins to your child if necessary. After he buys the items, let him be storekeeper and give you change after you buy the items.

3. Make price tags for several items around your house. In the beginning, use numbers that end in 5 or 10. Ask your child to play store with you to practice number recognition and money values.

4. When your child becomes comfortable with playing store, take him to a real store and allow him to buy a popsicle or ice cream.

Magazine Words

Reason

To help your child talk in complete sentences

What You Need

Magazine or newspaper pictures containing sentences on or near them, scissors

Time Needed

10 minutes

What to Do

1. Read a sentence from the magazine picture to your child. Then cover up one word and ask her what word is missing. Cut out the word and give it to her.

2. Follow this same procedure with two or three more sentences that are located near pictures. Keep the pictures and cut-out words together. Tell your child that these pictures and words are "word puzzles."

3. Show your child each picture, then ask her to find the appropriate cut-out words that will complete the picture's corresponding sentence.

4. Talk about the sentences that you read together. Leave off the last word in each sentence and ask your child to complete the sentence. Take turns.

Age of Child

5, 6, 7

Did It Work?

Can your child correctly arrange the cut-out words in the appropriate sentences? Can she finish a sentence you start?

Easier and Harder Ideas

1. Combine the magazine sentences into a story that you and your child make up together. Staple the pictures together for a "book."

2. For an older child, use longer sentences.

Homemade Poems

Reason

To help your child hear and discriminate between the sounds at the ends of words; to help your child identify ending sounds that match or rhyme

What You Need

Nothing (This is a good activity to do in a car, on a bus, or while waiting in line.)

Time Needed

10 minutes

What to Do

1. Talk about words that rhyme, such as *bake* and *cake*.
2. Tell your child, or have your child tell you, more words that end with the same sound: *take, lake, rake*.
3. Say another word, such as *hall*. Then ask your child to say a word that rhymes with it, such as *wall* or *fall*.
4. Make up a short sentence that contains two or three rhyming words. Say it aloud to your child. Ask him to tell you which words rhyme.
5. Write down some rhyming words and sentences. For example, "For goodness sake, I'm going to rake." Give these to your child and have him make a "poem book."

Age of Child

5, 6, 7

Did It Work?

Can your child think of one rhyming word to match a word that you say?

Easier and Harder Ideas

1. As you recite a list of words, have a younger child clap whenever you say a word that rhymes with a specific word that you choose.
2. Have an older child jump rope while you say rhyming words. Talk about the sounds in jump rope rhymes.

Math Puzzles

Reason

To help your child practice adding and subtracting

What You Need

Squares of cardboard or paper plates, scissors, marker or pen

Time Needed

10 minutes

What to Do

1. Write a simple addition problem on a piece of cardboard or a paper plate, such as 2 + 2 = 4.
2. Cut the cardboard or paper plate apart, making a zig-zag line between the problem and the answer. The pieces now form a puzzle.
3. Write other problems on other cardboard pieces and cut them apart with curving or zig-zag lines.
4. Mix up the problems and answers, then have your child complete the puzzles.

Age of Child

6, 7, 8

Did It Work?

Can your child match up one or two of the puzzle pieces correctly?

Easier and Harder Ideas

1. Make a set of subtraction problems this same way, or, match words and numbers, such as "dime = 10 cents."
2. For an older child, use multiplication problems or tables for the puzzles. Division problems are good, too. As with the other puzzles, have your child match the answer pieces with the problem pieces.

Waiting for Time

Reason

To help your child practice the skills needed for telling time

What You Need

A watch or clock that displays all 12 numbers (in addition, a digital clock can be used as a learning help)

Time Needed

10 minutes

What to Do

1. Show your child the minute hand on a watch or clock and ask her to see how long a TV commercial is.
2. When the commercial is over, help her figure out the length of time that has passed. One minute? Half a minute? Explain the marks on the clock; for example, tell your child that the five marks between two numbers in a row on a clock represent five minutes of time.
3. Have your child practice counting by 5s to 60: 5, 10, 15, 20, 25, and so on. Show your child how this method of counting relates to the marks on a clock's face. (Count by 10s if 5s are too hard.)
4. Help your child time other things, such as a song on the radio, how long it takes a traffic light to change, how long it takes to read a particular story, or how long her sibling may play with a toy she wants.

Age of Child

5, 6, 7

Did It Work?

Does your child understand what "wait 5 minutes" means? Does she talk about time more?

Easier and Harder Ideas

1. Talk to a younger child about the "thirties" and the "o'clocks" on a clock. Tell her that when both hands are at the top it is 12 o'clock. When the big hand is at the bottom it is 12:30. Explain that the small hand always tells the "o'clocks" and the big hand always tells the "thirties."
2. Use a "time-out" chair when your child misbehaves. Ask her to sit on a chair for 5 minutes and give her a watch or clock to hold and observe while she waits. This is a good way to interrupt a fight or a temper tantrum.

Home Chart

Reason

To help your child talk about and think about safety habits

What You Need

Piece of paper large enough to make a chart and a marker or pen

Time Needed

10 minutes

What to Do

1. Walk around your home with your child for a "safety inspection tour."
2. Look for electric cords that are frayed and for throw rugs that slide. Look for papers, rags, paint, laundry soap, or anything poisonous that is not stored safely and away from little children.
3. Make a chart of things that need attention. Write the needed safety repairs down the left side of the chart. Then write the days of the week across the top of the chart. Use this chart to record when things get done.
4. Plan a trip to the store to buy any supplies that will help in the needed safety repairs. These might include electrical tape for frayed cords or double-sided tape to secure a throw rug.

Age of Child

6, 7, 8

Did It Work?

Does your child think more about how safe things are? Does he enjoy putting check marks or stickers on the chart when repairs are made?

Easier and Harder Ideas

1. Talk to a younger child about safety rules. For example, "Look both ways before crossing the street. Don't run on stairs. Stay in your seat on the bus." Make a chart of these "safety activities" and allow your child to check them off.
2. Ask an older child to make a chart for another family member, with that family member's help. For example, he could make a chart that relates to the car: Check the tires; check the oil; check the transmission fluid.

Comparing Lengths

Reason

To help your child build number and comparing skills

What You Need

String or yarn, scissors

Time Needed

10 minutes

What to Do

1. Talk with your child about comparing the lengths of different items.
2. Cut a piece of yarn or string so that it is the same length as a particular piece of furniture, such as the dresser in your child's bedroom.
3. See how many times the piece of yarn is needed to measure the length of your child's bed. How many lengths are needed to measure the rug? The front door? The window?
4. Find out which item in your house needs the most lengths.
5. Measure your child and then yourself with the piece of yarn.

Age of Child

5, 6, 7

Did It Work?

Does your child notice that it takes more lengths of yarn to measure the bed than the dresser?

Easier and Harder Ideas

1. Ask your child to guess how many lengths of yarn it will take to measure an object.
2. Use a tape measure or a yardstick to measure the same pieces of furniture you measured with the yarn. Record the lengths of items and compare the lengths measured in inches.

HOME LEARNING ENABLER (#1)

A Box for Me

Reason

To help your child make a place that is her very own; she can use this for storing school things and private treasures

What You Need

A cardboard box, crayons or markers, scraps of fabric, comics from the newspaper or a piece of gift wrap, and glue

Time Needed

10 to 15 minutes

What to Do

1. Ask your child to decorate her "Treasure Box" with some of the materials listed.
2. Encourage your child to use the box to keep her things that she doesn't want to lose.
3. Suggest that she use the box to keep the booklets she makes at school and the things you two make together based on these home activities.
4. Explain to the rest of the family that this box is "off limits" to everyone but this child.

Age of Child

4, 5, 6, 7, 8

Did It Work?

Does your child enjoy using her box? Does she keep special toys or gifts in it?

Easier and Harder Ideas

1. A younger child can make a simpler box, perhaps using a shoe box and markers.
2. An older child can decorate boxes especially for each member of the family. These make good gifts.

Love Notes

Reason

To help your child practice writing

What You Need

Pieces of paper, pencil or pen

Time Needed

5 or 10 minutes

What to Do

1. Ask your child to write a short note to each family member. These notes might say, for example, "Good morning" or "I love you" or even "You can play with my blue toy today."
2. Together, have fun deciding where to put these notes so that each family member finds his or hers: in a lunch bag, on a pillow, on the refrigerator, or on a mirror, for example.
3. Encourage family members to write notes back.
4. Keep sending notes. Designate one day a week to be "note-writing day."

Age of Child

6, 7, 8

Did It Work?

Does your child enjoy sending and receiving notes? Does he write longer notes as his writing gets better?

Easier and Harder Ideas

1. Have a younger child draw a picture and tell you (dictate) the message he wants you to write on it.
2. At holiday time, add little gifts to the notes, such as a pencil or a piece of candy. Sign the notes, "From Secret Santa."

Problem-Solving

Reason

To help your child use hints and clues to guess the identity of an object or idea

What You Need

Nothing (This activity can be done in the car.)

Time Needed

5 to 10 minutes

What to Do

1. Describe an object that is in another room of the house. If you are driving, describe an object that you can't see in the car.
2. After providing a few hints, ask your child to guess what the object is; provide more and more hints if necessary.
3. If possible, after your child names the object, give her the object to look at and have her tell you how helpful your clues were.
4. Take turns. Have your child give you hints to help you guess an unseen object.

Age of Child

5, 6, 7, 8

Did It Work?

Does your child guess the objects more and more quickly? Does she give you better and better hints when it is her turn?

Easier and Harder Ideas

1. For a younger child, provide simpler clues.
2. With an older child (or adult), play "Twenty questions": Think of an object, then have the player ask you questions about the object. These questions should require either a "yes" or "no" answer. See if the player can guess an object by asking you less than 20 questions. Take turns.

Puzzle Comics

Reason

To help your child learn sequence skills

What You Need

Color or black-and-white comic strips (comics your child can read are best), scissors, envelopes

Time Needed

10 minutes

What to Do

1. Ask your child to cut apart the blocks of one comic strip. Then have him mix them up and put them in order again.
2. Cut up more comic strips and then put them back in order. Keep each set of comic strip blocks in a separate envelope.
3. Take one block out of one envelope. Ask your child to tell you what's missing. Or, ask him to make up the words or story for the missing blocks.
4. Do this for the other strips, too.

Age of Child

6, 7, 8

Did It Work?

Can your child put the comic strips back together again?

Easier and Harder Ideas

1. Find a comic strip with little or no words for a younger child.
2. Take out the ending block of a comic strip and ask your child to make up a new ending for the story. Ask him to draw the new ending.

Neighborhood Map

Reason

To help your child learn mapping skills; to help her see that she can draw a picture of places, which is what a map is

What You Need

Newspapers or brown paper grocery bags to make a large piece of paper, marker or pen, tape

Time Needed

15 minutes

What to Do

1. Tell your child you are going to draw a picture of your street. Explain that this picture is called a map.
2. Use a flattened, cut-open paper bag or newspaper, and draw your street. Add four or five houses or buildings on each side. Have your child show you on the map the location of your home and write your street number on it.
3. Attach more bags or newspapers to your original map and draw more streets and buildings.
4. Have your child name and draw several places (such as her school, a store, a gas station, etc.). Write in the signs for these places or have your child do so.

Age of Child

6, 7, 8

Did It Work?

Can your child locate one or two places on the "map"?

Easier and Harder Ideas

1. Have a younger child help you "map" the rooms in your home.
2. If you live near a river, railroad tracks, or a big street, have an older child map the area around it. What buildings are near this area that are different from those in your neighborhood? Look at the same places on a commercial map that you can get from a local gas station.

Making an Alphabet Line

Reason

To help your child learn to put things in alphabetical order

What You Need

Newspapers or shelf paper to lay out on the floor, a marker or pen

Time Needed

10 to 15 minutes

What to Do

1. On a piece of newspaper, write the first five letters of the alphabet in a row (use large letters).
2. Ask your child to find small objects that start with those letters, then have him put these objects by the appropriate letter on the "Alphabet Line." He can use toys (*ball, car*), groceries (*can, eggs, fruit*), or any other objects that are easy to carry.
3. Add more letters.
4. Take turns letting each other find objects to place on the Alphabet Line.

Age of Child

6, 7, 8

Did It Work?

Can your child place two or three things in correct alphabetical order?

Easier and Harder Ideas

1. Write the names of family members on slips of paper and place them on the Alphabet Line.
2. Cut out 10 words from the newspaper and ask an older child to alphabetize them. Let him cut out 10 words for you to alphabetize.

Timing Your Day

Reason

To help your child learn to plan activities

What You Need

Paper, pencil, pen

Time Needed

10 to 15 minutes

What to Do

1. Help your child make a chart for 5, 6, or 7 days that shows the days of the week.
2. In pencil, write in the times she eats breakfast, goes to school, participates in other activities, and goes to bed.
3. Ask your child to watch what times these activities actually happen, then, with a pen, write in those times.
4. On Saturday morning, use a pencil to write in any plans for the day. In the evening, use a pen to write in any changes that occurred.

Age of Child

6, 7, 8

Did It Work?

Does your child enjoy discussing with you the times she will do things? Does she enjoy comparing how close the estimated times were with the real times?

Easier and Harder Ideas

1. For a younger child who does not yet understand the concept of minutes, plan one day by the hour.
2. An older child can help plan an automobile trip. Write in the days you will be traveling, the estimated times that you will be arriving at specific places, and the distances between places. Later, compare the actual travel schedule with the planned schedule.

Measuring My House and Myself

Reason

To help your child practice measuring and numbering skills

What You Need

Yardstick, ruler, or tape measure; paper; pencil

Time Needed

10 to 15 minutes

What to Do

1. Talk with your child about measuring things. Measure a table, a chair, and your child's arm, then write down the numbers.
2. Ask your child to measure more things, such as the length of his shoe, the width of a doorway, the width of a window, the width of the TV, or the length of his little finger.
3. Ask him to guess the measurements of some things and have him write down these guesses (or estimates). Then have him measure these items and write down the actual measurements. Compare the estimates with the actual measurements.
4. Take turns measuring different objects.

Age of Child

6, 7, 8

Did It Work?

Does your child enjoy measuring things? Does he enjoy guessing or estimating a measurement and then checking it?

Easier and Harder Ideas

1. Have your child measure the pans in your kitchen.
2. With your child, find things you can measure outside: the width of the sidewalk, the height of a mailbox, or how far he can jump.

Newspaper Headline Puzzles

Reason

To help your child understand word sequence

What You Need

Scissors, tape, paper, envelopes

Time Needed

10 to 15 minutes

What to Do

1. Ask your child to cut out some newspaper headlines.
2. Cut apart the words of one headline. Ask your child to assemble the headline again.
3. After she succeeds, put that "headline puzzle" in an envelope. Cut up another headline to assemble.
4. Use the headline words to make sentences. Tape these sentences to a page and have your child illustrate the sentences to make a booklet.

Age of Child

6, 7, 8

Did It Work?

Did your child enjoy arranging the puzzles? Did she ask to do this activity again?

Easier and Harder Ideas

1. For a younger child, write on a piece of paper a simple sentence that she knows. Cut it up to make a puzzle.
2. For an older child, use harder and longer sentences. Trade places and let her make a puzzle for you. Use magazine headlines and sentences, too.

Do I Have Enough?

Reason

To help your child use household objects to practice adding and subtracting

What You Need

Silverware, food items, rocks

Time Needed

10 minutes

What to Do

1. Ask your child to set the table. Give her one or two fewer spoons than he needs. Ask him how many more spoons he needs to be able to complete the task.
2. Do this activity with fruit or any food you are serving. How many more servings do you need?
3. Outside, tell your child you want 10 rocks. Give him 7 and ask if he has enough.
4. Count out pennies to buy something. Have him tell you how many more pennies he needs to buy the item.

Age of Child

6, 7, 8

Did It Work?

Does he figure out the correct answer at least some of the time?

Easier and Harder Ideas

1. Take turns. Have your second grader or a younger child ask you if you have enough of something.
2. Practice subtracting. Give your child 10 spoons. Ask him how many he should give back to have enough left for the family.

Parent Papers

These Parent Papers may be given as handouts at parent meetings, added as an extra page to newsletters sent home with the children, or given as a single page for children to take home. Parents are important partners in children's learning. The goal of these Parent Papers is to help your center include parents in the learning process in a way that saves time and effort for you, while providing professional resources for parenting. By providing these resources to parents, the children at your center will be helped as well, since one of the most effective and inexpensive ways to reach children is to reach their parents. By providing a variety of formal and informal ways to keep in touch with parents, your center will build trust and two-way communication. Many parents find the guidance and support of knowledgeable adults to be invaluable. By learning some of the ways professional personnel interact with children, parents can feel more confident with their children at home. You may want to share this point of view with your staff at a staff meeting.

Parent Papers Set I

Teacher's Name

Goals of the Early Childhood Program Experience

Goals for Children

- Be themselves
- Express themselves by using art and play materials freely and constructively
- Learn to be tolerant, creative, cooperative, and imaginative
- Learn independence
- Learn limits of behavior
- Increase ability to handle emotions constructively

Goals for Parents

- Become more aware of your child's world and understand his or her behavior
- Achieve a more positive approach to child-adult relationships by taking advantage of professional guidance and sharing experiences with other parents
- Sympathize with and understand your child's feelings about his or her first experience away from home
- Participate in a worthwhile situation, outside of the home and job, by contributing your abilities and talents
- Learn constructive techniques of working with children

What We Teach . . .

- Is not always evident to the casual observer.
- Sets the stage by guiding unobtrusively.
- Maintains an atmosphere of freedom and friendliness within limits.

- Allows the children to develop their own ideas. Adults stay in the background ready to help if needed.

Objectives of the Early Childhood Program

I. Physical Development

A. Objective: To provide experiences, equipment, and activities that contribute to physical fitness and coordination. We plan:

   1. To provide each child with a balance of active and quiet activities.
   2. To provide the child with activities for small and large muscle development.
   3. To provide the child with balanced and nutritious meals or snacks.
   4. To help the child to achieve awareness and mastery of his or her physical self.

II. Intellectual Development

A. Objective: To provide experiences that increase the child's ability to solve problems by acting on the environment around him or her. This will include learning to observe, describe, discover, think, organize, and use the information he or she receives through the five senses. We plan:

   1. To develop language ability and vocabulary through all activities and experiences.
   2. To provide problem-solving and decision-making situations to enhance the child's thinking ability.
   3. To expose the child to as much of the world as possible through field trips and actual experience.
   4. To allow the child to express himself or herself creatively, and to manipulate and explore materials.
   5. To provide the child with a variety of learning experiences including cooking, art, water play, and dramatic play.

III. Emotional Development

A. Objective: To encourage children to develop and grow in positive feelings about themselves and their abilities; who they are; and what they can do. We plan, with your help:

   1. To develop self-confidence and feelings of achievement.
   2. To provide experiences that teach children to deal constructively with their frustrations.
   3. To encourage children to respect themselves, other children, adults, materials, and equipment.

4. To encourage children to take pride in their ethnic group, family, and community.

IV. Social Development

A. Objective: To help each child develop an awareness and appreciation of others, moving from preoccupation with self towards involvement with others. We plan:

1. To provide the child with opportunities to enjoy knowing and being with other children and adults.

2. To provide sharing experiences for the child and to provide for give-and-take relationships.

3. To help the child learn to trust adults outside the family and to be able to ask for help when it is needed.

V. Strengthening Families

A. Objective: To build a close and positive relationship with families of children in the program.

Teacher's Name

What Your Child Will Be Learning

We hope the activities in the program will offer your child a variety of ways to have fun. Play can include spontaneous and productive experiences that help children learn about their world and their relationship to it.

The *dramatic play corner* offers an opportunity for dramatic play through which children can assume the roles of a mother, a father, a baby, and many others. They can act out some of their feelings about people and events. Children can express their fantasies, their fears, their impulses, and their needs. They can have their turn with power.

Art activities such as easel painting, finger painting, and fruit and vegetable painting, allow for the discovery of colors, designs, and shapes. While exploring the creative possibilities of paint, clay, paste, and paper, children can find ways to express their feelings and experiences.

Sand and water play involve the sense of touch and the use of small muscles. In this relaxed play situation, children can use pitchers, funnels, measuring spoons, and sponges for pouring, measuring, and squeezing. This activity also helps future math learning.

Food experiences such as making juice and slicing bananas allow the different characteristics of food to be seen, tested, smelled, and touched. This is one way to help children become more aware of and sensitive to learning through their five senses.

Reading stories and making books available for children to use stimulate many interests. Books become recognized as sources of information. Through discussion of pictures, children observe details. Discussion also promotes language development and self-expression. Books can foster the sharing of experiences such as trips and visits from favorite friends and relatives.

Building with blocks stimulates and promotes creative play. Complex and imaginative structures arise. Selecting the blocks involves making comparisons and classifying sizes and shapes.

Outdoor equipment stimulates climbing, jumping, sliding, and balancing, and helps large muscle development and coordination.

We hope that through these activities, children will have the opportunities to gain confidence in themselves and their abilities. According to recent research, self-direction, interest, curiosity, and genuine pleasure in activities of all kinds promote the best possible intellectual development in children.

Teacher's Name

What to Expect

Ask yourself:

1. What do I expect from an early childhood experience?

   For my child:
   - the companionship and challenge of friends
   - the guidance and support of knowledgeable adults
   - the time and space and opportunity to explore many creative materials
   - the excitement and enticement of planned activities that provide foundation concepts and learnings
   - the strengthened feeling that he or she is a capable, active learner
   - the pleasure of a world of his or her own, apart from the family, where she or he is a valued individual
   - a head start on specific learnings and attitudes that will be expected in later school years

   For myself:
   - the assurance that my child is safe
   - the prospect that he or she will grow and gain knowledge, self-confidence, and social skills
   - the hope that he or she will be helped in his or her later school experiences
   - the chance to discuss my child and his or her needs with a caring teacher
   - the chance to observe other children and stages of development
   - the chance to extend my knowledge of effective alternatives in child-rearing practices
   - the chance to meet other families with similar-aged children who are facing the same or very different problems
   - the opportunity to be reliable in picking up my child and paying fees

   Note: Please remember—not everyone expects the same things from a program, so not all of these items will be important to everyone, nor will they all carry the same weight.

2. How can parents know how a program is operating, what it is achieving, and what is happening during the hours of operation?

By asking:

- Do the children in the program seem relaxed and sure of themselves, or do they seem tense and anxious?
- Do the children seem to like each other and get along (some of the time)?
- Are they interested in some activity most of the time?
- Do they seem comfortable chatting and explaining and questioning, or are they silent most of the time?
- Are they using all their senses to discover and handle their play materials?

By observing the teacher:

- Does the teacher welcome each child and seem to be aware of what each child is doing?
- Does the teacher speak naturally and directly to a child, stooping to his or her eye level most of the time?
- Does the teacher step in to stop fights or change activities before behavior becomes disruptive?
- Does the teacher seem upset or blaming when accidents occur?
- Does he or she show respect and genuine interest in a child's work?

By observing the program:

- Is the schedule a rigid timetable or a natural sequence?
- Are there activities for individuals and small groups as well as the whole class?
- Do some activities offer quiet experiences and opportunities for creating and exploring?
- Are the children's interests and comments taken into consideration in the planning of activities, or are all of the activities planned by the teachers?
- Are children permitted and encouraged to do things for themselves, such as hang up their clothes, pour their own juice, and manage art materials?

By observing the space and equipment:

- Is equipment sturdy and non-frustrating?
- Does the equipment upkeep show concern for the health and safety of the children, or are splinters and wobbles allowed to develop?
- Is there imaginative use of color and shape?
- Are there enough materials to really carry out an idea, or are there just a few blocks or dishes, for example?

- Are bathrooms clean, fresh-smelling, and equipped with sturdy step stools?
- Are examples of children's art work displayed around the classroom to be admired and shared?
- Are materials stored so that children may take them out and put them away independently?

By observing the outdoor area:
- Is there an enclosed space for outdoor play?
- Is the outdoor equipment sturdy and secure?
- Does the outdoor play equipment allow children the chance to run, stretch, pull, climb, yell, and in general, use up stored energy?

By asking about teacher and director credentials:
- Are certificates and diplomas that staff members received for training prominently displayed?

I can help this program and its activities in the following way:

Teacher's Name

Building Self-Esteem

Self-esteem or self-confidence affects how a person manages his or her needs, deals with others, produces in life, solves conflicts, and searches for meaning in life; these qualities also affect whether or not a person is able to develop close relationships and take responsibility for meeting others' needs. Self-esteem and a positive self-image go hand in hand.

The feelings of belonging and significance that a child gains in the family can help him or her to be successful in every area of life. Self-confidence and a sense of achievement can be built up in children the same way as it can in adults, but must be done in smaller steps. Children need to feel worthwhile and need to have a sense of self-respect just as adults do. Often, aggression in children is a symptom of a poor self-image.

Steps that build self-esteem include opportunities for decision-making. Children need a chance to make decisions. When providing such opportunities, limit choices to two or three, since too many choices are frustrating and confusing to young children. Some appropriate decision-making opportunities for a young child include:

1. Choosing which vegetable or fruit or dessert the family will eat for supper. Talk about color, smell, size, and taste. Alternatively or in addition, allow your child to choose the appropriate-sized dish to serve the food in—not too big and not too small.

2. Selecting the clothes he or she will wear. Again, allow your child to make selections from a limited number of options.

3. Sharing a grocery shopping trip with you. Make a "shopping list" for your child by pasting onto a piece of cardboard various labels from empty cans or boxes of food that you plan on purchasing during the shopping trip. Ask your child to find these items and put them in the cart. Your child will feel good because he or she is big enough to help, which boosts his or her self-image. You benefit, too, because the responsibility of helping keeps your child busy in a productive way.

4. Offering your child the opportunity to choose between two items to buy in the hardware or clothing store, when you have no preference for one or the other. How nice it is to have one's opinion valued and respected.

5. Offering a choice of alternatives to your child when he or she is absorbed in a behavior of which you disapprove. This opportunity can turn an unhappy situation into a learning experience. It also will help avoid a power struggle and will give your child the responsibility of making an appropriate decision. For example, you can explain to your child, "Crayons are for paper or coloring books, not for magazines (or walls). Which would you like to have, a coloring book or some paper?" This calm approach teaches the child something important: Some things are for coloring on, others are not. It may take several reminders before your child remembers and obeys the rule, but he or she has not been "put down" by a frustrated, angry adult. Your child has learned something, and he or she knows what materials to ask for next time.

More Ideas

Respect for children, respect for materials and equipment, and respect for adults could well be a "theme for the year" for many homes and centers. After two weeks, can you see your child's progress? Is he or she handling some object more carefully?

Teacher's Name

You and Children—Your Child is "Somebody"

1. *Treat your child as if he or she is "somebody."*   Call your child by his or her name. Help your child to feel that you like him or her. Try to learn what skills your child's age-group is capable of, then let your child know you think he or she is able to do those things. Be as polite to your child as you would be to an adult; for example, say "please" and "thank you" to your child.

2. *Try to see your child's point of view.*   The things children do make sense to them. Try to think like a child to discover why he or she is acting in a particular way. Find out why something makes sense to your child. It can be an enjoyable experience.

3. *Touch your child to get his or her attention.*   Put your hand on your child's shoulder, take his or her hand or bend down and put your arm around your child to get his or her attention. Speak in a quiet voice and speak slowly so he or she understands what you are saying. This method of gaining your child's attention takes more time, but it works better than does calling loudly across the room.

4. *Talk to your child.*   Talking to children builds their language ability. Give sincere approval when your child successfully masters a difficult situation: "Good job" or "Good idea." Try not to talk *for* your child, or *about* your child, in his or her presence.

5. *Listen to your child.*   Pay attention to children when they talk to you. This may take some time, but it lets children feel that someone thinks they are important enough to listen to. It also helps them develop their language abilities. This is a fine way to let children know they are worthwhile.

6. *Accept your child's feelings.*   Being sad, glad, lonely, or mad is part of being human. Try to let a child know you understand his or her feelings by saying, "You're angry that your brother took your doll," or "You're frightened by that loud noise that you heard," instead of telling a child to stop crying.

7. *Give your child choices.*   Whenever possible, give children a chance to choose. A young child, even a two-year-old, can choose between two things. "Do you want to wear the red shirt or the blue shirt?" A three- or four-year-old can manage three, four, or five choices. The offered choices should be as equal as possible; then be willing to accept what your child chooses!

8. *Give directions carefully.*   If you want your child to do something:
   - *Get* his or her attention.
   - *Explain* carefully what you want your child to do.
   - *Tell* your child why he or she should do it.
   - *Show* him or her how to do it.
   - *Give* your child appreciation. For example, you might say, "You picked up all your blocks." Then give your child a hug or do something else that shows you are proud of his or her accomplishment.

9. *Avoid comparing.*   Avoid making comparisons between your children. When you compare, one child thinks he or she is not as good as a sibling, or that he or she is better. For example, don't say, "Why can't you finish the food on your plate like Tommy does?"

10. *Let your child know you respect his or her decisions, wishes, and needs.*   Giving your child this respect will give him or her a brighter opinion of himself or herself. Your child will also be better able to demonstrate respect for others.

11. *Build your child's positive self-image with encouragement and praise.*   A child who THINKS he or she can succeed has a better chance of succeeding than does a child who expects to fail.

12. *Say to your child, "You're O.K.!"*   Tell him or her: "I will support your efforts, encourage your skills, respect your decisions, value your opinions, help you through rough spots, and watch you succeed!"

Additional Notes

Teacher's Name

Building Success and Confidence in Children

"Nothing succeeds like success." Children who learn this concept early—
that they CAN succeed in small efforts—will have confidence in their own
abilities to tackle greater tasks later. What children think about themselves
and their abilities will greatly influence their potential for success as they
grow older. It will also affect their enthusiasm for meeting new challenges
and will shape their outlook on life.

We can help children build a positive self-image by providing opportunities for them to prove to themselves that they are capable, worthwhile people who are worthy of our respect.

Cooperating and Carrying Out Tasks

1. Know your child's limits and abilities and provide only those tasks which
   he or she can complete successfully. At this age, your child's attention
   span is short, and muscle coordination is not fully developed. It takes a
   long time to accomplish things, and rushing won't help.

2. Your child will be confused and frustrated if you give too many directions
   at one time. It's best to keep jobs simple or give them one step at a time.
   For example, "Let's put some of the toys to bed in the toy box" is a less
   overwhelming instruction than is, "Clean up this mess!" Giving your
   child genuine praise after each successfully completed step keeps good
   behavior going and encourages your child to continue one step at a time.
   Too big a chore can result in failure and disapproval, and a negative
   self-image could follow.

Help A Child Help Himself or Herself

1. Let your child spread his or her own butter, jelly, or peanut butter.

2. Let your child serve himself or herself from bowls or plates of food at
   mealtimes.

3. Let children help set and clear the table. Build confidence and self-
   esteem by making this job a learning game. Talk about sizes, colors,
   numbers, and new concepts, such as the words *on, in, under, beside,* and
   on top of.

4. Even a young child can feel important when propped up on a stool and allowed to help his or her mother "wash" some dishes (unbreakable ones). Try this activity before mealtimes when young children may be underfoot and impatient to eat. Give your child an apron, a stool, some sudsy water, and the cooking spoons and pans you've finished using.

5. Encourage a child to dress himself or herself. This is a big accomplishment and one that a child can be proud of. Praise the effort and ignore the fact that the pants are on backwards. To redo it for your child tells him or her that he or she is not good enough to do it alone. As a result, your child may not want to try again. Try to buy clothing that is easy for your child to put on.

6. Remember, praising your child after he or she completes a job and does it well can help to build a good self-image.

Teacher's Name

Talking to Young Children

Between the ages of two years and four years, a child will have rapid language development—from a few words to an average of 2,000. Adults can help enormously with this development by reading and talking to young children. By helping their children gain new words, parents smooth many of the frustrations felt by young children when they can't explain what they mean. A child who is able to communicate frustration is ultimately a happier child.

What can a parent do to help a child see and describe:

- himself or herself?
- his or her actions?
- his or her world?

1. Play a game about the clothing you are wearing. Tell your child about something you are wearing and then ask him or her to tell you something about what he or she is wearing. For example:

   Parent: "I'm wearing blue pants."
   Child: "I'm wearing a red shirt." (Or, "I'm wearing a shirt with green stripes.")

   Work up to more and more comments until your child can tell you all about what he or she is wearing. Suggest that your child go in sequence from head to toes so he or she won't forget anything. An older child can tell you the materials that his or her clothes are made of, such as cotton or wool.

2. Tell your child about himself or herself as a baby and as a younger child. Often this becomes a favorite story. Point out all the things your child can do NOW that he or she couldn't do then. For example:

   Parent: "When you were a little baby, you couldn't tell me when you were hungry. You just cried and screamed. How do you tell me now?"
   Child: "I say, 'May I have something to eat?'"

   Build an older child's observation skills by having him or her describe a younger child in the family.

3. Ask your child to close his or her eyes and tell you everything that is in the room where you are. Write down what your child says. Then ask him or her to look around and find what was left out.

4. Play "Simon Says." In the role of Simon, ask your child to touch a part of the body that you name. Think of body parts that children don't always know, such as forehead, eyelids, knuckles, hips, elbows, and thighs. Then let your child be Simon. Talk together about parts of the body that come in pairs.

5. Play a game called "Giving Directions." For example, tell your child: "Go get the blue pencil on the table." Work up to two-part directions, such as, "Go get the blue pencil in the middle drawer of the desk upstairs." Add more directions until your child can remember three or four at one time. Add fun directions such as "Hop to the chair," "Jump two times," "Smile at the cat."

6. In the car (or anywhere), play the "Guess What I'm Thinking Of" game. For instance, say, "I'm thinking of something in this car that has two hands wearing mittens (or whatever)." Your child can answer, "That's me!" Let your child ask you to guess what he or she is thinking of.

7. Talk about the different emotions people feel. Look at pictures of people in magazines or in a photo album. Do they look happy or sad? Rushed or relaxed? Ask your child to tell you what makes him or her happy, angry, or worried. Share some of your feelings with your child. Talk about how the way we move around sometimes tells how we feel. Ask your child to show you how he or she would move when feeling happy, scared, or angry.

8. Sing any songs you know to your child. From babyhood on, a child's favorite voices are those of his or her mother and father. Your child doesn't care if you can't sing or think you can't. Sing lullabies, folk songs, holiday songs, patriotic songs, popular songs, or songs with motions that your child can participate in. Make up your own words. Any song that includes your child's name will be a big hit.

Books for Young Children

Ahlberg, Janet, and Allan Ahlberg. *Each Peach Pear Plum*. Viking, 1978. An "I Spy" story.

Anno, Mitsumasa. *Anno's Counting Book*. Crowell, 1975. Watercolor scenes take the reader through the year, with mathematical concepts suggested on each page.

Arkin, Alan. *Tony's Hard Work Day*. Harper, 1972. Tony wants to work too, and he proves that he can.

Asbjornsen, Peter C., and J. E. Moe. *Three Billy Goats Gruff*. Pictures by Marcia Brown. Harcourt, 1957. "Who's that tripping over my bridge?" roared the troll.

Bemelmans, Ludwig. *Madeline*. Viking, 1960. Twelve little French school girls in two straight lines, the youngest one is Madeline.

Birnbaum, Abe. *Green Eyes*. Golden, 1953. A white kitten experiences the four seasons of his first year.

Brenner, Barbara. *Bodies*. Dutton, 1973. We are all alike, yet we each have "a body and a mind, one of a kind." Also see *Faces* by the same author.

Brooke, L. Leslie. *Golden Goose Book*. Warne, 1906. Four stories: "Golden Goose," "Three Bears," "The Three Little Pigs," and "Tom Thumb," brought to life by the irresistible Brooke illustrations.

Brown, Margaret Wise. *Goodnight Moon*. Harper, 1947. A warm and cozy book for quiet night talk.

Burningham, John. *John Burningham's ABC*. Bobbs, 1964.

Burningham, John. *Mr. Gumpy's Outing*. Hold, 1970. The riders tip the boat, but all ends well with a grand tea party.

Burton, Virginia Lee. *Mike Mulligan and His Steam Shovel*. Houghton, 1939. Mike and Mary Ann accomplish great things.

Carle, Eric. *The Very Hungry Caterpillar*. World, 1970. An imaginative look at the life cycle of a butterfly.

Crews, Donald. *Freight Train*. Morrow, 1978. A colorful train experience—one of the best to come down the tracks.

de Brunhoff, Jean. *Story of Babar, the Little Elephant*. Random, 1933. Babar, born in a great forest, learns to enjoy the amenities of civilization. Also see more books about Babar by the same author and his son, Laurent de Brunhoff.

de Regniers, Beatrice Schenk. *May I Bring a Friend*? Illustrated by Beni Montresor. Atheneum, 1964. "Any friend of our friend is welcome here!" say the hospitable king and queen.

de Regniers, Beatrice Schenk. *It Does Not Say Meow*. Illustrated by Paul Galdone. Seabury, 1972. Animal riddle rhymes for guessing games.

Ets, Marie Hall. *Play with Me*. Viking, 1955. Small animals and a little girl meet quietly in a sunny window.

Flack, Marjorie, and Kurt Wiese. *The Story About Ping*. Viking, 1933. A duckling has a narrow escape before he reaches his houseboat home on the Yangtze River.

Fox Went Out on a Chilly Night. An old song illustrated by Peter Spier. Doubleday, 1961.

Teacher's Name

Reading to Young Children

One of the best ways young children learn new words is from parents reading out loud to them. A young two-year-old may be happy with a question-and-answer conversation about one or two of the pictures in a storybook. Reading two or three pages of a book and then discussing the story may be just right for a child who is almost three years old. The story line is not important at this age—identifying objects, enjoying time with Mom or Dad, and cuddling close are what is important. An older child may want the whole story.

Take your child to the library. Let your child pick out his or her own books. He or she may be ready for non-fiction books from the children's section of the library. Books about rockets, Native Americans, the Coast Guard, railroads, or almost any subject are great and can be used for the pictures alone. Discussing the captions of the pictures will help your child learn more about his or her world. Ask the children's librarian for book suggestions.

Repeat a Lot!

When young children (two- and three-year-olds) enjoy a story, they want to hear it over and over again. Help your children enjoy language by substituting new words for old ones and see if they catch you. Or, skip a section of the story and see if they notice. Make up a new ending to the story and then encourage them to do the same.

How Do You Read a Book to Young Children?

When reading to young children, use a lot of sound effects! Read enthusiastically and with drama. Encourage your children to observe details, ask questions, guess what happens next, and discuss what's going on. Point out that the page numbers change as you turn the page.

How to Tell If a Book Is Good

Do you and your child enjoy the experience?

- Are there brightly colored, realistic pictures? Can you tell what they are?

- Is the story simple and easy to identify with? Since two-, three-, and four-year-olds are the center of their own worlds, they like stories in which they can see themselves. They particularly enjoy and identify with talking animals or machines, such as in *Goldilocks and the Three Bears* or *The Little Engine That Could*.
- Is there a lot of repetition? A young child likes to know what to expect. This gives him or her a chance to join in the fun.
- Does it have clear language?
- Do the books show men and women, and people of all races, doing a variety of things?

More Benefits of Reading to Young Children

- It lets them know you think reading is important in your home.
- According to research, it helps your children do better in school.
- Reading together is a time for loving and warmth; it helps children associate this intellectual and stimulating experience with a warm and friendly time.

Books for Young Children

Freeman, Don. *Corduroy*. Viking, 1968.   A department store bear finds a friend named Lisa.

Gag, Wanda. *Millions of Cats*. Coward, 1928.   The rhythm and repetition of the text entice listener participation.

Galdone, Paul. *The Gingerbread Boy*. Seabury, 1975.   He eludes everyone but the wily fox.

Galdone, Paul. *The Little Red Hen*. Seabury, 1973.   The doughty little hen prevails over her lazy housemates.

Ginsburg, Mirra. *Mushroom in the Rain*. Pictures by Jose Aruego and Ariane Dewey. Macmillan, 1974.   A mushroom growing in the rain always shelters one more.

Gretz, Susanna. *The Bears Who Stayed Indoors*. Follett, 1971.   Five furry bears and their spotted dog find fun on a rainy day.

Grimm, Brothers. *The Wolf and the Seven Little Kids*. Translated by Katya Sheppard with pictures by Felix Hoffmann. Harcourt, 1959.   One of Hoffmann's most felicitous renditions of Grimm.

Harper, Wilhelmina. *The Gunniwolf*. Dutton, 1967.   Little Girl goes "pit-pat, pit-pat" and the almost scary Gunniwolf goes "hunker-cha, hunker-cha."

Hoban, Tana. *Count and See*. Macmillan, 1972.   Clear photographs illustrate and expand number concepts.

Hutchins, Pat. *Titch*. Macmillan, 1971.   The littlest one wins. Also try Hutchins' *Good Night Owl*.

Keats, Ezra. *The Snowy Day*. Viking, 1963.   All the wonder of snow seen through a little boy's eyes. See also *Whistle for Willie*.

Langstaff, John. *Oh, a-Hunting We Will Go.* Pictures by Nancy Winslow Parker. Atheneum, 1974. "We'll catch a fox and put him in a _____?" With piano and guitar accompaniment.

Lionni, Leo. *Swimmy.* Pantheon, 1963. Swimmy teaches other little fishes the advantage of working together.

McCloskey, Robert. *Blueberries for Sal.* Viking, 1948. Sal and her mother meet a mother bear and her cub on Blueberry Hill.

McCloskey, Robert. *Make Way for Ducklings.* Viking, 1941. Mrs. Mallard and her eight ducklings travel to the Boston Public Gardens with the help of the police.

Mother Goose: Ring o'Roses. Warne, 1922. A nursery rhyme picture book by L. Leslie Brooke. Incomparable pigs, and *the* Humpty Dumpty. See also *The Real Mother Goose* by B. Wright. Rand, 1916.

Petersham, Maud and Miska. *Circus Baby.* Macmillan, 1950. Mother Elephant tries to teach her baby table manners with hilarious results.

Potter, Beatrix. *The Tale of Peter Rabbit.* Warne, 1903. Naughty Peter explores Mr. McGregor's garden.

Rey, H. A. *Curious George.* Houghton, 1941. George's adventures on land and sea, in jail, and free.

Rice, Eve. *Sam Who Never Forgets.* Greenwillow, 1977. Dependable Sam feeds the zoo animals every day.

Sandburg, Carl. *Wedding Procession of the Rag Doll.* Harcourt, 1967. An unlikely but lively procession described by a poet.

Teacher's Name

Thinking, Talking, and Reading to Young Children

Thinking Activities for Young Children

Observing, noticing, and describing

Encourage your children to use all their senses when noticing. Making popcorn and walking in the rain are two activities that involve a lot of the senses. As you participate in different activities, ask your child:

How does it look?

How does it feel?

How does it taste?

How does it sound?

How does it smell?

Comparing

Have your child compare characters in a story or song.

Categorizing

Have your child make categories for things or feelings. For instance, ask your child to stack up all the red books, or stack up all the books he or she likes, or stack up all the books he or she dislikes. Have your child stack up all the little books. Another day, have him or her stack up all the big books.

Collecting and organizing

Help your child think in terms of groups and categories. For example, ask him or her:

What do you need for a backyard picnic?

What do you need for a family picture album?

What do you need for a birthday party?

Summarizing

Ask your child to give a new title to a story, a song, or a TV show.

Predicting and proving

Ask your child a question in which he or she must predict the correct answer. For example, ask: "Which box is heavier, the large one or the small one?" Then ask, "How do you know? How can you tell if your answer is true?"

Guessing

In science, guessing is called hypothesizing, but this activity is often discouraged in school. In the preschool years, encourage your child to guess what will happen next and to tell you why.

Talking Activities with Young Children

Ask children the following questions (only ask three or four questions at any one time):

What is happening?

What has happened?

What do you think will happen now?

How did this happen?

What caused this to happen?

What took place before this happened?

Where have you seen something like this happen?

How could we make something like this happen?

How does this compare with what we saw or did?

How can we do this more easily?

How can you do this more quickly?

Or ask:

What kind of a thing is it?

What is it called?

Where is it found?

What does it look like?

Have you seen anything else like it? Where? When?

How is like other things?

How is it different from other things?

How can you recognize or identify it?

How did it get its name?

What other names does it have?

What can you do with it?

What is it made of?

How was it made?

What is its purpose?

How does it work or operate?

Best Kinds of Books for Children

Simple stories, animal stories

ABC books that are clever and different

Counting books for beginners

Mother Goose rhymes

Learning books

Lullabies and bedtime/sleepy stories

Books about themselves and other people

Any book you think your child would enjoy

Books for Young Children

Seuss, Dr. *Horton Hatches the Egg*. Random, 1940.   Dedicated Horton is 100 percent faithful.

Slobodkina, Esphyr. *Caps for Sale*. Young Scott, 1947.   A tale of a peddler, some monkeys, and their monkey business.

Steig, William. *Sylvester and the Magic Pebble*. Windmill, 1969.   A careless wish turns Sylvester into a rock, but the tragedy is resolved with humor and tenderness.

Zemach, Harve, and Margot Zemach. *Mommy Buy Me a China Doll*. Follett, 1966.   From an Ozark song. Liza Lou has outlandish plans.

Zion, Gene. *Harry the Dirty Dog*. Pictures by Margaret Bloy Graham. Harper, 1956.   Harry has such fun getting dirty, but then Harry's family can't recognize him.

More Books to Read Aloud

Five-, six-, and seven-year-olds will enjoy these books, too.

Ackerman, K., and D. Ray. *The Banshee*. Philomel, 1990.

Alexander, M. *Move Over, Twerp*. Dial Books, 1981.

Alexander, S. *Dear Phoebe*. Little, Brown, 1984.

Aliki. *We Are Best Friends*. Greenwillow, 1982.

Allard, H., and J. Marshall. *Miss Nelson is Missing*. Houghton Mifflin, 1977.

Allender, D. *Shake My Sillies Out*. Crown Publishers, 1987.

Anno, M. *All in a Day*. Philomel, 1986.

Belloc, H. *Matilda. . . .* Knopf, 1991.

Base, G. *My Grandma Lived in Gooligulch*. Harry A. Abrahams, 1983.

Carle, E. *The Grouchy Ladybug*. Crowell, 1977.

Chorao, D. *Grumley the Grouch*. Holiday House, 1980.

Cohen, M., and L. Hoban. *Jim Meets the Thing*. Greenwillow, 1981.

Cole, J. *It's Too Noisy*. Crowell, 1989.

Coleridge, A., and R. Harvey. *The Friends of Emily Culpepper*. Putnam, 1987.

Conrad, P. *The Tub People*. Harper & Row, 1989.

Couzyn, J. *Bad Day*. Dutton, 1988.

Cuyler, M. *That's Good! That's Bad!* Holt, 1991.

Ehlert, L. *Fish Eyes*. Harcourt Brace Jovanovich, 1990.

Farber, N. *I Found Them in the Yellow Pages*. Little, Brown, 1973.

Gackenbach, D. *Harry and the Terrible Whatzit*. Houghton Mifflin, 1977.

Geissert, A. *Pigs from A to Z*. Houghton Mifflin, 1986.

Goode, D. *I Hear a Noise*. Dutton, 1988.

Holder, H. *Crows*. Farrar, Straus and Giroux, 1987.

Kellog, S. *Aster Aardvark's Alphabet Adventure*. Morrow, 1987.

Mahy, M. *The Great White Man-Eating Shark*. Dial, 1989.

Mayer, M. *There's Something in My Attic*. Dial, 1988.

Meddaugh, S. *Too Many Monsters*. Houghton Mifflin, 1982.

Merrian, E. *Fighting Words*. Morrow, 1992.

Nordqvist, S. *Willie in the Big World*. Morrow, 1985.

Parkinson, K. *The Enormous Turnip*. Whitman, 1986.

Pelavin, C. *Ruby's Revenge*. Punam, 1972.

Rice, E. *What Sadie Sang*. Greenwillow, 1976.

Sendak, M. *One Was Johnny*. Harper & Row, 1962.

Sendak, M. *Pierre, A Cautionary Tale . . .* Harper & Row, 1962.

Sendak, M. *Where the Wild Things Are*. Harper & Row, 1963.

Seuss, Dr. *The Sneetches*. Random House, 1950.

Seuss, Dr. *Thidwick the Big-Hearted Moose*. Random House, 1948.

Seuss, Dr. *Yertle the Turtle*. Random House, 1950.

Sheeter, B. *The Discontented Mother*. Harcourt, Brace, Jovanovich, 1980.

Slobodkin, L. *Excuse Me Certainly*. Vanguard Press, 1959.

Smith, L. *Glasses—Who Needs 'Em?* Viking, 1991.

Steig, W. *Amos and Boris*. Farrar, Straus and Giroux, 1971.

Steig, W. *Rotten Island*. Goldine, 1984.

Steptoe, J. *Mufaro's Beautiful Daughters*. Lothrop, Lee & Shepard, 1987.

Stevensen, J. *"Could Be Worse!"* Greenwillow, 1977.

Stevensen, J. *No Friends*. Greenwillow, 1986.

Stevensen, J. *That Dreadful Day*. Greenwillow, 1985.

Stevensen, J. *The Worst Person in the World at Crab Beach*. Greenwillow, 1988.

Stevensen, J. *Yuch!* Greenwillow, 1984.

Udry, J. *A Tree is Nice*. Harper & Row, 1956.

Ungerer, T. *No Kiss for Mother*. Harper & Row, 1973.

Ungerer, T. *The Three Robbers*. Antheneum, 1962.

Vincent, G. *Smile, Ernest and Celeste*. Greenwillow, 1982.

Viorst, J. *Alexander and the Terrible, Horrible, No Good, Very Bad Day*. Antheneum, 1972.

Vogel, M. *1 Is No Fun But 20 Is Plenty*. Antheneum, 1965.

Williams, L. *The Little Old Lady Who Was Not Afraid of Anything*. Crowell, 1986.

Zemach, M. *It Could Always Be Worse*. Farrar, Straus and Giroux, 1976.

Zion, G. *The Meanest Squirrel I Ever Met*. Scribner, 1962.

For these and more children's favorites, please see your children's librarian.

Parent Papers Set II

Teacher's Name

Understanding Two-Year-Olds

Every child is different, as every parent knows. Still, it is helpful to know what other children might be doing developmentally at a particular age. If your child doesn't fit this particular age group, read the Parent Paper that discusses older children or read other materials about younger children. By exploring and keeping in mind the general stages of child development, you may be able to better understand your child's everyday behavior as well as his or her occasional behavior.

Did you know that you (the parent) are your child's most important teacher? Research has shown this over and over, and research also shows that the most important thing for a child's success and development is for an adult to think he or she is wonderful.

General Characteristics of the Two-Year-Old

- Demonstrates unevenly developed motor skills. Large muscle coordination is good (the child can walk and climb), but small muscles and eye-hand coordination are still not well-developed.
- Goes through rapid language development. Vocabulary increases from a few words or short sentences to up to 2,000 words by age four.
- Gradually acquires skills in dressing and feeding self.
- Goes through changes in sleep patterns. He or she is gradually giving up daytime naps, but still needs a rest period and about 12 hours of sleep at night.
- Has almost a complete set of baby teeth.
- Often has begun to establish toilet habits and usually will be able to handle his or her own needs by age four.

Characteristic Behavior

- Plays alone, or plays beside, but not with, others.
- Does not share or take turns too well.
- Often says "no," but gradually becomes able to accept adult limits. Wants adult approval and likes to be close to mother and father.

- Helps around the house and is beginning to understand his or her surroundings and the demands of daily life. Likes to feel familiar with things and have a sense of security.
- Imitates language, manners, and habits.
- Is constantly active and shows tiredness by becoming irritable or restless. Seems to have an urgent need to explore.
- Gradually learns what is acceptable and what is not. Much repetition is important.
- Demonstrates great curiosity and asks countless questions.

Special Needs

- A need for love and affection from parents. Two-year-olds also need guidance and a pattern of behavior to follow.
- A need for time, patience, understanding, and genuine interest from adults.
- A need for simple, clear routines and limited choices.
- A need for opportunities to learn sharing and taking turns, to learn to play cooperatively with other children.

Teacher's Name

Understanding Three-Year-Olds

Every child is different, as every parent knows. Still, it is helpful to know what other children might be doing developmentally at a particular age. If your child doesn't fit this particular age group, read the selection on older or younger children in these Parent Papers. By discovering more about general stages of child development, you may be able to better understand your child's everyday behavior as well as his or her occasional behavior.

Did you know that you (the parent) are your child's most important teacher? Research has shown this over and over again; research also shows that the most important thing for a child's success is for an adult to think he or she is wonderful.

General Characteristics of the Three-Year-Old

- Demonstrates motor skills that are still unevenly developed. Large muscle coordination is still much better than small muscle and eye-hand coordination.
- Has a full set of baby teeth.
- Shows an awareness of the sequence of steps and the probable outcomes of his or her activities. The three-year-old begins to plan ahead.
- Continues to develop language ability at full speed. The most important and amazing verbal development occurs this year.
- Acquires more skills in feeding and dressing self.
- Goes through changes in sleep patterns, but still needs a daytime nap or rest period and nearly 12 hours of sleep at night. A three-year-old may get tired easily.
- Toilet habits are getting better.

Characteristic Behaviors

- Shows more interest in playing with other children. He or she still needs to play alone some, and is not ready to share or take turns too often.
- Wants adult approval and likes to cuddle. The three-year-old may reject the adult, but still needs him or her.
- Becomes even more interested in helping around the house.
- Likes to imitate language, manners, and habits.

- Experiments and explores within adult limits.
- Gradually learns what is acceptable behavior and what is not.
- Enjoys looking at picture and story books, and has a better understanding of words. A three-year-old shows great curiosity and still asks many questions.

Special Needs

- A need for the security of love and affection from parents, adult direction, and a consistent pattern of behavior to follow.
- A need for time, patience, understanding, and genuine interest from adults.
- A need for simple, clear daily schedules and limited choices.
- A need for opportunities to learn give-and-take, and to play with other children.
- A need for a wider scope of activity.

Teacher's Name

Understanding Four-Year-Olds

Every child is different, as every parent knows. Still, it is helpful to know what other children might be doing developmentally at a particular age. If your child doesn't fit his or her particular age group, read the material about younger children in these Parent Papers or look for material about older children. By finding out more about the general stages of child development, you may be better able to understand your child's everyday behavior as well as his or her occasional behavior.

Did you know that you (the parent) are your child's most important teacher? Research has shown this over and over; research also shows that the most important thing for a child's success and achievement is for an adult to think he or she is wonderful.

General Characteristics of the Four-Year-Old

- The desire to run, not walk, and the desire to yell, not talk. However, a four-year-old still wants adult approval.
- Motor development is still better in terms of large muscles than small muscles or eye-hand coordination.
- Rapid language development continues up to and past 2,000 words.
- Becomes quite skillful in feeding and dressing himself or herself, but may need occasional help.
- Develops sleep patterns that still incorporate up to 12 hours of sleep each night.
- Toilet habits are established. The four-year-old child usually takes care of his or her own needs by this age period.

Characteristic Behaviors

- Shows more independence and reliability.
- Has more interests in many things, including an interest in people and the way they act.
- Plays with real purpose, and engages in much more imaginative play. He or she begins to pretend to be other people or animals.
- Better understands his or her environment and enjoys trips. He or she asks searching questions about people and their relationships to others.

- Is able to accept necessary limits and restraints from adults.
- Likes to be close to mother and father.
- Is constantly active. Likes to help around the house, and imitates language and habits.
- Becomes capable of longer stretches of quiet activity as he or she approaches five.
- Learns many new words and asks many questions.

Special Needs

- A need for love and affection from parents. Four-year-olds also need guidance and a pattern of behavior they can imitate. They need to feel valued.
- A need for time, patience, understanding, and genuine interest from adults.
- A need for a wider scope of activity and limited freedom to move about, and to move away from the home surroundings.
- A need for opportunities to do things for him- or herself.

Teacher's Name

Discipline: A Learning Process

A *disciple* is someone who learns. *Discipline*, then, should be a learning process, not a process of scaring a child into NOT doing something. By explaining and helping a child to understand, you help him or her learn how you want him or her to behave. You also help him or her to communicate better and to develop self-control. A child who is scared into not doing something or saying something in front of one adult, may well say or do that very thing at school or in the center.

1. *Show children what to do instead of saying "Don't," "Stop," and "Quit."* Children learn how to act when you show them what to do. Just stopping their negative behavior doesn't teach them what to do next time. For example, telling a child, "Wait until the floor is dry" is better than saying, "Don't walk on the wet floor." Saying, "Hold it this way" is better than saying, "Don't drop it."

2. *Use substitutes.* If you have to take something away from a child, give him or her something different to play with. Provide active or noisy activities that are acceptable ways to let off aggression. Digging, shouting at the trees outside, and mopping are all good. (Saw about 2 feet off the handle of a mop for a very useful new toy.)

3. *Encourage little children to think of something else when they are unhappy.* Small children forget quickly. Call a child's attention to something else. This distraction will take his or her mind off the cause of the unhappiness. This works *very* well with children under two years of age.

4. *Show a child how to help you when he or she bothers you.* If a child is bothering you as you work, find something else for him or her to do. Show the child how to help. Giving him or her your attention may be more necessary right then than the job you are doing.

5. *Establish trust; build a positive relationship.* Build trust with your child by giving praise when he or she comes closer and closer to doing something the way you want him or her to do it. This is called "shaping behavior," and lets your child know you are cheering his or her efforts.

6. *Aim for consistency.* A little child learns best if the rules don't change too much. It's better to have just a few rules and then really stick to those few. If you have too many rules, you forget them and so does your child. Wait to add new rules until some old situations have been resolved.

7. *Consider your body language.* Cuing a child with a frown or a smile becomes more effective in shaping behavior as a child grows older. Explain your facial expressions to a young child. For example, say, "I'm smiling because _____" or "I am frowning because _____."

8. *Know your child.* Some children respond to different rewards or different instructions in different ways. This can be true even in the same family. Study your child and think what methods help him or her to understand. Learn what a child this age is capable of handling. By doing some research, you won't ask more of your child than he or she can deliver.

9. *Understand your own personal style.* Your child can get used to your style, but it helps if you both come to understand it. Try to respond to situations as a thinking adult rather than as a "super parent" or an infuriated child. (This is hard to do, but worth it.) You can tell your child what your style is. "I may not seem upset now, but if you do that three times, I'm really going to be upset." Some parents have a "quick to anger, quick to hug" style, while other parents are calmer.

10. *Consider your child's verbal development.* How well a child understands your directions and can express to you what he or she needs or wants can be the single most important factor in the smoothness of your relationship. The more you help your child learn new words by reading and talking with him or her, the faster frustrations can be resolved.

11. *Encourage decision-making.* Saying such things as, "Well, Michael, you make the decision—either this or this," helps your child build self-control. A decision your child makes is more interesting to him or her than one you make for him or her. This skill will also help your child in later life.

12. *Do some scheduling.* Children do best when quiet and active play are alternated. Think over the most difficult times of the day. Reflect on what a small (or large) scheduling change might accomplish. If both parents work, some singing in the morning might get the day off to a happier start, for instance.

13. *Set up rooms to make them "child-friendly."* Placing furniture and belongings so your child can do things for himself or herself greatly helps to remove frustrations and build his or her competence. The child who is helped to believe "I can do it" feels good about himself or herself, and develops self-control.

Summary

Think of something in the course of your childhood that helped to build *your* self-esteem and thus your self-control. It is important for a child to learn that his or her efforts toward a goal are as important as the goal itself. With this view, failure is less of a defeat because learning occurs along the way. "We'll try again and we'll learn from this" are wonderful words everyone likes to hear.

Parents' attitudes and moods convey either healthy respect to children or discouragement. If parents reinforce good behavior, children will grow to do what parents expect.

HELPING A YOUNG CHILD DEVELOP SELF-CONTROL (#2)

Teacher's Name

Self-Control

1. What is the most difficult task for *you* in the area of self-control in connection with your child?

2. What is the most difficult task for *your child* in the area of self-control?

3. What is the most difficult task for *you* in teaching and guiding your child to control his or her emotions and actions?

4. If you have visited our classroom, what are some of the ways the adults involved here tried to behave in a socially acceptable manner? (Adult behavior that a child *sees* is much more impressive than what an adult may say.)

5. Watch your child playing with some of his or her friends. At home, observe several children who are involved in frustrating situations. On another sheet of paper, describe the reactions of the children. Try to observe children older and younger than your own child, as well as children of both sexes.

Discussion

1. *Children may need different kinds of self-control for different situations.* A big concept for a young child to learn is to use such words as, "Please give me that. That's mine!" or "Stop it! I don't like that!" instead of using actions such as pushing, shoving, grabbing, or hitting to express themselves. Supply your child with the words he or she could use to replace unacceptable actions. For example, supply the words, "Please open the door!" Then say: "Do not kick the door when you want it opened." A child needs to be told what to do as well as what not to do. If your first attempts of the "use words and not actions" approach are not 100 percent successful, that's alright; your child is learning new words and will soon be able to use them at the appropriate time. Repeated trials will teach the idea. Try to use words and not actions yourself so your child will see you using acceptable behavior.

2. *Sometimes a young child needs to be completely removed from a situation.* If your child is playing with friends or with older children and is getting tired, removing him or her to a quiet activity may prevent a quarrel. A chair or place for a "time out" period can be quite successful. In this approach, the child sits with a book or a toy in the "time out" chair or place, until he or she feels like being with people again.

3. *Anticipate that when the parent is preoccupied, the child's self-control will deteriorate.* If a parent is visiting with guests, on the telephone, or occupied in some other way and a young child starts to fuss and whine, it is better for the parent to interrupt an activity briefly than to accept the formation of a bad habit. The parent can take the child to a quiet place, give him or her a book or toy, then say quite firmly, "You may not fuss while I am on the phone." Even if the child comes out again, the idea has been planted. If the parent does this every time there is a problem, the desired learning soon occurs. On the other hand, if the parent hands the child a cookie to quiet him or her, this will teach the child that if he or she fusses and whines while Mom or Dad are busy, a reward will be coming.

After one or two weeks, answer again the questions at the beginning of this Parent Paper. See if any answers have changed. If you have extra time, list good and bad examples of adults guiding children. Refer to this list of good examples when you need to. Some parents keep this list handy for a crisis moment.

Additional Notes

Teacher's Name

Children Need Adults for Guidance

As children grow, their need to be independent often leads them into trouble. Sometimes they put themselves in danger and often they put the people around them into uncomfortable situations. Frequently young children handle things too roughly, using small, eager, but awkward, fingers. This Parent Paper points out some planning ideas and techniques that can be used in your child's classroom or at home to redirect children's actions into acceptable behavior.

1. Look around your child's classroom. Consider the reasons why materials are placed where they are, and why specific amounts of each material are made available. What are some ways children are guided to use materials in a beneficial way?

2. What happens when there is a quarrel over materials or toys? What language does the adult who is dealing with the children use in this situation?

3. Children learn very quickly by imitation. Adult behavior that children see is much more impressive to them than what adults may say. How does the teacher show good relations between people? How does he or she show respect for others? How does the teacher demonstrate care for materials and equipment?

In guiding children, adults can:

- *Strengthen their self-control.* Often boosting the child's interest in what he or she is doing, or providing the child with extra materials, will accomplish this.

- *Reduce frustrations.* When a child can't reach his or her goals, the adult can:

  Remove temptations

  Restructure the situation; provide for a quiet activity; lend a helping hand

  See that the child's possessions are easy for him or her to get out and put away (i.e., check the child's room layout)

  Remove the child until he or she regains self-control (allow the child to ride a truck outside, go to his or her room with a book, or use the time-out chair, for example)

- *Appeal to understanding.* Explain how and why you want something done (or not done). You might say, for example, "Can you pick up two toys and I'll pick up two toys? How many toys do we have now?"

- *Use imagination.* Set up some role playing situations: "You be the Baby Bear and I'll be Mama Bear and then we can. . . ." Using special voices during role play is a big help in capturing the child's attention. Have children take turns giving you instructions.

Remember:

- A positive approach brings positive results.
- The ripple effect works both negatively and positively. A highly emotional approach to a situation distracts the family. If adults yell, children will too.
- Focus on what is being done rather than on feelings or on the child. Say, "Please paint on the paper and not on your chair."

More ideas:

- Give gifts that help with future quiet times, such as crayons, drawing paper, spiral notebooks, or photo albums.
- Have children make memory books of vacations. These books might include pictures, photographs, even pressed weeds from summer or from a walk with grandmother.
- Keep paper, old magazines, paste, blunt scissors, and other interesting materials in a special box for quiet times.

Evaluation

Have you tried two of these ideas in the last two weeks? Give yourself a blue ribbon or a pat on the back as a "Good Parent Award."

Additional Notes

Teacher's Name

Toys That Teach: What to Choose

When choosing toys, consider the major areas in which a child develops. Toys that teach and enhance development will be the result of careful selection. The major areas of a child's development are physical, mental, social, and emotional. The following list gives some ideas of appropriate toys for preschoolers that focus on developing skills in these four areas. Write your own ideas in the margins and keep this Parent Paper handy for birthdays, Christmas, calls from grandparents, or other special occasions.

Toys for Two- and Three-year-olds

Children this age especially need toys that build physical coordination, develop independence, and satisfy curiosity.

Physical Development ("Fitness")

Steps for climbing to reach sink and toilet

Large balls

Doll carriages

Large trucks to ride

Large, light, hollow blocks (See the Parent Paper "How to Make Toys for Your Child")

Swing set, climbing gym, tricycles, outdoor equipment

Outdoor sandbox

Mental Development ("Brainwork")

Simple inlay puzzles (just a few pieces to start)

Put-it-together train, boat

Colored beads to string

Legos™, table toys that interlock (store and use these in gift-type flat boxes with lids)

Blocks

Rubber animals and people to use with blocks

Picture books, song records

Shiny metal or unbreakable mirror

Water toys for bath tub or sink

Social Development ("Teamwork")

Housekeeping equipment

Dress-up hats and clothes for boys and girls (make-believe helps learning)

Large unbreakable washable doll

Ride-a-stick horse

Clothespins, clothesline for hanging art work, doll clothes

Paper bags, grocery boxes, and cans to play "store"

Tea set, plastic dishes, eggbeater, pots and pans

Small cars and trucks

Emotional Development ("Tension Releasers")

Rocking chair/rocking horse

Pounding toys

Large brushes, poster paints, crayons

Clay and/or play dough

Finger paint (use in bathtub for easy cleanup)

Sand and cups, pails, spoons, strainer, shovels, orange juice cans—for pouring, digging, modeling

Musical instruments—bells, xylophone, triangle, drums, pans

Straws to blow bubbles

Toys for Four- and Five-year-olds

Children this age have a special need for plenty of activity. They want to learn about their world by seeing and doing things. Their teamwork is getting better and toys that help with all these needs are sure to teach. All the toys listed for two- and three-year-olds are still good, along with the following:

Physical Development ("Fitness")

Old tires on the ground for jumping

Bean bags and baskets or boxes to throw them in

Large wooden or cardboard boxes to play train

Wagons

Mental Development ("Brainwork")

Blackboard and white chalk (materials that will be used in grade school)

Small-sized desk or table and chair

Bulletin board to pin up his or her works

Books and records with more detail than for age three

Puzzles with more pieces

Crayons, markers, paper of several sizes, including newspapers

More put-together toys

Lotto games

Scissors with rounded points

Glue or paste

Social Development ("Teamwork")

Small cars and trucks (play "gas station")

Finger and hand puppets

More blocks for the set he or she has started

Doctor kit, hospital kit

Flannel board and flannel cut-outs

More props for make-believe, such as costume jewelry and hats from different adult occupations

Emotional Development ("Tension Releasers")

More toys or cans for sand and water play

Eggbeater for water play

Hammer and nails for supervised woodworking

Painting of all kinds (plain water and a roller can be used outside in the summer)

Musical instruments and record player

Additional Notes

Teacher's Name

What Toys Can Teach

Math

Math learning begins when a child learns that two parts of a whole can be taken apart and put back together again. This realization can occur while cutting a cupcake or an apple in half, or while playing with blocks—one long block and two short blocks that combine in length to equal the long one. Learning the vocabulary for math is very important in early years. Using terms such as *how much, too much, half full, all gone, a quarter full,* and other measurement phrases can be incorporated into sand and water play.

Estimating is a process used throughout life and can be learned during block and water play. For example, watch a child estimate where to put two blocks to make the bottom of his or her bridge. This skill improves as three-year-olds become four-year-olds. During water play, ask a child to guess how many more spoons full (or cups full) of water are needed to fill up a pot. Fractions will not be so strange in elementary school if a child has been talking about them for years. Look for activities that require the child to make comparisons: More or less? Light or heavy? Thick or thin? Long or short?

Toys that help math learnings include:

Blocks

Sand or pouring materials that are contained within a large pan, such as rice, macaroni, bird seed, or cornmeal

Water, cups, and utensils

Ruler

Tape measure

Puzzles

Straws

Language/Prereading

A child must learn to talk and think before he or she can learn to read. Any activity that "gives" a child new words is valuable in the early years. Looking at and talking about a book or some pictures a few minutes every day will do a great deal to help your child in first grade. Records and songs also help children develop vocabulary.

Any toys that help a child to see sameness or difference in objects, pictures, shapes, colors, or symbols help build reading skills. Stringing beads, working with "fit-together" table toys, looking at details in pictures, and talking about what people are doing can all help to develop readiness and language skills.

Toys that encourage language/prereading skills include:

Books

Records

Lotto games (make your own from two matching catalogs)

Puppets

Games, especially board games

Old magazines that contain lots of pictures

Props that can be used to act out stories read in books

"Fit-together" toys

Dice or dominoes to match and do groupings

Sensory Learning

The more senses involved in a child's learning experience, the stronger the learning will be. An example of this is how the smells and tastes of holiday foods can take us back to certain times and events in our own childhoods.

In addition to *seeing* and learning to observe carefully, *hearing* samenesses and differences in sounds and recognizing common sounds are important for learning. *Touching* concrete objects, actually handling materials, is essential for young children and doubles or triples the impact of learning for adults, too. Learning to identify substances by their *smell* is fun for young children and can be a springboard to new conversations and thus to new words.

Children need to use their sense of *taste* to learn such words as *crunchy, sweet, sour, mushy,* and *sticky.* Most two-year-olds, who can barely talk, can tell you the name of their favorite cereal. Talking about food while you are eating with a child is a wonderful time to build vocabulary that identifies foods and their textures. For example: "This cracker tastes very crunchy and salty."

Toys and activities that help children learn through the senses include:

Musical toys or instruments

Objects placed inside small boxes for a listen-and-describe activity: rice, pebbles, pennies, beans. Fasten the boxes securely. For a younger child, make matching pairs of "listening boxes." Ask the child to find a box that sounds the same as yours.

Records, song books

Making popcorn

Kitchen items placed inside jars for a smell-and-describe activity: tea bag, mustard, peanut butter, chocolate

Objects placed inside a sock such as a stone, a stick, a pine cone, a spoon, or a cotton ball, to provide a feel-and-describe activity. Have the child describe what he or she feels.

Activities in the kitchen, such as tearing lettuce for salad, making instant pudding, and pouring ingredients into a bowl are good for young helpers.

Teacher's Name

How to Make Toys for Your Child

Toys or activities that are made at home are especially interesting to young children. They carry an extra ingredient of love and the child feels important, like "somebody special." The low price of homemade toys is especially attractive, and often the play value of these toys is long-lasting.

1. *Blocks*   Rinse out and stuff half-gallon milk cartons with crumpled newspaper. Tape the cartons securely closed to form a square end. You might also want to jam one carton inside a second to form a stronger block. These blocks can be covered with colored contact paper, but this is not necessary. Tip: This can be done two or three at a time while watching television.

2. *Puzzles*   Glue a colorful magazine picture onto a piece of cardboard. Cut the cardboard into three or four shapes for a two- or three-year-old; five to ten shapes for a four- or five-year-old. Store each puzzle in a separate envelope.

3. *Ride-in Train*   Line up three or four cardboard boxes to make a train that children can sit in. Add slips of paper for "tickets" and appoint a "ticket taker." This is a good activity for rainy weather.

4. *Play House*   Obtain a very large carton, such as a box from a washing machine or from a moving company. Use a marker to draw a door and windows onto the box. Cut out the doors and at least one window. This house will last about two weeks or more and is greatly appreciated.

5. *Tent*   Place a blanket over a card table. This makeshift tent allows children to invent games about camping, army, or whatever the child's imagination chooses. With a pillow inside and some books, the tent can be left up in a child's room as a reading corner.

6. *Puppets*   Stuff brown paper lunch bags with newspaper. Secure them with a wire twist-tie or rubber band. Draw faces and hair with markers. Show your child how to use a table as a stage by holding the puppets up from behind the table. Discarded white or light-colored socks also make good puppets. Draw faces on them with markers.

7. *Indoor sandbox*   Fill a large roasting pan or basin with macaroni, birdseed, cornmeal, or beans. Any substance that will pour is good. Provide cans, measuring cups, and a funnel. When your child is finished playing, store the "sand" in a plastic bag or cover the container with aluminum foil. (This activity is good for early math learnings.)

8. *Beads for Stringing*   Provide your child with empty spools and a shoelace. The spools can be painted if desired. Using a needle and thread to string round-shaped cereal (such as Cheerios™) for the birds is an activity young children enjoy. Rigatoni can be strung on a shoelace to make a "necklace" or a "bracelet." It also can be painted.

9. *Easel for Painting*   Tape paper to the bottom of the refrigerator door. Place newspaper on the floor beneath and let your child sit on the floor and create art work with crayons or paint.

10. *Homemade Paint*   Add food coloring to liquid starch to create some paints. For finger paints, use instant vanilla pudding that has food coloring added.

11. *Food Coloring*   During water play, put a few drops of red food coloring into the water. Later, add a few drops of yellow and ask the child what happens. Do this with blue and yellow and with red and blue. Freeze ice cubes of different colors. Put a red and yellow ice cube into a bowl and ask your child to tell you what happens. Add a squirt of liquid soap to the water to make bubbles.

12. *Play dough*   Mix or let your child mix 2 cups flour with 1 cup salt, 1/4 to 1/2 cup water, 1/4 cup oil, and a few drops of food coloring of your choice. Keep the dough in a plastic bag.

Additional Notes

Program Enrichment Papers

These program enrichment papers cover similar topics from three different early childhood education curriculum approaches: the activity approach, the subject matter approach, and the process skills approach. Programs favoring one particular philosophy can choose, from each series of three program enrichment papers, the paper that corresponds to the preferred philosophy. Many teachers and caregivers will want to use all three approaches. These different approaches can either be intermeshed in one day, or used on succeeding days to build a continuous flow in curriculum. The papers are meant to be removed from this text and individually posted in the classroom so that the teacher or aide can glance at them for reminders during actual teaching time. Visitors will benefit, too, from seeing an organized plan in action.

For each program enrichment paper, a particular month is indicated that a sheet might be used. Programs in warmer or colder climates will want to rearrange these to suit their particular locale.

As mentioned before, the three curriculum approaches selected are the activity approach, the subject matter approach, and the process skills approach. We at the Education, Continuing Education and Administration Institute (formerly the Early Childhood Education Administration Institute) believe that every curriculum's goal should be to develop the whole child—intellectually, socially, emotionally, and physically. However, goal titles will vary depending on the philosophy of a particular school or curriculum. Also, the ideas highlighted during a particular activity will reflect the curriculum approach being used. It is our opinion that a combination of all three approaches yields a rich and interesting program that contributes to the growth and development of children. However, since parameters are sometimes set by those outside the classroom, we have, to a degree, separated activities by the three different approaches.

Activity Approach

This is the traditional nursery school, whole child development curriculum. Goals and objectives are often listed by holidays, seasons, or units. This approach provides a wide range of experiences that build self-confidence and competence. The materials for this approach allow children to see, feel, smell, and interact with their environment. The child is encouraged to learn through ALL his or her senses and the materials provide for this.

Subject Matter Approach

This approach can be identified by goals that are academic and subjects that are the same as the ones the child will encounter later in schooling. Much of what is done in early childhood builds foundations for later learning in all approaches. By highlighting subject matter skills, this approach sometimes provides fewer concrete experiences and more teacher-directed learning than do other approaches. A good teacher can be aware of this pitfall and guard against it. Goals in the subject matter curriculum are listed by subject matter, such as language, math, science, or social studies.

Process Skills Approach

The process approach to the curriculum has as its goals the enabling of the child to adapt to an ever-changing society. As units or goals in this curriculum approach, creative skills, interactive skills, or cognitive skills are listed as headings. These skills or processes include decision-making, cooperating, caring, communicating, creating, perceiving, observing, loving, knowing, and problem-solving. The child is active in experimentation, exploration, construction, and selectivity. The child confidently acts on his or her environment and exhibits flexibility. The materials for this approach are much like those used in the activity approach, providing for visual discrimination, tactile sensitivity, perceptual motor development, and eye-hand coordination. Large and small muscle equipment is utilized to provide a wide range of experiences for the young child.

Organization of the Program Enrichment Papers

A distinct sequence is listed in each day's activity. The *Curriculum Approach* tells which philosophy is being highlighted. The *Goal* identifies particular learnings that are emphasized. The *Materials Needed* section lists materials and some ordering information. An attempt is made to keep materials simple, inexpensive, and readily available. The *Time Needed* is always shown, and can be expanded or continued for several days depending on the preference of the teacher and the age of the children. Reference is made to different times in the children's schedule, circle time, free choice time, outdoor time, and so forth. However, these activities can be fit into any schedule the program uses.

The *How To Do It* section gives a simple, step-by-step description of the activity. An effort is made to be brief and clear in this section. An effort also has been made to choose crafts and projects a child of three or four can do himself or herself. The process and fun of making the craft are more important than is the finished product. A child who is given a "pre-prepared" craft made from a pattern, and is expected just to put the finishing touches on so "it will look nice for mother," receives the message that he or she is incompetent to do it alone. Since children often may feel this way anyway—because most furniture at home is too big for them and they don't always understand what is going on with adults—it is important that their time in a children's group not add to these feelings of incompetence. With thought and planning, crafts can be chosen that give even a two-year-old a feeling of success and competency. Two-year-olds make lovely collages and attractive finger paint pictures, for instance.

The *Evaluation* section provides the teacher or caregiver with some evaluative information geared to the appropriateness of the age of the children, by describing observable signs of success. In the *Easier and Harder Ideas* section, number 1 gives adaptations of the activity or suggests another one like it for younger children, and number 2 provides ideas for older or more able children. This section also encourages teachers and children to adapt enrichment program activities and to create new ones themselves. The *Send-Home Ideas* section allows for the parent to be included as an active partner in his or her child's learning.

The program enrichment paper(s) that are to be in use on a particular day can be detached and posted in the classroom. Teachers can jot notes about the activity, the materials, or the children on the reverse side, and keep these in a folder as a resource.

Tasting Party

Curriculum Approach

Activity approach

Goal

Identifying foods that are considered good snacks; tasting and accepting a variety of foods

Materials Needed

Magazines, scissors, paste or glue, paper, fruits for tasting, raw vegetables, dry cereals, yogurt, crackers, lemons, honey

Time Needed

20 minutes during free choice time, 15 to 20 minutes at snack time

How To Do It

1. Ask the children to choose and cut out magazine pictures of "good" and "poor" snacks.
2. Make collages of good or poor snacks, or include both on one collage with a dividing line in the center.
3. Have a tasting party at snack time by allowing children to select a variety of snacks put out in small cups. This can continue for several days.
4. Discuss which foods are new to which children. Give a gold star or other reward to the child trying the most new foods, if desired. Discuss the texture and smell of the foods.

Age

3, 4, 5

Evaluation

Are the children able to divide the good and the poor snacks with some accuracy? Do most of them try at least one new thing?

Easier and Harder Ideas

1. Practice new words with the children, such as *crunchy, gooey, sour, slushy, sticky, crackly*, and any more that seem applicable.

2. Ask children to help prepare the tasting table as the week goes on. Using plastic or serrated knives, they can cut up fruit or vegetables under supervision. Encourage them to spread peanut butter or honey on their own crackers.

Send-Home Ideas

Suggest that parents have children point out good snacks and poor snacks when they are shopping together at the grocery store. Encourage parents to reward children in some small way when they try a new food. Let parents know that it builds eye-hand coordination when children are allowed to help prepare their own snacks.

Dear Teacher:

Thank you for your work with children. Did you know this is some of the most important work in the world? You are making a contribution to the future every day.

Textures, Smells, and Consistencies

Curriculum Approach

Subject matter

Goals

Developing science concepts by discovering different textures, odors, and consistencies in foods; building math concepts by measuring liquids

Materials Needed

Yogurt, pudding, apples, bananas, granola, apple sauce, peanut butter, juice, cups, crackers, nuts, measuring cups

Time Needed

10 minutes of free choice time extending into 20 minutes of snack time

How To Do It

1. Set up three discovery centers with appropriate foods for demonstrating different textures, odors, and consistencies.
2. Invite the children to measure half a cup of juice and pour it into paper cups.
3. Discuss each center and its foods with the children. Invite them to sniff the foods and describe the smells.
4. Have the children choose their snacks and eat them, along with the juice that they measured and poured. Discuss the consistency of the pudding and yogurt. Discuss the texture of the granola and nuts.

Age

3, 4, 5

Evaluation

Did some of the children realize the differences in consistency or texture and tell you about it, if only with one or two words? Could almost all the children recognize differences in smells?

Easier and Harder Ideas

1. Discuss smell, texture, and consistency of all snacks for several days.
2. Do some classroom cooking and discuss smells, textures, and consistencies, especially as these properties change during cooking.

Send-Home Ideas

To practice measuring, encourage parents to give children a set of measuring cups to play with in the bathtub. Stress that accuracy is not important, but math concepts such as one half, full, one quarter full, and so forth are important.

Dear Teacher:

Thank you for you work with children. Did you know this is some of the most important work in the world? You are making a contribution to the future every day.

Different-Sized Scoops

Curriculum Approach

Process approach

Goal

Observing, constructing, creating, hypothesizing, and cooperating

Materials Needed

Melons of different varieties, melon scoops of different sizes, lemon juice, other kitchen utensils, large paper for planning

Time Needed

20 minutes of free choice time, 10 minutes of snack time

How To Do It

1. In a group, have children cooperate to create a recipe for a good snack of melon balls.
2. Together with the children, estimate about how many scoops of each kind of melon each child should get. Write down the plan on the planning paper.
3. Develop the step-by-step execution. Discuss how many scoops you have and how many children could work at the same time.
4. Allow children to prepare the melon balls and have them at snack time.

Age

3, 4, 5

Evaluation

Did the children cooperate in the group planning? Did they enjoy creating the recipe for a combination?

Easier and Harder Ideas

1. Allow children to choose their own individual combinations. Offer additional fruit such as orange and banana slices and apple chunks.

2. Develop math concepts with the melon balls. Do simple addition problems, such as 2 cantaloupe balls and 2 honeydew balls and 1 watermelon ball make 5 balls total.

Send-Home Ideas

Encourage parents to let children create their own simple recipes at home. French toast is good for this, since the actual amount of eggs, milk, sugar, and vanilla can vary quite a bit.

Dear Teacher:

Thank you for your work with children. Did you know this is some of the most important work in the world? You are making a contribution to the future every day.

Learning about Insects, Worms, Caterpillars, and Spiders

Curriculum Approach

Activity approach

Goal

Recognizing, finding, and caring for insects

Materials Needed

Magnifying glass, 2 to 3 glass jars or other containers, egg cartons, paints and brushes, string, paper or cardboard, glue, book *A Very Hungry Caterpillar* by Carle, fingerplay "Eensy Weensy Spider," Teacher Resources *Nature Activities for Early Childhood* and *Resources for Creative Teaching in ECE* by Fleming, Hamilton, and Hicks (Harcourt, Brace Jovanovich) or similar storybooks and teacher resources

Time Needed

15 minutes outdoors, 20 minutes at free choice time, 5 minutes at story time

How To Do It

1. Go for a nature walk. Take along a magnifying glass and containers for collecting insects.
2. Collect insects, worms, and a caterpillar. Look on the ground and on plants. Put the insects in containers for children to observe in the classroom.
3. Cut egg cartons lengthwise so that children can make them into caterpillars. In the classroom, lay these egg carton sections out and invite the children to paint their "caterpillars."
4. Invite children to make worm (string) prints by gluing string to paper or cardboard. First paint the cardboard with a few strokes of white glue, then lay the string on it and let it dry. Read the story *A Very Hungry Caterpillar* and teach the fingerplay "Eensy Weensy Spider."

Ages

3, 4, 5

Evaluation

Do the children enjoy going for the nature walk? Do they enjoy viewing the insects in the containers?

Easier and Harder Ideas

1. Have two-year-olds and young three-year-olds make play dough with you, then together make play dough "caterpillars." Play dough recipe: 21/2 lbs. flour, 1/2 box salt, 1 to 2 tablespoons oil mixed in 1/2 cup of water that contains food coloring of choice. Mix dry ingredients together and gradually add more water to the dough until the consistency is right. Children should help pour and stir.
2. Dig up worms for a worm farm. Use a container with dirt in it to set up the farm in the classroom.

Send-Home Ideas

Ask parents to send in empty egg cartons and string. Suggest that parents praise and value the constructions and paintings their children bring home and perhaps use them as centerpieces on the kitchen table.

Dear Teacher:

Thank you for your work with children. Did you know this is some of the most important work in the world? You are making a contribution to the future every day.

Learning More about Insects, Worms, Caterpillars, and Spiders

Curriculum Approach

Subject matter approach

Goal

Developing science concepts by learning more about insects; building math concepts by counting groups of 3, 4, 6, and 8

Materials Needed

Bugs, spiders, worms, and ants collected from the activity approach Program Enrichment Paper; books showing the body parts of insects and spiders, with close-up pictures and names of body parts; story "Inch by Inch" and fingerplay "Roly Poly Caterpillar," or similar story and fingerplay (can be a teacher original)

Time Needed

10 minutes free choice time, 5 minutes at story time

How To Do It

1. Invite the children to study the close-up pictures of spiders and insects.
2. Talk about the names of the insects and spiders and together learn some of these names.
3. Talk about the names of the body parts of various insects and see if some of the children can learn the names of some of the body parts.
4. Using a magnifying glass, count the legs on one side of the ant (3) or on one side of the spider (4). Count the number of worms you found. Read the story "Inch by Inch" about a measuring worm, and teach the fingerplay "Roly Poly Caterpillar" (or use a similar story and fingerplay of your choosing).

Age

3, 4, 5

Evaluation

Do the children learn some names of insects?

Easier and Harder Ideas

1. Use a flannel board to display real ladybugs or flannel ladybugs. Have children count the number of ladybugs in different groups (1, 2, 3, and so forth).
2. Older children can count all the legs on ants (6) or on spiders (8). Discuss the difference between spiders and insects. Count the types of insects collected.

Send-Home Ideas

Tell parents that their children are learning the names of bugs, insects, and spiders and invite them to teach more about insects or to collect some insects at home to study.

Dear Teacher:

Thank you for your work with children. Did you know this is some of the most important work in the world? You are making a contribution to the future every day.

Discovery Skills

Curriculum Approach

Process approach

Goal

Developing observation and discovery skills by observing different types of insects and discovering where they are found

Materials Needed

Lettuce and cut leaves; magnifying glass; books and insects, bugs, and spiders used in other Day 2 enrichment papers; book *Terry and the Caterpillar* or a similar story

Time Needed

10 minutes of free choice time, 10 minutes outdoors

How To Do It

1. Find out how to feed and care for caterpillars and worms and watch them eat leaves and lettuce. Read the book *Terry and the Caterpillar* or a similar caterpillar book.
2. Find insects outdoors by listening for the sounds they make. Good examples are crickets, bees, and flies.
3. Look at an ant hill with a magnifying glass. Look at the ants, too.
4. Watch to see worms emerge from the ground after rain or after pouring water on loose ground. Put a stick in the ground where dirt is loose and shake it. Look at the worms and insects that emerge. Look also under rocks and trees.

Age

3, 4, 5

Evaluation

Do the children discover insects for themselves?

Easier and Harder Ideas

1. Look at leaves changing color outside. Have children collect some.
2. Watch a praying mantis lay eggs.
3. Watch a caterpillar go through a metamorphosis into a butterfly or a moth. Depending on the variety, this takes about 2 1/2 weeks.

Send-Home Ideas

Encourage parents to do listening activities with their children. Listening for insects, listening for sounds outside, and listening for sounds inside might be some suggestions.

Dear Teacher:

Thank you for your work with children. Did you know this is some of the most important work in the world? You are making a contribution to the future every day.

How Squirrels Prepare for Winter

Curriculum Approach

Activity approach

Goal

Learning to respond to verbal directions to perform specific motor skills

Materials Needed

Paper lunch bags, paper cut-outs of squirrel heads and tongues (allow children to cut them out, if possible), paste or glue, newspaper or other stuffing, twist ties, scissors, picture file, poetry and music books

Time Needed

15 minutes during free choice time, 10 minutes at story time

How To Do It

1. Have the children stuff the paper bags, fasten them with twist ties, and then glue on the squirrel heads and tongues to form a puppet. Talk about the materials needed to make the puppets and decide if more are needed.

2. Show pictures of squirrels gathering nuts. Talk about the reason squirrels gather nuts in the fall. If desired, introduce pictures of other animals preparing for winter.

3. Read the poem "Whiskey Frisky" or another squirrel poem. Invite the children to learn it with you if appropriate.

4. While the children are playing with the squirrel puppets, give the children verbal instructions to allow them to practice specific motor skills; for example, have the children stand up, sit down, turn around, sing a song, or look for nuts. Children can take turns having their puppets give the directions after you give a few directions to the children.

Evaluation

Did the children follow the directions correctly some of the time? When they were outside, did the children begin to notice squirrels more?

Age

3, 4, 5

Easier and Harder Ideas

1. Sing one or two songs about squirrels, such as the song "Let Us Chase the Squirrel," or sing the song "Ten Little Squirrels" to the tune of "Ten Little Indians" and do the accompanying fingerplay.

2. Dramatize the poem you learn about squirrels. Practice group decision-making. Who will be the tree? The squirrel?

3. Bring in different kinds of nuts still in their shells and learn the names of these different kinds.

Send-Home Ideas

Encourage parents to talk to their children about the ways in which animals and people prepare for winter. For example, do the children notice how dogs and cats grow thicker coats of fur? Parents could point out to children ways in which people get ready for winter by having children help in the family preparations, such as getting out warmer clothes and sweaters and putting up storm windows. Even in warm climates, people dress differently in winter and summer.

Dear Teacher:

Thank you for your work with children. Thank you for initiating a new activity with the children today. Creativity always gives people a gift—children and adults alike.

Counting Squirrels

Curriculum Approach

Subject matter approach

Goal

Understanding science and math concepts

Materials Needed

Squirrel puppets made in activity approach enrichment paper, flannel board, flannel squirrel heads, picture books showing what animals do to survive winter

Time Needed

15 minutes at circle time

How To Do It

1. Have each child bring a squirrel puppet to circle time.
2. Count the squirrels/children for a "roll call." Allow each child to place a flannel squirrel on the flannel board in his or her turn.
3. Talk about the one-to-one relationship that exists—one squirrel puppet to one child.
4. Read or talk about the picture books showing squirrels gathering nuts to prepare for winter.

Age

3, 4, 5

Evaluation

Do children put just one flannel squirrel on the flannel board at their turn?

Easier and Harder Ideas

1. In the housekeeping corner, have children pretend they are bears hibernating for the winter. Allow them to take turns getting into a sturdy doll bed and have another child cover the "bear" with a blanket.

2. Have children practice counting all the squirrel puppets in the class. Encourage children to do simple addition and subtraction problems by taking away 2 squirrels or having 2 more "visit."

Send-Home Ideas

Send home the puppets with the children and encourage parents to let their children make other puppets out of other paper bags. Suggest to the parents that for a bedtime story one evening, they allow their children to tell them a story using the puppet.

Dear Teacher:

Thank you for your work with children. Did you know this is some of the most important work in the world? You are making a contribution to the future every day.

Cause and Effect for Squirrels

Curriculum Approach

Process approach

Goal

Learning skills of decision-making, interaction, and cooperation

Materials Needed

Large piece of paper to make a mural, crayons, storybook about squirrels such as *The Lazy Squirrel*, real acorns, glue

Time Needed

20 minutes during free choice time, 10 minutes during circle time

How To Do It

1. Read the storybook *The Lazy Squirrel* or another story about squirrels.
2. Decide why the squirrel is gathering nuts and what would happen if he didn't.
3. Ask the children: "Could we make a forest?" "What would we need?" Suggest making a mural. Ask what materials would be needed. Encourage children to get to know each other by using their names while planning: Johnny and Susan could make trees; Prenetta and Tocci could glue on acorns.
4. Decide where the squirrel puts the nuts. Decide how this can be shown on the mural. Make the mural.

Age

3, 4, 5

Evaluation

Do some of the children understand what will happen if the squirrel *doesn't* gather nuts? Is there group cooperation in making the mural?

Easier and Harder Ideas

1. Take a "paper bag walk" and have children gather acorns and other seeds or interesting materials.

2. Make a seed collage by having children press seeds down into old play dough flattened on a paper plate. This will harden and can be sent home. Use glue if necessary. Older children might enjoy learning the names of some of the seeds.

Send-Home Ideas

Encourage parents to get to know other parents and to help their children remember names and get to know other children.

Dear Teacher:

Thank you for your work with children. Did you know this is some of the most important work in the world? You are making a contribution to the future every day.

Travel on Wheels

Curriculum Approach

Activity approach

Goal

Learning about trains and transportation

Materials Needed

Egg cartons, paint, brushes, song books

Time Needed

15 minutes at free choice time, 5 minutes at circle time

How To Do It

1. Talk about all the ways we travel on wheels. Ask: "Where do we go by car? By train? By bus? By bicycle?"
2. Sing the song "The Wheels on the Bus." Continue the song by adding verses: the mother, the father, the baby, and the driver. End the song by repeating the first verse: "The wheels on the bus go 'round and 'round . . ." Make appropriate hand motions.
3. Sing "Railroad" from *American Folk Songs for Children*, 1948. Sing "Transportation" from *American Folk Songs for Children*, 1942. Both are by Ruth Seeger (Doubleday, Garden City, NY).
4. Make trains out of egg cartons that have been cut lengthwise. Have children paint them.

Evaluation

Do children notice wheels on vehicles outside?

Ages

3, 4, 5

Easier and Harder Ideas

1. Paint big boxes and line them up to make a train children can sit in.
2. Older children can buy "tickets" to ride the train. Children can take turns being the "ticket person" and collecting tickets.

Send-Home Ideas

Ask parents to take their child on a short bus ride just for the experience. Have them talk about the driver, what you pay, and where the people might be going.

Dear Teacher:

Thank you for your work with children. Did you know this is some of the most important work in the world? You are making a contribution to the future every day.

Boats and Planes

Curriculum Approach

Subject matter approach

Goal

Learning science concepts about floating and sinking

Materials Needed

Tops of egg cartons, toothpicks, small pieces of paper for "sails," objects to float and sink, roaster pan full of water or a water table

Time Needed

5 minutes during free choice time, 10 minutes at circle time, or 15 minutes all at once at free choice time

How To Do It

1. Make boats from whole tops of egg cartons. Use them as is, or add "sails" fastened on with toothpicks.
2. Float the boats in the water. Talk about surface area helping boats to float.
3. Play float and sink. Ask children to predict which things will float on the water and which things will sink. Have on hand a penny, a rock, a feather, a piece of paper, a pad of steel wool, and a sponge.
4. Talk about how the steel wool and the sponge floated for a while and then sank. Have children put these items in the water again and watch to see what they do.

Evaluation

Do the children work up to being able to predict at least some of the things that will float or sink?

Ages

3, 4, 5

Easier and Harder Ideas

1. Have children make airplanes and boats from blocks. Put out blue paper to serve as sky or water.
2. Have children make airplanes at the workbench by hammering two pieces of wood together.

Send-Home Ideas

Ask parents to play float and sink at home with their child. Many objects will do. This can be played in the bathtub or the sink.

Dear Teacher:

Thank you for your work with children. Did you know this is some of the most important work in the world? You are making a contribution to the future every day.

More Travel by Wheel and Air

Curriculum Approach

Process approach

Goal

Creative problem-solving

Materials Needed

15 or 20 empty spools to do print painting with, paint, paper, *Pilot Small* by Lois Lenski, the record "Jet Plane" from Rhythm Time–Album I by Lucille Wood and Ruth Turner.

Time Needed

10 minutes during free choice time, 10 minutes during circle time

How To Do It

1. Show children how to do print painting by dipping the spool ends in paint and making "wheels" on their paper. Or ask children to paint some wheels "without using paint brushes." (Children are thus encouraged to use creative problem-solving.)
2. Add other objects that can be used for print painting as children get started. Suggestions include a potato masher and other kitchen utensils.
3. Role play the "Jet Plane" song at circle time.
4. Read *Pilot Small* by Lois Lensky. Discuss the pictures.

Evaluation

Do the children manage to paint without brushes?

Ages

3, 4, 5

Easier and Harder Ideas

1. Put out blue and green finger paint and have children make "water" (blue/green painted paper) for blocks made into boats (see subject matter enrichment paper).

2. Count aloud the number of wheels that each child makes on his or her print. Write the number on the picture.

Send-Home Ideas

Ask parents to collect spools for you. Suggest that they be aware of times when planes fly overhead, then to talk about it with their child. Recommend that parents and children listen together and talk about the sounds a plane makes.

Dear Teacher:

Thank you for your work with children. Did you know this is some of the most important work in the world? You are making a contribution to the future every day.

Making Ceremonial Jewelry

Curriculum Approach

Process approach

Goal

Observing, problem-solving, and learning classification and sequencing skills

Materials Needed

Rigatoni-type macaroni, red and blue tempera paint, brushes, newspaper, straws cut into one-inch pieces, string with taped ends

Time Needed

20 minutes of free choice time on 2 days, 5 minutes of circle time

How To Do It

1. Lay out newspapers on the table, pour paint into pie pans, and lay brushes and rigatoni on newspapers.
2. Invite children to paint the rigatoni different colors, and to let them dry overnight.
3. The next day, lay out the painted rigatoni, the string and tape, and the straw pieces. As the children show interest in making necklaces and bracelets, cut strings of the right length and then wrap tape around the ends to make tips.
4. Encourage the children to classify the red and blue rigatoni and the straws. Discuss the sequences they choose. See if they can make a second necklace or a bracelet to match the sequence they have made in the first necklace. At circle time, discuss Native Americans and the jewelry they wear for certain ceremonies.

Age

3, 4, 5

Evaluation

Do the children show pride and success in the achievement of creating the jewelry and wearing it? Do any of them succeed in making two matching items?

Easier and Harder Ideas

1. Use rigatoni, only, for younger children. The step of painting it can also be eliminated.
2. Add paper cutouts and wooden beads to the items for stringing to give children the opportunity to make more complex sequences. Tell about molecules making up all things around us, and how they have certain sequences too.

Send-Home Ideas

Explain to parents that stringing beads or rigatoni builds small muscle development and eye-hand coordination. Encourage them to allow their children to do this at home, perhaps using shoe laces. An older child might enjoy stringing round oat cereal pieces or other appropriate cereal for the birds. A needle and thread is best for this; an adult should work with the child. A loop can be made by tying the two ends of the thread together and then the "bird snack" can be hung on shrubbery.

Dear Teacher:

Thank you for your work with children. Did you know this is some of the most important work in the world? You are making a contribution to the future every day.

Native Americans and Pilgrims

Curriculum Approach

Subject matter approach

Goal

Understanding social studies concepts about other people from other times and places

Materials Needed

Storybook about the Pilgrims, baking mix (e.g., Bisquick™ or Jiffy™), sugar, cornmeal, milk, eggs, butter, utensils, bowl, paper muffin cups, and muffin pan

Time Needed

20 minutes during free choice time, 5 minutes at story time, 10 minutes at snack time

How To Do It

1. On a table, lay out a bowl, utensils, and ingredients for cornmeal muffins. Follow the recipe for muffins on the baking mix box, but substitute 3/4 cup of cornmeal for 3/4 cup of the baking mix.
2. Invite the children to participate in the preparation. Talk about measuring the ingredients and have children take turns pouring the ingredients into the bowl.
3. Have the children stir the ingredients and talk about the mixture as it changes consistency. Tell them about the Pilgrims coming to this country a long time ago and the Native Americans who taught them to use cornmeal so they would have food. Have the children place the muffin papers in the tin, pour the batter in, bake the muffins, and serve them at snack time.
4. At story time, show a picture book of the Pilgrims and Native Americans and tell about the first Thanksgiving.

Age

3, 4, 5

Evaluation

Did the children enjoy making the cornmeal muffins? Did almost all of them try a bite?

Easier and Harder Ideas

1. Talk about the smells and sounds associated with cooking. Have the children practice decision-making by asking them to decide who will pour in each ingredient next. Make the recipe over and over during the following months and the children will become able to do it with very little supervision. They can also decide who will stir first and next.

2. As the muffins are served, talk about one-to-one correspondence. Do this with all snacks. Mention the total number of children in the class and the total number of muffins served. (Do not count seconds, or the totals will not match!)

Send-Home Ideas

Ask parents to let children help them prepare simple mixes. On another occasion, have the class make enough muffins for the parents too, and send one home with each child.

Dear Teacher:

Thank you for your work with children. Did you know this is some of the most important work in the world? You are making a contribution to the future every day.

Turkeys

Curriculum Approach

Activity approach

Goal

Learning about Thanksgiving and turkeys

Materials Needed

Paper, crayons, picture book on the first Thanksgiving

Time Needed

2 hours to visit a turkey farm, 10 minutes of free choice time, 10 minutes of story time

How To Do It

1. Plan to visit a farm where turkeys are raised. Invite available parents to come along.
2. Look at the turkeys and discuss what they eat, where they sleep, and the noises they make. After visiting the turkeys, serve a morning snack of juice and crackers as a picnic, if the weather permits.
3. During the next free choice time, invite the children to make their own turkeys. Have the children draw around their outstretched hand on a piece of paper. Encourage children to color the "feathers."
4. At story time, read a picture/story book about the first Thanksgiving. Highlight the fact that the Native Americans introduced the Pilgrims to the idea of having turkey for food. Tell the story in your own words if the text is on an elementary-school level. Role play the Native Americans, the Pilgrims, and the turkeys if you like.

Age

3, 4, 5

Evaluation

Did the children enjoy visiting the turkey farm? Did some of them understand that turkeys for Thanksgiving come from a farm?

Easier and Harder Ideas

1. Look at the other animals on the farm. At story time, follow up with picture books. Plan to visit the farm again in the spring.

2. Sing the song "Ten Little Indians" with emphasis on the numbers. Substitute the word *turkey* in the song for the word *Indian*, and sing "Ten Little Turkeys." Do simple addition and subtraction problems using turkeys.

Send-Home Ideas

Ask parents to make a list with their child of all the things for which they are both thankful this year.

Dear Teacher:

Thank you for your work with children. Did you know this is some of the most important work in the world? You are making a contribution to the future every day.

Moving Day

Curriculum Approach

Process approach

Goal

Practice decision-making and discussing alternatives

Materials Needed

Furniture, toys, and equipment usually found in an early childhood classroom

Time Needed

15 to 30 minutes

How To Do It

1. Explain to the children that they are going to help you decide how to rearrange your room.
2. Start with one center, such as the dramatic play corner. Discuss how the furniture in that center might be placed differently. Ask how this rearrangement might help them play new games there. Discuss how each piece of furniture or equipment could be moved. For example, "Joe and Mary can push the stove and Timmy and I will pull it."
3. Talk about alternate outcomes. What would happen if you exchanged the block center and the dramatic play area? Would this make the room seem new for a new year?
4. Talk about what would be needed for each idea: "We could put the blocks in the wagon to move them." Discuss whether some parents might be needed to come in on Saturday and help. Talk about moving companies and moving vans.

Age

3, 4, 5

Evaluation

Did the children understand that something they decided could really be done? Did they explore at least two or three possibilities in some detail?

Easier and Harder Ideas

1. Discuss ways to rearrange the books on the book shelves. Should all the large books and all the small books be together? Or should they be sorted by color? Or should they be sorted by favorites and nonfavorites? With the children, redo the book shelves in the way chosen.

2. Rearrange at least three centers. First draw diagrams on a chalkboard or a piece of paper of all the possible alternatives. Then actually carry out three of these alternatives.

Send-Home Ideas

Encourage parents to discuss with children how their books and toys are stored. Have them arrive at a mutually agreeable plan for changing the storage arrangements and then carry it through.

Dear Teacher:

Thank you for your work with children. Did you know this is some of the most important work in the world? You are making a contribution to the future every day.

How Many Did We Move?

Curriculum Approach

Subject matter approach

Goal

Learning math concepts

Materials Needed

Furniture, toys, and equipment used by children

Time Needed

5 minutes

How To Do It

1. As children discuss rearranging their room or a center (see the process approach enrichment paper, Day 2) and then do it, have them count items as they move them. Take each child's abilities into account; for example, if a child can only count to three, ask him or her to move a set of three dolls to the doll area.

2. After a child successfully moves one set of three, four, or five items, ask him or her to move two sets of an item, such as blocks. For example, ask the child to move two sets of five blocks. Work up to three and four sets of five blocks. Ask children to further categorize by counting sets of long blocks, short blocks, square blocks, etc.

3. When rearranging books, ask a child how many sets of three books there are, perhaps focusing on books with a certain characteristic. For example, how many sets of three small books are there? Choose numbers within the grasp of the child.

4. Have children participate in addition and subtraction problems as you rearrange. For example, ask, "If you put two sets of three small books on the shelf, how many sets are left waiting to be placed?" Create simple addition and subtraction problems as you rearrange other materials.

Age

4, 5

Evaluation

Did the children collect some of the quantities correctly? Did some children manage to move two sets of three items?

Easier and Harder Ideas

1. When a child is playing with trucks or cars, one in each hand, say to him or her, "I see you are playing with a set of two cars." Use the word *set* in other conversations with the children; for example, at snack time, tell children that they each will get a set of two crackers.
2. Older children can work up to counting sets of seven, eight, nine, or ten items. For example, they might want to load two sets of ten blocks into the wagon. Children can be asked to create larger sets when they are playing with small toys or table toys.

Send-Home Ideas

Explain the concept of "sets" to parents. Ask parents to use this word when they work with their child while cleaning up his or her room. For example, a parent could ask: "Can you pick up three sets of two toys?" "That's great! Now can you pick up two sets of five blocks?" and so on.

Dear Teacher:

Thank you for your work with children. Did you know this is some of the most important work in the world? You are making a contribution to the future every day.

Large and Small Decisions

Curriculum Approach

Activity approach

Goal

Encouraging children to make choices

Materials Needed

An early childhood classroom that contains a variety of centers; discarded grocery boxes from cereal, pudding, raisins, etc. (perhaps left over from playing store); white glue in trays; paint brushes; newspapers

Time Needed

15 minutes at free choice and art time

How To Do It

1. As children enter the room, allow them to look around and choose a center in which to play.
2. In the art project area, have tables covered with newspaper, and spread grocery boxes out on top of the tables. Place white glue in pie pans or meat trays, and provide paint brushes for spreading it. (Brushes can later be cleaned in hot water.) Encourage children to build a box collage by having each child choose a box, then glue it to another box, and so on.
3. As a child finishes his or her collage, count the boxes used by the child, then write the child's name and the number of boxes on the collage.
4. Box collages can be painted, but are an interesting free-form sculpture just as they are. Boxes that have been brought in to play grocery store and have since become worn out are ideal for this project.

Age

3, 4, 5

Evaluation

Do children choose the center they will play in or wander aimlessly about? Do they take pleasure in choosing just which boxes will be right for their collages?

Easier and Harder Ideas

1. Ask children to choose between two books at story time.
2. Discuss simple math as the box collages grow: Three boxes plus one box makes four boxes, and so forth.

Send-Home Ideas

Suggest that parents use the collages for kitchen table centerpieces. Explain that creativity grows if it is praised and displayed in the home.

Dear Teacher:

Thank you for your work with children. Did you know this is some of the most important work in the world? You are making a contribution to the future every day.

Where Does Our Food Come From?

Curriculum Approach

Process approach

Goal

Learning group interaction and cooperation; developing observation skills

Materials Needed

Shelf paper and empty paper towel rolls to make a "scroll," scissors, glue, crayons, magazine pictures

Time Needed

15 minutes planning time before trip to market, about 2 hours for the shopping trip, 30 minutes art time after the trip

How To Do It

1. Ask the children where our food comes from. When they reply "the store," suggest that the group plan a trip to visit a supermarket and a fish market, if possible.

2. Have the children "brainstorm" things they especially want to see: the butcher, how trucks are unloaded, the storage areas, and so forth. Print these ideas on a chalkboard or on chart paper as a reminder to discuss these experiences later.

3. After the store trip, make a "movie" on shelf paper that shows how food comes into a store, goes out to homes, and is eaten. To make their "movie," have the children cut out magazine pictures and paste them onto the shelf paper. Then spread out the paper on the floor to dry. When it is dry, roll it up on the paper towel holder. Or, the shelf paper can be left flat and used for a mural.

4. Discuss the topics on the list that the children made before going on their store trip. Be sure pictures are drawn or posted on the "movie" of these topics.

Age

3, 4, 5

Evaluation

Did children build on each other's suggestions in planning the trip?
Did they work cooperatively on the "movie"? Did they observe carefully
enough to have several suggestions about what should be on the "movie"?

Easier and Harder Ideas

1. Ask one of the neighborhood grocers to visit the class and tell what he or
   she does.
2. Older children might enjoy making charts that classify food by food
   groups. They might also make a group scrapbook about their trip.
   Suggest that they make trips to a bakery and to a produce stand to add
   to the scrapbook later.

Send-Home Ideas

Ask parents to help their children develop observation skills. For example,
parents might have their children dictate the changes they see in a plant as
it grows from a seed or a cutting. The parent could write these observations
in a "plant diary." Allowing children to grow two or three carrot tops in a
saucer of water provides an interesting plant to observe.

Dear Teacher:

*Thank you for your work with children. Did you know this is some of the
most important work in the world? You are making a contribution to the
future every day.*

Planting and Grouping

Curriculum Approach

Subject matter approach

Goal

Developing science, health, and social studies concepts

Materials Needed

Tomato and avocado seeds, sweet potato and carrot tops, soil, water, planting containers, magazine pictures of food, paper, markers, paper plates

Time Needed

4 or 5 minutes a day for several days, 10 minutes during circle time

How To Do It

1. Place planting materials on a table and invite children to plant a vegetable.
2. Start the carrot tops, the sweet potato tops, and the avocado seeds in water, and start the tomato seeds in soil. Have the children make sure the vegetables have enough water, checking them each day for two or three weeks. Encourage the children to observe and compare the effect of water on these plants.
3. Make a chart with the children listing the four basic food groups: meat and protein; milk and cheese (dairy); vegetables and fruits; grains and cereals. Have the children "brainstorm" examples to go in each category.
4. Talk about how balanced meals have one item from each food group. Invite children to select and paste pictures of balanced meals on paper plates. An interested child might want to do several meals.

Age

3, 4, 5

Evaluation

Do children enjoy planting the vegetables? Do they seem interested in learning about the four kinds of food in a balanced meal?

Easier and Harder Ideas

1. Visit a supermarket and identify foods from different food groups.
2. Help children keep a chart showing the balanced meals they eat each day. (They may want to dictate to you the foods they have eaten while you write them on the chart.) Talk about what good foods do for the body. Ask the children to dictate a story about what good foods do for them.

Send-Home Ideas

Ask parents to talk with their children in the grocery store about the kinds of foods they are seeing. Encourage them to help children recognize plants and animals as sources for our food supply.

Dear Teacher:

Thank you for your work with children. Did you know this is some of the most important work in the world? You are making a contribution to the future every day.

Our Grocery Store

Curriculum Approach

Activity approach

Goal

Learning about foods and the food supply in the area

Materials Needed

The book *The Storybook of Food*, the poem "ABCD/Energy", and the song "The Apple" (or another book, poem, and/or song about food); food samples from each food group, such as apples, cheese or milk, carrots, sliced hot dogs, and crackers; brown paper or plastic grocery bags

Time Needed

2 hours for a trip to the supermarket, 5 or 10 minutes at circle time, 5 or 10 minutes at snack time

How To Do It

1. After the trip to the supermarket described in the process approach enrichment paper, Day 1 (or after another trip), talk with the children about how food is made available to us. Talk about the boxes, plastic wraps, and bags food is put into. Ask why grocers and farmers do this.

2. Ask parents to send in empty grocery boxes and packages. Use these to set up a store in the dramatic play corner. Have brown paper and plastic grocery bags available so "shoppers" can carry away their purchases.

3. At circle time, share the story, poem, and song listed in the Materials Needed section, or find other teacher resources that are similar to those suggested.

4. At snack time, present the idea of the four food groups and give children a small sample from each group: fruits/vegetables, dairy, bread and grains, and meat/protein. Allow children to have seconds if they wish.

Age

3, 4, 5

Evaluation

Do the children enjoy playing store? Do they understand that there is work involved in supplying, packaging, and buying food?

Easier and Harder Ideas

1. Look at pictures of food, talk about the food group that each pictured item belongs to, and encourage children to talk about eating these foods.
2. Give four- and five-year-olds play money to use in playing store. Slips of paper marked as ones, fives, and tens keep the money math manageable.

Send-Home Ideas

Suggest that parents allow their children to grow two or three potato tops in a saucer of water at home. Encourage parents to take their children to a wide variety of food stores, such as a fish market, a bakery, an oriental food store, or a meat market.

Dear Teacher:

Thank you for your work with children. Did you know this is some of the most important work in the world? You are making a contribution to the future every day.

Shadow Talk

Curriculum Approach

Activity approach

Goal

Learning about light and shadows

Materials Needed

Flashlight, sheets, paper, crayons, chalk

Time Needed

10 minutes of free choice time, 20 minutes during outdoor time

How To Do It

1. Indoors, hang up a sheet or drape a sheet over a table. Give the children a flashlight and invite them to create shadows.
2. Outdoors, have children stand with their backs to the sun so that they cast a shadow onto a piece of paper, or have them hold up a hand or an object to cast shadows onto paper. Allow other children to draw around the shadows. Then have the children switch roles.
3. Encourage children to experiment with shadows outdoors by seeing if they can make two shadows shake hands or touch without the children actually touching.
4. Use sidewalk chalk to draw around a child's shadow outdoors. Discuss how much larger the shadow is than the one who casts it.

Age

3, 4, 5

Evaluation

Are some children able to understand that blocked light causes a shadow? That a shadow may or may not be exactly the same as the object or person casting it?

Easier and Harder Ideas

1. Talk about how long daylight lasts at different times of the year. What effect does this have on shadows?

2. Have a shadow puppet show by allowing children to hold up familiar puppets behind a hanging sheet. Another child can hold the flashlight while the main "actors" recreate a familiar story in their own words.

Send-Home Ideas

Encourage parents to give their children a flashlight to use. Together, have them count all the different uses their children can find for the flashlight. Examples might include looking for boots in the corner of a closet, looking at pipes in the basement, and finding something in a room without turning on the light.

Dear Teacher:

Thank you for your work with children. Did you know this is some of the most important work in the world? You are making a contribution to the future every day.

Why Is It Dark at Suppertime?

Curriculum Approach

Subject matter approach

Goal

Learning beginning science concepts about the principles of light and dark; building math skills relating to sorting and classification; developing social studies understandings about other lands

Materials Needed

Books about Africa and Eskimos, magazine pictures of daily activities, paste or glue, paper

Time Needed

5 minutes at the beginning of the day, at lunch, and at the end of the day; 10 minutes during circle time

How To Do It

1. With the children, look at the position of the sun several times during the day and discuss its changing position. Record its position at the beginning of the day, at lunchtime, and at the end of the day, or look every two hours or so. Warn children not to look directly at the sun.

2. Use tape to mark on the window the position of the sun as it travels across the sky. If your window faces the wrong direction, tape newsprint to the wall and mark the moving shadow. Repeat this activity 4 to 6 months later and discuss the changes.

3. Discuss with the children whether certain activities are done during daylight or after dark. Suggestions include eating supper, eating breakfast, going to bed, playing outside, and so forth. Ask if the daylight and after-dark activities are the same in the summer as in the winter. Have the children paste pictures on daytime and nighttime collages. These will be different for different children.

4. Talk about people in other lands, the sun's position in those parts of the world, and the typical hours of daylight there. Read or tell a story from a picture book about Eskimos or Africa. Compare the sun's pattern in these two geographic areas.

Age

3, 4, 5

Evaluation

Do the children develop a gradual awareness of the sun traveling across the sky? Do they notice that the location of the sun at the beginning of the day is different from its location at the end of the day?

Easier and Harder Ideas

1. Discuss sunrises and sunsets with the children and the changes in color that occur in the sky. Put out pink, yellow, and orange paints and let the children paint a picture of a sunrise or a sunset.
2. Use a picture to introduce older children to the idea of the solar system. Explain that the sun doesn't really travel, the earth does. Encourage children to learn the names of the planets.

Send-Home Ideas

Encourage parents to discuss with their children how the shorter amount of daylight in December affects their daily lives. Ask parents to point out sunrises and sunsets to their children whenever possible.

Dear Teacher:

Thank you for your work with children. Thank you for initiating a new activity with the children today. Creativity always gives people a lift—children and adults alike.

Day and Night

Curriculum Approach

Process approach

Goal

Noticing, observing, and comparing the shortness of the days and the lengthening of the nights as winter approaches

Materials Needed

Children's books about animals hibernating, the book *Good Night Moon* by Margaret Wise Brown (Harper, 1947), paper, crayons

Time Needed

20 minutes of story time, 10 minutes of free choice time

How To Do It

1. Read the story *Good Night Moon* and discuss going to bed when it is dark versus when it is still light, as sometimes happens in the summer.
2. Show pictures of bears and other animals hibernating and introduce this idea.
3. Ask children to draw pictures of animals hibernating or encourage them to act it out by using stuffed animals in the bed in the dramatic play corner.
4. Call attention to the moon if it shows in the late afternoon. Talk about its shape and point out to the children its changing shape over 30 days. Record these changes on the calendar.

Age

3, 4, 5

Evaluation

Do children develop an awareness of the moon and the longer nighttime hours?

Easier and Harder Ideas

1. When the children are outside, have them look up and notice the clouds. Later, invite them to paint pictures of the clouds and what they saw. White paint on colored paper is effective for painting clouds.
2. Discuss what things in the sky look like. Ask which things move and which things move faster than others, such as tree branches move faster than clouds. Talk about which things are bigger or higher than others, such as planes are bigger and fly higher than birds.

Send-Home Ideas

Ask parents to let children look at the moon and stars at night for several nights. Ask them to record with their children the different locations of the moon in the sky and the moon's different shapes.

Dear Teacher:

Thank you for your work with children. Thank you for initiating a new activity with the children today. Creativity always gives people a lift—children and adults alike.

Hot and Cold

Curriculum Approach

Process approach

Goal

Studying cause and effect

Materials Needed

Saucer or bowl, large sheet of paper or flip chart, snow (or crushed ice if snow is not available)

Time Needed

15 minutes, along with a few minutes every hour

How To Do It

1. Use a saucer or a bowl to collect some snow and bring it inside.
2. Talk about what causes the snow to become water. Talk about the effect that the heat in your classroom has on the snow or crushed ice.
3. Ask what effect the heat in your room has on people. Answers include that people take off their coats, perhaps take off sweaters, and so forth. Have children look at the snow on the sleeves of their coats that they wore outside. Have them observe what happens to it.
4. Take a thermometer outside and have children notice the change in its reading. Bring the thermometer back inside and ask what effect the heat in the classroom has on the thermometer.

Age

4, 5 years

Evaluation

Did the children understand that heat and cold have certain effects? Can they apply this idea in other ways?

Easier and Harder Ideas

1. Put an ice cube into a bowl. Have children check on its progress as it melts.
2. Have the children dictate a "snow (or ice) melting diary" that you write on a large piece of paper or a flip chart. For example:

   10:30—snow half melted

   11:00—only water in the dish

Send-Home Ideas

Ask parents to talk about other cause-and-effect situations. For example, suggest that parents allow children to watch what happens when eggs are put into a hot frying pan. Have parents ask children the difference between uncooked carrots and cooked carrots. Remind parents to stress safety in the kitchen and not to let children touch hot things.

Dear Teacher:

Thank you for your work with children. Thank you for initiating a new activity with the children today. Creativity always gives people a lift—children and adults alike.

Snow Numbers[*]

Curriculum Approach

Subject matter approach

Goal

Learning science and math concepts

Materials Needed

Snow or sand; snow or play dough with which to make "snowballs"

Time Needed

15 minutes

How To Do It

1. When children are outside playing on a snowy day, have them use a magnifying glass to observe snowflakes that have fallen on their arms.
2. Make a number in the snow with your feet. Ask children who want to participate to make the same number or a different number. Stick to numbers under 5 unless you are sure children know quantities for larger numbers.
3. To provide practice in recognizing quantities, have children make snowballs and then count them. Ask the children to write in the snow the number of snowballs they each make. Show children how to make the numbers by tracking the outlines with their feet. (The numbers will be large, perhaps 2 or 3 feet high.)
4. If desired, discuss the following vocabulary words with children: melting, freezing, many, much, lots, drifts.

Age

3, 4, 5 years

Evaluation

Were children able to write at least some numbers correctly? When counting the snowballs, did they touch each one and understand one-to-one correspondence?

Easier and Harder Ideas

1. Talk about why the snow forms footprint outlines where a person has walked or on a path where many people have walked. Discuss how the heat from shoes melts the track or footprint in place.

2. When making snowballs, encourage children to do simple addition problems: How many snowballs do 2 snowballs and 2 snowballs make? How about 3 and 3? For older four- and five-year-olds, work up to numbers between 5 and 10. Try other combinations in math questions.

Send-Home Ideas

Any time parents and children are working with four or fewer items, ask parents to have their children count the items. Ask parents to make sure their child *touches* each thing he or she counts. Start with one or two items, if necessary.

Dear Teacher:
   Thank you for your work with children. Thank you for initiating a new activity with the children today. Creativity always gives people a lift—children and adults alike.

---

*Some of this activity can be done in sand if you are in a warm climate.

Snowy Wonders

Curriculum Approach

Activity Approach

Goal

Learning about winter and snow

Materials Needed

White and colored finger paints; a recording of music that sounds like whirling snowflakes; the book *The Snowy Day* by Ezra Jack Keats; two or three sleds for use outdoors; two or three small shovels

Time Needed

15 minutes of art time, 15 minutes of music time, 20 minutes outdoors, and 10 minutes of story time

How To Do It

1. *During free choice time*, put out finger paint materials for children who would like to choose this activity. As two or three children begin finger painting with colored paint, show them that a finger stuck in white paint and touched on top of the colors will make snowflakes on their pictures. Put out more materials as more children become interested.

2. *During music time*, talk about the motions snowflakes make as they fall. Put on some music and have the children pretend to be whirling snowflakes as they listen. Suggest that they act out a driving blizzard or gently falling snowflakes next. For more motion activity, ask the children to walk as if they were in deep, wet snow. Have a pretend snowball fight. Imitate shoveling heavy snow.

3. *At story time*, read *The Snowy Day*. Discuss the story. Talk about snow coming in winter only, and other aspects of winter.

4. *At outdoor time*, take the sleds and shovels outside for the children to use.

Age

3, 4, 5 years

Evaluation

Do children take more of an interest in snow? Do they understand that it can be heavy or light, whirling or falling straight? Have they discovered new ideas about snow?

Easier and Harder Ideas

1. Have children use cotton balls, pasted or glued onto paper, to create a collage of "snowballs."
2. Investigate icy snow and the ice crusts that form on snow in the shade. Talk about ice, icicles, and ice from the refrigerator. Put some water in a dish outside to see if it turns to ice.

Send-Home Ideas

Encourage parents to help children put on and take off their boots by themselves. Share the trick of putting plastic bags over shoes to slip them into boots that are very snug. Ask a helping mother to set up a boot exchange for your class or your center so that all children can have the right-sized boots.

Dear Teacher:

Thank you for your work with children. Thank you for initiating a new activity with the children today. Creativity always gives people a lift—children and adults alike.

What Melts Fastest?

Curriculum Approach

Process approach

Goal

Understanding more about cause and effect

Materials Needed

3 saucers

Time Needed

15 minutes at outdoor time, 5 to 10 minutes at free choice indoor time, and 5 to 10 minutes at group time

How To Do It

1. At outdoor time, collect snow in two of the saucers and put an icicle in the third saucer to bring inside later.

2. Make a snowman with the children. Have the children begin by rolling a small ball of snow around. As the ball increases in size, children should become aware that the snow will stick together and become compact.

3. Talk about the height and diameter of the snowman. Measure with a tape measure.

4. Look at ice forming on puddles, bird baths, or a pond. Look at the same area again later in the week.

5. Bring in the three saucers prepared in step 1. Add water to one of the snow saucers. Ask for predictions about which will melt fastest. Then ask the children to watch to see if their predictions were correct. At group time, check the three saucers again and talk about why the icicle melts more slowly. Accept all answers (e.g., "Maybe because it is pointed"). Help children learn to wonder, to observe, and to understand that the heat of the classroom is having an effect. Discuss the effect of adding water to snow. Why does this cause the snow to melt faster? Is it warmer than the snow? Have children feel the water and then the snow to find out.

Age

3, 4, 5 years

Evaluation

Do children understand that they can cause snow to melt faster by adding water to it? Do they understand that they can cause other effects? Do the children notice that it takes days for the snowman to melt?

Easier and Harder Ideas

1. Talk about cause and effect situations that occur with people. What makes us mad? What makes us cry? What makes us happy?
2. Play a float and sink game in the water by providing children with various objects, including a penny and a feather. Ask children why the penny sinks but the feather does not. Discuss the effects of weight and surface area.
3. Take a tape measure outside. Measure the snowman's height and diameter for several days running. On a chart in the classroom, keep track of the measurements. Discuss any changes the children observe and their causes.

Send-Home Ideas

Suggest that parents and their children make a snowman at home. If you have funds, send home a tape measure with every child and ask parents to help their children measure different household items. Accuracy is not important; however, using a number line together is important.

Dear Teacher:

Thank you for your work with children. Thank you for using resources around you to enrich the children's day: These program enrichment papers, a curriculum book or two from the library, ideas from a course you took. As you grow, the children will grow, too.

Snow or Sand Sounds

Curriculum Approach

Subject matter approach

Goal

Develop language abilities and knowledge of sounds

Materials Needed

None

Time Needed

10 minutes of outdoor time, 5 to 10 minutes of indoor time

How To Do It

1. During outdoor time, have the children use their feet to make tracks in the snow (or in the sand) in the shapes of letters. (The letters will be large.)
2. Have children start with hard consonants, such as *D, T, B,* and *P,* which have sounds that are easy to identify.
3. When inside again, ask the children what objects in the room begin with the same sounds as the letters they made outside. For example:

D	"duh"	"doll"
B	"bah"	"baby"
T	"tuh"	"table"
P	"puh"	"pan"

Age

4, 5

Evaluation

Do the children realize that the letters have corresponding sounds?
Can they get one or two of these four letters right?

Easier and Harder Ideas

1. Have children make other shapes in the snow or sand, such as a square, a circle, a triangle, or a rectangle.
2. In the classroom, have children look at other letter shapes to prepare for making these letters the next day.

Send-Home Ideas

Ask parents to have children tell them the names of objects at home that begin with the sounds for *B, D, T,* and *P.*

Dear Teacher:
Thank you for your work with children. Thank you for using resources around you to enrich the children's day: These program enrichment papers, a curriculum book or two from the library, ideas from a course you took. As you grow, the children will grow, too.

Crunchy Snowflakes

Curriculum Approach

Activity approach

Goal

Learning more about snow

Materials Needed

Tempera paint and brushes or finger paints, newsprint, pictures of snowflakes

Time Needed

15 minutes at art time, 5 minutes at story time, 10 minutes outdoors

How To Do It

1. *At free choice time,* direct children who want to paint to dabble paint on one half of their paper. Have them fold the paper in half, rub it, open up the paper, and then look at the print that resulted. Talk about the print being symmetrical and that snowflakes are symmetrical (matching on both sides). Look at pictures of snowflakes.

2. Look at other things in the classroom that are the same on both sides (books, balls, blocks). Then look at things in the classroom that are not the same on both sides (people, pictures, some toys).

3. *At story time,* talk about sounds related to weather and snow. Rain and thunder make one kind of sound. Allow children to imitate these sounds. Snow is very quiet, but it does make a sound when people walk on it: crunch, crunch, crunch. Snow makes another sound when it is melting and people walk on it: slip, slosh. Allow children to imitate these sounds as well.

4. During outdoor time, play a listening game. Encourage children to listen to the crunching snow when people walk; to cars driving past; to water dripping from trees; and to other sounds in the snow. Allow children to use the sleds and shovels brought in on Day 1.

Age

3, 4, 5 years

Evaluation

Do the children listen and describe at least some of the sounds they hear outside? Do some of them understand that two sides of something can be alike or different?

Easier and Harder Ideas

1. You or the children can tear up white paper into "confetti" snowflakes and have an indoor "snow storm." Later, use paper pieces for pasting.

2. Have older children fold round white paper in half, and then in thirds, and cut "snowflakes." Show children how to cut near the outer edges and to cut pieces from the folds. Open up the folds and point out to children that the sides match. Discuss the concept that every snowflake is different. Use a magnifying glass to observe snowflakes outside. Look at pictures of snowflakes and compare them with those the children made.

Send-Home Ideas

Send home the prints that the children made during art to be used as placemats. Write "Happy Winter Time" or some appropriate sentiment on each. Encourage parents to have children listen to sounds and describe them when they are outdoors, in the car together, at the store, or anywhere.

Dear Teacher:

Thank you for your work with children today. Draw or paste a gold star on this program enrichment paper when you are finished. Put stars on the other papers you've done too. Adults need rewards just as children do. Even small ones are nice!

Cooperation in a Family

Curriculum Approach

Process approach

Goal

Building cooperation skills for family living

Materials Needed

Video or storybook on the topic of getting along with others, paper, crayons or markers, puppets if desired

Time Needed

10 to 15 minutes at group time

How To Do It

1. During group time, have the children "brainstorm" ways of being good family members. Write these suggestions on a large piece of paper.
2. Encourage children to identify the rights and responsibilities of each person in the family. Talk about ways of solving conflicts within a family. List these also.
3. Describe ways of getting along with others. Compare situations within the family and situations outside the family. Show a video or read a book about getting along with others. (A teacher-original story is fine.)
4. Discuss things that make each child angry or sad and help him or her decide how to handle each situation. Have the group generate alternatives. Role play some or all of the alternatives. This may take several days.

Age

2, 3, 4, 5 to 100

Evaluation

Did the children each have several ideas about how to be a good family member?

Easier and Harder Ideas

1. Compare animal families and how they function. Squirrels put away nuts for the winter, birds bring worms to the young in the nest, baby birds take turns trying to fly, and so forth.
2. Ask older children to draw pictures of someone being cooperative.

Send-Home Ideas

Ask parents to share with their children the cooperative things they did with their families when they were young. If possible, call on grandparents to share more details of cooperative projects.

Dear Teacher:

Thank you for your work with children today. Draw or paste a gold star on this program enrichment paper when you are finished. Put stars on the other papers you've done too. Adults need rewards just as children do. Even small ones are nice!

Similarities and Differences

Curriculum Approach

Subject matter approach

Goal

Developing social studies concepts; identifying ways in which family members contribute to the health and happiness of others; identifying similarities and differences among family members; learning that all living things are interrelated

Time Needed

10 minutes at circle time, 20 minutes at art/free choice time, perhaps for several days

Materials Needed

Brown paper lunch bags, newspaper, twist ties, markers or crayons, paper, library books about family cooperation, video or storybook about being part of a family.

How To Do It

1. At free choice time, have materials available for making family member puppets, for those children who choose to do so. Children can make puppets by stuffing a lunch bag with newspaper and fastening the bottom with a twist tie.

2. Encourage children to use markers or crayons to draw features of different family members. Talk about what color hair and eyes each family member has. Yarn and glue can be used for hair, but this will take longer to dry. Discuss similarities and differences in features of family members. How many wear glasses? Does one have a mustache or a beard? It may take several days to make several puppets.

3. In the dramatic play area or the kitchen area, encourage children to use their puppets to role play family members working together.

4. At circle time, talk about ways their family members help each other. Show the video or read the book about being part of a family. On successive days, show and tell stories from library books that describe family cooperation. Leave these books on a table to allow children to browse through them.

Age

3, 4, 5

Evaluation

Do children identify one or two similarities or differences in family members' features? Do they tell at least one way a family member helps? Do they see themselves as helping, occasionally?

Easier and Harder Ideas

1. Use library books to compare animal families and how they function. Tell the story "Goldilocks and the Three Bears."

2. Have four- and five-year-olds use blocks of the same size to make a "Family Graph" on the floor. Children can estimate the relative heights of each family member and lay out the appropriate number of blocks for each person. Toilet paper that is rolled out also makes excellent graph material.

Send-Home Ideas

Encourage parents to talk with their children about how family members help each other or do things to make each other happy. Ask them to let their children draw pictures of family members working together.

Dear Teacher:

Thank you for your work with children. As you evaluate the children's achievements, take pride in your own achievements too. Give yourself:

- *A gold star for every new activity you've tried*
- *A hot fudge sundae or some other treat for the extra patience you had with boots and mittens*
- *Three new resource materials you've discovered and really love*

Whatever reward you chose, take pride in your achievement, because you are helping children have a better tomorrow.

What is Special About Me?

Curriculum Approach

Activity approach

Goal

Developing a positive self-image

Materials Needed

Piece of paper that is 3' x 4' (can be made by taping smaller pieces of paper together), markers, magazine pictures of people who have different facial expressions, Sesame Street and Hap Palmer recordings "All About Me," book *I Am Special*, video about self-esteem

Time Needed

20 to 30 minutes at free choice time, 5 to 10 minutes in circle time

How To Do It

1. Ask a child to lie down on a large piece of paper. Trace an outline drawing of him or her.
2. Ask the child to dictate what he or she likes about himself or herself. Record this on the paper and then share these thoughts with the group at circle time. Post the drawings.
3. During circle time, show children the cut-out magazine pictures and have the children tell what they think each person is feeling.
4. Using puppets or props from the dramatic play area, have children role play some of the feelings discussed. Show the video about self-esteem, read the book *I Am Special*, and play the records "All About Me."

Age

3, 4, 5

Evaluation

Can the children each say 3 or 4 things they like about themselves? Do they enjoy role playing feelings at circle time?

Easier and Harder Ideas

1. Ask the children to bring in more magazine pictures of people that display different feelings. Continue playing this game for several days.

2. Have the children make puppets as described in the subject matter approach Program Enrichment Paper, Day 1. Encourage children to draw happy, sad, or mad expressions on the puppet faces.

Send-Home Ideas

Ask parents to have each family member list what he or she likes about him- or herself and share it at a meal. Post these lists. Try having a "person of the week," during which time other family members do nice things for the person. Choose the person alphabetically.

Dear Teacher:

Thank you for your work with children today. Draw or paste a gold star on this program enrichment paper when you are finished. Put stars on the other papers you've done too. Adults need rewards just as children do. Even small ones are nice!

Learning About the Telephone

Curriculum Approach

Activity approach

Goal

Learning about the telephone

Materials Needed

Construction paper, scissors, glue or paste, yarn, crayons

Time Needed

10 minutes at free choice time, 5 minutes at circle time

How To Do It

1. Put out paper and yarn and encourage the children to cut out a telephone and attach a yarn cord, or to make a cordless telephone.
2. Put out crayons so that some children can draw a telephone. Comment on the children's art and encourage them to think about whether a telephone cord is straight or coiled.
3. Encourage children to play with their phones and act out conversations.
4. During circle time, talk about the order of conversation on the phone: First "Hello," then your conversation, then "Goodbye." Talk about how to dial and use a phone. Follow the suggestions in the subject matter approach and activity approach Program Enrichment Papers for Day 2.

Age

4, 5

Evaluation

Do the children enjoy their imaginative play on the telephone?

Easier and Harder Ideas

1. Practice answering the phone. Tape record sounds of a ringing phone or ring a bell to start off the practice.
2. Walk to a nearby phone booth and talk about the coins needed to make a call. Call up someone that you know will be home, or call your center.

Send-Home Ideas

Have children make a second phone and send both phones home with each child. Encourage parents to "talk" on these phones with their child. Parents may want to pretend they are other people or grandparents and practice possible conversations.

Dear Teacher:

Thank you for your work with children today. Draw or paste a gold star on this program enrichment paper when you are finished. Put stars on the other papers you've done too. Adults need rewards just as children do. Even small ones are nice!

Weather, Time, and Emergencies

Curriculum Approach

Subject matter approach

Goal

Learning math concepts, including number recognition, using a combination of numbers and number patterns

Materials Needed

A real phone

Time Needed

15 minutes during free choice time

How To Do It

1. Teach children to recognize the numbers 1 to 9 if they are interested in learning this. Show them the actual numbers on the phone.
2. Teach children to recognize the sequence of their own phone numbers by printing each child's number on a separate card. Teach children to sing their own phone numbers to the tune of "Twinkle, Twinkle, Little Star."
3. Encourage children to recognize their own phone number and practice dialing it.
4. Invite children to call each other up by dialing another child's number as it appears on their card.
5. Print out the numbers for weather, time, and emergency services (911 in some areas). Talk about when these numbers might be used. Practice using them if possible.

Age

4, 5

Evaluation

Do children enjoy using the phone? Do they understand that there is a relationship between a person's phone number and the ability to call a person?

Easier and Harder Ideas

1. Place the phone in the dramatic play corner. Invite the children to call up grandmother, Aunt Sue, Uncle Joe, and so forth.

2. Invite children to read out another child's phone number and ask, "Is that your phone number?" The child whose number it is stands up. Take turns doing this until a child can recognize his or her phone number.

Send-Home Ideas

Tell parents that you are learning about using the phone, and have introduced the idea of calling time and weather. Encourage parents to let their children actually make a call while the parents are present. Ask them to post a neighbor's or relative's phone number to call in case of emergencies.

Dear Teacher:

Thank you for your work with children today. Draw or paste a gold star on this program enrichment paper when you are finished. Put stars on the other papers you've done too. Adults need rewards just as children do. Even small ones are nice!

How to Get Help

Curriculum Approach

Process approach

Goal

Learning the skills of cooperating, thinking, and decision-making

Materials Needed

Real telephone, tape recording of sounds of a phone ringing

Time Needed

10 minutes at circle time

How To Do It

1. Think up an example of an emergency and discuss it with the children. Talk about how to get help.
2. Discuss and cooperate in deciding what kind of help is needed and who to call.
3. Act out an emergency, play the ringing phone tape, and have children take turns dealing with it.
4. Play the tape of the ringing telephone and ask the children to differentiate its sounds from other sounds, such as a record playing or children talking across the hall.

Age

4, 5

Evaluation

Do the children realize the telephone might be helpful in an emergency?

Easier and Harder Ideas

1. Using a toy telephone, play a listening game with the children. Say "ring" or ring a bell. When the child picks up the toy phone, give him or her a simple instruction, such as, "Hop on one foot." or "Clap your hands." Work up to giving two or three instructions at once.

2. Older children can dictate a list of their friends' names and their phone numbers. Write these on a piece of cardboard for the children to keep near the phone at home.

Send-Home Ideas

Send home the child's telephone list or ask parents to help the child make one. Suggest to parents that they allow a child to make his or her own phone call. This activity encourages independence and teaches the child to carry through on a sequence of numbers from left to right. Suggest they add emergency numbers to this list.

Dear Teacher:

Thank you for your work with children today. Draw or paste a gold star on this program enrichment paper when you are finished. Put stars on the other papers you've done too. Adults need rewards just as children do. Even small ones are nice!

Learning about Wind and Air

Curriculum Approach

Activity approach

Goal

Making kites and flying them; blowing and whistling

Materials Needed

Construction paper, hole punch, string, scissors

Time Needed

5 minutes during free choice time, 10 to 15 minutes of outdoor time

How To Do It

1. Show the children how to cut off the corners of a piece of construction paper to make a diamond shape. Draw lines for the children to cut along (or close to) if necessary.
2. Punch a hole in the corner of the diamond and attach a three-foot piece of string.
3. Have the children fly the kites outside by running and seeing if the air will lift them.
4. During circle time, talk about wind and air. Talk about air in the body. Ask children to put their hands on their chests and feel their lungs expand as they inhale air. Have them hold their hands in front of their mouths when they sing to feel the air that is exhaled. Have some fun pretending to whistle. Mention to children the idea that when they sing, they are instruments.

Evaluation

Do the children enjoy flying their kites?

Age

3, 4, 5

Easier and Harder Ideas

1. Let the children blow on things such as crumpled paper, a ping-pong ball, or a balloon. Ask if they can blow something toward themselves. They will find that wind coming from their mouths tends to blow things away.

2. Let older children do straw painting. Cut straws to three- or four-inch lengths. Have children blow watery non-toxic paint onto clean paper to make a design. One, two, or three colors can be used. Remind the children to breathe deeply between blowings.

Send-Home Ideas

Send home the kites and ask the parents to fly kites with their children. A tail can be added to these. Purchased kites may also be used. Schedule a parent-child kite flying on a Saturday.

Dear Teacher:

Thank you for your work with children today. Draw or paste a gold star on this program enrichment paper when you are finished. Put stars on the other papers you've done too. Adults need rewards just as children do. Even small ones are nice!

How Do We Feel the Wind?

Curriculum Approach

Subject matter approach

Goal

Developing counting skills and science skills

Materials Needed

A scarf or piece of filmy material for every child, large transparent plastic bag, collage materials, and dry leaves

Time Needed

10 minutes at music time, 5 minutes outdoors, 5 minutes at circle time

How To Do It

1. Ask the children how they are able to feel the wind while they are outdoors. Do they feel it in their hair? Rushing around their knees? In their eyes and ears?
2. At music time, take out the scarves and count them by colors, sizes, and sets. Invite the children to wave them around to music. Pretend they are the wind. See if they make any wind (breeze) from waving the scarves.
3. Fill the big plastic bag with collage materials and dry leaves and knot it. At circle time, show the children that they can see the materials moving around inside it.
4. Let the children see what happens when you let air escape from the plastic bag.

Evaluation

Can the children tell you many ways they feel the wind? Do they enjoy using scarves to music?

Age

3, 4, 5

Easier and Harder Ideas

1. Pick up a handful of dry grass outdoors. Let it fall as you talk about which way the wind is blowing. Hold out a handkerchief to see if the wind will blow it.

2. Hold up a wet finger outdoors. The side that dries first will feel colder. That is the side the wind is coming from.

Send-Home Ideas

Encourage parents to let children have a scarf or two to dance with while listening to music. Explain that this is good for large muscle coordination and that even two-year-olds have a sense of rhythm.

Dear Teacher:

Thank you for your work with children. Did you know that this is some of the most important work in the world? You are making a contribution to the future every day.

Moving Air and Watching the Wind

Curriculum Approach

Process approach

Goal

Observing and predicting

Materials Needed

Empty plastic liquid detergent bottle; soft white string; three cardboard rectangles (12" × 1", 12" × 3", and 12" × 6"); stick, dowel, yardstick, or clothesline

Time Needed

5 minutes during circle time, 5 minutes outside

How To Do It

1. Put the string in the empty detergent bottle so that 2 to 3 inches of string is left sticking out.
2. At circle time, squeeze the bottle so the children can see the string coming out of the bottle. Talk about how the moving air causes this. Make several bottles and pieces of string available for children to use during free choice time to make their own "string bottles."
3. Punch holes in the end of each cardboard rectangle. Tie a piece of string to each rectangle and tie the other end of the strings to a stick or clothesline.
4. Take the stick with the attached rectangles outside. Ask the children to observe it. Have children guess which pieces of cardboard will be blown highest by the wind. Talk about size and surface area.

Evaluation

Do some of the children correctly predict which cardboard rectangle will be blown the highest?

Age

3, 4, 5

Easier and Harder Ideas

1. Look for things the wind moves. For example, wind blows a piece of paper in a gutter, a ball on the grass, sail boats in the water, kites in the air, trees, and clouds in the sky.

2. Look for things the wind supports. Point out to children that air holds up birds, planes, parachutes, and gliders.

Send-Home Ideas

Encourage parents to make a simple paper airplane with their child or send one home. An airplane can be made from a standard piece of paper by folding it in half lengthwise, folding the sides to form a point at one end, then folding the sides back in quarters. Ask parents to fly this plane, or several different ones, with their child.

Dear Teacher:

Thank you for your work with children. Did you know that this is some of the most important work in the world? You are making a contribution to the future every day.

Learning About Frogs

Curriculum Approach

Activity Approach

Goal

1. To learn more about frogs through different activities in centers
2. To encourage discovery learning in small groups and individually
3. To encourage children to build upon different interests according to their abilities and learning styles

Materials Needed

Thematic materials for 3 or 4 centers, in this case related to learning about frogs: for a publishing center, supply books and materials on frogs (with a tape recorder to dictate fictional stories about frogs and crayons or paint to decorate the cover of a frog book); a library center; a frog center with a live frog or two in a see-through container; and a computer center with a software program or zoo CD-ROM disc that features frogs.

Time Needed

30 to 45 minutes

How To Do It

1. Introduce a frog storybook at circle time. Talk about frogs, what they do, and how they sound.
2. Practice hopping like frogs when you go outside. Play leap frog.
3. Sing a frog song or an adapted counting song, substituting frogs for the subject in the original song.
4. Role play "The Three Little Frogs" on the order of the "Three Bears" story.
5. Introduce materials in the centers, one center per day, for further exploration.

Evaluation

Did the children like one or more of the centers? Did they find the centers interesting? Are materials made that can go in a child's portfolio to share with a parent?

Age

3, 4

Easier and Harder Ideas

1. Younger children can follow this theme in the art center with a variety of green materials, paper, and paint.
2. Older children can use a microscope to examine the water that frogs live in from a creek or pond. They can compare it with tap water and note the differences.

Send-Home Ideas

Tell parents you are studying frogs this week and ask if they have any materials on frogs to send in (or any green material for costumes).

Dear Teacher:

Thank you for your work with children. Did you know this is some of the most important work in the world? You are making a contribution to the future every day.

Center Learning Experiences

Curriculum Approach

Subject matter approach

Goal

1. To encourage children to work independently and in groups of 2 or 3
2. To foster learning by discovery and by doing
3. To develop children's decision-making skills
4. To enhance and build upon children's different interests, abilities, and learning styles

Materials Needed

3 or 4 tables with materials on them arranged by academic area or subject matter: math, science, language arts, and social studies; different materials stored in labeled boxes; task cards at each center that tell aides and volunteers more uses for materials at each center

Time Needed

30 to 45 minutes

How To Do It

1. At circle time, introduce each new center, one a day, and the activities in it. Talk about how many children can be at each center at a time.
2. Show some of the activities. For the math center, for example, demonstrate dice, a game such as Candyland™, and manipulatives including Cuisenaire Rods™ or blocks.
3. Invite three children to try the center. Choose three more children for each remaining day in the week.
4. Have a folder or cubby at each center for work or art work that might not be completed at that center in the time allowed.

Evaluation

Did the children enjoy trying the materials in one or more centers?
Was work done in a center that could be saved in a portfolio to show parents at conference time?

Age

3, 4

Easier and Harder Ideas

1. Younger children can include the large blocks and all the puzzles in the math center area.
2. Older children might enjoy having mops and dress-up clothes from different countries in the social studies center.

Send-Home Ideas

Ask parents to send in materials for the different centers; for example, children could bring in materials for the art center and the science center one week, and items for the other centers another week.

Dear Teacher:

Thank you for your work with children. Did you know this is some of the most important work in the world? You are making a contribution to the future every day.

Center Learning Processes

Curriculum Approach

Process Approach

Goal

1. To encourage processes such as observing, comparing, and cooperating
2. To provide materials to foster discovery learning
3. To develop decision-making skills and to enhance and build upon children's different interests, abilities, and learning styles

Materials Needed

3 or 4 areas set up as process centers, such as a corner of a room, a wall, or a table; a box containing materials for process center topics such as art, music, observing and comparing, cooperating, and perhaps cause and effect (Materials for the observing/comparing center might include items from outdoors to observe and compare and perhaps an audio tape recorder to record children's comments; items for the cooperating center could include games and blocks and other materials that require two or more participants.)

Time Needed

30 to 45 minutes

How To Do It

1. At circle time, talk about one center each day. Talk about observing and comparing, for instance, and different things children can compare.
2. Introduce materials from one center and try some of the activities with the children who are interested. Talk about cooperating and working together.
3. The music center can include instruments and a tape recorder for children to record their favorite songs and their original songs. Demonstrate the recording process and play back some songs during another circle time.
4. Have available a folder or cubby at the art center in which children can place unfinished projects and projects to go home.

Evaluation

Did some of the children understand the idea of cooperating in a center setting?

Age

3, 4

Easier and Harder Ideas

1. Younger children can enjoy the art center if collage materials and liquid glue are provided. Pieces of crumpled gift wrap, tissue paper, and scraps of cloth can be stuck to the glue; these make a great collage.
2. Older children can play more elaborate games in the cooperating center such as checkers and even chess.

Send-Home Ideas

Tell parents you are learning about cause and effect and ask them to talk about this with their children, especially while cooking.

Dear Teacher:

Thank you for your work with children. Did you know this is some of the most important work in the world? You are making a contribution to the future every day.

Signs of Spring

Curriculum Approach

Activity approach

Goal

Learning that spring is the beginning of the growing season

Materials Needed

Paper, glue, cotton balls, tissue paper, twigs, construction paper, pictures of birds or bird pattern, crayons

Time Needed

20 minutes of outdoor time, 15 minutes of free choice time

How To Do It

1. Take a walk to look for signs of spring: grass turning greener, buds forming on trees and shrubs, flower shoots beginning to appear, more kinds of birds being seen, and so forth.
2. Discuss these signs of spring with the children. Make a booklet about spring. Include pictures or samples of pussy willows, forsythia, crocuses, trees, or whatever is appropriate in your region. Add pictures of birds or use a bird pattern to make some birds.
3. Visit a park with gardens and look for more signs of spring. Talk about early spring flowers.
4. Add new items to the booklet(s). Children can each make a picture or collage to go in the class booklet, or each child that wants to can make his or her own booklet.

Evaluation

Did the children become more aware of things beginning to grow?

Age

3, 4, 5

Easier and Harder Ideas

1. Bring some forsythia branches or a branch from a fruit tree inside. Put the branches in a container with warm water and place the container in a somewhat sunny location. Each day, add some fresh water to the container. It takes 3 or 4 weeks for these "dead" branches to blossom.

2. Plant a narcissus, hyacinth, or crocus bulb in some stones in a shallow container. Keep adding fresh, warm water. Wait and watch for it to blossom.

Send-Home Ideas

Ask parents to call their child's attention to birds they see or trees starting to bud. Ask them to read or tell a story about birds to their child. Remind parents that telling stories can be done while riding in the car.

Dear Teacher:

Thank you for your work with children. Did you know that this is some of the most important work in the world? You are making a contribution to the future every day.

Starting Small and Growing

Curriculum Approach

Subject matter approach

Goal

Understanding science concepts about growing plants and animals

Materials Needed

Seeds, tools (shovel, hoe, rake), calendar, symbols for growing, book *The Carrot Seed* by Ruth Krauss (Harper, New York), fertilized eggs in an incubator from a local hatchery

Time Needed

30 minutes of outdoor time, 10 minutes of circle time, 10 minutes of free choice time, 5 to 10 minutes a day for six weeks follow-up time

How To Do It

1. Use simple garden tools to plant seeds outdoors. Carrots and radishes are almost always successful. During circle time, read *The Carrot Seed*.
2. Keep a growth calendar by recording any change or lack of change noticed in the plants. Use symbols for rain, sun, and new sprouts. (These symbols may be either stick-on or hand-drawn.) Discuss the concept that growing takes time.
3. Cover some seedlings with a box and have children observe the difference this makes.
4. Hatch chicks in an incubator according to instructions from the hatchery. Watch them grow. Discuss the concept that animals need food, water, warmth, loving care, and rest to grow.

Evaluation

Do the children take an interest in the things they are growing? Do they observe changes with interest?

Age

3, 4, 5

Easier and Harder Ideas

1. Talk about the fact that everything alive starts small and then grows. Bring in pictures or stories of other examples, such as baby animals and seedling trees.
2. If you are in a cold climate or do not have access to a garden plot, plant seeds indoors in cans or egg cartons.

Send-Home Ideas

Ask parents to send in a labeled baby picture of their child. Talk about how all the children started small, too. Invite a mother to bring in a real baby to visit, if possible.

Dear Teacher:

Thank you for your work with children. Did you know this is some of the most important work in the world? You are making a contribution to the future every day.

Respecting and Appreciating Life

Curriculum Approach

Process approach

Goal

Observing, noticing, and valuing

Materials Needed

Paper towels, clear plastic cups, lima beans that have been soaked in water overnight, newsprint, markers

Time Needed

15 minutes during free choice time, 10 minutes at circle time

How To Do It

1. Invite children to place a lima bean in a clear plastic cup and cover it with a wet paper towel.
2. Watch a plant sprout from the seed. As the plant grows, talk about the root, the stem, and the leaves.
3. Write the children's observations on a large newsprint "calendar" each day. Encourage children to notice carefully any changes that occur.
4. Discuss living things and "brainstorm" ways that the children can appreciate and respect them. Suggestions might include not stepping on plants, playing gently with kittens and puppies, taking turns and respecting each other when using toys and materials.

Evaluation

Could the children report changes as they occur in their lima bean plants?

Age

3, 4, 5

Easier and Harder Ideas

1. Talk about seeds. Make a seed collage from many different kinds of seeds, such as apple, orange, melon, rice, corn, tomato, etc.

2. Have a pet in the classroom if possible, such as a rabbit, guinea pig, or even a goldfish. Talk about the pet's shape and how it moves. Have children take turns feeding it and caring for it.

Send-Home Ideas

Ask parents to talk with their child about pets, whether their own or a neighbor's. Talk about its shape, weight, movement, breathing, heartbeat, and body covering. Have a puppy or kitten or a cat or a dog visit your home, if possible.

Dear Teacher:

Thank you for your work with children. Did you know that this is some of the most important work in the world? You are making a contribution to the future every day.

Making Bowls

Curriculum Approach

Activity approach

Goal

1. To learn by all the senses
2. To learn some words for numbers and colors in Spanish (Another language, such as French or German, can be used another day.)
3. To appreciate that songs and folk stories can be told with some or all Spanish words
4. To see a child's primary language as a valuable resource to be nurtured and expanded, both for children who speak English as a second language and for English-speaking children
5. To encourage natural and functional learnings for all speakers
6. To learn words in a new language through meaning and content activities

Materials Needed

Homemade play dough that can be dried and sent home; red, yellow, and blue paint; library books with Spanish folklore stories and songs

Time Needed

30 to 45 minutes

How To Do It

1. Introduce the play dough and talk about making bowls in many ways. Show one way yourself by rolling out a "snake" and coiling it around to make a bowl. Introduce any Spanish words you know that relate to the activity, such as the words for bowl and rolling or coiling. Pat the bowls dry.
2. When the bowls are dry, talk about painting them. Introduce the Spanish words for red, yellow, and blue. Paint the bowls and count them, in Spanish, in sets of five.
3. Read a story from the Spanish folk stories that you checked out of the library.

4. Sing a song in Spanish. Have Spanish-speaking children help you or even choose the song. Ask them to each find a partner and together practice saying the Spanish words for numbers and colors.

Evaluation

Do the children enjoy learning three Spanish words? Do they enjoy learning one new word from a partner?

Age

4, 5

Easier and Harder Ideas

1. A younger child can make other clay objects without painting them.
2. An older child can help cook a simple Mexican food such as tacos.

Send-Home Ideas

Ask parents to display the bowl, perhaps as a kitchen table centerpiece. Ask them to tell their children other Spanish words if they know some.

Learning Spanish Words

Curriculum Approach

Subject matter approach

Goal

1. To learn several Spanish words
2. To develop an appreciation for words in another language that are names of familiar objects or concepts
3. To develop the self-image of children who already speak Spanish as a first language
4. To provide context-embedded new learnings

Materials Needed

Classroom materials relating to numbers, letters, and science; artifacts with a Spanish origin for a social studies center

Time Needed

20 to 30 minutes

How To Do It

1. Name the numbers 1 through 10 in Spanish, and as you say each number, put the numeral up on a board (chalkboard, flannel board, bulletin board). Ask children to say the numbers with you.
2. Ask the children to print their names on graph paper. Put the names on the board under the numerals that correspond to the number of letters in each name. Ask the children, "Who has the most letters in his or her name?" (Have the named child go and point to his or her name.) "Who has the least?" Count the letters in the names of the other children.
3. Any child in the group who is a native speaker of Spanish can help model the ways to pronounce the numerals and other words.
4. Talk about the Spanish names for items in the science center. Do the same for the social studies center. Have a Spanish-speaking parent or volunteer help you. On chart paper, write out each word as it is spoken.
5. Put the words up around the classroom.

Evaluation

Did the children enjoy learning at least three new Spanish words?

Age

4, 5, 6

Easier and Harder Ideas

1. A younger child can learn to sing a song in Spanish.
2. An older child can substitute French words and numbers after learning the Spanish words.

Send-Home Ideas

Ask parents to look, along with their children, for Spanish words in print in the community. Food items such as tacos, tortillas, and salsa are several common examples.

Uno, Dos, Tres

Curriculum Approach

Process approach

Goal

1. To develop thinking skills in observing, comparing, categorizing, and sequencing
2. To learn to count and to learn a few Spanish words
3. To enhance the self-esteem of any Spanish-speaking children in the class
4. To provide discovery learning

Materials Needed

Spanish dictionary or knowledge of Spanish words for observing, comparing, counting, and colors; Spanish song or songs

Time Needed

20 to 30 minutes

How To Do It

1. Say the numbers 1 to 6 in Spanish (uno, dos, tres, cuatro, cinco, seis). Compare how many sets of three children there are in the group. How many sets of four are there? Of five? Of six?
2. Talk about the names of three colors in Spanish: red (rojo), yellow (amarillo), and blue (azul). Count how many children are wearing each color. If the number goes above six, break into sets again.
3. Ask the children to stand up if they are wearing a color that you call out. Talk about the categories of "up" and "down." Count the number of children in each category.
4. If children in the group are Spanish-speaking, have them help lead the class in pronouncing words.
5. Sing a number song, with the numbers in sequence in Spanish.

Evaluation

Could the children observe and compare using Spanish numbers?

Easier and Harder Ideas

1. A younger child can color objects in sets of numbers with red, yellow, and blue.
2. An older child can learn the numbers from 1 to 10 and to count by tens to 100.

Send-Home Ideas

Encourage parents to count things with their children in English and Spanish.

Visit the Zoo

Curriculum Approach

Activity approach

Goal

Visiting the zoo and identifying zoo animals

Materials Needed

Extra adults and cars to help with a trip to the zoo; *Sesame Street* magazine, May 1982; *A Visit to the Zoo*, Hallmark Children's Edition; *The Animals' ABCs*, Hallmark Children's Edition; *The Zoo Book* by Jan P. Floog (Golden Press); *Animals: My Happy Book* (Dolisha Press); *Animal Kingdom: Star Book* (Seigo Publishers); circus and zoo songs from *This is Music Book I* by Sur, McCall, Fisher, and Tolbert (Allyn and Bacon, 1962); the record "A Trip to the Zoo" by Young People's Records (Other books and records about zoo animals may be substituted.)

Time Needed

2 hours for the zoo trip, 15 minutes a day at circle and music time for 3 to 4 days

How To Do It

1. Over a period of several days, read and discuss the books on zoo animals. Practice identifying different animals.
2. Involve the children in planning a trip to the zoo. What is needed? What are the rules for behavior? Sing zoo songs from "This is Music."
3. Visit the zoo and enjoy the animals.
4. Reread the books on zoo animals and see how many animals children can now identify.

Age

3, 4, 5

Evaluation

Are some of the children able to identify some of the animals? Can they do this at the zoo as well as from books?

Easier and Harder Ideas

1. Act out the story in "Train to the Zoo."
2. View videos about the zoo or zoo animals and then have children draw pictures of zoo animals.

Send-Home Ideas

Encourage parents to take their child back to the zoo for a family picnic. The whole family can enjoy identifying animals and can help the young child increase his or her store of animal names.

Dear Teacher:

   Thank you for your work with children. Did you know that this is some of the most important work in the world? You are making a contribution to the future every day.

Counting Animals

Curriculum Approach

Subject matter approach

Goal

Learning the concepts of numbers from 1 to 5

Materials Needed

Extra adults and cars to help with a trip to the zoo; *Your Big Backyard* by National Geographic; *World Book Encyclopedia*, Volume A (Animals) or Volume Z (Zoo) and *Childcraft*, Volume 5 (About Animals); toy zoo animals or puppets and a cardboard box or strips of paper

Time Needed

2 hours for the trip to the zoo, 10 minutes at circle time, 5 minutes during free choice time

How To Do It

1. Have children practice counting anything and everything for several days before the trip. Choose groups of things that contain five or less items.
2. During circle time, lay strips of paper on the floor or use a cardboard box to be a "cage." Place varying numbers of toy animals (up to five) in the cage and have children take turns counting the animals in the cage. Continue this activity during free choice time.
3. Using the encyclopedia or books as resources, share pictures and information about zoo animals with the children.
4. Visit the zoo. Count the number of animals in each cage that contains five or fewer animals.

Evaluation

Were some of the children able to count the animals accurately?

Age

4, 5

Easier and Harder Ideas

1. Count the number of animals in each cage at the zoo and in the classroom up to the number 3.
2. Ask children to draw five animals that they saw at the zoo.

Send-Home Ideas

Ask parents to count up to five objects with their children. Suggest counting soup cans, steps, laundry, mittens—almost anything will do. Parents can incorporate this activity into a clean-up game: "Can you pick up five toys off the floor?" Encourage parents to make pick-up time a counting time.

Dear Teacher:

Thank you for your work with children. Did you know that this is some of the most important work in the world? You are making a contribution to the future every day.

Categorizing Large and Small Animals

Curriculum Approach

Process approach

Goal

Observing various characteristics of zoo animals, categorizing large and small animals

Materials Needed

Trip to the zoo, as described in Day 2 activity approach and subject matter approach enrichment papers; record "A Trip to the Zoo" by Young People's Records

How To Do It

1. Ask the children to name the large zoo animals.
2. Ask the children to name the small zoo animals.
3. Ask different children to choose and act out the actions of a favorite zoo animal. Observe and comment on the various characteristics of the animals.
4. Play the record "Trip to the Zoo" and act it out.

Time Needed

15 minutes during circle time

Evaluation

Did most of the children get the large and small animals in the correct category?

Age

3, 4, 5

Easier and Harder Ideas

1. Ask children to draw a picture of their favorite zoo animal.
2. Encourage all the children to plan and cooperate in making a mural that shows different animals. Glue dried twigs and grass to the mural to make the earth more interesting.

Send-Home Ideas

Ask parents to talk with their children about the concept of large and small, perhaps having them match or group similar objects. Encourage them to read "Goldilocks and the Three Bears" to their children.

Dear Teacher:

Thank you for your work with children. Did you know that this is some of the most important work in the world? You are making a contribution to the future every day.

Have a Happy Summer

Curriculum Approach

Activity, subject matter, and process approaches

Goal

Finding an interesting activity/learning experience for each day

Materials Needed

An adult to read the activity of the day to the child, other materials as listed, copier machine to copy this sheet to send home with each child

Time Needed

5 minutes a day

How To Do It

1. Ask the children to do one activity a day.
2. Ask them to find the date listed for the day's activity, and then cross it off when they do the activity.
3. Sing the alphabet song with the children. Encourage them to print their names.
4. Send home the following activities for the days listed.

Age

4, 5, 6

Send-Home Ideas

June 10	Get a library card from the library or bookmobile. Choose a book.
June 11	Make your own bed and put away all your things.
June 12	Sing the alphabet song with your mom or dad.
June 13	Do 5 jumping jacks. Hop 5 times on your left foot and 5 times on your right foot.
June 14	Write the numbers 0 through 5. Draw a set of something to go with each number.
June 15	Listen to a story that someone reads to you. Tell the story back to him or her.

June 16	Ask for an allowance of 25 cents or 50 cents a week.
June 17	Buy something that costs less than your allowance. Ask your mom or dad to tell you how much money you have left.
June 18	On Father's Day, do something special for your dad.
June 19	Make a sandwich. Get someone to cut it in the middle. Cut the smaller pieces in the middle. How many pieces do you have?
June 20	Set the table for your parent. Be sure to give everyone everything they will need.
June 21	Print as many of the capital letters as you can.
June 22	Draw a pretty summer picture. What is today?
June 23	Find 5 pretty stones. How many different sets can you make using them?
June 24	Find 10 pretty stones. How many different sets can you make using them?
June 25	Practice printing your name.
June 26	Write the numbers 0 through 10. Draw a set of something to go with each number.
June 27	Plan a summer picnic. Draw a picture of what you would like to eat.
June 28	Look for 5 pretty flowers. Don't pick them until you get permission from someone.
June 29	Tell stories about the pictures you see in a nursery rhyme book or "read" it to someone.
June 30	Do 10 jumping jacks. Hop 10 times on your left foot and 10 times on your right foot.

More Happy Summer Days

Curriculum Approach

Activity, subject matter, and process approaches

Goal

Finding an interesting activity/learning experience for each day

Materials Needed

An adult to read the activity of the day to the child, other materials as listed, copier machine to copy this sheet to send home with each child

Time Needed

5 minutes a day

How To Do It

1. Ask the children to do one activity a day.
2. Ask them to cross off the activity number after they have done the activity.

Age

4, 5

Send-Home Ideas

July 1	Make a July calendar. Draw a picture of the weather each day on your calendar.
July 2	This is a good day to help your mother do whatever she is doing.
July 3	Sit very still in your yard for 5 minutes. Draw a picture of things you see and hear.
July 4	Happy Independence Day! Find out how old America is today.
July 5	Watch the clouds. What kinds of sky animals can you see?
July 6	Look for insects and see if you can find one you can name.

July 7	Get a *big* pan of water. Find 5 things that sink and 5 things that float.
July 8	Count all the doors in your house. Draw a house that has one more door than your house has.
July 9	Say the alphabet to someone. How many letter *sounds* can you say?
July 10	Tell your parent(s) how much you love them. Do something nice to show them.
July 11	Write all the numbers from 0 to 15. Make a set of stones to go with each number.
July 12	Have you been to the library or bookmobile lately? Read or look at a good book.
July 13	Make a sandwich. Can you cut it to make 2 rectangles? 4 rectangles? Get your parent to cut it for you.
July 14	Get a *long* piece of string. Use the string to measure your table. Find five things that are not as *wide* as your table is. Keep your string!
July 15	Draw a picture of everything you eat today. Did you eat a lot?
July 16	Make a purchase with your allowance. Save up several weeks' allowance if you need to.
July 17	Are you making your bed and putting your things away every day? Start today if you are not doing this yet.
July 18	Make a picture. Use only red and yellow. Is there another color on your paper?
July 19	Count all the doorknobs in your house. Are there more doors or doorknobs? Or are there the same number of each?
July 20	How many different leaves can you find in your yard? Ask someone if you can pick them. Trace around them and color them.
July 21	Ask your Mom to buy a melon and let you make melon balls for dinner. Make a set of 5 for each family member.
July 22	Take a paper bag outside and collect 10 interesting things. Tell someone about each item in your collection.
July 23	Get your piece of string (or get a new piece of string if you can't find it). Measure your arm. Find 10 things that are shorter.
July 24	Practice printing your name.
July 25	Take a walk around your yard. How many insects do you see? Don't bother them.
July 26	Get your piece of string. Measure your foot. Find 10 things that are *larger*.
July 27	Write as many of the small letters of the alphabet as you can.
July 28	Ask Mom if you can stay up late to listen to all the night sounds. Do you know what they are?

July 29	Count all the windows in your house. Are there more or less windows than doors?
July 30	Have you read a library book lately? Read one to your parent(s).
July 31	Look at your July calendar. Were there more sunny days or more rainy days? Less rainy days or less cloudy days?

Happy August Days

Curriculum Approach

Activity, subject matter, and process approaches

Goal

Learning or doing one interesting thing each day

Materials Needed

Materials are listed in each activity description.

Time Needed

5 minutes a day

How To Do It

1. Copy this sheet and send it home with all the children.
2. Ask children to do one activity a day.

Age

4, 5

Send-Home Ideas

August 1	Sit very still in your yard. How many different bird songs do you hear?
August 2	Set the table for *all* the meals today. Don't forget anything.
August 3	Make a picture. Use only yellow and blue. Do you see another color?
August 4	Ask your parent for an old magazine. Find five pictures with names that begin with the same sound as "sun." Cut them out.
August 5	How many stones do you need to make 5 sets with 2 stones in each set? Try it!
August 6	Make a picture of the sky after a storm. Is there a rainbow?
August 7	Draw a picture of what you would like to do on your next vacation.

August 8	Ask Mom for some grocery boxes to play store with.
August 9	Have you gone to the library or bookmobile lately? Read a book to someone.
August 10	Count all the chairs in your house. Can you write the number?
August 11	Draw a picture. Use only the shapes of a circle, a square, a triangle, and a rectangle. Ask a parent to draw these shapes for you to help you remember.
August 12	Read a nursery rhyme book to a friend.
August 13	Do something special for your Mom. Don't forget to tell her how much you love her.
August 14	Count all the beds in your house. Are there more beds or more chairs?
August 15	Ask your parent(s) if you can have a goldfish in a glass bowl. Give the fish a name.
August 16	Practice printing your name. Learn to print the goldfish's name.
August 17	Find an old magazine. Find or draw three things that rhyme with *can*. Now find three things that rhyme with *tree*.
August 18	Make a sandwich. Can you cut it to make 2 triangles? 4 triangles? Get a parent to help you cut it.
August 19	Do you still have your measuring string? Measure how *high* the sofa is. Find 3 things that are higher.
August 20	Ask your parent if you can go to the grocery store with him or her. Ask if you can put three things in the basket.
August 21	Show your parent(s) how well you can make your own bed.
August 22	Find 12 stones. Make 6 sets with 2 stones in each set. Make 4 sets with 3 stones in each set. Can you do it other ways?
August 23	Say the alphabet to yourself. Say it again to someone else.
August 24	Count all the months until Christmas. Say the names of all the months that you can.
August 25	Draw a picture of what today's weather is like. Can you draw a picture of the weather every day?
August 26	Count all the rooms in your home. Which room is largest? Smallest? Longest? Shortest?
August 27	Help your Dad do whatever he is doing today. Tell him how much you love him.
August 28	Ask if you can have a bucket of water outside. Float a boat or leaves in it.
August 29	With a rock or chalk, make lines on the sidewalk. Make 5 lines. Then add 5 more.
August 30	See if the whole family can plan a picnic. Help make a list of what you will need.

Have a happy year!

The University Children's Educational Center

After some initial planning meetings had been held for an on-campus child-care center, the following resolution was submitted to the president of the university:

WHEREAS the University recognizes the ever-growing societal need for child-care services, and
WHEREAS the University recognizes the trend of an increasing number of women returning for postsecondary education, and
WHEREAS the University has demonstrated a need for child-care services on the campus,
AND TO THAT END, the University is committed to serving the needs of human society in general and the needs of the campus in particular to providing high-quality educational opportunities for all ages;
THEREFORE, BE IT RESOLVED that the University accepts and supports the formation of the Children's Educational Center as a service provided on the campus of the University.

The Graduate Student Association had initiated this request with the Associate Dean of Students the year before. After the resolution was presented in May, the center opened 16 months later in August. A phased-in orientation program allowed for enrollment to begin with 10 children in August, and 10 more started on September 1. A planning committee met regularly the year before start-up, and their accomplishments and time line appear later.

The nature of the child-care center was to be a service provided by the university for the university community. It would have a highly qualified director and teachers, it would encourage parent participation and drop-in visits, and it would be self-supporting from tuition fees paid by the enrollees. Two snacks a day were to be provided, but the children were to bring their own lunches.

The center would be open to faculty, staff, administration, and students, and would serve 20 children from the ages of two and a half to five years of age. The Assistant to the Dean for Re-Entry Student Services in the Dean of Students Office would supervise the center. A Board of Directors would develop policies and direct the operation of the center. This Board was to be made up of 55 percent parents, in addition to the Director and interested administrators and persons from the university community. A start-up grant of $10,000 from the Graduate Student Association (GSA) would provide start-up costs and equipment costs. The GSA would also provide three scholarships of $1,715 each for the first year, with first priority to be given to graduate students. The tuition for the start-up year was $55 per week, along with a $30 application fee. The center would, of course, meet all health, safety, and insurance requirements of the District and the University Insurance Company. The Children's Education Center would plan to be consistent with the aims of the university community. (The names have been adapted in the following description to make it applicable to others.)

Summary of Planning Activities—Time Line

Fall, Year I

1. Discussion on formation of a center took place between the president of the Graduate Student Association and the Associate Dean of Students.

Spring, Year II

2. These two parties requested that the Associate Dean of Students work with the Graduate Student Association on formulating a child-care center. The Graduate Student Association appropriated $3,000 in start-up funds.

February 24, Year II

3. A meeting took place between the Associate Dean of Students and the Dean of University College, regarding interest in child care.

May 5, Year II

4. A planning meeting was held between the new president of the Graduate Student Association and the Associate Dean of Students.

June 10, Year II

5. The planners visited the site of a nearby university child-care center.[*]

June 11–13, Year II

6. Planners attended the National Day Care Council Conference in Washington, D.C.

June 29, Year II

7. Bimonthly meetings of the Day-Care Advisory Board began. These meetings dealt with site, philosophy, recognition, program, funding, etc.

July 7, Year II

8. Planners attended a session on day-care center licensing sponsored by the District Office of Licensing and Regulations.

August 3, Year II

9. Planners surveyed space available in the university neighborhood.*

September, Year II

10. Needs assessments were distributed to students, faculty, and staff.*

September 9, Year II

11. The Chair of the Day-Care Advisory Board met with the president of the university.

September 17, Year II

12. Approval was received from the Dean of Students for the child-care center to be under the auspices of the Dean of Students Office.

September 20, Year II

13. A meeting was held with the Assistant Director of Resident Life and Food Services regarding the use of space in College Hall (a dormitory).

October, Year II

14. The Graduate Student Association began to consider a resolution to appropriate an additional $7,000 to the Children's Education Center.

October 21, Year II

15. A meeting was held for interested parents and the Advisory Committee to discuss plans for the Center. Committees were organized for parents to help write bylaws, order equipment, and interview Director/teacher candidates.

October 22, Year II

16. A prelicensing inspection of possible spaces was made by the District Office of Licensing and Regulations.

November 9, Year II

17. A budget presentation was made to the Graduate Student Association.

November, Year II

18. A meeting was arranged with Resident Advisors and Residence Hall Representatives from College Hall to discuss the possibility of College Hall being used for the Center. A letter was sent out to all residents of College Hall, and a meeting was arranged with all the residents to discuss the possibility of College Hall being used for the Center.

Early December, Year II

19. Meeting was held with representatives of East Hall, College Hall, West Hall, and South Hall dormitories regarding the use of College Hall for the Center.

December, Year II

20. Site was chosen and approved by the appropriate offices of the university.[1]

December, Year II

21. A brochure was planned that would describe the Center, especially noting the philosophy for child care (whole-child developmental philosophy).

---

1. Most centers might start here at step 20, in addition to completing steps 5, 9, 10, and 16 (the starred items).

January, Year III

22. The brochure was printed and distributed.

February, Year III

23. The Director/teacher hiring process began; incorporation papers with bylaws were filed.

March, Year III

24. Necessary repairs and renovations to the Center facility were begun (fire doors, child-size toilet facilities, fencing, etc.).

April, Year III

25. Applications were made available for children.

May, Year III

26. Equipment was ordered; a Director/teacher was hired. (Salary was to begin August 15. The early hiring was meant to allow the Director/teacher to have input into planning.)

June, Year III

27. Supplies were ordered; repairs and renovations were checked; the hiring process began for Center aides.

July, Year III

28. The Center facility was painted; the installation of equipment was arranged. An inspection was arranged to obtain the licensing and occupancy permit.

August 15, Year III

29. The rooms were set up and the Center was readied for the opening.

August 20, Year III

30. The Center was opened with approximately 10 children, which is 1/2 capacity.

September 1, Year III

The Center was in full operation. Twenty children were enrolled, which was full capacity at that time. A sample on-going budget worksheet follows.

Expenses
_____

Category	Month		Year To Date	Budgeted Year	Est. Left for Year	Est. Left for Month	This Month	Profit or Loss / Year
Expense								
Salaries				$ %				
Food								
Household								
Utilities								
Materials								
Maintenance								
Accounting								
Insurance								
Rent								
Advertising								
Postage								
Annuity (reserve)								
Equipment								
Prof. Fund								
Miscellaneous								
Total								

Recommended

Teachers' Salaries	70%
Utilities and Maintenance	6–12%
Insurance	1%
Custodial Help	3%
Permanent Equipment	8%
Expendable Supplies and Food	7–14%
Miscellaneous and Other	6%
	100%

Requesting Help from the University[2]

In order to provide the quality child care needed for the children of members of the university community, the Advisory Board of the Children's Education Center requested the following from the sponsoring university:

- Approval of the proposal
- Acceptance of the Children's Education Center as a service to the parents in the university community
- Support for the Center through the use of the first-floor (south) lounge in College Hall, including utilities
- Repairs to the site that fall under usual university maintenance, such as replacing cracked windows and torn screens, scraping peeling paint and repainting, and so forth
- Hiring the Center's professional staff as staff employees of the university, eligible for university benefits, but with salaries to be paid through Center income

The first-floor lounge space in the south end of College Hall was offered by the Office of Resident Life and Food Service as a possible site for the Children's Education Center. In a review of other possible facilities, no other site that was comparable to the College Hall lounge was available.

On October 22, Year II, with the agreement of the Office of Resident Life and Food Service, a preliminary licensing inspection by the District Department of Human Resources was held at the College Hall site.

This inspection indicated that the following renovations and/or repairs were needed:

- replace all broken windows and screens
- cover exposed radiators
- scrape and repaint window sills and other peeling areas
- replace urinal with standard toilet

The Department of Human Resources representative indicated that the site was a good one, large and well-lit, and met the necessary health and safety procedures required by law, including two means of egress.

A meeting was held with representatives of the College Hall Resident Advisor staff on November 22 to address any concerns and questions that

---

2. This same procedure could also be used with any large sponsoring organization.

residents/students might have regarding the use of dormitory space for a child-care center. The Resident Advisor representatives' response was very positive, and a meeting of residents was held on December 2, Year II, as described in the time line.

The Center opened as described in Year III, and has been running successfully since that time. The students enjoy seeing the children, and the service to the university has helped retain staff, faculty, and adult students.

APPENDIX E

Motivator Activities

The following Motivator Activities represent a few ideas for making changes in the motivator variables in your center as described in Chapter 5. These changes should help to build recognition, self-esteem, growth, a sense of achievement, and a sense of the worth of the work for staff members, parents, and children. Many other "motivators" are possible as discussed in Chapter 5. The hygiene variables are easier to address and many personnel books contain ideas for improving rules and regulations, hours, pay, and interpersonal relations. Of course, these motivator ideas also help to improve interpersonal relations.

Alumni Day

Motivators

Sense of achievement, self-esteem, and worth of the work

Time Needed

2 hours a year

Materials Needed

Invitations, refreshments

How To Do It

1. Formally invite alumni and parents to the child-care center.
2. Encourage former students to tell about their present successes and experiences.
3. Encourage parents to express their gratitude to teachers.
4. Offer refreshments.

Did It Work?

Does the staff want to do this again? Encourage feedback from the staff.

Other Possibilities

1. Invite local media, child-care administrators, and politicians to this event.
2. Give teachers a flower or a big decorative name tag to wear for the day.

"We're Proud" Open House

Motivators

Growth, self-esteem (other benefits include sharing ideas with other child-care center staff)

Time Needed

2 hours twice a year

Materials

Refreshments, which can be prepared by the children and can highlight nutrition, if desired

How To Do It

1. Formally invite staff from a nearby child-care center.
2. Encourage the hosting staff to allow visitors to view their rooms and activity ideas.
3. Encourage informal conversations about your program and teaching techniques. Encourage visitors to share their ideas.
4. Offer refreshments.

Did It Work?

Do employees want to do this again? Ask for feedback about how to improve this activity the next time. Ask staff what they gained from this experience.

Other Possibilities

1. Visit the center of the other staff.
2. Invite parents and grandparents to the same open house.
3. Have a "drop in" afternoon once a month to encourage staff from other centers and parents to visit. Coffee or simple refreshments may be set up in a central location.
4. Provide recognition in general for the center by printing the center's logo on helium balloons.
5. Invite a local newspaper photographer to take pictures of a center event relating to the community, such as a story hour in the library or attendance at an Arbor Day event.

Mountain Climbing

Motivators

Esteem, achievement

Time Needed

5 minutes

Materials

A badge with a picture on it of a mountain climber who has reached the top (this can be drawn as a stock figure or can be clipped from a magazine); book about a curriculum topic of interest to the receiver

How To Do It

1. Honor teachers or other staff who have completed a course or degree.
2. Have a ceremony and deliver the badge during morning opening exercises.
3. Decorate the teacher's lunch table and have his or her food delivered to the table as special music is played or sung.
4. Present the gift-wrapped book.
5. Allow for the book's expense in the training section of the budget. Encourage the use of this book for planning.

Did It Work?

Was the teacher surprised and pleased? Do you give more books each year?

Other Possibilities

1. Give a "You're Number One!" badge.
2. Honor the teacher who has been with the school the most number of years.
3. Honor teachers for other large or small reasons, for example, give a prize for the brightest smile on the second floor.

The Political Game of Life

Motivators

Responsibility, growth, autonomy (other benefits include enhancing awareness of the political establishment, improving child-care services for all persons)

Time Needed

1 hour during a staff meeting

Materials

Writing paper (personal stationery is fine); envelopes; stamps; addresses of local, state, or federal legislators

How To Do It

1. As a group, select one child-care law or bill that is under consideration.
2. Encourage each staff member to write his or her feelings about the bill and send it to a political official.
3. Invite the official to visit your center at any time or for an upcoming event with parents. Enclose a copy of your newsletter or other information about your center. (Some legislators do not know what good child-care programs look like.)

Did It Work?

Does the staff want to do this again? What did they gain from this project? Was the bill or law passed or defeated? Repeat the activity several times.

Other Possibilities

1. Encourage parents and staff at other centers to participate in this project.
2. If a legislator visits your center, pin a badge on him or her saying, "Friend of Children."
3. Have a newspaper or other media representative present to photograph and report the visit.
4. Take a snapshot of the official wearing the "Friend of Children" badge and enclose a copy of the photo the next time you write that legislator about supporting child-care services.

Ice Breaker Nutrition Game

Motivator

Responsibility, growth

Time Needed

30 to 45 minutes

Materials

Empty food boxes, cans, and grocery bags; large (4' x 4') white sheet, cloth, paper, or oil cloth divided into 4 blocks representing the 4 food groups (a bed sheet is fine). Cut out and paste pictures that represent a particular food group into the corresponding box.

meat fish poultry	dairy
breads cereals	fruits vegetables

Hint: Have parents send in empty food containers for 3 or 4 weeks beforehand; in addition to being available for this activity, children can later use these containers to play store or to play in the housekeeping corner.

How To Do It

1. Have the mat or sheet lying on the floor where all can see it.
2. Give each parent a prefilled bag of groceries as he or she comes in.
3. Start the game by explaining the food groups.
4. Ask each parent to come up and put each article of food on the mat in the proper food group block. Parents might also do this as they gather for a meeting.
5. All "junk" food should be placed off the mat.
6. When everyone has finished, see how many items have been placed in the proper food blocks. Read the ingredients lists on items that have been misplaced.

Did It Work?

Do parents agree that it is important to look at ingredients on food boxes?

Other Possibilities

1. Display refreshments on a table after organizing them by food groups and labeling them.
2. Have handouts available that give several recipes for parents to take home.

Center Decorations

Motivators

Growth, sense of achievement (other benefits include gaining new decorations for the center, promoting positive parent/child interaction, boosting parent creativity and encouraging home decoration, increasing parents' skills in saving money, helping staff and parents realize that scrap materials can be creatively recycled)

Time Needed

1 to 2 hours at the end of the center day

Materials Needed

Decorative pieces of scrap paper, egg cartons, pieces of wood, scrap pieces of plastic, tempera paint, glitter, shoe polish, egg shells, ribbon, scissors, glue, string, plastic bottles, milk containers, foam pieces, empty spools, wall paper scraps (Hint: Request that parents send in these items for 3 to 4 weeks before the event.)

How To Do It

1. Have children make bologna or peanut butter sandwiches and cut up some fruit to eat as a snack with parents when they arrive.
2. Lay out supplies on tables. Talk about some possibilities, then break into small groups to brainstorm. Assign different bulletin boards or planning locations to different groups.
3. Start and have fun. Give a lot of praise.

Did It Work?

Do children and parents display their work? Is staff and parent interaction benefitted? Does the group want to decorate again for other seasons? Do other centers copy the idea?

Other Possibilities

1. Have parent and staff workshops to help parents make a Christmas present for their children. Ideas for presents might be puppets, simple toys, games, bean bags, or stuffed animals. Provide a babysitter and let parents share the cost.
2. List ideas in an "Idea Book" that parents can take home, or devote a page in the newsletter to ideas contributed by parents and staff.
3. Make Christmas or holiday cards or ornaments.

"My News for Mom" Calendar

Motivator

Autonomy, responsibility (other benefits include promoting communication between parent and child, providing opportunities for language development, and recalling activities for child)

Time Needed

5 to 10 minutes for parents, and 5 to 10 minutes for teachers to prepare

Materials Needed

Copies of calendar forms, enough to send home one with each child

How To Do It

Teachers prepare each child's calendar on Thursday to send home with him or her on Friday.

Monday	Tuesday	Wednesday	Thursday
Susie brought turtle to school. Learned finger play "there was a little turtle who lived in a box."	Policeman came to school. Ask me how to cross the street safely.	Painted with Q tips. I'll tell you the colors I used.	Made play doh. Here's the recipe: 2 cups flour, 1 cup salt, ½ cup water, ¼ cup oil, food coloring. Let's make it at home!

Did It Work?

Do the parents feel more involved with the child's school life? Does the child communicate more readily about school activities?

Other Possibilities

1. Include one or more home learning activity suggestions with the calendar.
2. Make a calendar with activity suggestions for each day in December to use at home. Some example activities might include feeding the birds, singing holiday music together, or making Christmas or holiday cards.

Father-Grandfather Hour

Motivator

Recognition, growth (other benefits include introducing fathers and grandfathers to the program the center or school offers; giving the children a time with important males in their lives)

Time Needed

1 hour or more at the end of the center day or on a Saturday morning

Materials

Magic markers, paint, cardboard, collage materials, and a snack, if desired

How To Do It

1. Have the staff plan the schedule so that everyone starts all together in a big room with a music person. Sing easy songs that adults can join in on, then end with a circle dance.
2. Using materials in the child's classroom, have fathers, grandfathers, and children make a game to take home. Serve a snack if this is planned.
3. Close the session with a good-bye song.

Did It Work?

Is there positive feedback from all? Did the staff have a good feeling about the evening? Are the children pleased about it?

Other Possibilities

1. Have a Mother/Grandmother Hour.
2. Do this activity with Executive Board members or other adults who need orientation to good child care.
3. Have a special day (perhaps a Saturday) to involve spouses who are usually prevented from involvement by work. Plan a special center project that these adults can participate in.

Car Chatter

Motivator

Growth (other benefits include making the ride to and from the child-care center a "quality time," and promoting language development and initial sounds concepts)

Time Needed

A few minutes

Materials

None

How To Do It

1. Play an "I see _____" game that focuses on beginning sounds. For example, say, "I see something in the front seat that starts with 'buh'." The child might guess blue jeans, book, bottle, etc.
2. Try other starting sounds.
3. Trade roles with the child or children.
4. Try a variation of this game: "I'm thinking of a (toy, person, or animal) whose name begins with the sound 'duh'." The child might guess Dad, dog, doll, etc.

Did It Work?

Does the child ask to play the game again? Will he or she play both roles? Are some sounds easier for the child than others? Is the ride pleasant?

Other Possibilities

1. Use the same game format with colors, shapes, or descriptions.
2. Talk about what you are thinking, feeling, seeing, or hearing. Then ask the child to tell you what he or she is thinking, feeling, seeing, or hearing.

I Did It!

Motivator

Recognition, achievement, and self-esteem (other benefits include a reward for learning the rules)

Time Needed

1 minute

Materials

Construction paper, magic marker, safety pin

How to Do It

1. Make a badge for whatever goal you are working on with a particular child.
2. Write the goal on the badge.
3. Reward the child with the badge when he or she remembers to do what was requested.

Did It Work?

Does the child ask for the badge when he or she has reached a particular goal?

Other Possibilities

1. Suggest that parents use the badge idea at home.
2. Make a badge for eating vegetables, helping a friend, learning to button, or putting away toys.
3. Take a picture of the child wearing the badge and send the picture to a special relative.

Use Your Great Big Voice

Motivator

Recognition (other benefits include getting a child to talk in a voice louder than a whisper)

Time Needed

A few minutes weekly, over a 3-month period

How To Do It

1. Have the children as a group discuss talking loud enough for friends to hear you.
2. When a particular child speaks too softly, have the children tell this child that they can't hear what he or she is saying.
3. Allow the child to use the tape recorder to record and play back his or her voice. Encourage him or her to take deep breaths while talking. (This relaxes the vocal cords.)
4. Ask the staff to give verbal and physical praise (pats on the back) when the child talks in a louder voice.
5. Ask other children to give the child verbal and physical praise when the child talks in a louder voice.
6. Encourage the parent to give a reward to the child when the teacher communicates that the child is talking louder at school.

Did It Work?

Does the child speak with normal loudness 80 percent of the time?

Other Possibilities

1. Refer the child to a speech pathologist.
2. Encourage the parent to take turns at storytelling at home with the child. Allow the child to use the tape recorder and play it back at home.

Spring Garden Project

Motivator

Worth of the work, achievement (other benefits include involving parents, teachers, and children in a cooperative venture; learning about nature and the growth patterns of plants)

Time Needed

2 to 3 months

Materials

Garden plot, garden tools, seeds

How To Do It

1. Have a Saturday or Sunday "Sowing Social." Invite parents, children, and teachers to get the garden soil ready. Have parents purchase the seeds and allow the children to plant them in a corner of the outdoor play area.
2. Caring for the garden and additional planting can be done by children and teachers during outdoor activity times.
3. Discuss ways of growing food and the principles of good nutrition with the children.
4. Have a harvest picnic and/or dinner when the garden is ready for harvest. For example, lettuce, radishes, and carrots could all go in a salad. Children could make the salad the afternoon before the planned event.

Did It Work?

How successful was the harvest? Did children learn about growing crops and about nutrition? Did parents, children, and teachers cooperate together?

Other Possibilities

1. Keep growth charts for different vegetables.
2. Have each family grow something at home in a flower pot, garden, yard, or orange crate lined with a trash bag.

Leadership Enablers

The following leadership enablers represent just a few ideas for making changes in causal variables. These changes should help to build loyalty, gratitude, or a feeling of self-worth in persons, and thus may lead to a climate conducive to higher quality child care. Many other types of causal variables might be considered when deciding to make changes, such as encouraging workers to take courses and workshops, improving personnel policies, creating more flexible hours or schedules, and any others discussed in Chapter 7 of the text. In these leadership enablers, the causal variables that are addressed are described in the "How To Do It" sections. Output variables and intervening variables are described in the "Did It Work?" sections.

A Certificate of Recognition

Benefits

Building the self-esteem of staff members and encouraging them to foster positive attitudes towards the program; showing that the staff's efforts are noticed and appreciated

Time Needed

30 to 45 minutes per month

How To Do It

1. Make certificates or "Happy Grams" based on notes in each teacher's file. See the following example:

> _____ Day Care Center
> Date _____
>
> A Personal Note
> To: Susie Williams
>
>   Thank you so much for previewing the
> new six month goals for Child Development
> at our total staff meeting. You did a great job!
>
>
> _____
>   Director

2. Present the certificate at a staff meeting or share the information and appreciation at a staff meeting.

Did It Work?

Was the certificate appreciated? Was the work attitude of this staff member changed? Did it make a difference? (Intervening variables)

Other Possibilities

Give similar certificates to children or parents.

(Your Center Name) Child Care Center Seal of Approval

Benefits

Developing a staff file of arts and crafts activities to be used in the center program

Time Needed

1 hour

What You Need

Arts and crafts books borrowed from the library

How To Do It

1. Everyone takes a book and looks for *good* activities; when an activity is found, its place is marked with a bookmark.
2. The staff votes on the selected choices (i.e., gives them the "Seal of Approval").
3. The chosen activities can be filed under appropriate titles, such as pasting, printing, cutting, etc.
4. Activities can also be filed according to the ages they serve: 6- to 12-year-olds for the after-school program; 2- to 4, or 4- to 6-year-olds for your child-care program.

Did it Work?

The Director or head teacher can ask at staff meetings for feedback on activities tried and for any success reports (output variables). Did teachers appreciate having new activities at their fingertips? (interviewing variable)

Other Possibilities

Find books about games, music, woodworking, or any other topic on which the staff wants to build a file.

Teacher of the Month

Benefits

Building self-esteem and feelings of self-worth for teachers

Time Needed

30 minutes once a month

How To Do It

1. During a staff meeting, make a chart of teacher goals, jobs, and activities that are important to the group.
2. Casually observe class areas or classrooms at 3-day intervals.
3. Keep a record in the form of a checklist of teachers who are meeting the goals or implementing the activities discussed at the staff meeting.
4. Choose a "Teacher of the Month" based on goals met. Make a bulletin board that features a different teacher each month.
5. Give a special small gift to the teacher chosen, or buy him or her lunch.

Did it Work?

After a few months, take note of whether teachers are working towards the goal of "Teacher of the Month" (output variable).

Other Possibilities

1. Choosing a "Teacher of the Year" based on the same criteria used for choosing a "Teacher of the Month."
2. Feature a "Child of the Month" for perfect attendance or for meeting other criteria.
3. Choose a "Parent of the Year" or "Parent of the Month." Brainstorm criteria and activities at a parents' meeting.
4. Recognize six months of perfect attendance for teachers.
5. Do a bulletin board on yourself if you accomplish a difficult task or meet important goals.

Staff Recognition at Board Meetings

Benefits

Building self-esteem of staff members and reinforcing staff strengths; keeping the Board informed and giving the Board knowledge of "good" child-care activities; improving staff and parent and/or staff and Board relations

Time Needed

5 minutes every 2 months

How To Do It

1. Mention in a parent newsletter that the Director would welcome notes from parents praising teachers' strengths.
2. Keep a file and present the notes at Board meetings.

Did It Work?

Does the Board seem to have more concrete or positive feelings about the program or the teachers? Do they seem to be learning through this experience? Is the Director's choice of staff reaffirmed? Does the staff enjoy receiving additional recognition from someone other than the Director? (Intervening variables)

Other Possibilities

Encourage parents to verbally praise teachers for their efforts, or parents might put together a "Staff Scrapbook" to present to the staff on a special day. This scrapbook can be shared with the Board also. These scrapbooks can include children's artwork and make wonderful end-of-the-year (or five- or ten-year) "award" presentations when done individually.

Secret Santa or Holiday Fun

Benefits

Building concern and understanding about each other; building staff interaction

Time Needed

5 minutes a day of school/center time for 5 days, and 15 minutes a day of home or work time

How To Do It

1. Each staff member hangs a stocking in a central place.
2. The staff draws names for a person for whom each will be "Secret Santa."
3. Each day, each Secret Santa sneaks a "gift" into the stocking of the person whose name he or she drew.
4. Inexpensive, homemade, funny, and creative gifts are to be used. For example, if the teacher likes burned popcorn, Santa fills the stocking with burned popcorn one day. Obviously, Secret Santa has to learn a lot about his or her "person."

Did it Work?

Do teachers want to do similar things throughout the year? Do teachers ask to draw names in October so they have plenty of time to think of gifts? (Intervening variables)

Other Possibilities

Have a "Secret Ghost" at Halloween or a "Secret Bunny" at Easter. Instead of stockings, have staff members hunt for gifts each day in a scavenger hunt.

Meet the Staff

Benefits

Informing parents and other staff members about a particular staff person so they can get to know him or her better; motivating staff, building self-esteem, and giving recognition

Time Needed

15 to 30 minutes once a month

How To Do It

1. Write an article for the parent newsletter that features a different staff person each month. Include information such as his or her background, skills, hobbies, family, etc.
2. Interview the staff person or let him or her help write the article, if you wish.

Did it Work?

Is the chosen staff person proud to see the article and to be recognized or "chosen?" Is he or she happier and more motivated? Do other staff members look forward to their turns? (Intervening variables)

Other Possibilities

Try selecting a "Child of the Month" or "Child of the Week."

Swap Day

Benefits

Encouraging teaching diversity and sharing ideas

Time Needed

15 minutes 2 days per week

How To Do It

1. On the first day, ask teachers to spend 15 minutes writing an informal classroom activity. List how the activity is done and what materials are needed.
2. On the second day, use the 15 minutes to discuss the activities with another teacher. Swap places with him or her and implement the activity.
3. Directors can do this too, but must be very tactful, as the goal is creativity, not evaluation.

Did It Work?

Did this activity generate enthusiasm and teacher interaction? Did it encourage creativity? (Intervening variables)

Other Possibilities

Swap classrooms for longer parts of the day or for a full day.

Staff Recognition Day

Benefits

Recognizing special achievements and highlighting the worth of the staff's work

Time Needed

About 2 hours sometime during the year; the Director will have to spend some time planning and setting this up

How To Do It

1. Call in substitute teachers or parents to stay with the children and invite all the staff to a tea (or whatever you decide).
2. Have special refreshments.
3. Talk about how worthwhile the work of providing quality care for young children is, and how well it is being done.
4. Give each staff person a small gift, such as a small pin that is a symbol of their dedication and hard work.
5. Give something special to staff members that have accomplished something unusual during the year, such as having received a degree, having good attendance, or having been with the center a long time.
6. Invite other interested persons in addition to the staff.

Did it Work?

Does the staff ask if it will be done every year? Is the staff morale improved? (Intervening variable)

Other Possibilities

Write about special achievements in a staff newsletter.

INDEX